MOVING OUT OF POVERTY, VOLUME 2

Success from the Bottom Up

About the Series

The Moving Out of Poverty series presents the results of new comparative research across more than 500 communities in 15 countries on how and why poor people move out of poverty. The findings lay the foundations for new policies that will promote inclusive growth and just societies, and move millions out of poverty.

The series was launched in 2007 under the editorial direction of Deepa Narayan, former senior adviser in the World Bank. She earlier directed the pathbreaking Voices of the Poor project.

Titles in the Moving Out of Poverty series:

Moving
Out of
Poverty

VOLUME 2

Success from the Bottom Up

Deepa Narayan,
Lant Pritchett, *and*
Soumya Kapoor

A COPUBLICATION OF PALGRAVE MACMILLAN
AND THE WORLD BANK

PALGRAVE MACMILLAN

Palgrave Macmillan in the UK is an imprint of Macmillan Publishers Limited, registered in England, company number 785998, of Houndmills, Basingstoke, Hampshire, RG21 6XS.

Palgrave Macmillan in the US is a division of St Martin's Press LLC, 175 Fifth Avenue, New York, NY 10010.

Palgrave Macmillan is the global academic imprint of the above companies and has companies and representatives throughout the world.

Palgrave® and Macmillan® are registered trademarks in the United States, the United Kingdom, Europe and other countries.

ISBN: 978-0-8213-7215-9 (*softcover*)   eISBN: 978-0-8213-7216-6 (*softcover*)
ISBN: 978-0-8213-7836-6 (*hardcover*)   DOI: 10.1596/978-0-8213-7215-9
                                           ISSN: None

Library of Congress Cataloging-in-Publication Data has been applied for.

Cover design: Drew Fasick
Cover photograph: Brice Richard

Printed in the United States

Dedication

To the thousands of women, men, and youths who took the time
to share with us their experiences, their hopes, and their dreams

and

To Charles Tilly (1929–2008)—adviser, guide, and friend

Contents

Tables

Figures

Boxes

Foreword

The global *Moving Out of Poverty* study is unique in several respects. It is one of the few large-scale comparative research efforts to focus on mobility out of poverty rather than on poverty alone. The study draws together the experiences of poor women and men who have managed to move out of poverty over time and the processes and local institutions that have helped or hindered their efforts. It is also the first time that a World Bank report draws on people's own understanding of freedom, democracy, equality, empowerment, and aspirations—and how these affect poor people in different growth, social, and political contexts. By giving primacy to people's own experiences and how they define poverty, the study provides several new insights to develop more effective strategies to reduce poverty.

I want to draw attention to two striking findings that will help focus our approach to poverty reduction. First, half of the people who participated in the study show some mobility either up or down the socioeconomic ladder. By dampening downward mobility, we can dramatically affect poverty rates. In Malawi, for example, while 10.4 percent of people moved out of poverty, 10.6 percent fell into poverty, completely netting out all upward movement. Two important reasons for falling into poverty were declining local levels of economic prosperity and health shocks. These findings have important policy implications. Reducing vulnerability is critical. We must help people build permanent assets to reduce their chances of being thrown back into poverty by unexpected shocks such as food and fuel price increases, illness, natural disasters, or loss of jobs. We must provide basic social safety nets, including provision of basic health services to prevent setbacks from becoming catastrophic events. And we must expand local-level economic opportunities so that poor people have fair access to jobs and markets.

Second, the study finds that poor people take lots of initiative, in many cases even more than those who are better off. There are millions and millions of tiny poor entrepreneurs. The investment climate of these tiny entrepreneurs has not been a centerpiece of poverty strategies. Too often, poor people do not face a level playing field. Despite the micro credit revolution, poor people remain outside of most financial services; and large lenders remain reluctant to lend to microenterprises and microentrepreneurs. New institutional models and financial instruments are needed to serve poor people's financial needs and give them the capital they need to expand their businesses and connect to markets.

The book will be of interest to all who care about ending poverty. We hope you will be inspired to take action by the voices of 60,000 poor or recently poor men and women in Sub-Saharan Africa, Latin America, and East and South Asia.

Danny Leipziger
Vice President and Head of Network
Poverty Reduction and Economic Management
The World Bank

Study Team and Acknowledgments

This book draws on the contributions of many people who supported the Moving Out of Poverty research project at different stages. We first want to acknowledge the governments, the research institutes, and the 60,000 people who participated in the global study.

The project was led and managed by Deepa Narayan, who served from 2002 through 2008 as senior adviser in the Poverty Reduction and Economic Management (PREM) Network of the World Bank, first in the Poverty Reduction Group and subsequently in the vice president's office within PREM.

The project would never have started if not for the insistence of John Page, then director of the Poverty Reduction Group, and Gobind Nankani, then vice president of PREM. Successors to both continued their support, including Luca Barbone and Ana Revenga, directors of the Poverty Reduction Group; Sudhir Shetty and Louise Cord, sector managers in the Poverty Reduction Group; and Danny Leipziger, vice president of PREM. We also gratefully acknowledge Lyn Squire and his successor, Gobind Nankani, of the Global Development Network for their support throughout the project.

The team was split between Washington, DC, and New Delhi. Deepa Narayan was based in New Delhi but traveled to and fro. Lant Pritchett served as economic adviser to the study and provided stimulating overall guidance particularly on the quantitative data analyses. In Washington, Patti Petesch ably served as the project coordinator until the end of 2006. A succession of young research analysts provided valuable management and research support, including Bryan Kurey, Sarah Sullivan, Sunita Varada, Mohini Datt, Emcet Oktay Tas, Katrinka Ebbe, Kyla Hayford, and Sibel Selcuk. Four students from Stanford University—Jeremy Gordon, Nithya Rajagopalan, Rahul Shaikh, and Sumeet Bhatti—provided able support during their stints with the project. Others who worked for short periods included Ursula Casabonne, Katy Hull, Kazuhiro Numasawa, and Elizabeth Radin. Administrative support was provided by Oykiao Koo Tze Mew, Nelly Obias, and Jae Shin Yang.

In the New Delhi office, Soumya Kapoor was involved in the entire project and coordinated the South Asian studies. The office was successively supported by Kaushik Barua, Divya Nambiar, and Mohini Datt. Administrative assistance was provided by Sunila Andrews, who held us all together.

A range of local and international research institutes headed the country studies. Without their collaboration there would have been no study. Their contribution is so vital that we have listed them separately in appendix 1. We also gratefully acknowledge the teams who led the pilot studies conducted in Ethiopia, India, Peru, the Philippines, and Romania.

The project was supported by a loose network of advisers, all of whom provided valuable guidance and encouragement at different stages of the project. They included Stefan Dercon, Alan Gelb, Ashraf Ghani, Naila Kabeer, Ravi Kanbur, Steen Jorgensen, Praful Patel, Amartya Sen, Rehman Sobhan, Eva Tobisson, and Ashutosh Varshney. Charles Tilly was an invaluable adviser in so many ways. He was brave enough to join us in a technical workshop held in St. Petersburg, Russia, in January 2006, that guided our analyses. His untimely death in April 2008 remains a loss to us all.

Several World Bank staff members and others helped us initiate the country studies or provided technical guidance or both. They included Kathleen Beegle, Louise Fox, Johannes Hoogeveen, Jennie Litvack, Antonio Nucifora, and Quentin Wodon (Africa); Nisha Agarwal, Jehan Arulpragasam, Gillian Brown, Tim Conway, Scott Guggenheim, Mia Hyun, Priyanut Piboolsravut, and Kaspar Richter (East Asia); Jairo A. Arboleda, Gillette Hall, Harry Anthony Patrinos, Jaime Saavedra, and Maximo Torero (Latin America); and Nilufar Ahmad, Christine Allison, Maitreyi Das, Elena Glinskaya, Stephen Howes, Valerie Kozel, Rinku Murgai, Ashish Narain, Ambar Narayan, V. J. Ravishankar, Shonali Sardesai, Binayak Sen, and Tara Vishwanath (South Asia). We are also grateful to all the World Bank country directors who extended their support to the study, particularly Michael Carter, without whose support the large India study would not have been possible.

Data analysis was a huge task. The quantitative data analyses were guided by Lant Pritchett and Deepa Narayan and involved several researchers over time. These included Nina Badgaiyan, Kalpana Mehra, and Denis Nikitin, with support from Jeremy Gordon, Kristin Himelein, Flora Nankhuni, Kazuhiro Numasawa, Saumik Paul, Rahul Sheikh, and Sunita Varada.

The huge qualitative data set was analyzed partially by the ACNielsen team in India and by other researchers over time, including Kaushik Barua, Nandita Bhan, Chester Chua, Mohini Datt, Chris Gibson, Reema Govil, Soumya Kapoor, Huma Kidwai, Molly Kinder, Mahima Mitra, Divya Nambiar, Yukti Pahwa, Brice Richard, Manzoor Ali Sait, Niti Saxena, and Gitima Sharma.

The design of the research project evolved through brainstorming workshops held at different points in the project. We want to thank participants in the workshops and particularly the following people, who played key roles: Ian Bannon, Bob Baulch, Louise Cord, Stefan Dercon, Raj Desai, Francisco Ferreira, Gary Fields, Christiaan Grootaert, Johannes Linn, Kai Kaiser, Phil Keefer, Stuti Khemani, Stephen Knack, Caroline Moser, Giovanna Prennushi, Binayak Sen, Lyn Squire, Anand Swamy, Ashutosh Varshney, Quentin Wodon, and Michael Woolcock.

We are particularly grateful to Ravi Kanbur, T. H. Lee Professor of World Affairs at Cornell University; Frances Stewart, Director, Centre for Research on Inequality, Human Security and Ethnicity at the University of Oxford; Louise Cord, sector manager, Poverty Reduction Group; and Nora Dudwick, senior social scientist, Poverty Reduction Group. They reviewed the entire manuscript and provided feedback that was tremendously helpful. Pratap Bhanu Mehta, President, Centre for Policy Research, New Delhi, provided invaluable guidance on the democracy chapter. Internal reviewers of individual chapters included Robert Chase, Anis Dani, Shanta Devarajan, Alexandre Marc, Andy Norton, and Michael Woolcock. We owe a deep debt of gratitude to all, though any errors remain our responsibility.

The study was financed by several governments and donors. We especially wish to thank the government of Sweden, which provided untied funds to support the project. In addition, we gratefully acknowledge generous grants from the governments of Denmark, Finland, Luxembourg, the Netherlands, Norway, Thailand, Uganda, and the United Kingdom, as well as the United Nations Development Programme and the World Bank. In addition to the support through PREM, World Bank assistance to the project included a grant from the President's Contingency Fund under Jim Wolfensohn and a grant from the Post-Conflict Fund to the Global Development Network.

We thank the team at the World Bank Office of the Publisher, including Mary Fisk, Pat Katayama, and Nancy Lammers, who managed publication of the *Moving Out of Poverty* series. We deeply appreciate Cathy Sunshine's meticulous editorial work and eye for detail that helped us through successive drafts and resulted in this book.

About the Authors

Deepa Narayan is project director of the 15-country World Bank study titled *Moving Out of Poverty: Understanding Freedom, Democracy, and Growth from the Bottom Up*. From 2002 through 2008, she served as senior adviser in the Poverty Reduction and Economic Management (PREM) Network of the World Bank, first in the Poverty Reduction Group and subsequently in the vice president's office within PREM. She has development experience in Asia and Africa while working across sectors for nongovernmental organizations, national governments, and the United Nations system. Her areas of expertise include participatory development, community-driven development, and social capital, as well as use of these concepts to create wealth for poor people. Her recent publications include *Moving Out of Poverty: Cross-Disciplinary Perspectives on Mobility* (World Bank 2007); *Ending Poverty in South Asia: Ideas That Work* (with Elena Glinskaya, World Bank 2007); *Measuring Empowerment: Cross-Disciplinary Perspectives* (World Bank 2005); *Empowerment and Poverty Reduction: A Sourcebook* (World Bank 2002); and the three-volume *Voices of the Poor* series (Oxford University Press 2000, 2001, 2002).

Lant Pritchett is professor of the practice of economic development at the John F. Kennedy School of Government at Harvard University. He is also a nonresident fellow of the Center for Global Development, a senior fellow of BREAD (Bureau for Research and Economic Analysis of Development), co-editor of the *Journal of Development Economics*, and a consultant to Google.org. He held a number of positions at the World Bank between 1988 and 2007, working in Indonesia and India as well as in Washington, DC. He has been part of the teams producing many World Bank reports, including *World Development Report 1994: Infrastructure for Development; Assessing Aid: What Works, What Doesn't, and Why* (1998); *Better Health Systems for India's Poor: Findings, Analysis, and Options* (2003); *World Development Report 2004: Making Services Work for Poor People*; and *Economic Growth in the 1990s: Learning from a Decade of Reforms* (2005). He has authored or coauthored more than 50 papers published in refereed journals, as chapters in books, or as articles.

His monograph, *Let Their People Come: Breaking the Gridlock on Global Labor Mobility,* was published by the Center for Global Development in 2006.

Soumya Kapoor is a consultant in the Social Development unit of the World Bank in India, where she works on issues of social exclusion and environment as they relate to poverty reduction. She was a key member of the Moving Out of Poverty study team between 2003 and 2008. Before joining the World Bank, she worked as a corporate banker with a leading bank in India and as a credit analyst with an arm of Moody's. Her research interests center on social exclusion and participatory development and on how private enterprise can help reduce poverty while increasing profits. In addition to her writings for the Moving Out of Poverty project, she is the author of a chapter (with Deepa Narayan) in *Assets, Livelihoods, and Social Policy* (World Bank 2008).

Abbreviations

ACE	aggregate consumption expenditure
AIDS	acquired immune deficiency syndrome
BNS	Bangladesh Nutrition Survey
BPS	Statistics Indonesia
BRAC	Bangladesh Rural Advancement Committee
BREAD	Bureau for Research and Economic Analysis of Development
CASEN	National Socioeconomic Characterization (Chile)
CDA	community development assistant
CDD	community-driven development
CEPA	Centre for Policy Analysis
CFAF	Communauté Financière Africaine Franc
CGAP	Consultative Group to Assist the Poor
CILSS	Côte d'Ivoire Living Standards Survey
CNEF	Cross-National Equivalent Files
CONGUATE	Coalition of Guatemalan Immigrants
CONIC	National Indigenous and Campesino Coordinating Committee
CPL	community poverty line
CRECE	Centro de Estudios Regionales, Cafeteros y Empresariales
ECHP	European Community Household Panel
EDI	Economic Initiatives
EHM	Household Sample Survey (Venezuela)
EIHS	Egypt Integrated Household Survey
ENAHO	National Household Survey (Peru)
ENEU	National Survey of Urban Employment (Mexico)
EPH	Permanent Household Survey (Argentina)
ERHS	Ethiopia Rural Household Survey
ESRF	Economic and Social Research Foundation
EU	European Union
EU-15	pre-2004 members of the European Union
EUHS	Ethiopia Urban Household Survey
FENACOAC	Federación Nacional de Cooperativas de Ahorro y Crédito (Guatemala)
FMHS	Farm Management and Household Survey (Côte d'Ivoire)

FODIGUA	El Fondo de Desarrollo Indígena de Guatemala
GDP	gross domestic product
GUATENET	National Congress of Guatemalan Organizations in the United States
HACE	headcount measure of absolute expenditure
HBS	Household Budget Survey (Poland)
HDI	Human Development Index
HHP	Hungarian Household Panel
HIES	Household Income and Expenditure Survey (Bangladesh)
HIV	human immunodeficiency virus
HTA	hometown association
ICRISAT	International Crops Research Institute for the Semi-Arid Tropics
IDB	Inter-American Development Bank
IETS	Instituto de Estudos do Trabalho e Sociedade (Brazil)
IFAD	International Fund for Agricultural Development
IFLS	Indonesia Family Life Survey
IFPRI	International Food Policy Research Institute
IHS	Integrated Household Survey (Uganda)
INS	Immigration and Naturalization Service (United States)
IOM	International Organization for Migration
IRCA	Immigration Reform and Control Act (United States)
IRNet	International Remittance Network
KHDS	Kagera Health and Development Study (Tanzania)
KICS	Kenyan Ideational Change Survey
KIDS	KwaZulu-Natal Income Dynamics Study (South Africa)
LAC	Latin America and the Caribbean
LDF	Local Development Board
LMI	Local Knowledge Management Institute
LOM	leave-out means
LPM	linear probability model
LSMS	Living Standard Measurement Survey
MFI	microfinance institution
MIF	Multilateral Investment Fund (of the IDB)
MK	Malawi Kwacha
MOP	Moving Out of Poverty
MPI	mobility of the poor
NASFAM	National Smallholder Farmers' Association
NCAER	National Council of Applied Economic Research (India)
NGO	nongovernmental organization

NPI	net prosperity index
OBC	other backward castes
OECD	Organisation for Economic Co-operation and Development
OI	original interviewee
OLS	ordinary least squares
PCA	Principal Components Analysis
PDS	Public Distribution System (India)
PIDI	Integrated Child Development Project (Bolivia)
PREM	Poverty Reduction and Economic Management
PSID	Panel Study of Income Dynamics
Q	quetzal
REDS	Rural Economic Development Survey (India)
RHS	Rural Household Survey (China)
RIMCU	Research Institute for Mindanao Culture (Philippines)
RLMS	Russian Longitudinal Monitoring Survey
Rs	rupees
SACCO	Savings and Credit Cooperatives
SC	scheduled caste
SES	socioeconomic status
SEWA	Self-Employed Women's Association
SHGs	self-help groups
SLID	Canadian Survey of Labour and Income Dynamics
ST	scheduled tribe
TAMPA	Tegemeo Agricultural Monitoring and Policy Analysis Project (Kenya)
TAOs	Tambon Administrative Organizations
TPDS	Targeted Public Distribution System (India)
UNDP	United Nations Development Programme
UNHS	Uganda National Household Survey
UPPAP	Uganda Participatory Poverty Assessment Project
USAID	U.S. Agency for International Development
VLSS	Vietnam Living Standards Survey
WMS	Welfare Monitoring Survey (Kenya)
WOCCU	World Council of Credit Unions

Note: All dollar amounts are U.S. dollars.

Study Regions

Abbreviation	Country or state	Policy focus
AFG (Conf)	Afghanistan	Conflict
AP (SHG)	Andhra Pradesh	Self-help groups
ASSAM (Conf)	Assam	Conflict
BAN (Empow)	Bangladesh	Women's empowerment
COL (Conf)	Colombia	Conflict
INDO (Conf)	Indonesia	Conflict
MAL (Infra)	Malawi	Infrastructure
MEX (Ethn)	Mexico	Ethnicity
MOR (Mig)	Morocco	Migration
PHI (Conf)	Philippines	Conflict
PHI (Panel)	Philippines	Panel study
SEN (Infra)	Senegal	Infrastructure
SRI (Conf)	Sri Lanka	Conflict
TAN (Ruv)	Tanzania	Ruvuma
THAI (Ineq)	Thailand	Inequality
UGA (Panel)	Uganda	Panel study
UP (Caste)	Uttar Pradesh	Caste
WB (Landdist)	West Bengal	Land distribution reforms

Indexes

MOP   Moving out of poverty index
Measures extent of upward mobility by the poor across the CPL in a community.
MOP = initially poor who move above CPL ÷ initially poor.

MPI   Mobility of the poor index
Measures extent of upward mobility by those who were initially poor.
MPI = initially poor who move up ÷ initially poor.

MRI   Mobility of the rich index
Measures extent of upward mobility by those who were initially above the CPL (nonpoor or "rich" by the study's definition).
MRI = initially rich who move up ÷ initially rich.

FI   Falling index
Measures extent of all downward mobility in a community.
FI = all households that move down ÷ total number of households.

FPI   Falling of the poor index
         Measures extent of downward mobility of the initially poor.
         FPI = initially poor who move down ÷ initially poor.

FRI   Falling of the rich index
         Measures extent of downward mobility of the rich.
         FRI = initially rich who move down ÷ initially rich.

FRIP   Falling of the rich into poverty index
         Measures extent of downward mobility of the rich across the CPL.
         FRI = initially rich who move below CPL ÷ initially rich.

NPR   Net poverty reduction
         Measures changes in the share of poor over study period.
         NPR = % ending poor – % initially poor.

NPI   Net prosperity index
         Measures extent of net upward mobility (upward less downward) in a
         community.
         NPI = (all households that move up – all households that move down)
         ÷ total number of households.

NPP   Net prosperity of the poor index
         Measures extent of net upward mobility (upward less downward) of
         the initially poor.
         NPP = (initially poor who move up – initially poor who move down)
         ÷ initially poor.

PI   Prosperity index
         Measures extent of all upward mobility in a community.
         PI = all households that move up ÷ total number of households.

Variable Prefixes and Suffixes

h   household questionnaire
c   community questionnaire
a   current (at time of study, about 2005)
b   initial (approximately 10 years ago, about 1995)
r   variable was recoded
T   total number of groups
m   male focus group discussion
f   female focus group discussion

MOVING OUT OF POVERTY, VOLUME 2

Success from the Bottom Up

The Moving Out of Poverty Study: An Overview

Poverty is a dark stain that darkens the whole world.

—MEN'S DISCUSSION GROUP,
Villa Rosa, Colombia

The longer I live the more convinced am I that—except in purely abstract problems—the statistical side must never be separated even for an instant from the nonstatistical.

—ALFRED MARSHALL,
English economist, 1906

The goal is clear: to end poverty. And to do that we must begin by answering the question of why poor people are poor. Beliefs about the poor and the underlying causes of poverty determine the actions that development practitioners pursue, the policies that national politicians devise, and the actions that we as concerned citizens take. Our assumptions about the underlying causes of poverty, therefore, will play a part in whether families living in communities in Mississippi, Malawi, Manchester, Mexico, or Morocco will have a chance to move out of poverty. Our unspoken, unexamined, and often unconscious beliefs about poor people are critical, as these determine whether poverty is defined as a problem at all. And if it is a problem, whose problem is it? Is it their problem or is it our problem? Beliefs about the nature of poverty and "the poor" can motivate action—or rationalize inaction.

Our book is not about ideology, whether right or left. It is not about bleeding heart liberalism or rugged individualism. It does not take a position for or against free markets or big government. It is not pro-globalization or anti-globalization. It is not about a clash of civilizations or about Protestant values as opposed to Catholic, Islamic, or Hindu values. It is not about paradigm shifts.

Our book is about local realities, and about the urgent need to develop poverty-reducing strategies informed by the lives and experiences of millions of poor people in communities around the world. To do so, we must put aside our assumptions. When we look closely at the local realities of communities rather than at countries, we see movement, not only stagnation. Despite the odds, some poor people in places from Bangladesh in South Asia to Mexico in Latin America are moving up and out of poverty. At the same time, others in the same communities are stuck in poverty or falling down. We set out to find out why and how.

3

We begin with the lives of three individuals from different parts of the world who either moved out of poverty or remained stuck in poverty.

Meet Three People . . .

Ayesha from Bangladesh

Forty-year-old Ayesha lives in the farming village of Pirjadi in Narshingdi district in Bangladesh. A divorcee, Ayesha has been reviled and derided by people in her village for her marital status. She has fought hard to achieve what little she has today. Unlike other women in the community, she now owns the small mud-brick house she lives in, and she has a small poultry farming business. She lends money to her neighbors.

It was not always this way. About a decade ago, Ayesha recalls, "My condition was very bad. I did not have food, and I used to stay in others' houses. I passed my days covering my body with this sack." (She points to a soiled jute gunny bag). "But those days are gone. Now I am fine."

Ayesha is illiterate, and her mother died three days after she was born. Married at 15, she was stuck in an abusive marriage, with her husband frequently "going to other girls." She left him when she was about 20 and started working as a maid in a neighbor's house. She received no salary for the first six years and worked only for food and clothing. After prodding from others, she asked for a salary and started receiving 50 taka a month (about 75 cents). She also worked as a wage laborer and sold the rice that her employers provided for her evening meal. "For three years, I did not have rice at night," she says proudly. With her miniscule wages and the money she received from selling her food, Ayesha saved bit by bit and was able to buy a chicken and a goat and some clothes for herself.

At the age of 32, Ayesha applied for a small job at the union parishad (local council) office. She worked there for four years and received 1,200 taka (about US$18) each month. At the time our field team met her, Ayesha had substantial savings from her union parishad job—savings that she had invested wisely. She had returned to Pirjadi, where she reared and sold ducks and chickens; she had her own house and her own piece of land that she bought to cultivate rice. She says that she feels lonely with no family of her own: "Nobody is with me. If I lie down in this room for the whole day, nobody will call me." Yet she is proud of what she has achieved. "I have my own house," she says. "That is why I have been able to entertain you, no? I'll tell you my secret: unity, courage, and hard work."

Mamba from Malawi

Mamba is a 35-year-old farmer who lives in chronic poverty in the village of Kalugeni in Dowa district in Malawi. He loves his country, his village, his people, and his family and has no desire to leave his village, despite droughts and periods of acute hunger.

Mamba started his education late, at the age of 15, and he had to leave school two years later because his family could not afford his school fees and uniform. He started farming maize and groundnuts and later added sweet potatoes, which he raised both for consumption and for sale. But in 1998 Mamba stopped growing sweet potatoes because the cuttings for the crop dried out due to improper storage. He got new cuttings from a friend in 2000, but he did not manage a good crop. "There was hunger in the land at that time. I was spending a lot of time doing *ganyu* [farm day labor]. As a result, my garden was neglected and the harvesting was affected."

The next two years were a period of widespread hunger in the community. Villagers ate sugarcane waste and wild roots that had to be boiled three times to make them edible. Some people died. Farm work became increasingly difficult to find, and Mamba went from place to place looking for work and food. He survived by molding and selling bricks. In 2002 the government started a fertilizer and seed distribution program for poor families, but Mamba's village received only 28 starter packs for more than 400 families. "The big programs that top leaders make do not reach us here," Mamba says. From 2002 to 2004 Mamba toiled on his garden, but yields were low due to poor rains. His break finally came in 2005, when he secured employment on a road maintenance project.

Looking back at his life, Mamba sees that he has not been able to accumulate any assets except for a chair that he had bought for visitors; it had broken and he pointed to it, hanging from the roof. "Never in my life have I been able to hold money. There have always been ups and downs. I cannot afford fertilizer because it is too expensive. The government is not helping us by controlling its price. If this is hard, then they should restore farm clubs so that we can obtain fertilizer loans from them. Maybe if the starter packs were to be distributed to all people in the village, things would have been better, but they just distribute it to only 20 or 15 people."

Mamba has suffered many losses, including the deaths of two sons, who died from hunger and lack of medical care. His friends are his lifeline. They extend help when needed, from giving him a hoe for farming to stitching his clothes for free. Despite all he has endured, Mamba feels confident. "I am an energetic man, and I believe that if I have fertilizer I can do better. This confidence has been growing, since I am a man who has a family. I have failed to move forward in well-being, yes, but the way I see it, the respect that I receive within my family has increased over the last 10 years. This is because I do not love to do a lot of things like chasing skirts, drinking beer, and smoking tobacco. I just love to play football. . . ." And he smiles.

Adolfo from Mexico

In the small mountainous community of Guadalamoros in Oaxaca, Mexico, Adolfo, age 29, is busy in his *tiendita*, his small store. Thanks to the store, Adolfo is "economically independent," according to his friends. But things were not always so. After he completed secondary school, Adolfo had to help his father in the fields, for which he received no pay. To escape the drudgery, he decided to migrate to the United States, and at the age of 20 he crossed the border, undetected, for the first time. "I suffered a lot," he recalls. "At 3 p.m. we left Tecate walking, and we walked for an entire day. We had nothing to eat."

Adolfo began working in a restaurant in California. He knew no English, but his brother, who worked in the same restaurant, helped him. "It was easy because my brother worked there so I didn't need to know the language." But the separation from his family was hard. "Migration splits the family and it is not with money that you can cure the effects [of the separation]."

He returned to Mexico two years later with some savings, but they soon ran out. "I lasted a year and a half in Guadalamoros, and then I had to return to California again because I needed more money. There is no money, no jobs here in Guadalamoros," he says. In 2000 Adolfo, now age 24, went back to California. This time the border crossing was more difficult. He first tried to cross at Mexicali but was caught and sent back. The Mexican border patrols treated him very badly (he does not say how). He finally crossed at Tijuana. "Tijuana is the saddest city. You have to protect yourself against our government and authorities. Instead of helping migrants, they hurt them."

A year later Adolfo returned once more to Guadalamoros—this time, he says, for good. He used savings from his work in California to set up his store. He prefers living in Mexico, but he also recognizes that without migration he would not have been able to go into business. "I pray to God that I will never have to return. Not for fear of work, but for fear of leaving the family and for fear of the risks you have to take to cross the border." Adolfo insists that it is not "correct" to leave one's country for good and that he could never live outside Mexico permanently. "Mexico is my land, my country, my people" (*México es mi tierra, mi país, mi gente*).

One study . . . thousands of narratives

The lives of poor people like Ayesha, Mamba, and Adolfo push us to look beyond simplistic ideological divides or economic formulas. We are forced to come to terms with our flawed and discipline-constrained diagnosis of why there are still so many poor people in our prosperous world. As we trace backward to root causes, we see that the underlying assumptions and residues of ideologies about poverty have left deep imprints on policy choices. Confronting these assumptions leads us to a series of questions. Are poor people dysfunctional or are the contexts in which they live dysfunctional? Is poverty the result of lack of initiative among the poor, or is the problem lack of opportunity?

We build our case from the bottom up. Our "data," our "case material," are narratives from 60,000 people: poor or formerly poor women, men, and youths in over 500 communities across 21 study regions in 15 countries of Africa, South Asia, East Asia, and Latin America.[1] Some of these people have escaped poverty over the last decade even as others in their communities have remained poor or have fallen into poverty; a few have never been poor. We learn from thousands of discussions—some animated, some angry, some tearful, some filled with laughter. We start with questions, not theories. We use an inductive approach to gradually aggregate, life story by life story, discussion by discussion, the threads that tie these experiences together. In doing so, we lose some of the rich details of each local context, but we gain insights into the underlying processes by which people either escape poverty or remain stuck in chronic poverty.[2] These insights guide our concluding reflections on policy and action that call for innovations on a large scale by civil society, businesses, and governments, informed by poor people's realities.

This opening chapter now turns to a brief discussion of the principles grounding our study and the multiple methods, both qualitative and quantitative, that we used to understand people's lives over time. We then summarize seven key sets of findings that emerge from our inductive analyses. These findings frame the structure of the book. We end this chapter with a discussion of the conceptual framework that evolved as we pored over thousands of pages of field notes, reflecting primarily on individuals' life stories and group discussions.

Principles and Methods

The Moving Out of Poverty study is a follow-up to the earlier Voices of the Poor study (Narayan et al. 2000, 2001, 2002). Its purpose is to explore from the bottom up how people move out of poverty. Our approach builds upon and has been influenced by the work of many colleagues, some of whom contributed to the first volume in the Moving Out of Poverty series (Narayan and Petesch 2007). This second volume is based on new qualitative and quantitative data gathered for this study.

Individual voices, local context, and change over time

Three principles guided this study. First, each individual is the expert on her or his own life. Poor people are no different. Hence, we give primacy to the voices of thousands of people, living primarily in rural communities, who shared their life experiences and insights with us. This is not methodological naïveté. We are well aware that subjective data, especially subjective data about the past, are subject to a variety of distorting factors. These include biases in recall (Gibbs, Lindner, and Fischer 1986; Withey 1954), the ways in which individuals frame narratives about themselves (Tilly 2006; Bertrand and Mullainathan 2001), sensitivity of responses to the research method and questions (Krueger and Schkade 2007; Kahneman and Krueger 2006), social context and power structures (Chambers 2002), and just plain errors. An additional concern in poverty studies is the incentive facing poor people and poor communities to give answers that "please" in the hope of gaining funds and programs. Our data are not immune to any of these problems. At the same time, we believe that how people recount their own experiences is intrinsically of interest. Moreover, we believe in methodological pluralism, in the need to investigate a phenomenon from multiple perspectives using multiple methods. This study is meant to complement and not substitute for the enormous body of existing quantitative and qualitative work on the topic of poverty.

The second principle is that local context matters. Hence, we locate individuals and households *in their community contexts* and go beyond the exclusive focus on individual or household characteristics that is typical of poverty surveys. We pay particular attention to the rules, regulations, informal norms, and expectations that govern the local social, economic, and political institutions with which poor people interact.

Third, our interest is in change over time, in the dynamics of poverty mobility. Most studies present a snapshot, a static picture of individuals frozen in time. We want the movie. We seek to understand in some depth the processes through which people rise out of—or fall into—poverty.

Study sites

The study was conducted in 15 countries:

- In Africa: Malawi, Morocco, Senegal, Tanzania, and Uganda
- In South Asia: Afghanistan, Bangladesh, India (the four poorer states of Assam, Andhra Pradesh, Uttar Pradesh, West Bengal), and Sri Lanka
- In East Asia: Cambodia, Indonesia, the Philippines, and Thailand
- In Latin America: Colombia and Mexico

While for convenience we refer to our results by country—for example, the results in Senegal or in the Philippines—we never take these results to be representative of the whole country (or in the case of India, of the state). We sacrifice national representation to study in depth a smaller number of communities in order to reveal relationships and processes that lead to poverty outcomes. Altogether we conducted 21 studies. In several countries—the Philippines, Sri Lanka, and Tanzania—we conducted two studies, each with its own focus. As a reminder that our studies are not nationally representative, we mostly refer to results by study region.

Selection of study regions within countries took into account the availability of local research institutes with the interest and capacity to carry out the multidisciplinary study. In addition, the study team held intensive dialogues with government and civil society representatives, academics, and World Bank staff to identify specific policy questions that were of interest. In the Philippines, for instance, two study regions were identified. The Bukidnon study built on a panel data set to examine the role that physical assets, human capital, and governance play in mobility. In the region of Mindanao, however, the focus was on local-level conflicts to investigate how conflict in different growth contexts affected people's ability to move out of poverty.

We did more intensive study of a small number of communities, 8–20 in every study region (except in the four Indian states, where the number of communities ranged from 50 to 110). Communities were chosen through stratified randomized sampling with purposive stratification that depended on the regional context. In some regions stratification was based on high- and low-growth regions, in others on high or low availability of infrastructure, in still others on conflict (see appendix 2, table A.2, for a list of study regions and selection criteria for communities).

Data collection methods

We used 10 different data collection methods, in part to overcome by triangulation potential distortions. Sometimes we probed the same issue with the same people using different methods, such as a questionnaire followed by a life story interview. At other times we asked different people to discuss the same issue, presenting the same question, for example, to separate focus groups of men, women, and youths. Our core tools include individual life stories, the ladder of life exercise, focus group discussions on various topics, and household interviews using questionnaires. All 10 methods are summarized in appendix 3.

Individual life stories. We examined over 5,000 life stories from more than 500 communities in the 15 countries. The individual life story is an open-ended interview that complements the household questionnaire. Its purpose is to gather people's own perceptions of key events in their lives over time. We graphed people's life histories along five dimensions: their migration history; their occupational history; their economic history; their social, cultural, and psychological history; and their education. People discussed the impact of each event on their well-being and identified the turning or tipping points. These discussions and graphs made visible to them and to us the sequencing and interaction of factors over time. Most people loved talking about their lives; invariably the interviewer rather than the storyteller was the one to gently bring the session to a close.

Ladder of life. We conducted nearly 1,000 discussions to obtain local definitions of poverty and wealth and causes of mobility with focus groups of men and women. These discussions used a tool called the ladder of life, described in more detail in the next section. The groups clarified local understandings of how someone moves out of poverty or falls into poverty and why some people in the community are rich and others poor. The focus groups then categorized actual households in their community according to their well-being status at the time of the study (2005) and a decade earlier (1995), allowing us to see the extent of upward and downward movement in the community.

Focus group discussions. We conducted more than 1,500 discussions to understand key events that helped or hindered community prosperity. We also held more than 2,000 focus group discussions on the topics of livelihoods, democracy, freedom, and power.

Household interviews. We conducted approximately 9,000 household interviews using questionnaires that investigate a household's economic, political, and social life. These interviews provide most of our quantitative data.

Use of these various tools generated a massive body of evidence spanning multiple contexts. Analyzing this diverse data set has taken time. Although we use statistics and statistical analyses even of the qualitative data obtained from life stories and group discussions, these are located in the "thick" descriptions gathered. These narratives were systematically analyzed over thousands of hours, both manually and using an anthropological software package, Nudist. We struggled with letting individuals express themselves while at the same time starting the process of aggregation to allow common themes to emerge.

Most important, we let poor people and those no longer poor speak for themselves. We are fully aware that such individual narratives are inevitably complicated by the social interaction of the interview and by people's natural desire to present themselves in ways that are positive and consistent with their social ideals. But by the same token, the ways in which people choose to describe their experiences reveal a great deal about how they think their worlds are ordered and how they think their worlds *should* be ordered. Of necessity, we also bring in the literature—the perspectives of technocrats, policy makers, world leaders, economists, political scientists, philosophers, and anthropologists who have influenced the poverty debates. But while expert representations add an important dimension to our overall understanding of poverty, we do not focus on them, because these voices have already been heard. We present them sparingly, as needed. They should not drown out the voices of the poor.

What Is Poverty? Who Is Poor?

Poverty is timeless.
> —Women's discussion group, Tecamín, Mexico

Poverty is a cruel wild animal. If you doze, it eats you up. So people are not sleeping; they are working to prosper.
> —Kevina, a 60-year-old female farmer, Bukwaime, Uganda

If one is to understand poor people's lives and how they move out of poverty, poverty has to be defined and measured. When the World Bank dreams of a world free of poverty, the World Bank defines poverty. When heads of state gather at the United Nations to pledge an attack on poverty, the U.N. defines poverty. In our study, we do not define poverty. We let local people define poverty for themselves.

The ladder of life

We use a tool called the ladder of life to establish each community's own definition of poverty and wealth and determine who in the community qualifies as poor. A typical ladder of life discussion group has 6–15 participants who are purposively selected to represent different social and economic groups in the community. The discussions last from two to four hours; where possible, they are held separately with men and women.

The activity starts with an icebreaker exercise in which the group discusses the most important factors that have facilitated and hindered prosperity in their community. Participants then create a figurative ladder of well-being, with the bottom step representing the poorest or worst-off people found in that community and the top step the wealthiest or best-off. Participants discuss and describe the household characteristics that define each step of the ladder and the typical ways in which households can move up or down the ladder.

The group then sorts up to 150 households in the community onto the ladder steps. They identify each household's placement initially (approximately 10 years ago, around 1995) and currently (in 2005). Based on these rankings, we develop a community mobility matrix that shows which households moved up or down the ladder or stayed at the same step over the 10-year study period. Examples of the mobility matrixes are presented in chapter 3.

After sorting the households, the focus group identifies a community poverty line (CPL). The CPL is drawn between two steps of the ladder: households at steps below the line are considered poor and those at steps above the line are considered not poor. Just as different focus groups create ladders with different numbers of steps (usually four to six), they can set the poverty line wherever they think is appropriate for their own community. In the example shown in table 1.1, the focus groups set the line between steps 2 and 3 in a village in Andhra Pradesh and between steps 4 and 5 in a village in Uganda.

The mapping of households onto the community mobility matrix allows us to categorize them in terms of their poverty mobility or lack of mobility during the study period. Households may have moved up or down or remained stuck at the same step of the ladder. Those that have moved may or may not have crossed the community poverty line. Throughout the book, we refer to four mobility categories:

- *Movers:* households that were poor in 1995 but had moved out of poverty by 2005
- *Chronic poor:* households that were poor in 1995 and remained poor in 2005

- *Never poor:* households that were not poor in 1995 and remained not poor in 2005
- *Fallers:* households that were not poor in 1995 but fell into poverty by 2005

Thus throughout our study, the terms "poor people" and "poverty" refer to households identified by the ladder of life focus groups as poor. No more. No less. Each discussion group's definition is what it is. Mobility status is not assigned by the outside researchers, nor is it assessed by the household itself.

Poverty is a problem of the many, not the few

There is no economic inequality here. Everyone is poor.
                                —Men's discussion group, Chakax, Mexico

When you give a person that much [income at the official poverty line], also prepare a prison for him or her, because after a few hours she or he will already start stealing.
                        —Discussion group, Chubaka, Kagera, Tanzania

Construction of the ladder of life and the community mobility matrix allows us to gain an overall picture of poverty and wealth in a community. Using the community-created definitions of poverty, there is no question that poverty is perceived as a problem of the many, not the few. In a typical country or study region, more than 60 percent of households were classified as currently in poverty, and in every single study region, the fraction of households classified as poor was more than 40 percent (figure 1.1).[3] And as the focus groups recall it, things used to be even worse: in the typical country more than 70 percent of households were poor 10 years ago, in 1995.

These poverty percentages are much higher than those that would result from applying the "$1 a day" measure often used in international circles as the poverty line. Our focus group perceptions often aligned fairly closely with a standard based on $2 a day—sometimes higher, sometimes lower, but nearly always closer than to the $1 a day standard.

Is this expansive definition of poverty reasonable? The key debate is around two alternative conceptions of poverty. One defines poverty down: the poor are the destitute, the wretched, those on the fringes of society, the poorest of the poor. This characterization makes the poor seem different from the rest of us and casts poverty as a problem of the few. Some (but not all) focus groups did associate such characteristics with the households at the very bottom step of the ladder of life. That is, in some villages the focus groups reserved the bot-

TABLE 1.1

Sample ladders of life from two villages in Andhra Pradesh and Uganda

	Ladder constructed in Kamalapur, Andhra Pradesh	% of households	Ladder constructed in Bufkaro, Uganda	% of households
Step 6	Landlords: Employ servants to cultivate their lands, own huge buildings, and command high respect in the village. Only 2 families in the village are at this step.	4	They can pay for a piece of land worth 400,000 shillings in one day. They have permanent, well-furnished, beautiful houses, a means of transport, and at least 5 cows. Their friends are also rich and can give them loans if they get into a problem.	1
Step 5	Big farmers: Own 15–25 acres of ancestral property plus 4–5 houses, motorbikes, fans, and cattle. Land gives good yields. Cultivate crops like cotton, chilies, soybeans. Banks provide loans. Educate their children and can live without working.	6	They own painted cement houses, a bicycle, and livestock, including 2 cows, 2 goats, and 3 sheep. They can afford to buy a bar of soap every week. Even when their children are sent away from school, they are able to pay the fee next morning.	6
Step 4	Medium farmers: Own 5 acres of land. Some have government jobs. Own houses with cement walls, cattle, borehole wells, televisions, fans, and cots. Eat fine rice. Women wear gold ornaments and children study in good schools. Banks provide loans.	25	They save money to educate their children above primary 7. All household members sleep on mattresses, and the house has furniture. They own livestock—about 3 goats, 1 cow, and a chicken. But they are forced to sell off the animals because they have no land for grazing them.	14

Step 3	Small farmers: Own 3–5 acres of land. Own houses and cattle but do not have wells. Their lives depend on rainfall. During periods of drought, they migrate to towns or work as agricultural labor. They are a little bit educated.	28	They own about 1.5 acre of land, which they cultivate. They have iron-roofed houses, mattresses, and blankets. Each member of the family can afford at least 2 shirts, 2 trousers, and 1 coat. People at this step also do manual labor. Parents are able to educate children up to senior 2, but after that the school sends the child away for want of fees. Children at this step dress in secondhand clothes and shoes.	48
Step 2	Laborers with small landholdings: Own 1–2 acres of land. Land is rarely fertile and they have to do wage labor; some serve as bonded labor. Don't have proper houses. They are illiterate and belong to backward and scheduled castes. Every day is a struggle.	26	They usually sell their land so they can build a house and have a decent place to stay. Most people do not have shoes. They eat meat only on big days like Christmas and Easter. Most children complete primary 7, but with a lot of struggle. They are sent away from school for want of uniforms.	29
Step 1	Landless laborers: Lack proper food, proper clothes, and proper houses. Don't find work regularly and are able to work only 12–15 days a month. They are usually illiterate, and their children cannot attend school because they have to work.	11	The "unplanful": They work as casual laborers for others. They are unemployed and have no money. They do not care about cleanliness and have only one pair of clothes that they rarely wash. When paid money for labor, they use it to buy alcohol.	2

Source: Male ladder of life focus groups in Kamalapur, Andhra Pradesh, and Bufkaro, Uganda.

Note: Bold lines indicate the community poverty line.

FIGURE 1.1
More than half of all households were classified as poor in 2005

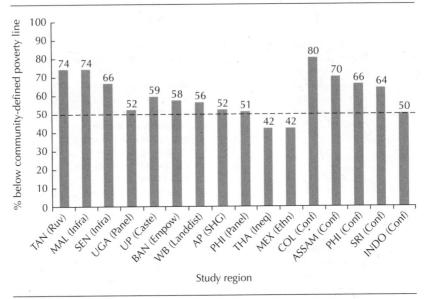

Study region

Source: Ladder of life discussion groups.

Note:
AP (SHG) = Andhra Pradesh, Self-help groups
ASSAM (Conf)= Assam, Conflict
BAN (Empow) = Bangladesh, Women's
  empowerment
COL (Conf) = Colombia, Conflict
INDO (Conf) = Indonesia, Conflict
MAL (Infra) = Malawi, Infrastructure
MEX (Ethn) = Mexico, Ethnicity
PHI (Conf) = Philippines, Conflict

PHI (Panel) = Philippines, Panel study
SEN (Infra) = Senegal, Infrastructure
SRI (Conf) = Sri Lanka, Conflict
TAN (Ruv) = Tanzania, Ruvuma
THAI (Ineq) = Thailand, Inequality
UGA (Panel) = Uganda, Panel study
UP (Caste) = Uttar Pradesh, Caste
WB (Landdist) = West Bengal, Land distribution
  reforms

tom step for those with problematic behaviors (e.g., too much drinking) or physical disadvantages (e.g., disability) or social stigma (e.g., widows with no sons). But this category, where it existed, was usually very small, many times containing only one or two households. As seen in table 1.1, people in the bottom category in Bufkaro, Uganda—some of whom spend their meager wages on alcohol—represented just 2 percent of all households. They were a small minority even of those considered the bottom poor.

In the alternative definition of poverty, the poor are those who have some things but lack enough of the important things that they are considered poor. This is clearly the concept of poverty that, by and large, the focus groups used. They typically did not single out the bottommost group as "the poor," but rather included several categories on the lower end of the ladder as collectively experiencing poverty.

Table 1.1 shows ladders of life constructed by men's focus groups in two sample villages in Uganda and Andhra Pradesh. Both groups created ladders with six steps. As people move up the ladder, they accumulate more assets and no longer engage in casual or bonded labor. Vulnerability declines. There are some discontinuities, particularly in relation to owning permanent housing, but overall there are few sharp distinctions just below and just above the poverty line. The groups distinguished households by some mix of six characteristics:

- *Occupation and land ownership.* In Kamalapur, Andhra Pradesh, the step just below the CPL includes laborers with small landholdings of 1–2 acres. Just above the CPL are small farmers with 3–5 acres, who may also do wage labor during periods of drought. The bottom category consists of landless laborers who do not find regular work.
- *Assets and savings.* In Bufkaro, Uganda, households just below the CPL own mattresses and some furniture. They also have a few animals— "three goats, one cow, and a chicken"—but often have to sell them off. Those just above the CPL own more livestock, typically two goats, three cows, and three sheep. In Kamalapur, households below the CPL don't have proper houses; those above the CPL own houses, which become larger and finer as one moves up the ladder.
- *Consumption.* In Kamalapur, those at the bottom of the ladder "lack proper food" while those two steps above the CPL "eat fine rice." In Bufkaro, lack of clothing partly defines those low on the ladder. Those at steps 1 and 2 have just one soiled set of clothes and no shoes, but at step 3 each person can afford at least two shirts, two trousers, and one coat, although children are clad in secondhand clothes and shoes.
- *Education of household head and children.* In Kamalapur, people at step 1 are illiterate, and their children cannot attend school because they have to work. By step 3, just above the CPL, people are "a little bit educated," and at step 4 their children "study in good schools." In Bufkaro, step 2 households can give their children seven years of primary schooling, but it is a struggle. At step 3, children can go up to "senior 2" but cannot progress further because families cannot afford school fees. Households at step 5, above the CPL, have no problem paying the fees. The desire to educate children appears in all categories; what varies is the ability to send children to school.

- *Behavioral characteristics.* Households in the very lowest category in Bufkaro "when paid money for labor . . . use it to buy alcohol." Apart from this, there is no mention of behavior.
- *Social status.* High status and respect is only mentioned in the very top categories. Households at step 6 in Kamalapur "employ servants" and "command high respect in the village." In many other village ladders, the top category consists of bosses and landlords, those who can tell others what to do.

Across our study sites, as in Kamalapur and Bufkaro, there is decreasing vulnerability as people rise up the ladder and accumulate assets. Although some of our focus groups identified a small category of destitute and dysfunctional households on the very bottom rung of the ladder, this is not their overall view of poverty. Rather, they see poverty as a condition that affects the majority of the population—and is a risk to nearly all.

One women's discussion group in Assam described people just below the poverty line this way: "Their behavior is good. They work hard and have food daily. They also have 2–3 bighas of land. Their houses are usually made of mud walls with a tin roof." A similar description would apply to many, perhaps most, of the households in our study communities. For the overwhelming majority of people in these communities, then, the definition of poverty can be summed up in a few words: the poor are us.

Key Findings

Seven key findings emerge from our research. These findings, highlighted here and discussed in depth in subsequent chapters, link to our conceptual framework that defines mobility largely as the interaction between two concepts: the *initiative* poor people take to move out of poverty and the *opportunity* they have to do so, facilitated or constrained by local-level social, political, and economic institutions.

Poor people are not trapped in a culture of poverty

> *People want to work, want to improve. They're getting organized. Isn't that something good?*
>> —Doralis, a poor woman, Villa Rosa, Colombia

> *Poor people have aspirations but they are not met. Rich people have aspirations that can be achieved.*
>> —Suka, a 45-year-old woman, Tattantok, Indonesia

I couldn't have come to this position if I hadn't labored, dealing in rice and paddy. You have to maintain prestige and at the same time work hard. Doing both, I have been able to get my children educated. That's the best achievement in my life.

— Abdus Salam, a male mover, Satgailijhara, Bangladesh

Three ideologies have long shaped thinking about poverty and "the poor." The first two can be traced back to the Industrial Revolution, when large numbers of poor people emerged in the cities of England. The Victorian view is that people are poor because of their character deficits and moral failings; hence charity combined with uplifting moral instruction is the appropriate solution. Marxists, by contrast, argue that the system is stacked against the poor, and thus the poor can be helped only by changing the system. Poor people are rightly fatalistic, by this logic, and their own initiative has no role to play. Although these two worldviews differ radically, both deny poor people their agency.

In the past century, American anthropologist Oscar Lewis posited a "culture of poverty" (1959, 1966). He described it as a complex of many characteristics including alienation, passivity, laziness, feelings of powerlessness and unworthiness, and low aspirations, not to mention addictions, alcoholism, and crime. These cultural deficits, he argued, are passed from generation to generation within families. His views have informed debates and policy making on welfare in the United States. There is still a persistent belief, though it may be vehemently denied, that poor people have no one to blame but themselves for their plight. Most recently, Charles Karelis (2007) uses cultural factors to explain the persistence of poverty in the United States and around the world.

In our study, we find very little evidence that poor people are trapped in a culture of poverty. Even in the desperately poor country of Malawi or conflict-torn communities in Indonesia and the Philippines, poor people seldom seem apathetic. Instead, they take initiatives, often pursuing many small ventures simultaneously to survive and get ahead. Some do manage to move out of poverty. In country after country, when we asked movers to name the top three reasons for their move out of poverty, the answers most frequently emphasized people's own initiative in finding jobs and starting new businesses (figure 1.2). The distribution is very similar when we examine the reasons given for any upward movement by the chronic poor. This picture, detailed in chapter 2, is far removed from a culture of laziness, passivity, and criminality.

FIGURE 1.2
Movers most frequently cite initiatives as reasons for their move out of poverty

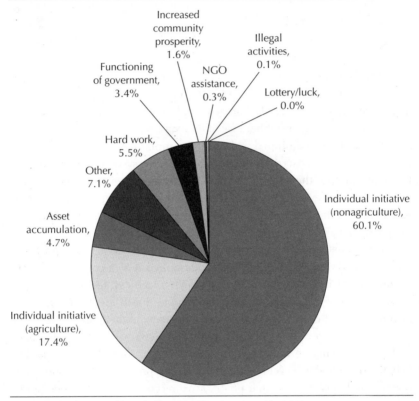

Source: Authors' analysis of household survey; all study regions; N = 3,991 movers.

Note: Figures are percentages of reasons cited by movers when asked to name the top three reasons for their movement out of poverty. "Individual initiative (nonagriculture)" includes finding jobs, investing in business, adding new sources of income, and migration.

Such initiative taking is common even among people who do not succeed in moving out of poverty. In India, where we did detailed analyses of 2,700 life stories, we find the chronic poor taking as many initiatives as the rich. Yet they have stayed poor. We find little evidence that poor people are poor because of laziness, drunkenness, or disinterest in work and saving. On the contrary, a refrain heard in country after country was the importance of hard work and of a healthy body to do hard work. A men's discussion group in Bufkaro, Uganda, summed up by saying, "The capital of a poor person is his physical strength. He uses his strength."

FIGURE 1.3
Gambling, drugs, and alcohol are rarely cited as reasons for falling

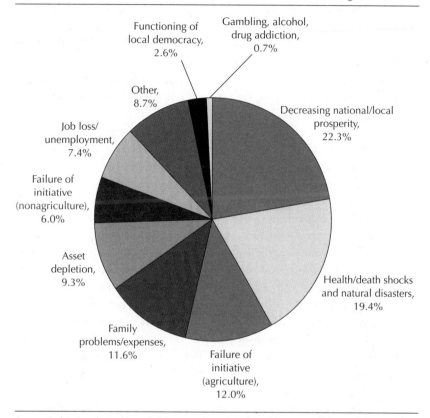

Source: Authors' analysis of household survey; all study regions; *N* = 3,661 (all four mobility groups).

Note: Figures are percentages of reasons cited by respondents in all mobility groups when asked to name the top three reasons for their downward movement.

Poor people are not saints. In a few communities in every country, and particularly in the conflict-affected contexts, we do find a few of the households at the lowest step afflicted by alcoholism, drugs, family disintegration, and hopelessness. But such severe problems affect a very small percentage of those who are poor. Gambling, drugs, and alcohol are seldom mentioned as reasons for falling by any group (figure 1.3). Instead, declines in national and local economic prosperity, health and death shocks, and family expenses play the most important roles in the downward slide.

The majority of poor people in our study do not lack confidence, although confidence is reinforced by the positive experience of moving up. Even in conflict-affected contexts, people display courage, tenacity, and goal orientation. Pedro, a 32-year-old who lives in the crime-ridden barrio of Santa María in Colombia, says, "I feel confident because I like setting goals for myself. I like moving on, overcoming obstacles."

Self-confidence and initiative should go hand in hand with high aspirations for the future. Indeed, we find that 78 percent of all households interviewed believe that their children will be better off in the years to come. Strikingly, more than 90 percent of households in the low-income contexts of Bangladesh, Senegal, Afghanistan, and Andhra Pradesh had high aspirations for their children's future. Clearly, most poor parents are not transmitting expectations of poverty to their children.

These findings have three important implications for poverty reduction strategies. When countries experience mass poverty—when more than 60 percent of the nation is poor, as in Zambia, or half the nation, as in Malawi, or one-third of the nation, as in India—this cannot be the result of large numbers of people engaging in bad conduct. Charity-oriented and other paternalistic programs may ease the pain for a few in the short run, but they are totally inadequate to lift entire nations or communities out of poverty.

Poverty assessments, the main diagnostic tools used by organizations concerned about poverty reduction, also focus on measuring the characteristics of the poor in the bottom quintiles and measuring and describing how they differ from the better off. Implicitly, they assume that poor people's characteristics are the problem. Instead, studies should focus much more on understanding the contextual constraints to poor people's initiatives and how to expand economic opportunity at the local level.

When economic prosperity is low and half the population is poor, redistributive programs that are supposed to give everyone a little may help poor people cope. But they rarely build permanent assets that reduce vulnerability: the resources they provide are often tiny, and they seldom reach everyone. In Malawi, a discussion group described a food-for-work program in their village. "It has brought social inequality because in the whole community, they only chose two people. . . . Development work is not supposed to choose. . . . You only get two people. How are these two people going to improve the whole community?"

Such programs cannot lift large numbers of people out of poverty. Social protection programs should be generous enough to enable poor people to survive shocks *and* build assets to lift them out of poverty. Moreover, the focus has to shift to increasing local-level economic prosperity, unblocking opportunity, providing business know-how so that poor people's initiatives pay off, and stopping the bleeding from health shocks. Chapter 2 explores these findings in greater depth.

Poverty is a condition, not a characteristic

My father's illness is our family problem, because I even fear to imagine what our life would be without our father, in whom lay all our hopes and aspirations.

—Munmi, a female youth, Thengal Gaon, Assam

A poor person is like a prisoner. Circumstances deny him freedom to join others in doing things. He is always anxious about how he will get food and clothing to cover his body. . . . It's not like dressing to look better, but dressing just to cover up the body because his clothes are dirty.

—Men's discussion group, Matdombo, Malawi

Is being poor more like being left-handed or like having a cold? This question may sound a little crazy, but that is the point. The question describes two different aspects of the human experience. One consists of stable, permanent characteristics like our biological sex, or our adult height, or left-handedness. These characteristics tend to be integral to our identity, although that is not always the case. The other consists of short-term, contingent situations or conditions that people experience, like wearing a red shirt or having a cold. They may persist for a long or short time, but they are not by definition permanent and they do not define our identity.

There are now hundreds of organizations seeking to address the problem of poverty. There is more and more talk of "the poor." Who are "the poor"? Where do "the poor" live? How will "the poor" be affected by globalization? But the term "the poor" is itself misleading, because it lumps together individuals who may have nothing more in common than a transitory experience of poverty.

There is nothing intrinsically wrong with creating an empirical category based on a characterization of the fraction of the population having a certain experience. For example, statisticians can, and do, identify the fraction of people who were pregnant at the time of a household survey. This group, "the pregnant," would share some demographic characteristics (they would all be women, in a limited age bracket), and they would probably tend to have certain social characteristics and behaviors (in a marriage/partnership, sexually active) in common as well. Yet no one would think of "the pregnant" as identifying a stable set of *individuals*. We all recognize pregnancy as a transitory condition that is an experience or situation of individuals at certain points in their lives.

Using our analysis of the community mobility matrixes in the study villages and the qualitative data in the life stories, we find, most boldly stated, that poverty is not a problem of "the poor." That is, although there might be a small group of people for whom "poor" is a stable ascriptive identity, for most people, poverty is a *situation*. Poverty is not, by and large, a permanent characteristic of households. It is a condition, something households *experience*.

How do we know this? Our analysis yielded three key insights, all of which point to poverty as an experience. One, people in our study communities do not see being poor as an identity. Two, there is lots of movement up and down the ladder. Three, there are strong location effects; that is, which community you live in matters. Chapter 3 explores these findings in greater depth.

There is no evidence that poor people or others in local communities see being poor as an identity. In the ladders of life, described above, there were typically more similarities than differences between households just above and households just below the poverty line. This is not consistent with the notion of being poor as an identity. Moreover, if poverty were a socially constructed identity—either self-ascribed or imposed by society—then one could not talk of escaping it through individual effort. Yet when asked how one could move out of poverty, nearly all groups, including disabled people, emphasized individual effort, self-reliance, and initiative. These are pathways out of a situation, not an identity. In life stories too, people clearly identify periods of poverty—but they emphasize that this was a situation to be coped with, not a permanent fate.

If "the poor" were in poverty because of some stable, permanent characteristic (such as being illiterate), we wouldn't have seen them experience any upward climb in the short run without a change in that characteristic. Yet our evidence suggests that there is considerable upward movement of people in poverty within localities in rural areas. This is not to say that there are no "poverty traps," only that most people currently in poverty are probably not in a poverty trap because of their personal characteristics. In the typical study region, almost half of all households that began in poverty moved up by at least one step on the ladder of life. The average proportion of households moving out of poverty altogether was almost a quarter.

Statistics of net reduction or increase in poverty levels at any point in time hide two opposing effects: movement out of poverty and movement into it. To find the net reduction in poverty, we must count those who move out of poverty *less* those who fall into poverty over the given period. Our sampled communities in Malawi, for instance, registered a marginal increase in net poverty of less than 1 percent. But this stagnation did not mean calm. Looking more closely, we see that 10.2 percent of all Malawi households sorted for the ladder of life exercise had moved out of poverty. At the same time, nearly 10.6 percent of households fell into poverty. The extent of falling thus negated the positive news on upward movement.

Across study regions, our evidence suggests very high levels of mobility, both up and down. In the typical study region, three times as many people moved up or down as the net number of people who moved out of poverty. This fluidity of households is important for policy. If "the poor" were a fixed group, then they could be identified and reached by narrowly targeted transfer programs. But with so much rising and falling, the underlying vulnerabilities of large numbers of people have to be addressed. Poverty-reducing strategies have to help people build permanent assets and livelihoods to help them cope with fluctuating life circumstances in tight economies.

No one doubts that living in a country with sustained, rapid economic growth improves one's chances of moving out of poverty. But absolute poverty reduction at the national level often hides enormous local variability. Our data suggest that local conditions do matter significantly for poverty mobility. Two key findings support this result. First, we find large variation across villages both in prosperity levels and in upward movement from poverty. There are communities in which a majority moved out of poverty and communities in which almost nobody did. Second, the differences seem to be largely local. In fact, a simple analysis of variance across communities shows that only 25 percent of the variation in upward movement of the poor can be attributed to the study region or country; the remaining 75 percent depends on the community of study within a country. When community-level effects are so strong, poverty is clearly not just an individually determined characteristic.

Economic, social, and political factors make a difference to community mobility. Positive factors that favor movement out of poverty include overall economic prosperity (especially ease in finding jobs), the physical presence of markets in a village, and proximity to cities and roads. Local government responsiveness also makes a positive difference. On the other hand, mobility is hindered by the presence of a large proportion of poor people in a village and by deep social divisions, which impede fair access to markets, facilities, and services. Somewhat less obviously, propensity toward collective action is also negatively related to mobility. Our qualitative evidence shows that in highly socially stratified communities—as in caste-dominated India, for example—poor people are excluded from the networks of the rich and pursue collective action with each other to cope and survive because they are poor; hence the negative sign.

Together, our findings belie the notion that poverty is a permanent or semi-permanent characteristic of individuals. If people were permanently trapped in poverty because of some stable identity, we wouldn't have observed large upward movements out of poverty. Nor would we have observed such high levels of movement of households up or down (churning). Finally, if mobility from poverty were largely an individual or country-of-residence phenomenon, village-level differences wouldn't matter.

The search for solutions should thus go below the national level to focus on local communities. The emphasis needs to shift to contextual efforts to increase local prosperity by providing roads and markets, improving local government attentiveness, and working to smooth social inequalities, including through organizations of poor people. Diagnostic tools to aid poverty reduction need to take into account local contexts and the factors that facilitate community prosperity. They should seek to answer the question that arises next: If poverty is a temporary condition, what determines whether households escape poverty or not?

In general, as our study in Kagera, Tanzania, demonstrates, existing economic models are better at predicting falling than at predicting movement out of poverty.[4] Our study seeks to do a better job of explaining which people move out of poverty, and how they do it, by examining local processes in depth and locating individuals within these local contexts. Our analysis is guided by a conceptual framework that examines the interactions between poor people's initiatives and opportunities within the context of local-level institutions. We examine the extent to which social stratification conditions poor people's access to economic and political opportunities, either individually or collectively. The framework is discussed in greater detail at the end of this chapter.

Power "within" can help a person move up

What restricts me is just the amount of money I get. But I am not confined inside. I think big.

        —Milward, a man in chronic poverty, Guluteza, Malawi

Power is capability. Every person who has capability is able to be in command of everything. For example, though we are poor, if we have strong will then we can do anything.

        —Discussion with young boys, Patobako, Indonesia

In thousands of conversations with men and women in our study, inner strength and confidence emerge time and again as a key factor in moving out of poverty. Moreover, self-confidence increases quickly as poor people experience some success. In fact, poor people soon start looking very similar to the rich in their sense of confidence and inner strength.

During the household interviews, we asked people to rank themselves on a 10-step ladder of power and rights, with a ranking of 1 meaning they feel totally powerless and a ranking of 10 meaning they feel powerful and in control. We use this measure as a proxy for self-confidence, defining those on the top seven rungs as feeling empowered and those on the bottom three rungs as feeling powerless (figure 1.4).

Three patterns are striking. First, it is the fallers, those who were not poor 10 years ago but who are poor today, who feel the least confident and power-

FIGURE 1.4

The never poor and movers score themselves higher in power and rights

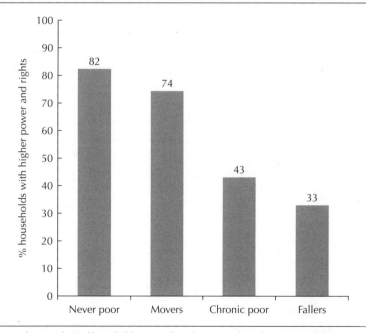

Source: Authors' analysis of household survey; all study regions where data were available; N = 8,319.

Note: Households with "high" power and rights were those that rated themselves at 4 or above on a 10-step ladder of power and rights in 2005.

ful. Only 33 percent of the fallers feel empowered, compared to 43 percent of the chronic poor.

Second, while the chronic poor on average rate themselves lower in power than movers and the never poor, almost half do feel empowered. This makes it difficult to argue that there is a generic lack of confidence among "the poor."

Third, confidence appears to be dynamic and related to experience. We see this when we compare people's rankings 10 years ago and today. Ten years ago, when they were not yet poor, nearly 60 percent of the fallers felt empowered; only 33 percent feel empowered today. Conversely, only 42 percent of the movers scored themselves as empowered 10 years ago, when they were still poor; now that they have escaped poverty, nearly 74 percent feel empowered. This implies that the well-off lose a sense of power as they experience a decline and the poor gain confidence as they move up. There are no inherent differences in confidence between the poor and rich; it is a matter of circumstances. A men's discussion group in Boodanpur, Uttar Pradesh, confirms the virtuous cycle of poverty escapes: "People start feeling more powerful after coming out of poverty because their relations with other people start improving. There is a common saying: a hungry man only invites further drought and is not welcome anywhere. A rich man, however, is welcome everywhere."

Chapter 4 highlights the importance of self-confidence and personal agency in movement out of poverty. Our evidence emerges both from multivariate regression analysis and from life stories. In the regression analysis, our measure for a household's movement out of poverty is constructed using the community perception, not the household's own rating of its status. This reduces the potential bias that could arise from regressing a person's own declaration of mobility against his or her perception of a host of other factors, including psychological well-being. We construct a measure of power and control by combing the self-ratings on power and another question on extent of control over daily decision making. We make no claims of causality; for that, we turn to the life stories. These chronicle and sequence events over a person's lifetime, with particular attention to the last 10 years.

Our results from multivariate regression analyses suggest strong associations between self-rated power and mobility in several countries, even after controlling for 22 or more other community and household variables, including education and assets. The orders of magnitude are illustrative. In the Indian states of Uttar Pradesh and Assam and in Bangladesh, Indonesia, and Uganda, the association is strong and positive. In Bangladesh, for instance, a

2-unit increase in individual control is associated with a 15 percent increase in the probability of moving out of poverty. We find even stronger and more consistently positive associations for another psychological variable, aspirations for the future, in 10 of the 15 study regions for which we have quantitative data. In West Bengal, a 2-unit increase in aspirations is associated with a 35 percent increase in the probability of escaping poverty.

Milward, a chronic poor man in Guluteza, Malawi, emphasizes the importance of personal agency. "I have struggled over the years and have been able to pass through. This has increased my confidence. Now I depend on no one. Whenever there is anything to be solved in our family, I do it alone with my wife. I have to mention here that having my wife at my side increases my confidence." Milward's self-confidence has expanded as he has gained social standing and respect in the community. He was recently chosen to be the clan overseer in his village. "I sit down and think how people can have confidence in me like that. And I think to myself what I should do so people take me to be responsible enough? Then I put on more courage."

Paradoxically, while poor people sometimes describe poverty as a python squeezing the breath out of them, they simultaneously express strong belief in their own ability to overcome the odds. As 60-year-old Gudelia from Los Rincones, Colombia, says, "We don't think in negative terms, and that is why we are able to bear our situation."

Yet poor people are not naïve about the environment in which they live or the amount of influence they have. During group discussions, they draw a clear distinction between good power and bad or coercive power. They are aware of inequality but for the most part accept a certain amount of inequality as a given. Across countries, one of the most common metaphors about inequality uses the hand and fingers: "See my hand. Are the fingers equal? No, one will always be tall."

Poor parents contain their fears and mostly do not transmit them to their children. In discussions with youths about their aspirations, we found that most young people do not see themselves as locked into their parents' occupation. They have big dreams of doing better than their parents—by starting businesses, becoming lawyers and doctors, having salaried jobs, modernizing their farms, and fighting for justice in their communities.

A range of assets and capabilities can facilitate or hinder the exercise of personal agency. One of the biggest hindrances is health shocks, which lead to reduced earnings, additional expenditures, and sometimes the death of the main breadwinner. A greater sense of control, not surprisingly, is associated with lower incidence of health shocks, as well as with more household assets, house ownership, and an educated head of household. People who scored high on the ladder of power and rights were also more likely to have engaged in political activities, such as by contacting their local politician for a personal favor.

Our findings on personal agency are also important for *how* development is done. Development interventions should be carried out in ways that respect and increase—rather than detract from—people's confidence in themselves and their families. Participatory and community-driven approaches reinforce people's own sense of agency. Entrenched gender inequalities can be addressed in part through investment in organizations of poor women. Steps to increase material assets, particularly permanent housing, can reinforce poor people's self-confidence and give them an economic foundation to build on. Equally important are strategies to prevent and buffer health shocks. Finally, it is crucial to direct poor people's initiatives to activities for which there are markets.

Belief in self can take people far, but it cannot make up for lack of economic opportunity and blocked access to opportunity in the communities where poor people live. Skewed opportunity structures thwart poor people's initiatives. Unblocking these opportunity structures requires changes in three basic institutions: markets, local democracies, and poor people's collective groups. These changes are taken up in the remaining chapters of the book.

Equal opportunity remains a dream

There is a ditch in front of us and a well behind us.
   —Women's discussion group, Govindapalle, Andhra Pradesh

The rich are moving very fast because they have many economic opportunities. When you buy a matchbox from the rich person's shop, you are adding him with more money and as for you, you lose. The poor are moving slowly, because there is limited economic change for them. The rich do not want to share with the poor.
   —Discussion with men, Bupungi, Uganda

Poor people face agonizingly limited economic choices, very different from the gilded choices of the rich. We probed opportunity sets, or the choices available to the rich and poor within communities. In most places, even those where the local economy is booming, we find that equal opportunity remains elusive.

Let us compare two life stories from Bangladesh. Nobi is a 51-year-old man who has never been poor; indeed, by the standards of his community he is rich. Rahimuddin, age 50, has always been poor. Both men live in the relatively prosperous village of Pirjadi, where 3 out of 10 people moved out of poverty in our study, higher than the average for Bangladesh (2/10).

Nobi's father owned about 22 acres of land in Pirjadi. "He spent money like anything," says Nobi. "With so much land, it was possible to live with luxury." Nobi's father enrolled him in school at the age of six but Nobi dropped out at 14, saying studying did not interest him. Nobi joined a local theater company and toured with them until he was 25. His father tried to stop him, but Nobi resisted. "We were in a good position, and there was no scarcity in the house," Nobi says. "Money was not as important as entertainment."

Nobi did start farming, at the age of 17. He tried sugarcane, then vegetables. He invested in machinery and a tubewell for irrigation and then diversified into other businesses. He bought and supplied insecticides, he opened a nursery to sell saplings, he started cultivating pineapples, and he tried farming fish. At the time of the interview, Nobi had successfully sent one of his sons to Saudi Arabia, which he called the highest point in his life. "Sending my son was a question of respect and honor," he adds. "If someone stays abroad then the house develops automatically."

Nobi also provides financial support to his two other sons, neither of whom turned out to be a great worker. His life has been relatively free of shocks. Two years prior to the interview, he suffered a stroke, but he was able to afford treatment in a good hospital in Dhaka. Reflecting on his good fortune, Nobi adds, "I know I inherited a lot of property. But proper utilization of inherited property is also important."

Rahimuddin's life unfolded much differently. He was born in another village to a destitute family, and his father died before he was born. His mother begged alms to raise him. Unlike Nobi, who had the choice of going to school, Rahimuddin is illiterate. He says, "In this life, I have no idea what is a school. My mother fed me by begging. How could I get educated?"

His first job was at the age of five, when he worked as a domestic servant to a middle-class family in his village. "I stayed at my employer's house. I worked there for years for food in lieu of wages. I was in a good condition there. My mother would also stay with me. My employer would give me 70 taka in a year, which I would give to my mother. I would do all kinds of work: rearing cows, weeding land, doing errands, everything."

Rahimuddin continued to work as hired help until he turned 21. He married in 1976 and migrated a year later to Pirjadi to work as a daily wage laborer. He tried other work as well: he made hand fans from grass and grew chilies on a sharecropping basis. But his income didn't increase. "There is no income. People buy one fan in a year. Some people don't even buy that. Still, I make them if someone wants them," he says of the only skill he knows. Of chilies, he says, "I have leased two gondas of land. I give half of the crop to the landowner. The soil is not good for cultivating paddy [rice] so I grow chilies in it. I don't even get 100 taka by selling it." He also thinks the landowner mixes powdered husk into the chilies.

To supplement his meager income, Rahimuddin's wife now cleans other people's houses. His elder son works as a tailor in a nearby town. Both he and his wife are constantly ill, but they cannot afford to see a doctor. He hears insults from the relatives with whom he lives because he does not own a home. He cannot marry off his daughter because he cannot afford a dowry. He concludes sadly: "I feel like going somewhere, leaving everything behind. But where should I go? Wherever I go, I'll have to work as a day laborer for my stomach. . . . There is no upward movement. My 50 years of life is entirely a loan. There is no capital. There is no way to repay. If I die now, I will be buried in someone else's land. People will even have to donate my shroud."

Rahimuddin lives in a community with a growing economy. But given all his disadvantages and lack of any sort of capital, he has stayed poor despite a lifetime of work. Clearly, if one is poor, it is better to live in a prosperous area than in a generally poor area. But local prosperity offers no protection against exploitation. Even poor people in booming economies may find themselves cycling through a series of low-value, dead-end activities.

In the coffee-growing area of Ngimyoni, Tanzania, traders often cheat poor producers while weighing the coffee brought to the market for sale. Such trickery even has a name, *masomba*, which means making the coffee as weightless as a sunflower. So the small farmer who hands over 60 kilograms of coffee may be paid for only 50 kilograms. Stretched thin, small coffee cultivators in Ngimyoni often borrow money from the better-off in their community, but here too they may be cheated. Before giving the farmer a loan, the lender may force him to sign an agreement saying he has borrowed three times the amount actually lent.

Poor cultivators across study regions, with their one bag of coffee or clutch of bananas, find themselves in no position to negotiate with bigger buyers. Their immediate cash needs often force them to accept the miserable prices offered or cave in to exploitative terms when taking a loan. Farmers in Bamlozi, Malawi, noted that "the small easily suffocate. It is very easy to eat up the little capital you have due to food insecurity in the home."

Chapter 5 discusses interventions to increase prosperity at the local level and make markets work more fairly for poor people's tiny enterprises. The business climate for poor people is very different from the one that large businesses enjoy. We call for liberalization from below. This includes removing restrictive government regulations; expanding access to markets, especially by providing connectivity through roads, bridges, and telephones; and integrating poor people's businesses on fairer terms in new business models. Poor people's economic organizations and business know-how are very important in helping them overcome problems of scale and move up the value chain in order to get higher return for their labor. Collective action is so important that we have devoted an entire chapter to this issue, chapter 7, where we also discuss moving toward poor people's corporations. We also offer two important insights about credit from our data. One is that the tiny loans usually provided under microcredit schemes do not seem to lift large numbers of people out of poverty. Poor people need credit that enables them to go beyond meeting immediate consumption needs and build permanent assets. Second, credit is more likely to be used productively when it is combined with improved local infrastructure, particularly rural roads, and with help in connecting to and producing for markets.

When new economic possibilities open up, whether through construction of roads, liberalization of markets, or introduction of new commercial crops, for approximately two years there seems to be a period of openness to social change. During this time it is possible to increase equality of opportunity and effect change in social relations across lines of caste, ethnicity, or religion. Eventually, however, new elites emerge—and new cycles of suffocation begin.

Responsive local democracies can help reduce poverty

Democracy is like a pond. In the pond there are several kinds of fish. The pond has not only the fish, but also other animals like frogs and snakes. The snakes catch the frog, while the big fish eat the small fish. Democracy, too, is a pond where man eats man. People elect a leader. But later, this leader becomes corrupt and exploits the people.

—Discussion with men, Raja Pukhuri, Assam

We have not been forgotten by God. We have been forgotten by politicians.

—A 38-year-old man, Guadalamoros, Mexico

Local democracies work imperfectly. Corruption abounds. Despite these imperfections, most poor people value democracy, which they equate with the freedom to vote, to think, to speak, to move, to protest, and to work. "Democracy and freedom are the same," said women in a discussion group in San Dogon, Philippines. "We cannot experience freedom if there is no democracy."

We focus on the effectiveness of democracy at the local level, irrespective of the state of democracy at the national level. At the local level, we find that there is much more variation within countries than across countries; indeed, 93 percent of the variation in the quality of local-level democracy is explained by within-country variation. Hence, the importance of understanding how local politics affects poor people's efforts to move out of poverty.

In theory, responsive local governments can play a significant role in shaping opportunities for movement out of poverty. They do so through two channels—one community-wide, the other individual. They can provide essential community services like health and schooling, secure law and order, and make and enforce rules and regulations that favor livelihoods and poor people's initiative. Local officials also distribute government aid to households, including food, agricultural inputs, houses, and land. They may provide skills training through a variety of agricultural extension and nonagricultural training programs.

We set out to learn whether the practice of democracy lives up to this promise. We wanted to find out whether there is an association between local democracy that is viewed as responsive and the likelihood of poverty escapes. We combine several measures to gauge responsiveness. Do people trust their officials? Does the local democracy take into account citizen concerns? Are people able to contact their local democracy and influence its actions? Are they satisfied with their local democracies?

Our evidence, presented in chapter 6, suggests that responsive local democracies may help people move out of poverty. We find that communities with more responsive local governments do in fact have better access to clean water, schools, doctors and nurses, and public health clinics (figure 1.5). Furthermore, the quality of education and health services also registers more improvement in these communities, as does the incidence of roads and the level of community safety. Communities where local government is responsive also have much lower corruption. The association with individual poverty escapes is more mixed: strongly positive in some of the South Asian contexts and negative in some of the conflict-affected sites. To examine these processes, we turned to communities that had experienced a

FIGURE 1.5

Communities where governments became more responsive were likely to report increased presence of services over the past 10 years

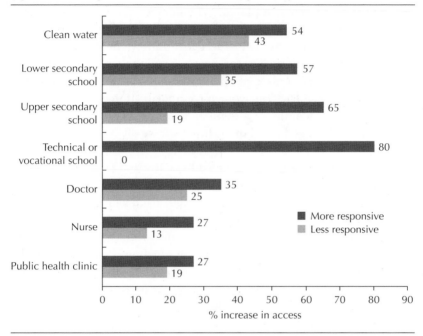

Source: Authors' analysis using data from the community questionnaire with key informants and responses to the question: "Compared to 10 years ago, does the local government now pay more, about the same, or less attention to what people like you think when it decides what to do?" *N* = 420 communities.

dramatic improvement in responsiveness of local democracy over the previous decade.

The village of Mintang in Bukidnon, Philippines, was among those that experienced a shift in democracy, from being nonresponsive 10 years ago to being responsive, just, and accountable to the residents of the community today. The turning point was the election of a good leader. Nora, a woman in Mintang, said of the village head, "Before, only the relatives of the officials were privileged to work with them. But now, even if he [the leader] is my cousin, I am still obliged to submit an application. He levels down to the people. He is one of us." Andresa added, "We just have to approach him and ask for help, even for personal reasons. Other politicians are not similar to him. They think only of themselves."

Officials at higher levels of local government were also credited with bringing projects such as health programs and solar dryers for farming that increased community prosperity. A male discussion group in Mintang spoke of the role they had played. "The number one factor that helped Mintang improve is the implementation of different projects by the barangay officials. Also, it is the style of leadership shown by the politicians in the higher government such as the governor and the senator. They are the ones who provided our place an opportunity to improve. If they ever press us down, we will suffer." The women continued, "If the current barangay chairman goes to Manila for a seminar, he never misses to report to the people the purpose and result of his trip. Now we often conduct assembly meetings."

Elections in Mintang were reported to be free and fair. In a discussion group, men claimed, "There is no coercion. We vote for someone dictated by our conscience." Assembly meetings were regular and transparent, with open discussions around issues like budgets. "The budget is shown to us during assembly. We have access to it any time," the men said. High levels of collective action and associations within Mintang supported democracy. Women praised the unity, mutual understanding, and respect within the community. "Just like a broomstick. A broomstick symbolizes unity. The midribs should be bound together to create a broomstick. If cooperation and unity are evident among people, there is democracy."

Villages like Mintang, while they exist, are hardly typical. Far more commonly, poor people find themselves facing political institutions that are captured by the elite. Becoming a local politician or affiliating oneself with the right political party is a sure way to riches. The makeup of the elite in any community changes over time, but the system of political clientelism and corruption persists. Both the rich and the poor flock to the powerful for favors. The poor typically have to wait outside, and wait longer.

In the village of Mpusola in Malawi, drought and floods brought widespread hunger between 2002 and 2005. To avoid mass starvation, the government undertook a food distribution program. The distribution of maize and targeted inputs was conducted by a government marketing agency that has since been shut down. Discussion groups all agreed that poor farmers were at a disadvantage as they could not afford to fill the pockets of officials in order to obtain the grain. They described how corrupt staff sold the maize that was intended for distribution, leaving a shortage in the depots. "There were times when the maize did come to the depots. Strangely enough, the maize would be sold at night using back doors. By the next morning, there was no maize stock in the depots. People could starve even with money in their pockets. Many people mixed sawdust with maize flour in order to have enough to meet the demands of the entire family."

A male youth group explained how political and economic alliances worked in the village. As in politics at higher levels, political alliances determined who gained membership to powerful committees and who chaired them. The stakes were smaller than at the national level but could still mean the difference between survival and starvation for poor people. "There is oppression here," said the youths. "One person is chairing eight committees. We do not have freedom of speech. When something comes to the village, the village headman and his close friends make sure that they are the first beneficiaries. We just hear later that a particular organization came to the village and it has gone." They added, "The friends and relatives of the village chief do not get intimidated as they have the law on their side. The chief is the law! Why will they be afraid?" The group went on to say that because of preferential treatment in the distribution of government programs, the community has lost interest in "community participation." They concluded, "The chief chooses only those people whom he sees will remember him when that person gets some materials. The chief is also fond of calling just those people who he is used to in making deals to form a committee. . . . Then all you will hear the next day is that 'we are in such and such committee.' All done to continue their fraudulent ways."

Government largesse in poor countries can be extremely limited, and elite capture—as in Mpusola—often leaves little for the poor. Under such circumstances, moving ahead becomes a zero-sum game: if I win, you lose. Thus, it should not be surprising that we find poor people at times locked in struggle with each other in a fight over limited resources. We found evidence of this in both our qualitative and quantitative data.

There are, fortunately, ways of uncapturing local democracy. One-third of the communities visited reported that their local government had become more responsive over time, suggesting that change is possible. Mechanisms included having good leaders; holding free and fair elections; providing access to information, particularly about local government activities; and promoting people's participation and demand-side pressure through poor people's organizations. Local leaders can play a particularly important role in expanding local economic opportunities and supporting liberalization of economic rules and regulations that unbind from below.

The most important implication of our findings is simply that poverty reduction strategies cannot ignore local politics, and that when they do, poor people are the losers. If one is to understand democracy, the focus has to be on the local level. Demand-side pressures through self-help groups and other organizations of women, men, and youth, even when their members are illiterate, help make local politicians more accountable. Availability of information at the local level, particularly about local politicians and government, is key to making democracy work for all.

Collective action helps poor people cope but not get ahead

How good are these loans? We have to repay them in installments each week. The amount they give finishes off quickly.
—Asiya, a poor woman, Hasanbagh, Bangladesh

People have developed well with the help of women's self-help groups. They have more knowledge. They are becoming partners in politics. They want to know about government programs and form good, bad opinions on parties.
—Discussion with men, Bestharapalle, Andhra Pradesh

I place a lot of importance on relations with my neighbors. They are my only capital in life.
—Aziza, a woman in chronic poverty, Abzif, Morocco

Poor people in a community frequently come together to pool their labor or their cash or their skills. This pooling involves tiny, tiny resources. The paradox of this collective action is that while it may enable poor people to cope and survive, it typically does not help them move out of poverty. Even though it involves thousands of poor people helping each other in groups, since the groups are scattered rather than connected or aggregated, they have not been able to achieve the advantages that come with scale. We discuss ways out of this deadlock in chapter 7.

Ironically, the real benefit of poor people's collective action is to society. Working together in small groups creates unity, trust, social cohesion, and a sense of social belonging to units larger than the immediate family. It fosters a sense of citizenship essential to functioning, stable, and cohesive democratic societies. This is the beginning of civil society.

In Mbata, Ruvuma, Tanzania, women came together in *nsango* groups to survive the economic crisis that followed the dismantling of government-run coffee cooperatives. Each group has 10–15 members who contribute a small sum each week to a collective savings pool. The contributions are primarily used to buy clothes for group members and their children or to support tiny businesses. Women may buy wheat to bake a few loaves of bread, or sorghum to make a local brew. If the business takes off, women are able to help others, save, and meet daily household needs. Salome says, "The money enables us to help one another in case of an emergency. For example, when one of the group members has a problem, she would be the first to receive the contributions. Men do not have such groups because they own property like livestock."

People in Ruvuma also form collective labor groups called *ngoro*. These consist of 5 to 15 men or women who help each other cultivate the region's steep and infertile slopes. With no cattle to provide manure, people pool their effort to dig pits (*ngoros*) that are used to compost grass, weeds, and crop residues. Crops are rotated so soil fertility can be maintained. All members work on one member's farm for an agreed number of days, then move to another member's farm, and so on, until all of their farms are cultivated.

We found several instances of small, spontaneous groups like the nsango and ngoro across our study regions. Although helpful, such groups on their own did not lift people out of poverty. Poor people as a group lack cash, assets, education, market know-how, and connections with the rich and powerful. When poor people associate only with each other, they bring only their own meager resources to the table. Poor people understand these constraints and affirm that "there is a limit to how much one hungry man can feed another." The challenge is to extend these positive local traditions of mutual help so that they reach across social lines to involve those who can bring in new resources, ideas, and skills.

This is difficult, however, and in practice, most people rely on the institution closest to them: their family. In the 2,700 life stories from India, the family was the most frequently mentioned institution that helped people accumulate assets. People rated help from family as more important than help from public institutions like the government, more important than help from civil society, and more important than engagement with the private sector (figure 1.6). This was true for all four mobility groups: the movers, fallers, chronic poor, and never poor.

Given the universal dependence on kin, we analyze the characteristics of successful families and discuss how other types of organizations, from small groups to cooperatives to equity firms owned by poor people, might mimic some of their features. We discuss a few large-scale successful efforts such as Grameen Bank in Bangladesh, the women's self-help movement in Andhra

FIGURE 1.6

Families are rated the most important institution for asset accumulation by all mobility groups in Indian study regions

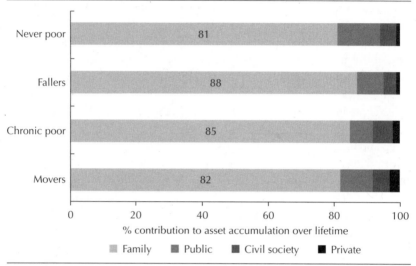

% contribution to asset accumulation over lifetime

■ Family   ■ Public   ■ Civil society   ■ Private

Source: Narayan, Nikitin, and Richards (2009), using coded data from life stories gathered from the Indian study regions; N = 2,700 life stories.

Pradesh, and the community-driven development program that has spread to over half the villages in Indonesia.

Nongovernmental organizations (NGOs) are hardly mentioned as a support in moving out of poverty. NGO assistance accounts for only 0.3 percent of the reasons cited for poverty escapes (figure 1.2). This does not mean that NGOs are not present or doing important humanitarian work. It means either that NGOs affect only a small number of people or that their work is not perceived to have a direct effect on poverty. Collective action that involves federated organizations of poor people has the potential to transform lives by connecting poor producers to markets and involving them in economic activities higher up the value chain. But creating such organizations takes time and financial resources and does not produce immediate returns; as a result, this is an area of investment failure on a massive scale. Such a transformation in thinking and practice is not easy. It requires the coming together of people who understand local realities and community organizing, on the one hand, with people who possess capital, business skills, and market access, on the other. As long as these two groups, civil society and private business, remain

at war, poor people will remain excluded from markets, and important innovations, including poor people's corporations and changes in mainstream
business models to ensure fairer returns, will not be achieved.[5]

Poverty reduction should be guided by lessons from poor people

Freedom means having opportunities.
                        —Discussion with women, Chinxe, Mexico

In sum, our evidence suggests that poor women, men, and youth doing
day labor like Mamba, tending tiny plots like Ayesha, and working in small
businesses like Adolfo do not lack the drive to do well and improve their
lives. Some, like Adolfo and Ayesha, are successful; others, like Mamba, are
not. Yet the great majority of those who are stuck in poverty do not give up;
they continue to aspire to better lives, for themselves and for their children.
Chapter 8 provides our ideas on creating poverty-reducing strategies that
build on poor people's agency and reflect what we learned from them about
how people escape poverty.

The people we met defy the various Victorian, cultural, and Marxist inter-
pretations of poverty that classify "the poor" as a group unable to help themselves. Poor people are not in any collective sense lazy, drunk, or stupid. They
work hard to eke out a living and seize opportunities as they arise. Indeed, a
major finding of the study is that there is no such fixed group as "the poor."
Poverty is a condition, not a permanent identity.

Given the inadequacies of existing approaches to poverty reduction, in
our concluding reflections we offer three principles that should guide future
efforts. These principles are based on lessons from poor and recently poor
people themselves—the thousands who participated in sharing their experiences with our field teams.

The first principle is that all actions should seek to *expand the scope for
people in poverty to utilize their agency*, in both the public and private spheres.
Poor people have needs but reducing people to just their needs robs them of
their aspirations, dreams, ambitions, and skills—in short, of their ability to
help themselves. Poor people's agency is important at the individual level and
also the collective level through organizations of the poor. When these organizations gain some scale and connect with markets and the public sector, poor
people become important players in decisions that impact their lives.

Across the study regions, we were struck by the faith poor people still
place in the marketplace. Faced with enormous barriers there, they still believe

that markets will work, and they want to do business on an equal and fair footing. Thus, the second principle is that actions should seek to *transform markets so that poor people can access and participate in them fairly*. There are several keys to expanding fair access: scaling up and linking poor people's livelihood activities; providing "connectedness" through roads, telephones, electricity, and irrigation; easing access to loans that can be used for production; and providing information, business know-how, and skills to connect to mainstream markets.

Similarly, poor people still believe that governments and their local democracies can do good, and they want to participate in them. Freedom and democracy are of both intrinsic and instrumental value. The third principle, therefore, is that *well-functioning local democracies can help people move out of poverty*. We saw many examples of poorly functioning local democracies. Governance at the local level is all too often a zero-sum contest for spoils, marred by pervasive corruption that creates opportunities for some and barriers for others. But the combination of good local leaders, fair elections, improved access to information, participation, and collective action can enable poor people to demand accountability from local leaders. Local leaders can do much to liberalize and expand economies from below.

The Conceptual Framework

We started our research with broad questions. What are the processes that result in some poor people moving out of poverty while others in the same community remain stuck in poverty? What is the role of social relations in moving out of poverty? How important are psychological factors and personal agency? Does local democracy make a difference? We deliberately did not adopt any particular conceptual framework because we knew that early marriage to concepts and measuring tools limits what you see. We wanted to explore before we started limiting.

We deliberately collected too much data, using 10 different measuring tools to probe the whys and hows of poverty escapes and stagnation. We expected that this would create an enormous challenge in data analysis, and it did. We are not recommending this as a research strategy to everyone, but we think it is important in poverty studies to cast a wide net and to look beyond what one might first assume to be the correct explanation.

Our data analyses proceeded in three stages. In the first phase, which took six months, we used an inductive approach to develop a coding system for the analysis of life stories. We let the data speak to us. After reading 200 life stories, we developed categories that would "catch" most of the information emerging from people's descriptions of the key events in their lives and the processes that facilitated or hindered their accumulation of assets.

In the second phase, we analyzed 60 community pairs. The communities in each pair were selected to vary in terms of one particular variable: social stratification or democracy, collective action, and economic opportunity. In one pair, for instance, community A might differ from community B only in levels of social stratification, holding other variables constant. We analyzed these communities using a variant of the SOSOTEC technique that we learned from Robert Chambers during the Voices of the Poor study.[6] We read reports, interviews, and descriptions, cut them into strips, and sorted the ideas, gradually compiling them into subsets and larger sets and diagramming the relationships between them. Given our huge data set, this process also took several months. The diagrams became very elaborate as our teams mapped relationships across communities and country contexts. This technique appears disorganized and time-consuming but surpasses all others in "letting voices emerge" during the analysis phase. In particular, it delays the imposition of expert concepts until much later.

Figure 1.7 shows one such diagram created by our team, for the village of Bufkaro in Uganda. In this predominantly poor community, villagers cultivate sorghum, beans, and sweet potatoes. Poor people have limited options to invest in business opportunities, and credit is hard to get. "It is not feasible to start a retail shop because one cannot afford to buy the items for the fear that the loan acquired to start the business may be wasted," explained one discussion group. The local government is not helpful. "No government programs operate in this village because our leaders are not serious at all," lamented another discussion group. "No community meetings are held between the community members and the local council authorities." Lack of such meetings is cited as one of the reasons why the community does not receive timely information about development programs.

While poor people struggle with daily wage labor, the handful of rich people in the village face very different opportunity sets. They own shops and vehicles and have money to invest in other profitable ventures to expand their sources of income further. Their friends are other rich people who can loan them money if the need arises. One discussion group said, "When you are rich, you are more powerful because people respect you so much. If a poor person is going to a rich person's house, he fears to talk to the rich person."

Poor people in Bufkaro come together to cope with their circumstances, sometimes among themselves and sometimes in community-wide groups.

FIGURE 1.7
Collective action helps people cope in Bufkaro, Uganda

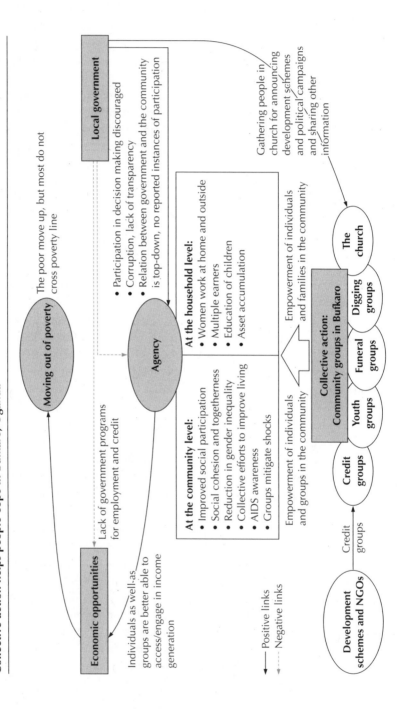

Some of these groups are supported by NGOs. They include mutual aid and burial societies that use contributions of money and labor from members to transport sick people to health facilities or organize funerals. "Before the association, the bereaved families would sleep on an empty stomach; sometimes they would even sell part of their land for [funeral] celebrations," recounted a group of women. "Now when a member loses someone, the burial groups use the money to buy food, a coffin, and other requirements for the funeral." Women also join digging societies, working land for the well-off households in the community and using the money to buy household items and pay school fees. The local church serves as a vital source of information about development schemes and community programs.

"If you do not belong to any group in this village, then you cannot survive," said women in a ladder of life discussion. Group activities help poor people in Bufkaro cope with few resources, but they do not seem to help them move out of poverty. While some poor people manage to move up, most do not cross the poverty line.

Is movement out of poverty in Bufkaro low because poor people, for whatever reason, lack initiative? Or do poor people fail to escape poverty because their initiatives meet resistance and are blocked? Or are poor people simply excluded from the economic, social, and political opportunities that the well-off enjoy? How does collective action by the rich and poor block or facilitate economic and political opportunities?

The interplay of factors revealed in the community diagrams eventually led to the conceptual framework adopted for the quantitative analyses carried out in the third year. This conceptual framework, described below, guided the third and final phase of our data analysis, which was quantitative. This included multivariate regression analyses to test the role of local-level institutions in the movement out of poverty while taking into account other community and household features.

Key concepts: Initiative and opportunity

In studying hundreds of diagrams from individual communities, the two overarching concepts that emerge are *initiative* and *opportunity*. The interaction between these two largely structures the movement out of poverty (figure 1.8).

In studying these movements, we can make an analogy with flows from physical systems. If we see that a weak flow of electric current is causing a bulb to glow faintly, it could be either because the power source is weak or because

FIGURE 1.8

Initiative and opportunity interact to produce upward movement

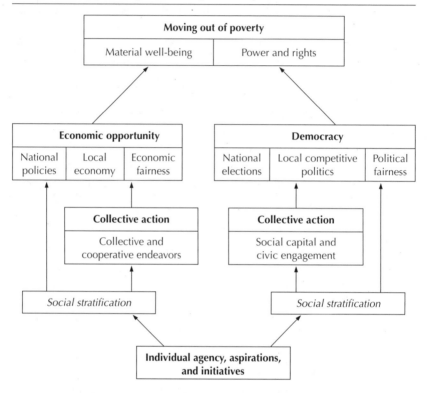

the resistance to the flow of power is high, so the power is dissipated in heat. Or if we see a trickle of water flowing past us, it could be because there was little water at the source or because obstacles are blocking the flow.

We start with poor people. At the source of poverty reduction are the initiatives that millions and millions of individuals and households take to better their lives.[7] Such initiatives may involve growing new crops, using new agricultural techniques or equipment, accessing new markets, starting a business, getting a job, or migrating for employment. People take initiatives based on their self-confidence, agency, aspirations, and empowerment—their sense that what they do matters and has the potential to succeed.

Initiative can also be embedded in collective action, from pooled labor or savings to cooperation in marketing to fully cooperative firms. Both the poor and the rich can act collectively, either through formal organizations or through informal groups and networks. Both usually associate with their own kind—the rich with the rich and the poor with the poor. At times, the interests of the rich and poor may converge, as when everyone wants to solve a community-wide problem. At other times, the rich and poor compete for influence and access to limited resources. Collective action by the poor will then meet with resistance from the rich.

It is a reality that most societies are divided, most often along lines of caste, ethnicity, gender, religion, or wealth. Economic, social, and political organizations and networks fissure along the same social divides, leading to "durable inequality" between social groups (Tilly 1999). Across all study regions and all topics, we find social stratification to be a conditioning factor that affects both initiative and opportunity.

Whether economic initiative, either individual or collective, leads to upward movement depends on the opportunities available and access to them. We consider three aspects: national policies, local economies, and economic fairness. As detailed in chapter 5, there is no question that progress in overall national prosperity has an enormous influence on the pace of poverty reduction. But our study is not primarily about the link between national policies and poverty, a field of inquiry for which our techniques are not well suited. Instead, we focus on the local level. How do opportunities at the very local level (as small as the village) structure the movement out of poverty? How does the fairness of economic opportunity—whether individuals from all walks of life are able to effectively participate in the economy—influence poverty reduction, at the local level and hence also at the national level?

In the political sphere too, people participate both individually and collectively. We acknowledge the importance of electoral democracy at the national level in framing political freedom. But our focus is again at the local level. It is participation in open, competitive, *local* political processes that determines access to and influence over local governments and government-financed programs. Poor people can participate individually through elections. But organized collective action is just as important, as the ability to express common interests is key to successful participation and representation, especially among marginalized groups. Moreover, the structures of political opportunity strongly influence whether local politics helps or harms poor people in their efforts to improve their well-being. We are concerned with the efficacy of electoral accountability, the presence of political clientelism, and the extent of fairness in opportunities to participate in public decision making. An important aspect of the latter is the degree of discrimination against women.

In reality, of course, the boundaries between the political and economic are blurred and contested. Political power can thwart or create economic opportunity, and economic success can increase power and influence in the political sphere. We stress these interconnections throughout the book.

We have written this book to give voice to thousands of poor people—women, men, and youths—who shared their life experiences, their hopes, and their dreams with us. Ayesha, Mamba, and Adolfo in our opening stories seized whatever tiny opportunities they could find. And there are millions and millions of others just like them.

Poor people do not give up. They try again and again. Poor people are ready to work with businesses, NGOs, foundations, students, concerned citizens, governments—with any of us—to innovate and invest in their lives and communities. Can we find the courage and imagination to try again with them?

Notes

Epigraph: The letter from Marshal to Arthur Lyon Bowley is from *The Correspondence of Alfred Marshall, Economist*, vol. 3, *Towards the Close, 1903–1924* (New York: Cambridge University Press, 1996).

1. So this book could protect the privacy of individuals, all local-level communities in the study (villages, barrios, etc.) are identified by pseudonyms in this book. Higher-level entities (blocks, districts, provinces, regions, states, and countries) are identified by their real names. To increase readability when we use materials from the 21 country studies commissioned for the Moving Out of Poverty project, we reference only the name of the village and country. The names of the team leaders for the country studies and researchers are in appendix 1. The country reports can be found on the Moving Out of Poverty study Web site at http://go.worldbank .org/8K2Q8RYZ10.
2. Forthcoming volumes in the Moving Out of Poverty series will probe specific contexts in greater depth. Volume 3 will focus on India, and volume 4 on conflict-affected communities.
3. The ladder of life discussion was not conducted in all study communities. For instance, some studies that built on existing panel data sets (Kagera in Tanzania, and Cambodia) did not use the ladder of life exercise and instead identified household mobility status using information in the panel. Only qualitative data were gathered for the Sri Lanka tea estate and Morocco studies. While discussions around the ladder were held in the Afghanistan study sites, the households sorted for the community mobility matrixes were too few to be quantified. Figure 1.1, therefore, is based on ladder of life data from 16, not 21, study regions.
4. The study in Kagera, based on a panel data set and led by Joachim De Weerdt, found that although 78 percent of the fallers were predicted correctly, only half of those who were predicted to move out of poverty actually did so.

5. An increasing number of experiments are attempting to create new partnerships between NGOs and businesses and new financial instruments that allow poor people to scale up their businesses and move higher up in the value chain. The Clinton Global Initiative has mobilized US$30 billion in commitments since 2005, and it is effectively bringing many different actors together across political and ideological divides to innovate on a large scale on behalf of poor people (see http://www.clintonglobalinitiative.org).
6. SOSOTEC stands for Self-Organizing System on the Edge of Chaos. The exercise is done in groups.
7. We often use the terms "individual" and "household" interchangeably, although we recognize that complicated gender dynamics inside the household can keep the household from acting as a single unit.

Stories of the Poor,
Stories by the Poor

*The African peasant only knows the
eternal renewal of time, rhythmed by the
endless repetition of the same gestures
and the same words. In this imaginary
world where everything starts over and
over again, there is no place for human
endeavor or for the idea of progress.*

—NICOLAS SARKOZY, PRESIDENT OF FRANCE,
lecture at the University of Dakar, Senegal, 2007

*I did not sit idle. I started the business
of baking bread and selling it in the
village market. To increase our income,
we were also selling extra food crops
from our food harvest and selling coffee
from the farm. Sometimes I also worked
in the factory as a casual laborer.*

—ALTENZIA, A 42-YEAR-OLD PEASANT WOMAN,
Ngimyoni, Ruvuma, Tanzania

CHAPTER 2

We start our exploration of underlying assumptions about "the poor" and causes of poverty with the 18th-century Scottish economist Adam Smith. In his seminal work *The Wealth of Nations*, Smith (1776) wrote:

> By necessaries I understand not only the commodities which are indispensably necessary for the support of life, but what ever the customs of the country renders it indecent for creditable people, even of the lowest order, to be without. A linen shirt, for example, is, strictly speaking, not a necessary of life. The Greeks and Romans lived, I suppose, very comfortably, though they had no linen. But in the present times, through the greater part of Europe, a creditable day-laborer would be ashamed to appear in public without a linen shirt, the want of which would be supposed to denote that disgraceful degree of poverty which, it is presumed, nobody can well fall into, without extreme bad conduct.

This brief excerpt suggests several conclusions about the nature of poverty. One is that the definition of poverty is a *social* construct: it varies depending on the particular context and time. People must have the commodities and conditions that their own society deems essential in order to be considered decent, to belong, and to walk without shame. More recently, Amartya Sen (1999) has argued for an expansion of the notion of poverty from one based on commodities to one based on a broader set of human capabilities and freedoms.

But there is another important message in Adam Smith's text: that not having what is customary is cause for shame and is evidence of bad behavior. Smith implies that poverty is a disgrace because it can be avoided. If opportunities to avoid poverty are widely available, then it follows logically that one cannot fall into a "disgraceful degree of poverty" except by "extreme bad conduct." His remark is a wonderfully concise statement of the view that being poor is a poor person's fault.

Today's free market proponents espouse a similar ideology. Since markets provide ample and equal opportunity, as they contend, then the cause of poverty must lie with a lack of initiative on the part of poor people. This could be due to a lack of self-confidence or to a belief that action is futile and will not pay off in results. It could reflect a vicious cycle of behavioral pathologies such as laziness, drug addiction, and crime. Whatever the cause, there is a "culture of poverty" and the culture of poverty is the cause of poverty. Poverty is poor people's fault.

The exact opposite stance is that there is no opportunity for the poor: the poor are caught in a structural trap not of their own making and from which their own efforts cannot extract them. Proponents of this view also believe in a culture of poverty, but they see it as effect rather than cause. People who must cope with inexorable poverty create a culture of poverty as a defense. In this fatalistic view, poor people's supposed low aspirations and reluctance to take initiative are rational responses to the world as they find it. This plays out in political life as well, where the poor are trapped in political structures that exclude them.

Few people would admit to holding either of these views so starkly expressed. Among many economic elites there is a sense that opportunity is not sufficiently equal. In a historical irony, several countries with Marxist governments such as China and Vietnam now offer a wide array of market-based opportunities for the poor. Nevertheless, like old ghosts, these notions still rattle around upstairs and it is useful to bring them out into the open and exorcise them.

Let us examine the stories that people tell or have heard about "the poor"—and the contrasting stories poor people told us themselves. Stories, myths, and legends reside deep in the human psyche and often persist despite facts to the contrary. These tales of a culture of poverty are harmful and should be dismissed; they limit our imagination about the potential of poor people and strategies for ending poverty. Poor people are not the obstacles to poverty reduction. Rather, they are the most important actors and contributors to meaningful change.

Is Poverty Poor People's Fault?

I feel confident because I like setting goals for myself. I like moving on, overcoming obstacles.

—Pedro, an internally displaced poor man, age 32,
Santa María, Colombia

At age 15, I began work, breaking rocks. Later, I rented land to grow tobacco. The first time I planted tobacco, I just copied the way others did it. But it rained, so I didn't produce anything. Even now the biggest obstacle is rain. If the tobacco is good, it sells. I can eat.
        —Dul, a man in chronic poverty, Tattantok, Indonesia

The term "culture of poverty" is strongly associated with the work of American anthropologist Oscar Lewis, who first advanced the notion in his 1959 work on five families in urban Mexico. That ethnographic study proposed 70 characteristics that Lewis believed were frequently found in members of the "underclass." They included no sense of history, short time horizons, no savings or future orientation, low aspirations, an unreliable work ethic, unstable families, and unwed mothers. Children of the poor, he argued, are socialized into believing that they deserve to be poor, leading to low aspirations, low effort, and an inability to escape poverty.[1] Lewis further elaborated his theory in an ethnographic study of Puerto Ricans (1966). His ideas have persisted in the popular imagination for decades, but they have often been misunderstood: many have cited the "culture of poverty" as a cause of poverty, rather than as an adaptive response to and consequence of persistent poverty, as Lewis proposed.

Some scholars have extended Lewis's theory from the household to the country level, suggesting that entire societies are caught up in a culture of poverty. In their edited volume *Culture Matters*, Lawrence Harrison and Samuel P. Huntington (2000) link lack of economic progress in many developing countries to religious and cultural values. In his foreword, Huntington contrasts Ghana and South Korea: they had the same per capita income in the 1960s but diverted dramatically by the 1990s, when Ghana had one-fifteenth the gross national product of South Korea. He concludes that the critical difference is that Koreans "valued thrift, investment, hard work, education, organization, and discipline" while Ghanaians had "different values" (xiii). Several contributors to the volume offer typologies of values that supposedly distinguish a dynamic culture from a stagnant one. Harrison lists 10 values related to time, work ethic, frugality, education, community orientation, justice, authority, and secularism. Mariano Grondona offers a similar list of 20 characteristics presumed to be absent in societies that remain economically backward. These and similar lists resonate depressingly with the concept of a culture of poverty.

At the country level, it is easy to deconstruct these cultural explanations as the ex post rationalizations they often are. Country economic growth accelerates and decelerates, sometimes almost overnight. Intellectuals derided India for its "Hindu rate of growth" and China as a nation of communist ideologues. Such cultural explanations can hardly account for the transformation of India and China from basket cases in the 1960s and 1970s to the "dancing giants" that are already shaping the 21st century (Winters and Yusuf 2007).

But perhaps there is a culture of poverty at the individual or household level? If so, we did not find it.

Amid poverty, high aspirations

I am expecting to make my kid progress in life. He wants to be an industrial engineer, and his goal is my goal.
       —Sara, a 35-year-old displaced woman, Villa Rosa, Colombia

It was in 2004 that Joy gave birth to our son. The feeling was unexplainable when I first saw him. That was the time that I told myself that I have to work harder for the future of my son and for our family.
       —Naem, a 27-year-old man, Bakimati, Philippines

At the end of the household interviews, we asked people about their expectations for themselves and for their children. We use this question as a proxy for aspirations. A majority of all respondents, 66.5 percent, said that they hope to be better off in the future, while 22 percent expect to remain in a situation similar to their current one. Only 11.5 percent expect to be worse off.

There were no noteworthy differences between study regions in South Asia, Africa, and Latin America, nor did the conflict-affected sites differ significantly from others. Compared to other settings, higher percentages of households in two African contexts, Uganda and Ruvuma, Tanzania, expect to be worse off. However, in the African country of Senegal, 94 percent expect to be better off. Also expressing hope for a better future were 92 percent in poverty-stricken Bangladesh, 81 percent in war-torn Afghanistan, and 77 percent in Uttar Pradesh, one of the poorest states of India. Even among the chronic poor, 60 percent across the study contexts hold positive expectations for their own future. Despite bone-grinding hard work and privation, people manage to remain optimistic.

People have even higher expectations and aspirations for their children than for themselves. Overall, 77 percent of households feel that their children will be better off in the future. Another 15 percent say their children will be in a similar situation to their own, and only 8 percent are pessimistic about their children's future. No major differences were observed across study regions.

Over 90 percent of parents in Bangladesh, Afghanistan, Senegal, and Andhra Pradesh have positive aspirations for their children. People in the African study regions other than Senegal, though, are slightly less optimistic (figure 2.1). These findings mirror results from wider surveys such as the one undertaken by the Pew Global Attitudes Project (2007).

More importantly, we found very little evidence that parents were transmitting expectations of poverty to their children. A large majority of the chronic poor, 69 percent, had positive expectations for their children's future (figure 2.2). This was close to the average for all four mobility groups. Not

FIGURE 2.1
Majority of all households have high aspirations for their children

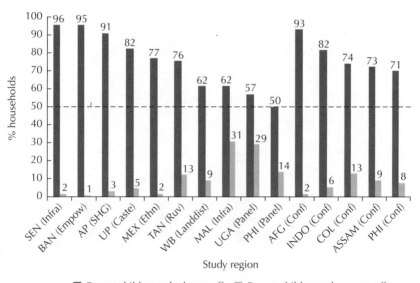

Source: Authors' analysis of household survey; all study regions where data were available; *N* = 8,298.

Note:

AFG (Conf) = Afghanistan, Conflict
AP (SHG) = Andhra Pradesh, Self-help groups
ASSAM (Conf)= Assam, Conflict
BAN (Empow) = Bangladesh, Women's
   empowerment
COL (Conf) = Colombia, Conflict
INDO (Conf) = Indonesia, Conflict
MAL (Infra) = Malawi, Infrastructure
MEX (Ethn) = Mexico, Ethnicity

PHI (Conf) = Philippines, Conflict
PHI (Panel) = Philippines, Panel study
SEN (Infra) = Senegal, Infrastructure
TAN (Ruv) = Tanzania, Ruvuma
UGA (Panel) = Uganda, Panel study
UP (Caste) = Uttar Pradesh, Caste
WB (Landdist) = West Bengal, Land distribution
   reforms

unexpectedly, there were some group differences: movers and never poor were slightly more optimistic, chronic poor and fallers slightly less so.

Not only do people aspire for a better future for their children, but also they actively take steps to ensure it, especially by sending them to school if they can. Poor men and women across the study regions spoke of how education was the only inheritance they could leave for their children. In ranking levels of well-being, ladder of life focus groups drew clear distinctions based on people's ability to educate their children. In Kramrrak, Indonesia, for example, people at step 1 (*teri*) were described as the unemployed, "Those whose children have to start working after finishing elementary education." Those at step 2 (*tongkol*) are usually fishermen who are able to send their children to senior high school but cannot afford to send them to college. Those at step 3 (*kakap*) are large landowners and rice traders. Their children are college graduates.

FIGURE 2.2

Movers and never poor have higher hopes, but even chronic poor and fallers have high aspirations for their children

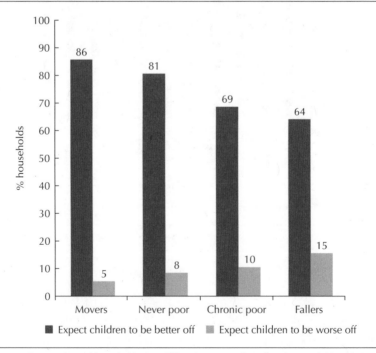

Source: Authors' analysis of household survey; all study regions where data were available; N = 8,298.

In a female discussion group in Ponky Kda, Cambodia, young girls said, "Education is the most important asset in the world. An educated person never fears facing financial insecurity because he or she gets a permanent job, even if it is as a worker in a garment factory. Those who have no education do not have such fortune. They become mobile laborers, a more risky job." Across the oceans, young Habiba in Ferjama, Morocco, agreed. She wanted to start her own folk dance group but felt she lacked the education to do so. "I am illiterate. It limits my thoughts and capacities."

Despite overwhelming optimism, a sense of anxiety persists. People fear becoming ill and losing family members to illness. Health and death shocks were cited as one of the most common reasons for falling into poverty. Social shocks like divorce or marital separation or a rift in the family also affected mental well-being. People spoke about the loss of tangible assets such as health but also about a range of intangible assets, including happiness and peace of mind.

Anxiety about war is common in conflict-affected contexts. Sivapakyam, a woman who returned to Sri Lanka after the ceasefire between the government and rebel troops there, still feared the war. She said, "I hope that the war won't restart, and we will not have to go through the same experiences again. We live in fear always. We sometimes question why we came back. Is there a purpose in living like this? Now we are afraid and panic at the sound of firecrackers."

Hard work as a route out of poverty

The capital of a poor person is his physical strength. He uses his strength.
                              —Men's discussion group, Bufkaro, Uganda

People do not recognize any exhaustion. Never let go of any chances. If fishermen still have time after seafaring, they will use the time to do other things.
                              —Men's discussion group, Kramrrak, Indonesia

Eat whatever namak [salt] and roti [bread] you get through your own hard labor, but don't extend your palm toward others begging.
                              —A poor woman, Shekh Dahir, Uttar Pradesh

There is sometimes an interesting confluence of diametrically opposing political viewpoints. Many people argue that the reason for poverty is that poor people do not work hard. Of those who believe this, some say the problem is the deficient attitude of the poor themselves—that they are lazy.

Others say that poor people do not work hard because they believe the system is rigged against them and therefore hard work will not pay off. In other words, poor people do not try, and they are right not to try; they are right to be fatalistic. Using data from the World Values Survey, Alesina, Glaeser, and Sacerdote (2001) report that twice as many Americans as Europeans think the poor are lazy (60 percent versus 26 percent). Europeans tend to place more credence in the existence of poverty traps.

These beliefs are mirrored in policy choices. U.S. tax rates and social spending are sharply lower than those in Europe, reflecting the notion that everyone will work harder and prosper more if there is less government help to fall back on. Although the average employee in the United States works 1,600 hours a year compared to 1,200 hours in Europe (Alesina and Angeletos 2005), hours worked by the bottom quintile are comparable in both settings (Alesina and Glaeser 2004). And although Americans are more likely than Europeans to believe that hard work pays off, actual mobility out of poverty is *higher* in Germany and the Scandinavian countries than in the United States (Bénabou and Tirole 2006).

What do people in poverty say? The primary refrain we heard in story after story, in discussion group after discussion group, and in country after country was the importance of hard work and persistence as a means to move out of poverty. Even rural people surviving on next to nothing in some of the poorest countries in Africa—the sample includes Malawi, Senegal, Uganda, and remote regions of Tanzania—voiced strong belief in the importance of hard work and tenacity. This theme also emerged repeatedly in communities beset by conflict, as in Afghanistan.

Across the study regions, hard work emerges as important even when people are working for next to nothing. Poor men and women almost everywhere report working for a pittance in order to get a start. In Chakax, Yucatán, Mexico, 46-year-old Tomás said, "You have to work hard to move ahead. When I began, I earned 60 pesos a week, and in the end I earned up to 300 pesos." In Upper Deuri, Assam, a men's discussion group insisted that if daily wage laborers, whom they placed at the lowest step of the ladder, want to move up, they have no choice but to take any job available. "The laborers have to work hard and concentrate. But most importantly, they should have a sense of responsibility and consciousness for any work. They have to do whatever work they get. Otherwise their families would starve."

In other places, too, people emphasize the importance of a good work ethic. Poor men and women who engage in vegetable trading or have small grocery kiosks need to have what the men in Upper Deuri called "a consciousness not to be a slave to laziness." A men's discussion group in Galalolo, North Maluku, Indonesia, said, "A good work ethic is displayed by a person who works well and becomes trusted by his boss and business associates. This includes working promptly, being punctual, and doing high-quality work to get repeat orders." Interestingly, it is only when people become well off that special importance is given to having a "a good moral character," which involves an ethic of helping others. For example, government employees in Upper Deuri who are classified as nonpoor can progress if they have "good human qualities and help others." Selfishness or lack of altruism is looked down upon. The men said, "If they engage in illegal work, corruption, and don't help others, their position will move down in society."

The importance of hard work among poor people who are resource-constrained also emerges in the quantitative analyses of life stories from India. The inputs that go into supporting agricultural initiatives reveal an interesting pattern (figure 2.3). Compared to the never poor, the chronic poor more often

FIGURE 2.3

Movers and never poor support their agricultural initiatives through purchase of assets, while chronic poor rely on hard work

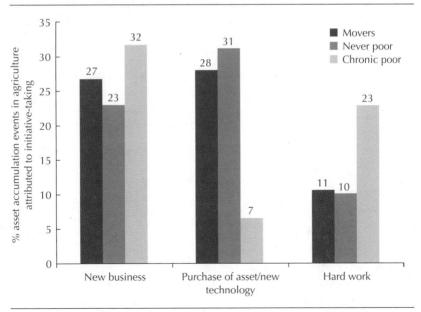

Source: Narayan, Nikitin, and Richards (2009), using coded data from life stories gathered in the Indian study regions; $N = 2,700$ life stories.

start new businesses. However, in the absence of capital to invest in new technologies and equipment, poor people's primary input is "sheer hard work." In other words, the capital-constrained chronic poor invest more of their labor—this is almost the only input that their circumstances allow. In contrast, the movers and especially the never poor support their agricultural initiatives by adopting new technologies and purchasing new assets like threshers and combines.

Those people who are worst off, affected by displacement, drought, or conflict, seem to work the hardest, a finding that goes against the predictions of the "culture of poverty" theory. In Villa Rosa, Colombia, people displaced from their homes do anything they can to survive. Esteban, age 78, said, "I'm very old, but if they were to give me work, I would do it." Displaced men with skills find themselves doing hard unskilled labor, often hurting themselves, lugging heavy construction lumber or pushing carts in the sun all day. In a men's ladder of life discussion group in the Moroccan community of Abzif, Mohamed said, "After successive years of drought, agriculture changed so deeply. I decided to work in the quarries, even if this will cause me to die under the stones of these caves, without leaving any insurance for my children. I only thought to make a small saving that I exploited in partnership with my friends to buy a cow."

In all the war-ravaged communities visited in Afghanistan, hard work was the most important factor that could help a household progress on the ladder (table 2.1). Not working hard enough was cited as one of the main reasons that

TABLE 2.1

All villages in Afghanistan report hard work as a factor in moving out of poverty

Factor	Village						Score
	K1	K2	N1	N2	H1	H2	
Hard work							
Hard work	•	•	•	•	•	•	6/6
Support							
Support from children	•	•	•	•	•	•	6/6
Remittances from abroad	•	•	•	•	•	•	6/6
Support from government	•			•	•	•	4/6
Support from the community					•		1/6
Support from NGO			•				1/6
Support from others		•					1/6
Assets							
Ownership of a house	•	•	•	•	•	•	6/6
Access to (more) land				•	•	•	3/6

Factor	Village						Score
	K1	K2	N1	N2	H1	H2	
Financial							
Savings	•	•	•	•	•		5/6
Investment		•	•	•			3/6
Access to credit				•			1/6
Sound management of domestic economy				•			1/6
Employment							
Work for NGO	•		•	•	•	•	5/6
Find work regularly			•		•	•	3/6
Promotion at work		•		•	•		3/6
Migration to Saudi Arabia, United Arab Emirates, Iran					•	•	2/6
Agriculture							
Better access to agricultural inputs		•	•		•	•	4/6
Improvement in markets		•		•	•	•	4/6
Poppy cultivation		•	•				2/6
Increased land productivity			•		•		2/6
Access to storage						•	1/6
Education							
Education	•		•	•		•	4/6
Skills improvement					•	•	2/6
Other							
Overall economic growth				•	•	•	3/6
Economic diversity		•				•	2/6
Good relations in the government	•						1/6
Luck	•						1/6

Source: Ladder of life focus group discussions.

Note: K1, K2 = Kabul province villages; N1, N2 = Nangarhar province villages; H1, H2 = Herat province villages.

people remained stuck in poverty. Sabera, a 38-year-old female carpet weaver in Shazimir, said, "It is difficult to move from one step to the other if people are not interested in working hard. If they work hard, it is not difficult."

Clearly, then, poor men and women realize the importance of hard work, and they believe in passing on a strong work ethic to their children. In the community of Preysath, Cambodia, when we asked a men's discussion group what the term "power" meant to them, they said, "It is advising children to work hard and earn money." Young people below the age of 20 also focused on the importance of developing a good work ethic. In Kramrrak in East Java, Indonesia, young men said, "Get experience from people who are already successful; work hard; be disciplined with time and prepare yourself mentally to carry out change." The final word comes from a men's discussion group in a poor indigenous community in Guapa del Mar in Oaxaca, Mexico. "Laziness, if you allow it to take possession of you, you limit yourself. You will stay at the first step. . . . You shouldn't worry about obstacles, you just have to find out how to get around them."

Self-confidence and empowerment

> *If someone does not have self-confidence, it will be difficult to develop ideas. If there is initiative without any self-confidence, it will fail. That is why self-confidence is needed. Self-confidence is the capital.*
> —Suno, a 53-year-old man, Patobako, Indonesia

> *I can perform any work if I try. Having this confidence is power.*
> —Discussion with young girls, Bahana, West Bengal

In his recent book *Poor People*, William Vollmann (2007) gives graphic accounts of poor people he has met in his travels around the world. Like Henry Mayhew 150 years earlier, Vollmann trains his gaze on the prostitutes, drunks, drug addicts, and beggars who inhabit the streets. When he asks these people, "Why are you poor?" they tell him it is destiny, accidental, or in God's hands. Vollmann concludes that "poor people's answers are frequently as impoverished as their lives." The poor in his book come across as broken and desolate, beset by feelings of worthlessness. This view of "the poor" is not uncommon; it often underpins charitable efforts that seek to change poor people in order to change poverty.

Our data suggest that among poor people themselves, this view of poverty is limited to a very small group. In the thousands of conversations with poor men and women, we found that most have confidence and believe in themselves. It is true that those stuck in chronic poverty rate themselves as lower in power and confidence than others. But we also find strong evidence of dramatic shifts in ratings of power and self-confidence as the poor move out of poverty and experience some success. In fact, in this regard they very quickly start looking similar to the rich.

During the household interviews, we asked people to rank themselves on a 10-step ladder of power and rights, with those at step 1 feeling totally powerless and those at step 10 feeling powerful and in control. We use this measure as a proxy for their confidence in themselves, defining those on the top seven rungs as feeling "empowered" and those on the bottom three rungs as feeling "powerless." The results show that feelings of empowerment are dynamic and situational. Nearly 74 percent of movers but only 33 percent of fallers place themselves at step 4 or above on the ladder of power and rights. The poor gain confidence as they move out of poverty, and the rich lose confidence as they experience a decline. There are no inherent differences between the poor and the nonpoor in this regard; it is a matter of circumstances.

Unhappy people are usually lower in confidence, so we also examined happiness ratings, using a similar 10-step scale (figure 2.4). A similar pattern emerges: while 64 percent of the fallers put themselves in the bottom three happiness categories, only 49 percent of the chronic poor, 19 percent of the movers, and 16 percent of the never poor do so. So while about half of the chronic poor are unhappy, their unhappiness drops dramatically as they move out of poverty.

Although not all poor people are happy or confident, many express a spirit of self-confidence and grit even in the face of adversity. Wilmar, an internally displaced person who ended up in a violent barrio in El Gorrión, Colombia, said, "I believe in myself, because I have proved to myself that I am capable. My self-confidence has increased, because even though I fall, I

FIGURE 2.4
Fallers and chronic poor are more likely to be unhappy

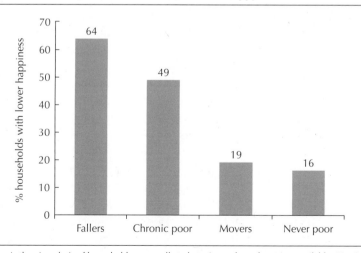

Source: Authors' analysis of household survey; all study regions where data were available; N = 8,295.

am able to pick myself up. If I fall 10 million times, 10 million times do I pick myself up, more now than ever before."

An abundance of initiative

> *It fell to me to do work that I never thought I would do. I worked as an odd-jobs man in order to survive, lugging wood to the point of drawing blood from my shoulders. When I arrived here, I ended up being a helper to a bricklayer, something I had no knowledge of.*
> —Milciades, a displaced man, Villa Rosa, Colombia

> *Those who want to get educated are doing farming to raise money to pay for school fees. Those who want to run a business have already started running small businesses like selling fried fish. Those who want to be farmers have already started farming but on a smaller scale; they are growing cabbage, tomatoes, and some vegetables in the river banks.*
> —Group of young men and women, Guluteza, Malawi

Just as we find poor people's laziness to be a myth, we find very little evidence that poor people in general are passive, fatalistic, and lack initiative. The life stories of Ayesha, Mamba, and Adolfo, recounted in chapter 1, were among the thousands we gathered that showed poor people's enterprise and resourcefulness. Poor people take risks, migrating to foreign shores to earn and save money. They emerge as diligent entrepreneurs, managers of a diversified portfolio of assets. But the rewards to their initiatives are constrained by limited capital, limited knowledge of and access to markets, and, at times, by limited exposure to ideas beyond what they see in their immediate environment.

Consider the life of Beauty, a mover from the village of Mirabari in Kurigram district in Bangladesh. Married at the age of 13, she is illiterate. Yet she is very astute when it comes to decisions regarding her business and livelihood.

Early in the marriage, her mother-in-law forced Beauty and her husband Rashid to move out of their home. "I had nothing but a single thatched house. I had nothing to sleep on, nothing to cook." Beauty worked to support her husband so they could improve their income. At first she helped him in his rice business. "He used to buy paddy, and I would dry it in our neighbors' houses because we did not have sufficient space in our home. Then I would husk it in the machine. After that, my husband would sell the rice in the market. But this business was laborious, with minimum profit. So I suggested to my husband that we shift to vegetable selling. He would buy a variety of vegetables, I would wash and dry them, and then he would take them to the market. My husband would sell the vegetables on market days and on rest days he would pull a rickshaw. On days when the market was closed, I would sell vegetables from my home." Recalling those years, Beauty said, "I worked very hard. At that time I woke up at 4 a.m. and slept at 1 a.m. For this reason I could improve my economic situation."

When her husband fell sick and could no longer pull rickshaws, Beauty suggested that they open a tea stall, as there was none in the village. "Keeping a chair, table, and two benches in front of our house, my husband started a tea stall. He sold only tea and biscuits at that time. Now from oil to soap to all necessary goods are available in our shop," she said with much pride. A loan from Grameen Bank helped. Beauty now manages the tea stall herself. Following their example, five other tea stalls have opened in the village. In the past, people spoke down to her for being a woman and sitting in the open without purdah. "Now everybody says that due to Rashid's wife his family is leading a better life now."

Beauty is not alone. Striking evidence of poor people's initiative emerges from the 2,700 life stories from India, which we analyzed to identify the triggers for accumulation of assets. Every life event was coded into one of four primary categories: inheritance, initiative, institutions, and infrastructure. Initiative emerged as the most frequent trigger through which people accumulated assets—more than help from institutions, informal or formal, more than inheritance, and more than accumulation using publicly available infrastructure (figure 2.5).

It is possible that these results are prone to psychological bias. Success is hailed as a result of one's own effort while failure is blamed on others. (Certainly this is how most of us behave!) If this is true, we should expect to find that the never poor and movers report taking more initiative than the chronic poor and fallers.

But we do not find that. On average, there are no significant differences between the chronic poor and the never poor in the rate of reported initiative taking as a trigger for asset accumulation (table 2.2). It seems likely that the key difference is not the frequency of initiative taking but the nature of the initiatives taken. Lacking capital, poor people keep trying different low-capital activities in often saturated markets. They cook and sell food, raise chickens or goats, sew clothes, make and sell charcoal, pull bicycle rickshaws, or fashion mud pots, brooms, or grass fans for sale. Compared to the resource-endowed endeavors of the better off, these are marginal activities with low rates of return.

Individual initiative features prominently in the explanations that households give for their upward movement over the past decade (figure 2.6). The

FIGURE 2.5

Respondents in India rate initiative as most important trigger for accumulating assets

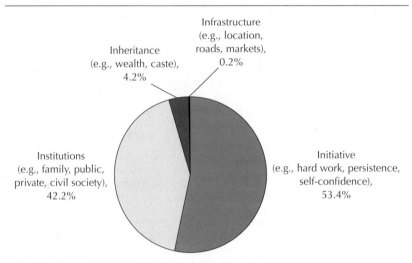

Source: Narayan, Nikitin, and Richards (2009), using coded data from life stories gathered in the Indian study regions; N = 2,700 life stories.

Note: Figures are percentages of asset accumulation events in life stories, broken down by primary trigger. N = 35,076 events across 2,700 life stories, all four mobility groups (one life story may have multiple asset accumulation events).

TABLE 2.2

Movers in India take more initiative, but chronic poor take about as much initiative as never poor

	% of asset accumulation events where initiative taking was primary trigger			
State	*Mover*	*Never poor*	*Chronic poor*	*Fallers*
Uttar Pradesh	53.9	52.1	46.0	45.3
West Bengal	59.3	46.6	45.7	42.1
Assam	55.1	52.3	52.2	45.9
Andhra Pradesh	57.6	58.1	60.9	64.2

Source: Narayan, Nikitin, and Richards (2009), using coded data from life stories gathered in the Indian study regions. N = 35,076 asset accumulation events across 2,700 life stories, all four mobility groups (one life story may have multiple asset accumulation events).

FIGURE 2.6
Initiative features prominently, luck hardly at all as reasons for moving up

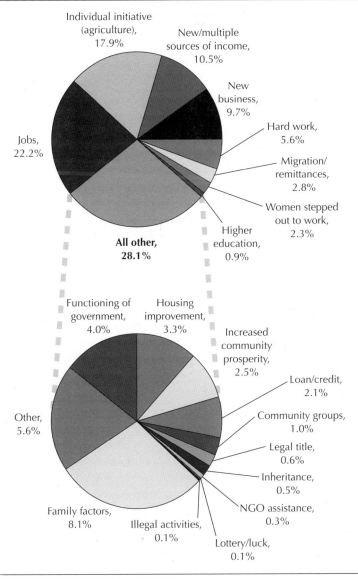

Source: Authors' analysis of household survey; all study regions; *N* = 8,966 from all four mobility groups.

Note: Figures are percentages of reasons cited by respondents when asked to name the top three reasons for an upward move.

great majority credit some initiative that their household has undertaken in either agricultural or nonagricultural activities. Agricultural initiatives include attempts to diversify crops or improve yields through better seed, technology, or fertilizer (17.9 percent). Nonagricultural initiatives include getting a job (22.2 percent), starting a new business (9.7 percent), or juggling multiple livelihood activities (10.5 percent). Overall, only 0.5 percent of households relate their upward movement to inheritance.

The limited role of luck

> *To take birth as a poor man itself is a big punishment.*
> —Discussion with men, Appilepalle, Andhra Pradesh

People seldom cite luck or fate as a principal cause of upward or downward movement. Luck (or the lottery) was mentioned only seven times as a reason for moving up. It was one of the top three reasons only 0.1 percent of the time (figure 2.6). Among the movers, those who started poor and escaped poverty, only one person attributed his success to good fortune. Across the study regions, luck was mentioned more frequently in describing the reasons for moving from step 4 to 5, the top step in some communities. In Saré Ogicol, Senegal, for instance, destiny was more important for the rich than for the poor (figure 2.7). In this village, bad luck hardly featured in people's explanations of moving out of poverty or falling into poverty.

Although luck is seldom mentioned as a reason for movement up or down, people are aware of the disadvantages of being born into a poor family. Those of humble birth lament especially the fact that they could never become educated, but must work to contribute to the family pot. Conversely, the never poor are aware of the advantages they enjoy by birth. Rama, a man from Konapuram, Andhra Pradesh, explained, "When I was born in 1970, our family conditions were good. We had a very good yield of cultivation and were reckoned to be rich. Love and affection and good filial relations prevailed in our family." In Nachni Ghat, Uttar Pradesh, Arshad stated, "The reason of remaining rich for me is that my parents are rich. My forefathers had good agriculture. We have always done hard labor and never did any wrong work. We always had the grace of God." Similarly in Riah Khillaw, Afghanistan, 40-year-old Sediqa described the affluence into which she was born, surrounded by family land, gardens, and animals. She then married an educated man with his own lands and gardens who got a government job.

Poor people are exposed to a series of misfortunes from which they have little protection. Prominent among these are widowhood and accidents or illness that leave people disabled. For people who have no savings and live in countries with few social protection policies, such shocks can plunge them into destitution. Across the study regions, the bottom step of the ladder of life includes widows, disabled people, victims of stroke and accidents, and the blind.

There is almost universal agreement that the lives of widows are very harsh. "Widows have no power because they don't have a husband," said a group of female youths in Mexico. In Lamraab, Morocco, the household of Aziza, 38, dropped from step 6 to step 1 on the ladder after her husband's death. Her husband's prolonged illness exhausted the family savings, and Aziza, who knew nothing of her husband's business, had to sell his truck to pay the debts. Earlier, she "never lacked anything." Now, when she crosses paths with her husband's friends, they ignore her. "Nobody likes the poor," she concluded. In Cambodia, households with widows live in huts made of palm leaves and rely on collecting flowers such as morning glory and insects for sale and for food.

In villages in Africa, divorce and separation from husbands is as damaging as becoming a widow. A 42-year-old woman in a village in Kagera, Tanzania, got nothing after she separated from her husband. Because traditional laws exclude women from inheriting land, houses, and livestock after their father's death, she could rely only on her brothers after her separation. Initially, she moved in with her younger brother, taking care of his farms, but she had to move out again after he married. At the time of the interview, she was living with the widow of one of her other brothers. She realized that she could be thrown out at any time. "When my brother's children grow up and get married, they have the right to eject me. So does their mother."

Possibilities for the disabled vary with the nature of the disability and presence of services. "The worst lameness is being blind, but if one has one hand or one leg crippled, one can work self-reliantly," said Mussa, a disabled farmer in Namdenye, Ruvuma, Tanzania. So important is the health of the body, particularly among the poor, that people often describe power in the physical sense. In West Bengal, poor youths said, "Those who have physical strength have power."

Mahesh, born into poverty and still poor in Raipat village in Assam, did not lose his spirit even after many misfortunes. He related, "My mother died in 1995. I was overpowered by sorrow after her death. I had no money to perform her last rites and so I borrowed 3,500 rupees from a savings group [self-help group] in the village. I still have to return a part of that money. In 1996, my house was blown away by a devastating cyclone. In 1997, my wife

FIGURE 2.7
Ladder from Saré Ogicol, Senegal: Destiny matters for moving up at the top

Reasons for moving up

From step 4 to 5: They rise because of their destiny. They diversify their income sources through agriculture, cattle breeding, and remittances. Cultivation of groundnuts and sale of cattle are used to pay the costs of emigration.

From step 3 to 4: Success of adult children and diversification of income sources explain their rise. They have enough laborers and farming materials to cultivate large areas. Successive good harvests bring them additional income.

Step 5: Gallo or "bosses"
- Are usually big agricultural producers with more than 100 animals
- Have farming materials (sower, hoe, barrow, cart) and farm or exploit wide areas
- Easily build houses with zinc roofing and have transportation means
- Have some members of the household who draw a monthly salary
- Have families that eat good food (three meals a day)
- Are able to cure their illnesses
- Regularly provide their families with good clothing
- Have nice skin and complexion
- Help people with gifts and loans

Step 4: keb-do or "owners"
- Cultivate their fields with the help of the poor
- Own at least 10 nanny goats, 10 sheep, 10 chickens, 1 horse, and 2 donkeys
- Own a barrow, a sower, and a cart
- Live in houses so good that the bosses can visit or even sleep there
- Get enough to eat (three meals a day)
- Can afford medicines and take care of illness without reliance on bosses
- Can provide their wives with special clothes for feast days
- Are well-educated and open-minded; trust veterinarians if livestock fall sick

Reasons for moving down

From step 5 to 4: Excessive practice of usury payable with interest can lead to complaints and sanctions by authorities. Stealing of cattle, serious diseases, death of the household head, and numerous divorces can also cause a decrease in well-being.

From step 4 to 3: A failure to honor debt commitments to the bosses can lead to a fall, for the latter can seize their properties. Death of a household head can lead to sharing of properties. Serious diseases may also cause a fall.

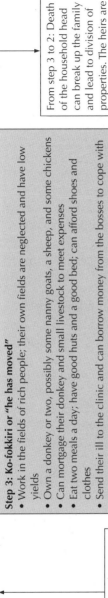

From step 3 to 2: Death of the household head can break up the family and lead to division of properties. The heirs are often forced to sell part of their inheritance to meet their needs. Disabling diseases and divorces can also cause a fall.

From step 2 to 1: Big family size, death of the household head, and laziness of children can cause a fall.

Step 3: Ko-fokkiri or "he has moved"
- Work in the fields of rich people; their own fields are neglected and have low yields
- Own a donkey or two, possibly some nanny goats, a sheep, and some chickens
- Can mortgage their donkey and small livestock to meet expenses
- Eat two meals a day; have good huts and a good bed; can afford shoes and clothes
- Send their ill to the clinic and can borrow money from the bosses to cope with illness
- Are more open-minded and literate than they were 10 years ago, therefore, are more competent to manage their properties and meet their needs

Step 2: Fouddi ma hebde or "one who is moving up from poverty"
- Possess 5 to 10 chickens
- Have at least one daily meal regardless of the quantity
- Have women who cook without caring about the taste of the meals
- Usually rely on their social solidarity to satisfy needs such as health

Step 1: Basso
- Cannot practice agriculture well because they lack materials
- Work in other people's fields
- Don't have a comfortable hut
- Rarely eat daily, and if they find rice, they cannot make sauce for it
- Cannot take care of their family illnesses; rely on other people's help
- Know that the richest people will not grant them a loan because they have no guarantee
- Have wives who cannot afford to braid their hair

From step 2 to 3: They borrow farming materials to meet their food needs and have additional sources of income such as flexible jobs.

From step 1 to 2: Before they can progress, they must meet their food needs by obtaining farming materials and a sufficient workforce. The support of children and relatives can fill the gaps.

Source: Discussion with men, Saré Ogicol, Senegal.

suffered from typhoid. I thought she would die but she survived. I had to spend a good amount of money on her treatment. In 2000, one of my hands was fractured due to an accident when I was plying a [bicycle] rickshaw. A Maruti car knocked me down and I was injured. I couldn't work for four months. Now I am sometimes able to earn 60 rupees a day as many Tata Sumos [vans] and tractors are also plying the same route."

Although the poor are buffeted by risks and shocks of all kinds, even the chronic poor people in our sample reject the view that they are poor because of personal misfortune. Not even Mahesh, who has suffered a cyclone, his wife's typhoid, and being hit by a car, said he was poor because he was unlucky.

Bad behavior as a cause of poverty

The lack of work and the emptiness of their lives lead young people to take drugs and do bad things.
                      —Women's discussion group, Tindyata, Morocco

I donated blood in a blood donation camp, and I was pleased mentally because I have not much ability to do something for our society. But this donation of blood could help our society, so I was happy.
                      —Nisit, a chronic poor man, Anakha, West Bengal

A pernicious belief that surfaces in all societies from time to time is that "the poor" as a group are immoral and prone to addictions and drunkenness. Such people are incapable of taking any initiative, it is said, except to feed their addictions. Work for them has no meaning, and economic opportunity is irrelevant. Thus, the poor deserve what they get and are unworthy of support except for morally uplifting charity.

This myth traveled around the world with colonizers and has proved resistant to extinction. During the Victorian era of the late 19th century, social observers in England cast poverty as a moral and social problem to be met with charity, social works, and compassion. The focus was on the deviant behavior of the poor.[2] In one of the earliest such studies, Henry Mayhew (1851) described the rough underclass of London, the street performers, beggars, and prostitutes of the city's streets. His dramatic descriptions captured the popular imagination and came to dominate perceptions about all poor people. Toward the turn of the century, Charles Booth (1889) conducted the first serious investigation into the lives of the London poor. He distinguished between four classes that together made up nearly a third of the population.

Lowest on the ladder was a small "hereditary" class made up of criminals, barbarians, beggars, and bullies. The "very poor" were more numerous: while in a state of chronic want, they seldom worked and were prone to drinking. The "poor," by contrast, were not in want, but they had irregular employment and struggled to make ends meet. They were "not worse morally than any other class though shiftless and improvident." Above them were those with regular employment but low wages—"decent steady men, paying their way and bringing up their children respectably (45–50)." Speaking of the top category, Booth recommended that governments target this "deserving" group in an effort to reduce poverty. The very poor were viewed as a lost cause, even as a dangerous influence on others.

The belief that poverty had a moral underpinning was reflected in economic thinking as well. Alfred Marshall, in his classic *Principles of Economics* (1890), defined poverty as a state of "physical, mental, and moral ill health." Marshall also suspected a hereditary "taint of vice" in poor people.

A century later, studies of American poverty still reveal a widely held notion that the poor are morally flawed. In a 2001 survey of Americans by National Public Radio, the Kaiser Family Foundation, and the Kennedy School of Government at Harvard University, 70 percent of those polled rated drug abuse as a major cause of poverty in their country.[3] A recent book, *The Persistence of Poverty* (Karelis 2007), identifies five causes of poverty in the United States and other places: drinking, crime, low education, not working, and lack of savings.

Do these stories and beliefs about poor people being drunks, addicts, and deviants hold true for poor men and women in countries like Malawi, where a large proportion of the population lives in abject poverty? No matter which data collection tool we consider, drunkenness, drug abuse, and prostitution do not emerge as defining characteristics of the poor people in our study. Nor does vice figure as a central reason for falling into or remaining stuck in poverty. The ladder of life discussions reveal community perspectives on the characteristics of both the poor and the nonpoor. Drinking and drugs are only associated with the very poorest people, and even in this group there are many other reasons for poverty, including low education, widowhood, disability, physical weakness, and old age.

Poor people are aware of the dangers of drinking, drugs, and promiscuity. Parents warn children and friends remind friends to keep away from such "evil." There is a recognition that these behaviors can lead to falling down into poverty or being left behind. Around a bonfire lit at night during the field visit to the community of Maguli in Ruvuma, Tanzania, young boys and girls danced and sang about how HIV/AIDS and immoral behavior could "messy me up."

In the household questionnaire, people were asked to name the three most important reasons for their downward movement over the last decade. Among those who had fallen into poverty, gambling or addiction to alcohol or drugs was mentioned among the top three reasons only 1.1 percent of the time. Instead, the primary triggers of falling were economic conditions in the community or country (high inflation, a worsening economy) and health and death shocks to the family. The distribution of reasons was very similar when considering all downward movement among the poor and nonpoor.

In many communities people describe drinking as a *consequence* of prolonged poverty and unemployment rather than as the initial cause of poverty. In the village of Butmuli in Uganda, 46-year-old Mbualamoko had no land and survived as a casual laborer. His only asset, his house, had washed away in torrential rains, and his second wife left him. Frustrated, sick, and weak, he said, "I know I drink. I know my marriages failed because of my excessive drinking. But each time, I return home more frustrated than I went. I hate myself, feel cursed, and resort to drinking to cover my feelings. I drink *waragi* and other types of alcohol only to force sleep when poverty bites." Mbualamoko had to surrender his two goats to creditors in settlement of accumulated debts soon after the interview.

Women sometimes take a less benign view of male drinking. They often report that men's dysfunctional behavior—alcohol or drug abuse, domestic violence, extramarital affairs—leads to income declines and family breakups. In the village of Welumbe in Sri Lanka, a woman stuck in chronic poverty said her husband's alcoholism made it difficult for her family to improve its condition. A bus driver, he spent about three-fourths of his income on drink. The family survived by doing odd jobs—the mother and daughter rolled cigars and the son worked as a mason. In Pothupana, Ampara, Sri Lanka, women said, "If people are falling it is because of gambling and alcohol. It is only those at the bottom steps that waste money this way. Men drink alcohol saying that it is all because of depression or because they are tired. But this increases the women's grievances even more."

In conflict-affected areas, alcohol abuse is mentioned more frequently. In some communities in Sri Lanka, community members express concern that drinking among adults sets a negative example for young men. Drinking the local brew and smoking marijuana sometimes cycles from generation to generation, reducing the possibility of moving out of poverty in the long term. In Cambodia, increasing drug addiction among youth is rapidly turning into a security concern. Drug users in several communities engage in gang fighting, theft, and violence, particularly against women. In a group discussion in Sastaing, young girls voiced their fears. "The use of drugs is very popular now in our country. Therefore, the criminal has been created. Nowadays if you ask the question between humans and ghosts, which one do you fear? I will answer that I am more afraid of humans because the ghost cannot cause me any problems while humans can."

Drug abuse among youth is linked to unemployment. In a discussion group in Tindyata, Morocco, women said, "Our children don't find a job. Even those that have a diploma in their pocket don't manage to find jobs. They become disappointed and they begin to sniff drugs and we are not able to control them." Young men in the poor rural community of Lamraab, Morocco, agreed, but said they had no other diversions to occupy them. In one Moroccan community, a young doctor was credited with keeping local youths away from alcohol and drugs. His solution was simple: he played soccer and basketball with them every night.

Abstinence from unsafe sexual behavior is a critical concern, particularly in the African communities hit hard by HIV/AIDS. In Namdenye, Ruvuma, Tanzania, mothers are derided for sending their young daughters to bus stands to solicit men. When youths in Guluteza, Malawi, were asked what they were doing to prepare for the future, they said, "We are taking care of ourselves by abstaining from immoral practices. When you get infected with this disease [AIDS], then it can be very difficult to say that you are preparing for the future. Because getting this disease means you are dooming your whole future."

Even when they are hungry, poor people often display what Adam Smith calls "sympathy" and sentiments for their fellow human beings. In one way or another, many people spoke about the importance of having "a good nature, good will, and good heart." A discussion group in Chintada, Hyderabad, Andhra Pradesh, defined freedom as "sharing our happiness with others and being friendly to everyone; cooperation with community members to share their problems. . . . Freedom lies with the good-hearted people." From some of the poorest villages in conflict-affected Assam come accounts of caring for others and doing good works. Ahmed, from Barbakara, Assam, who grew up in abject poverty, spoke about helping maintain the local mosque and plastering the floor. Betha Ram, who started life as a daily wage laborer, donated two fans to the hospital. Bhuwaneshwar makes and donates wood images of gods to the local temple, without any payment.

In West Bengal, Ali, age 60, talked about the joy of helping his neighbors when they fell ill by rushing them to the nearest hospital. Many people reported donating blood, as this is one commodity that even poor people have to give. Anup, a chronic poor man from Tola, West Bengal, summed up the fellow feeling displayed by many poor people across the study regions. "I am a daily laborer. When men give me work, I earn 62 rupees a day. To be alive, we should live well and in a good way with everyone. I am not involved with social work. But if there is any blood donation camp or any cultural program, then I spend what I can. For this I get mental peace."

Our evidence suggests that falling into poverty is first and foremost a consequence of economic conditions, poor health, death in the family, and failed enterprises, causes that affect large numbers of people. Only 1–2 percent of poor people, it seems, are poor primarily because of personal character deficits or bad behavior. Poverty is, therefore, not a moral problem. Poverty is an economic problem. Poverty is a political problem. The proper policy response is not charity or moral uplift, but broad-based action to improve and unblock the economic opportunity sets available to poor people including young girls and boys.

The Hunger for Freedom

> *Freedom is an element of development, and to some extent development is an element of freedom. Is it possible to develop without being free? Freedom is a sign of development. That is why we women who are always ranked below men cannot say we are developed. When you have developed, you have freedom. You can hardly have a free non-developed person. Development is part of freedom.*
>
> —Mixed discussion group, Kijuronga, Kagera, Tanzania

> *Freedom is . . . the freedom to choose and work out your dream.*
>
> —Len, a 34-year-old woman, Baroygor, Philippines

The notion that the people of developing nations lack the capacity for freedom and self-rule pervades European and American political history. Speaking in the British Parliament in 1833, Lord Macaulay justified the role of the East India Company in India as saving people who had sunk to the lowest depths of slavery and superstition. British rule, he claimed, would make them worthy of the privileges of citizens. In 1899, Rudyard Kipling wrote *The White's Man Burden* to urge the United States to wield imperial power in the

Philippines, extending a paternalistic rule over natives that Kipling described as "half-devil and half-child." The era of Manifest Destiny was built on the belief that racial superiority gave white Americans the right and obligation to rule over and "civilize" poorer lands.

A common theme in these colonial and imperial rationalizations was that people do not need freedom if they live in conditions of want. Our study emphatically refutes this notion. It is true that many poor people are hungry and that finding food, work, and money is a pressing concern. But this does not mean that they no longer care about dignity, goodness, community, or rights. Across the study regions, poor men, women, and especially youth made clear that they value and long for freedom. Echoing the Universal Declaration of Human Rights, poor people defined freedom as the right to choose what they truly value (Nussbaum 2000; Alkire 2002; Moser and Norton 2001). For them, freedom has both intrinsic value, as a way to live with dignity, and instrumental value, as a means to access and profit from economic opportunity. Their comments evoke the work of Amartya Sen (1999), who describes freedom as having both constitutive and instrumental importance for development.

Freedom as an intrinsic value

Five key concepts emerged in people's ideas of freedom as an intrinsic value. They are freedom of mind; freedom of choice; freedom to live with dignity and respect; freedom from fear and oppression; and freedom of movement (box 2.1).

Freedom of mind. Poor people, like all human beings, value the freedom to think without restriction and to speak their mind. In discussions, they said freedom of mind is primary since one has to think before one speaks. Poor people are aware that their ability to speak up is constrained by their dependence on others to make a living. Cleopatra, a 17-year-old farmer in a village in Tanzania, said, "When you walk with your own head without wearing the other's head then you have freedom."

Freedom of choice. Everywhere, women, men, and youths express a longing for autonomy—the freedom to choose big and small things on their own and to live according to their beliefs and desires. Small, simple, everyday acts give happiness. Tentulia, a woman in Kismopara, Bangladesh, defined freedom as "listening to music or going to work at my own will." For Lovely, a woman in the same village, "planting trees at my own free will" is freedom. For Rinu, a woman in Upper Deuri, Assam, "weaving my own cloth on my handloom and wearing it" is freedom. Cory, a 42-year-old in Baroygor, Philippines, said, "You

BOX 2.1
What is freedom? Voices from the field

Freedom of mind
Freedom is to express your opinion and to express ideas.
—Discussion with women, Sian-Ha, Mexico

Freedom means we dare to talk. We have rights to express our opinion on what is right and what is wrong. But if we have no money, our voice becomes bullshit.
—Discussion group, Kdadaum, Cambodia

Freedom to think, freedom to tell a story.
—Discussion with women, Galalolo, Indonesia

A poor person has spaces to be free. Your thoughts surround you, and then you struggle.
—Neftali, a 49-year-old man, Los Rincones, Colombia

Freedom of choice
You need to be the boss of yourself, otherwise this is nonfreedom.
—A woman, Kijuronga, Kagera, Tanzania

Freedom is to live independently and having handful of work and eyeful of sleep.
—Discussion with men, Chedulla, Andhra Pradesh

To be free is to always have the choice to decide what we need.
—Discussion with men and women, Sindar, Morocco

Freedom to live with dignity and respect
You do not have a hundred shillings to buy a Panadol [fever medicine] for your dying child and you say you are free. . . . You will start begging, and there your freedom ends.
—Discussion with men and women, Nyakahora, Kagera, Tanzania

For me, what becomes important in freedom is doing something with self-assurance, and at the end nobody opposes me and disturbs what I have done. Otherwise, I just become a slave.
—A man, Bugokela, Kagera, Tanzania

To live a life of dignity and respect: that is freedom.
—Harinath, Mondal, Kathalbari, West Bengal

Freedom from fear and oppression
To protest against injustice is freedom.
—Aditya, a poor man, Nababpur, West Bengal

BOX 2.1 continued

People now know their rights, the rights of their partner, of their neighbors. Once people know their rights and are free to express themselves, freedom becomes automatic.

—Discussion with men, Kodola, Uganda

I was asleep. A local guard came in my home and commanded me to go and transport bricks on my head in order to build a school. Am I free? Am I not a slave in my own community and country?

—A poor man, Bugokela, Kagera, Tanzania

Freedom is peace, nondisturbance, no threats, and love.

—Discussion with men, Bugokela, Kagera, Tanzania

I live with courage. That is my freedom.

—A man, Donekal, Andhra Pradesh

Freedom of movement

To be free is to move, to travel, without restrictions.

—Discussion with women, Mbata, Ruvuma, Tanzania

Freedom is the ability to work in the fields without my husband's permission, the ability to go to market without my husband's permission, and the ability to visit my father's house at will.

—Discussion with women, Digbari, Bangladesh

---

are happy because you are free to get whatever you want, to dream whatever you want, and to live the kind of life that you want." Not being able to do what one feels like doing leads to feelings of oppression. "Chained" is how Vanyen, a woman in Baroygor, described it. "It is as if you are being controlled from doing what you want because somebody had already set a plan."

Some people feel that poor people have more freedom than others because they have nothing to lose. Men and women in a discussion in Nyakahora, Kagera, Tanzania, said, "Sometimes poor people are the freest; they do not worry about anything but their lives. A rich person worries a lot more. What is the difference between this man [a rich man] and the one who is in prison? That this one has chosen to imprison himself rather than being imprisoned by the police." Others feel that poor people have no freedom because they need to be constantly looking for work and money. Everywhere, people qualified freedom by saying that it permits actions that are within the bounds of law and that do not hurt or disturb others. Freedom to choose which God to worship was mentioned in every country.

Freedom to live with dignity and respect. People want to enjoy self-respect and to be respected by others, even when they must depend upon or work for others. Poor people express their yearning for dignity in simple terms. For Sergine in Ndagiel, Senegal, "Freedom is to have sufficient for daily expenses so others respect you." For Kam, a woman in Mexico, "Freedom is how we are now: nobody beats us." And women in Rajapurmalhua, Uttar Pradesh, suppressed for decades in a highly patriarchal society, long for freedom in the form of "respect and honor for our voice."

Freedom from fear and oppression. To be free is to live in peace and security, to have the right to protest and to vote. Discussions on this aspect of freedom were often long and involved. Poor people treasure their right to vote, even when they perceive clearly the mismatch between their own interests and the interests of the political elite. They express great vulnerability in the face of wrongdoing and frequently lament their helplessness to protest against exploitation. But they express both hope and frustration about the ability of the justice systems of their countries to protect them. People's knowledge of their rights appears to be increasing; armed with this knowledge, poor people sometimes feel free to speak out against injustice. In Kaludoma, Ruvuma, Tanzania, young girls defined freedom as "being free to enjoy one's citizenship without a problem such as being jailed, being free in life without being anguished, humiliated, beaten, or interrogated at one's home." In the conflict-affected state of Assam, people called frequently for freedom from abuse and threats by the police and army. In Kandulimari, a village in the state, men defined freedom as "the justice of the government and freedom of mind. On the contrary, the threatening of the army, the police to innocent people is not called freedom."

Freedom of movement. Geographic mobility is important to both men and women. For men it is linked to looking for work wherever they can find it. For women, freedom of movement implies a loosening of the restrictions and controls imposed by husbands and society. This yearning to move, to come and go, emerges everywhere. A group of men in Gabunazi, Kagera, Tanzania, explained, "Freedom is when you can go out without asking for permission or bidding farewell. I feel free because I can go out and I am sure that I shall come back. I do not need anybody to escort me."

Across a wide swath of societies, from India, Afghanistan, and Bangladesh to Mexico, Malawi, and Tanzania, women express anger at restrictions on their movement. Some compare their experience to living like "a bird in a cage." In Surjana, Uttar Pradesh, a group of women said, "We should have freedom to unveil our face, because when an elder man is present in the house, we have to cover our face. We have to be closeted in one room. We cannot move about. We should have freedom from these customary regulations." In Afghanistan, some women said that not wearing a chador is freedom; many more spoke about the desire to walk along a road alone, without anyone's permission and without being accompanied by anyone. In Chiksisi, Malawi, women spoke of their desire to wear high heels and trousers but said they would be chastised if they did. "If you wear a trouser, your husband is going to ask you whether you want the household to have two men!"

Women who breach customary restrictions often are ill treated by their husbands, so women's desire for freedom of movement is linked to their desire for freedom from domestic violence. Women in Chakax, Mexico, spoke of the abuse they face; for them, marriage is the opposite of freedom. Fear of abandonment also restricts women. Nasima asked, "Where is your peace of mind, considering that you sleep in this house and your husband leaves you?" In Pueblo de León, Mexico, one woman who was not abused declared, "I go out all the time and talk with everybody, and my husband does not hit me. I am free."

Instrumental freedom for economic opportunity

In addition to being an intrinsic good, freedom has an instrumental value, making it possible for people to find and seize economic opportunity. Both men and women hanker for the freedom to find good work, to control their money, to conduct business freely, to own property and goods with no legal hassles, and to sell their property whenever and to whomever they choose.

For men across the study regions, freedom means practicing the livelihoods they want without restrictions. In Kramrrak, Indonesia, people feel free when they can "work in any fields; nobody commands; nobody obstructs." Men also talked about "freedom of selling, freedom of getting a loan from banks, and freedom to be fishermen and teachers." In Patobako, another village in Indonesia, men spoke about the "freedom of running a business; freedom of looking for a loan from a bank because many people here need financial capital but can't find it because they are on the blacklist."

The ability to establish a business without restrictions is a valued freedom in the African study states too. Freedom to pursue economic activities "without interference in whom one transacts with and where" is important in Ruvuma, Tanzania. In Uganda, people are concerned with the freedom "to pursue activities that generate income," and in Malawi, "to transact in the market without bureaucratic harassment." In Butmuli, Uganda, a man explained, "I do whatever I want with my cow as compared to the past, when we used to give a share to the village chairman."

Engagement in Family and Community

Losing adult children is very painful. It is like a pot breaking when you have already washed your hands to eat. He [an orphan she raised] is like a son. He grew up with me, he cares for me. It is a consolation, the only thing that keeps me alive.

—A woman, Kakyango, Kagera, Tanzania

Sometimes young people come together to help each other but most of the times, we just meet to have fun, play sports, or celebrate an event, a wedding, a holiday.

—Discussion with female youth, Zakwak Ulya, Afghanistan

The flip side of the myth that poor people are too fatalistic to take advantage of economic opportunity is the myth that they are too obsessed with subsistence to care for their families, participate in their communities, or play a role in the broader society. These myths often affect the design of government and charitable programs that treat "the poor" not as agents of their destiny but as the objects of actions by others—as "beneficiaries" but not participants. Our findings, by contrast, show poor people to be engaged in their families and in their communities as well.

An assumption often made about poor people is that they have broken homes and chaotic family lives. But nearly every life story told to us—by movers, chronic poor, never poor, and even fallers—depicts people striving to create better lives for their families, particularly their children. The love of family is palpable everywhere, and it motivates men and women to keep on against the odds. Life stories are filled with expressions of joy at the birth of children, particularly boys, and grief at the illness or death of kin. A woman in Glikati, Philippines, said, "I was so depressed when my mother died because I felt so empty. It was the same feelings that I had during the time that my children died."

In a remote community in Mexico, Victor, a 35-year-old man stuck in chronic poverty, called his family the most important relationship in his life. "The family, my children, that's who you think about in order to make the family move ahead a little." His daughter fell ill and needed to be hospitalized, but he had no savings. He said, "You have to fight. You have to make an attempt to solve the problems." A chronic poor man in Assam described how his father had insisted on his schooling despite their poverty. "In that season, he got no work. There was no fire in our house. Three or four days we lived in hunger. One piece of *chappati* [bread] was not in our luck. My mother had died during my birth time. . . . My father loved me too much. He introduced me to school." Men rejoice when after years of savings, they can buy clothes for their children, a sari and gold jewelry for their wives. Pramod, a 34-year-old man in Atkona, Uttar Pradesh, recalled, "In 1997, when I bought clothes for all the members of the family by my own earnings, it gave me happiness and a lot of satisfaction."

For poor men and women across the study regions, family emerges as the central economic institution in their lives. Families manage their portfolios of assets jointly. All family members, including children, typically contribute to the household's support, whether by working to earn money or by getting an education to prepare for future work. The frequent decision to educate sons rather than daughters is based in part on a calculation of economic returns, since until recently girls could not work outside the home. Diversification of income is based on deploying different members of the household in different activities, sometimes in different places. Families often arrange for one or more members to migrate, either to a city in the same country or to another country; the remittances sent home by the migrant become a crucial part of the extended family's livelihood portfolio. In the ladder of life discussions, the top step of the ladder often includes people who have adult children working overseas.

Poor people's sense of belonging and solidarity extends beyond the family to the larger community. The importance of getting along with others and living together amicably emerges time and again. Men in Korrapadu, Andhra Pradesh, define freedom as "living together happily, mixing up with unity, without having any hurdles or hindrances and without causing inconvenience to others." In Devupuram, another village in the same state, a men's group said, "People enjoy freedom when they maintain good relations with people. They are admired by society. People who never maintain good relations with people have less freedom." Social discrimination and marginalization, whether based on caste or some other criteria, is painful. In Jambugumpala, Andhra Pradesh, a group of men said, "Restraining the backward classes of people from moving about this way or that, asking them to speak with folded hands, further keeping them penniless and in a helpless state, is negative freedom and against freedom."

Celebration of festivals reaffirms identity and social ties (Rao and Walton 2004a; Banerjee and Duflo 2006). Poor youths in our study emphasize the importance of festivals in bringing people together across caste and income groups and enabling them to forget their misery for a day. In Chintada, Andhra Pradesh, a village with low social stratification along caste lines, young people said, "We all come together during festivals like Bhathukamma or Dusshera. We just can't express the happiness we get in those days." In Bhosi, also in Andhra Pradesh, festivals provide youths with their only diversion. "On these days, we groom ourselves in new clothes and enjoy our time with friends. We also come to help each other, do some small works." In Bangladesh, almost every community reported celebrations to mark graduations, weddings, the Muslim holiday of Eid, and independence day. In Mexico, patron saint celebrations include basketball games for youth. In Morocco, people participate in folk groups that entertain during weddings and the summer festivals.

Living in contexts of little government support for childrearing, education, illness, old age, or death, poor people are keenly aware that their survival depends on others. In African communities, especially, many people belong to mutual aid groups such as savings and credit groups and burial societies. People across the study contexts describe community solidarity and unity as a lifeline. A discussion group in Saré Ogicol, Senegal, said, "In the village, there is solidarity. The men have an informal grouping, and Sellou is the president. They have collective activities, and they club together. With the incomes they get from these activities, they have started to build a mosque in the village."

Having a circle of friends is important. Mamba, a chronic poor man in Malawi, recounted with great joy and affection his list of friends. "Ezekiel is a friend of mine who helps me when I am in need of money to buy soap. He also assisted me with maize seeds last year. When he has Irish potatoes he gives me. Innocent, this one has a vegetable garden and he assists me with money for maize milling. He gives us vegetables for he says we can't buy them." About Blessing he says, "When my child is sick, he helps me with money for transport. He also gives me medicine which he gets from a private clinic. Chiwengo, this one has a sewing machine, and he sews my clothes for free." About Meke, he says, "This friend is like the others; we do help each other. There was a time in 2004 that I had no hoe, and he gave me one. We also advise one another not to go in the way of chasing skirts."

The importance of belonging and staying together becomes even more evident in crises, such as periods of conflict or mass displacement and relocation. Rubiela, a 40-year-old woman in El Gorrión, Colombia, described the solidarity that developed in the process of reconstruction of their neighborhood. "Something remarkable is respect. We all used to sleep in the same bed, live in the same house, just separated by a piece of canvas. We learned to love each other. The other thing is the understanding. We learned to know our needs. When someone got sick we used to take care of each other. We watched so no one would get into our territory."

The absence of a mutual support network is associated with privation. A women's ladder of life focus group in Satgailijhara, Bangladesh, said, "There are six categories of people in our village. At the bottommost step are the Huduirra or Humainna, those who have no friends to turn to and no resources to fall back on."

Conclusion

Poor people are neither saints nor villains, neither victims nor superheroes. There are few differences between the poor and the nonpoor in their aspirations for themselves and their children, in their belief in hard work as a means of getting ahead, in their initiative, or in their morals. Poverty is not an affliction of the few but a condition of the many. In almost half the countries in our study, 50 percent of the population is poor. These hundreds of millions of people cannot all be drunken, lazy, criminal, or unable to imagine and plan a future for themselves and their children.

Myths about poor people and about the causes of poverty have led to policy choices that have not helped those in poverty. Our research reveals the wretched opportunities that confront poor people in contrast to the gilded choices that the rich enjoy. To break out of poverty, poor people need the same opportunity sets as the rich. This requires fresh thinking and new mind-sets about poor people and the scale of poverty.

The problem is us, not poor people. We have to change. If only we can make the world look like what poor people think it really is—a place where hard work pays off, where there is equality of opportunity—we will see mass poverty reduction in our time. Imagine a world in which we listen to poor women, men, and young people, and fix what they think isn't right.

Notes

1. There is a vast psychological, anthropological, and sociological literature on this subject. See Lane (1959), Lerner (1982), Boudon (1973), Bourdieu and Passeron (1970), Appadurai (2004), and Rao and Walton (2004a).
2. For one of the best overviews of this time period, see Himmelfarb (1992).
3. See "Poverty in America," NPR Online, http://www.npr.org/programs/specials/poll/poverty.

Poverty Is a Condition, Not a Characteristic

I know that if one had a small job, one could slowly save and in the future be able to meet any emergencies or make the most of whatever opportunity presented itself. One knows that it is better to teach a person to fish than to hand out a fish. But the state has left us abandoned!

—ALICIA, A DISPLACED WOMAN,
Villa Rosa, Colombia

With my earnings from agriculture, I bought 10 used bicycles and a sewing machine. I repaired them myself and sold them. Then I bought a radio, 15 goats, and pigs. I also bought a car, though an old one, to make my life better. But my ambition is not fulfilled.

—ODWIN, A 52-YEAR-OLD MALE MOVER,
Ngimyoni, Ruvuma

There is a story, possibly apocryphal, about a researcher measuring the size of rats' bodies. The study concluded that the largest rat body was six inches long. A colleague, looking over his paper, thought for a while and then asked, "How big is your largest trap?" "Six inches. We don't need them any larger as that is the size of the biggest rat" was the researcher's confident reply.

All scientists know that the tools used to observe the world limit and structure what we observe and even shape our concepts. Using multiple tools to measure the same phenomenon broadens our understanding. The most common tool for investigating poverty has been a household survey, usually administered to a sample chosen to be representative for the nation (and perhaps also for a subnational unit like state or province). This tool does two things well. First, it can answer this question: "What is the *current* level of a poverty measure for the national (or state or provincial) population?" An attempt to determine whether poverty has gone up or down strains the tool of the household survey to its limits, because comparability issues are so bedeviling.[1] Second, the household survey can compare differences between "the poor" and "the nonpoor" in the specific characteristics—age, sex, occupation, education, household size—that a large-scale survey can capture. The World Bank has carried out hundreds of poverty assessments using these tools to present poverty profiles showing levels of poverty and the characteristics of "the poor."

However, while the household survey as a tool has proven its value and has deepened the understanding of poverty in some ways, it also presents two conceptual dangers.

The first danger lurks in the very words "the poor." At any point in time, individuals can be described in an infinite variety of ways, some of which are relatively permanent *characteristics*. Persistent characteristics can be fixed in part by biology, like height (for adults) or being left-handed, or they can be chosen by individuals (political party affiliation), or they can be some mix of choice and circumstance (like religion or ethnicity). But the descriptions of specific individuals at a given point in time also include current but perhaps temporary *conditions* that people are experiencing, like having a cold, or wearing a red shirt, or being tired. A snapshot cannot distinguish between characteristics and conditions. A cross-sectional survey cannot tell whether an individual who is counted as one of "the poor" is experiencing permanent poverty (like being left-handed) or temporary poverty (like having a broken right hand).

Our study has used a different collection of tools to examine poverty. Local community-based focus groups were asked to construct a ladder of well-being categories for their community, called the ladder of life. The groups then subjectively ranked each household in their community, placing it on a step of the ladder according to its current status and, based on recollection, its status 10 years ago (in 2005 and 1995). The findings from this exercise strongly confirm the conclusion that has emerged from the increasing use of surveys that track the same individuals over time: poverty is a condition, not a characteristic. Although one can talk about the collection of people who are experiencing an episode of poverty as "the poor," this should not lead us to the dangerous assumption that for most of these people, being poor is a relatively permanent characteristic (like being left-handed or tall) or even a stable ascriptive identity (like ethnicity or religion or party affiliation).

A second limitation of the household sample survey is that it pays attention exclusively to large units—nations, states, provinces (although recent work constructs local snapshots using survey and census data).[2] This leads to the conceptual danger that one may rely exclusively on national policies and programs in addressing poverty. As we get dressed on a January day in the United States, the average nationwide temperature doesn't matter much—it may be a bitter 7 degrees Fahrenheit in Duluth, Minnesota, but a balmy 70 degrees in Phoenix, Arizona. How heavy a coat we put on depends on where we are. Locality matters.

Our study sampled communities, not nation-states. Within each community, we then produced rankings of the changes in prosperity and poverty of all (or nearly all) households. We show that locality matters: villages in the same country have very different experiences in poverty reduction. Even in the countries with rapid economic growth, some villages were stalling, and even in countries where poverty was increasing, some villages were thriving.

This comprehensive approach to measuring mobility at the community levels means we could also examine inequality at the local level, attempting to discover to what extent the fortunes of the (relatively) rich and poor *within the same village* move together. We show that the degree to which the poor and nonpoor move together varies widely across the study regions.

The findings of this chapter, showing that individual- and locality-specific features are an important part of the overall experience of poverty, give rise to the questions addressed in the rest of the study: What are the conditions of households and localities that facilitate moving out of poverty?

Household Dynamics and Poverty

We constructed a community mobility matrix (CMM) for each village on the basis of the focus group rankings of households on the steps of the ladder of life.[3] For each of the communities in the 18 study regions for which we have sufficient data, we have a community mobility matrix like the one shown for Fateh Garh village in Uttar Pradesh (figure 3.1). The steps on the ladder in this village go from step 1, the poorest, to step 6, the richest (recall that each village creates its own ladder and defines the steps). Each number in any cell represents a particular household (the household numbers are just arbitrary labels). A household's placement in the matrix is determined by its position on steps of the ladder now and 10 years ago, as perceived by the focus group. The community mobility matrix thus reveals the stability or mobility of households over time. In figure 3.1, for example, the household (arbitrarily) numbered 1 remained at step 1 in both periods, while household 107 moved up from step 1 to step 3. Household 34 made the amazing rise from step 1 to step 6 over the 10-year period. Some households fell: household 2 moved from step 4, well above poverty, to the lowest rung.

Adding the community-defined poverty line to the matrix enables us to see which households moved out of (or into) poverty. In the example from the village of Fateh Garh, the community poverty line was set between steps 3 and 4 of the ladder of life, so the focus group considered households on steps 1, 2, or 3 of the ladder to be in poverty (figure 3.2). The dark gray region in figure 3.2 shows the "movers"—households (like 34 or 20 or 78) that started out poor but moved up sufficiently to escape poverty (moving out of poverty, or MOP). The light gray region shows poor households (like 23 or 107) that experienced some upward mobility but not enough to cross the community poverty line. Both gray shaded regions together show "upward movement of the poor" (mobility of the poor, or MPI)—initially poor households that experienced any upward mobility, irrespective of whether they crossed the poverty line. Finally, the striped region identifies households (like 74 or 18) that were initially non-poor but fell into poverty (falling of the rich into poverty, or FRIP).

FIGURE 3.1
Community mobility matrix from Fateh Garh, Uttar Pradesh, shows types and magnitude of household mobility

Steps		1	2	3	4	5	6	Total
10 years ago	1	1, 3, 4, 5, 6, 7, 8, 10, 11, 12, 13, 15, 19, 21, 22, 24, 25, 26, 27, 28, 29, 30, 32, 46, 47, 48, 49, 51, 53, 56, 57, 83, 84, 85, 110, 112, 113, 114, 116, 117, 118, 123, 124, 125, 126, 128, 133, 134, 135, 139, 149, 150	14, 23, 33, 50, 59, 64, 108, 109, 119, 120, 122, 129, 130, 131, 132, 137, 138	107	20, 76, 82, 86, 87, 136	93	34	78
	2	42, 44, 45, 67, 95, 111, 140, 141, 145, 147, 148	9, 16, 17, 38, 39, 40, 41, 43, 54, 58, 65, 66, 68, 69, 70, 71, 72, 73, 80, 89, 94, 127, 142, 143, 144	36, 37, 52, 55, 60, 61, 62, 63, 75, 103, 104, 115	81, 88	78	79	53
	3			35				1
	4	2, 106, 121	74		91	92		6
	5	18, 31				77		3
	6						90, 96, 97, 98, 99, 100, 101, 102, 105	9
	Total	69	43	14	9	4	11	150

Now

Households discussed as examples in the text

FIGURE 3.2

Community mobility matrix from Fateh Garh, Uttar Pradesh, shows household movement out of poverty, within poverty, into poverty, and among the nonpoor

	Steps	Now						Total
		1	2	3	4	5	6	
10 years ago	1	1, 3, 4, 5, 6, 7, 8, 10, 11, 12, 13, 15, 19, 21, 22, 24, 25, 26, 27, 28, 29, 30, 32, 46, 47, 48, 49, 51, 53, 56, 57, 83, 84, 85, 110, 112, 113, 114, 116, 117, 118, 123, 124, 125, 126, 128, 133, 134, 135, 139, 149, 150	14, 23, 33, 50, 59, 64, 108, 109, 119, 120, 122, 129, 130, 131, 132, 137, 138	107	20, 76, 82, 86, 87, 136	93	34	78
	2	42, 44, 45, 67, 95, 111, 140, 141, 145, 147, 148	9, 16, 17, 38, 39, 40, 41, 43, 54, 58, 65, 66, 68, 69, 70, 71, 72, 73, 80, 89, 94, 127, 142, 143, 144	36, 37, 52, 55, 60, 61, 62, 63, 75, 103, 104, 115	81, 88	78	79	53
	3			35				1
	4	2, 106, 121	74		91	92		6
	5	18, 31				77		3
	6						90, 96, 97, 98, 99, 100, 101, 102, 105	9
	Total	69	43	14	9	4	11	150

MPI   MOP   FRIP

Note: Bold lines indicate the community poverty line. FRIP = falling of the rich into poverty; MOP = moving out of poverty; MPI = mobility of the poor.

In the next two sections, we use the CMM to examine both the overall mobility of households and how the movements in measured poverty rates over time are related to household mobility.

Household dynamics on the ladder of life: Mobility and churning

Using the CMM, we calculate the "mobility index" that shows how many households moved up or down at least one step on the ladder of life over the 10-year period.[4] If all households remained in exactly the same category, the mobility index would be 0, while if every single household moved (either up or down), then it would be equal to 1.

The extremely high level of mobility is striking (table 3.1). The proportion of households that moved at least one step either up or down over the past 10 years was more than half in 10 of the 18 study regions and above 40 percent in all but three regions. Movement across the categories is thus very fluid. Note that this mobility index does not itself distinguish direction. In some regions, mobility is primarily upward, as in Indonesia, where 46.3 percent moved up but only 6.6 percent moved down. In others, it represents "churning" as households rise and fall, as in Malawi, which had almost the same amount of upward (38.1 percent) and downward (34.8 percent) movement.

Two visual metaphors can help distinguish different notions about the process of moving out of poverty.

Imagine a narrow escalator on which people are standing. All riders move up at the same rate and hence retain their relative rankings. In this metaphor of poverty reduction, an individual's progress is determined by the pace of the escalator he or she is on.

An alternative metaphor is a broad staircase. On these stairs, many people are headed in both directions, moving at different speeds. Some are running up, and some might be inching up, while others are headed down. Measured poverty reduction or net upward movement over time is the result of both net movement and churning as people go up and down.

These two metaphors can be used to illustrate a hypothetical example involving 10 people in which poverty reduction is 20 percent in both cases. Figure 3.3 shows people on a narrow escalator, with all households retaining their relative rankings and movement out of poverty entirely a matter of the uniform upward movement common to all households. In the escalator, everyone moves up one step at the same time. Poverty falls from six people to four people, with no churning. The proportion of initially poor is 60 percent; upward movement of the poor is 100 percent (all six of the initially poor move

TABLE 3.1
Over half of households moved up or down at least one step on the ladder of life over 10 years

Study region	Average households ranked in CMM per village	Mobility index: movers up plus movers down (%)	Movers up (%) PI[a]	Movers down (%) FI[b]	Net upward movement: movers up less movers down (%)[c]	Churning index: ratio of total movers to net upward movement
Uganda	62	76.0	48.8	27.3	21.5	3.5
Malawi	54	72.9	38.1	34.8	3.3	21.9
Colombia	108	71.5	66.9	4.6	62.3	1.1
Tanzania	111	69.6	46.5	23.1	23.4	3.0
Senegal	68	69.5	43.0	26.5	16.5	4.2
Mexico	80	68.8	65.5	3.3	62.2	1.1
Bangladesh	143	55.8	37.9	17.9	20.1	2.8
Afghanistan	96	55.4	41.3	14.2	27.1	2.0
Indonesia	144	52.9	46.3	6.6	39.7	1.3
West Bengal	150	52.3	36.9	15.4	21.6	2.4
Thailand	106	49.4	40.2	9.2	31.0	1.6
Morocco	111	47.5	28.4	19.1	9.3	5.1
Andhra Pradesh	148	44.4	32.2	12.2	20.1	2.2
Philippines (conflict)	145	43.0	26.4	16.6	9.8	4.4
Sri Lanka (conflict)	99	42.1	32.6	9.6	23.0	1.8
Uttar Pradesh	153	36.9	25.1	11.8	13.3	2.8
Philippines (Bukidnon)	71	30.0	25.2	4.8	20.4	1.5
Assam	146	28.0	16.7	11.3	5.4	5.2
Median	109	52.6	38.0	13.2	21.0	2.6

Source: Authors' calculations from ladder-of-life data.

a. Prosperity Index (PI) = gross proportion of all households that moved up.
b. Falling Index (FI) = gross proportion of all households that moved down.
c. Net Prosperity Index (NPI) = net proportion of all households that moved up less households that moved down.

FIGURE 3.3
Narrow escalator model illustrates moving out of poverty with all households retaining their relative rankings

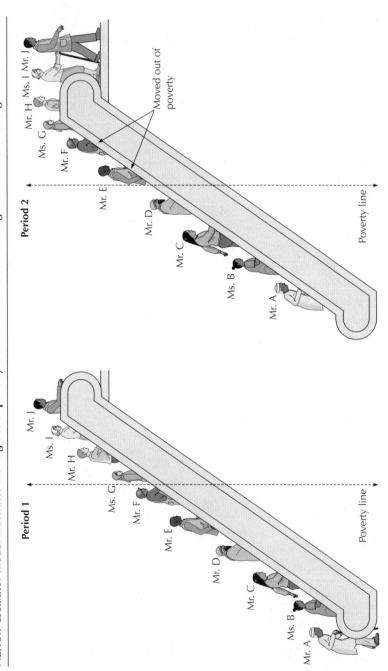

up); movement out of poverty is 33 percent (two of the six initially poor cross the poverty line); upward movement of the nonpoor is 75 percent; and net poverty reduction is 20 percent.

Figure 3.4 shows a broad staircase with households churning in both their absolute and relative status. In the staircase, three people moved out of poverty, and one person fell into poverty. As in figure 3.3, the proportion of initially poor is 60 percent. Upward movement of the poor is 67 percent (Ms. B, Mr. C, Mr. D, and Mr. F moved up). Downward movement of the poor is 17 percent (Mr. E fell). Movement out of poverty is 50 percent (Ms. C, Mr. D, and Mr. F moved out of poverty). Upward movement of the nonpoor is 50 percent (Mr. G and Mr. H moved up). Downward movement of the nonpoor is 50 percent (Mr. J and Ms. I fell).

The community mobility matrix can distinguish *gross* mobility (how many people moved up or down) from *net* prosperity—the net proportion of households that moved up. Table 3.1 shows very different dynamics across the study regions. Contrast the study regions in Mexico and Malawi (again, neither region was chosen to be typical of the entire country). They have similar indicators of mobility, with roughly 70 percent of households having moved on the ladder of life. In the small sample in Mexico, nearly all households moved up, so this is like the narrow escalator model; there was very little churning. Malawi, however, illustrates the broad staircase model. There is a lot of movement, but most of it consists of households churning up and down on a stationary stairway: 38 percent of households moved up, 35 percent of households moved down, and hence the *net* upward movement was only 3 percent of households.

The "churning index" is the ratio of total moves to net upward moves. The lowest this number could be is 1 (because a net upward move is a total move), but if upward and downward moves are similarly balanced, it can be very high. In Malawi, the churning index is 22—meaning 22 times as many people changed places as the net number of people who moved up—because the net upward movement was so small. Repeated household surveys would see only that overall well-being was "about the same"; this would miss the huge upward and downward movements that households experienced.

Poverty dynamics: Rising out of poverty and falling into poverty

Now that we have discussed general household mobility, let us turn to mobility in and out of poverty. Table 3.2 shows the relationship of household movements to the community poverty line in each study region. This table reveals three key points.

FIGURE 3.4
Broad staircase model illustrates moving out of poverty with households changing both their absolute and relative rankings

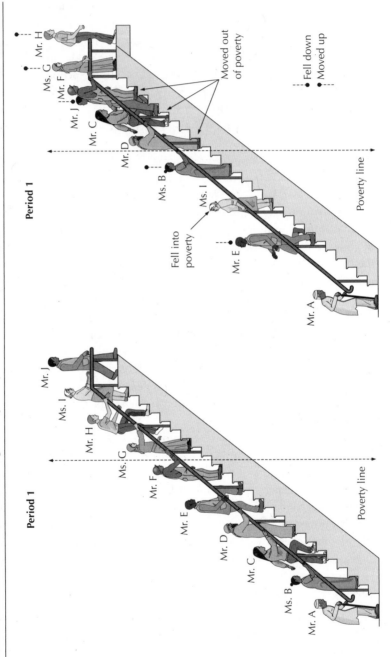

TABLE 3.2
Movements up and out of poverty are only one part of overall poverty dynamics

Study region	% of initial poor who moved out of poverty[c]	% starting poor	Movers as % of total households	Fallers as % of total households	Net change in poverty[a] (%)	% of all poor who moved up at least one step	% of poor who moved down at least one step	% of nonpoor falling into poverty	Churning[b]
Bangladesh	32.1	69.8	22.4	10.2	-12.2	47.5	7.4	33.9	3.2
West Bengal	29.7	63.3	18.8	7.8	-11.0	44.5	7.9	21.1	2.9
Indonesia	30.6	76.2	23.3	4.2	-19.1	54.1	0.8	17.5	1.9
Afghanistan	45.9	59.6	27.4	9.8	-17.6	52.3	1.8	24.1	2.5
Mexico	50.5	87.6	44.2	0.6	-43.6	70.9	2.3	5.0	1.7
Thailand	35.4	62.6	22.2	2.9	-19.3	51.3	2.1	7.7	1.8
Uttar Pradesh	19.2	66.7	12.8	5.5	-7.4	31.7	5.7	16.5	3.2
Philippines—conflict	17.3	72.4	12.5	10.5	-2.0	32.9	6.4	38.1	16.7
Andhra Pradesh	16.8	63.4	10.6	3.5	-7.1	38.0	6.7	9.6	3.8
Tanzania	19.6	82.9	16.3	6.7	-9.6	53.9	15.4	39.5	6.5
Sri Lanka—conflict	29.8	85.2	25.4	4.5	-20.8	53.7	9.5	30.7	2.7
Uganda	30.3	63.9	19.3	8.5	-10.8	57.4	16.3	23.6	5.8
Senegal	24.4	73.9	18.0	10.1	-7.9	46.9	15.9	38.7	7.9
Morocco	13.9	69.2	9.6	6.4	-3.2	34.6	11.2	20.8	11.6
Assam	9.6	71.1	6.8	5.4	-1.4	20.0	6.0	18.7	14.7
Colombia—conflict	12.6	89.1	11.3	3.8	-7.4	67.1	2.7	35.1	8.8
Philippines—Bukidnon	17.3	61.6	10.7	2.0	-8.7	29.3	1.3	5.1	2.8
Malawi	13.4	76.2	10.2	10.6	0.4	43.5	24.7	44.7	164.3
Median	22.0	70.5	17.2	5.9	-9.1	47.2	6.6	22.4	3.5

Source: Authors' calculations from ladder of life community mobility matrixes.

a. Figures in this column show poverty reduction.
b. Churning is defined as movers out of poverty plus movers into poverty plus movers within poverty (up and down) over the net reduction in number of poor.
c. MOP is based on the subsample of households that started out in poverty.

First, over this period, there was considerable upward movement of people who began in poverty. In the typical study region, almost half (47.2 percent) of all households that began in poverty moved up by at least one step on the ladder of life, and almost a quarter (22 percent) of the initially poor moved out of poverty altogether.

This is not to say that poverty traps do not exist—only that most of the people currently in poverty are probably not in a poverty trap. One needs to distinguish, as in chapters 1 and 2, between the very small percentage of poor people who have personal characteristics (such as chronic illness, alcoholism, or physical disability) that may keep them in extended episodes of poverty, and the much larger number who are poor at a given point in time. There are poverty traps, but not all poverty is a trap.

Recent studies have emphasized this point in different ways. For instance, Carter and Ikegami (2007) emphasize that poverty mobility can be affected by poor people's endowments of assets and capabilities. These models can lead to substantial poverty dynamics even while there are "intrinsically chronically poor" who "lack the ability or circumstance to achieve a nonpoor standard of living in their existing economic context" (5).

The Chronic Poverty Research Centre (2008), in its current report on chronic poverty, estimates that 1.2 billion people were in absolute poverty (below $1 a day) in 2002. Between a quarter (320 million) and one-third (443 million) of those in absolute poverty were trapped in "chronic poverty"—an episode of poverty that lasts for many years, often a lifetime. The report attributes chronic poverty traps to five factors that correspond to many of the same issues our study explores:

- *Insecurity.* Insecurity of assets and income may be caused by conflict, economic crisis, and especially health shocks.
- *Limited citizenship.* This factor includes lack of voice and participation in governance and service delivery.
- *Spatial disadvantage.* People are disadvantaged by living in chronically deprived countries (identified based on per capita gross domestic product, child mortality, fertility, and undernourishment). Even in countries that are otherwise progressing, some locations may be unfavorable because they are remote and politically marginalized, have poor agricultural and natural resource endowments, or are not well connected to infrastructure like roads and markets.
- *Social discrimination.* Important social divisions include those along lines of gender, race, and caste.

- *Poor economic opportunities.* Even where there is local economic growth, economic opportunities may be inaccessible to some people.

The recent chronic poverty report and ours are strikingly consistent on some points. There is enormous fluidity in poverty: only a fraction (by their estimates, from a quarter to a third) of those who are in an episode of poverty at any point in time are in an extended episode of poverty. Even for those in chronic poverty, their plight has less to do with individual characteristics than with the opportunities—and the barriers to opportunities—that households experience.

A second point that emerges from the analysis of poverty mobility is that similar net reductions in poverty in the different study regions can mask very different poverty dynamics. For instance, in West Bengal about 30 percent of those who began in poverty moved out, while only about 17 percent of the initially poor moved out of poverty in Andhra Pradesh. But the net reduction in poverty was only 4 percentage points larger in West Bengal. Why? Because in West Bengal, 21.1 percent of the nonpoor moved into poverty, and in Andhra Pradesh, this movement was only half as large. The dynamics of the nonpoor matter for poverty reduction as well.

The extent of falling into poverty is particularly striking in Africa. Malawi's communities registered a marginal increase in poverty (less than 1 percent). But this apparent stagnation does not mean there was no movement. In Malawi, 45 percent of the households that were classified as nonpoor 10 years ago were considered poor today. Equally impressively, 43.5 percent of those in poverty moved up at least one step—but 25 percent of those already in poverty moved down. The lack of net increase in poverty hides enormous churning in economic status among households.

Similarly large fractions of the nonpoor are falling into poverty in other parts of Africa and, not surprisingly, in the conflict regions we studied. In Ruvuma, Tanzania, and in Senegal, 40 and 39 percent of nonpoor households were reported to have fallen below the community poverty line. In those study regions that sampled households affected by conflict, nearly a third of nonpoor households fell into poverty. It is interesting that in the conflict-affected region of the Philippines, 38 percent of the nonpoor fell into poverty, but only 5 percent did in the nonconflict Bukidnon region of that country.

This attention to movement into poverty is important. In designing poverty reduction strategies, one might be tempted to consider only how the economy and programs affect those who are now poor. But as the study regions show, how the nonpoor fare can be just as significant for the evolution of the overall poverty rate.

Third, the final column of table 3.2 shows very high levels of churning. In the typical study region, the number of people who moved at all is three times the net number of people who moved out of poverty. So, setting methodological issues to one side, a repeated household survey would have been able only to identify a net reduction in poverty of, on average, 9.1 percent of households over this 10-year period (shown in column 6). What would have been missed is everything else—repeated surveys examining poverty headcounts would have missed the fact that 22 percent of poor households moved out of poverty, but 22 percent of nonpoor households moved in. It would have missed that 47 percent of the poor moved up (so roughly twice as many moved up as moved out). It would have missed that 6.6 percent of people already in poverty moved down.[5]

Our examination of the community mobility matrix is a new method, but it confirms what has been found almost whenever economists have been to able produce data linking households over time (often called "panel" data). These studies have measured massive income mobility, very fluid poverty dynamics, and high levels of vulnerability to episodes of poverty.[6] Using data from Indonesia, Pritchett, Suryahadi, and Sumarto (2000) find that transitions into and out of poverty mean that almost twice as many households have at least one episode of poverty as do those who are poor at any given point in time. Even over very short periods, measures find very large transitions. For instance, when Dercon and Krishna (2000) compared two surveys in Ethiopia less than a year apart, they found that only 32.8 percent of households were in the same quintile in measured consumption expenditures. Even over that very short time, 13.7 percent had moved out of poverty and 16.4 percent moved into poverty.[7]

Implications of household poverty dynamics

Are these metaphors of escalators and staircases really relevant for thinking about poverty programs and policies? Indeed.

One direct policy consequence of these high levels of churning is that programs that attempt to target benefits to "the poor" are unlikely to succeed on any static criteria. If the poor were a fixed group (either absolutely or relatively), then they could be accurately identified and reached by transfers or income generation programs. Poverty is a condition, a situation households find themselves in, and the households in this situation turn out to be very fluid; hence, "the poor" today are not "the poor" of tomorrow. The poor today are just those households currently experiencing an episode of poverty; they are a mix of the chronically destitute, those moving up, those with a temporary spate of bad luck, and lots of people who fall between categories. A classic study by Jalan and Ravallion (2000) followed the same households in China over six years and found that a precise identification of those who were poor in the first year did not help improve targeting much compared to a simple uniform transfer to all households.

A second consequence of churning is that it shapes how one thinks about distributional issues during episodes of reform. Ravallion (2004) introduced the important distinction between changes in vertical inequality and changes in horizontal inequality.[8] This distinction draws on a traditional distinction in the economics of public finance between vertical equity (that richer households pay as much or more in taxes than do poorer households) and horizontal equity (that people who are similarly situated are treated similarly). He argues that much of the confusion in the discussion about globalization stems from the fact that pro-globalization advocates focus on vertical equity, claiming that globalization has been good for absolute poverty reduction, while anti-globalization advocates focus on the fact that there are winners and losers—that people who before were equal are made unequal by change. As Ravallion points out, if one person moves up and another down, the aggregate measures of income and inequality might remain exactly the same. But the political and political economy consequences would be very different, as this churning "is unlikely to go unnoticed by the people involved" (20).

Kanbur (2008) points out that focusing only on the "snapshots" and ignoring the movie may give rise to particular concerns about economic transformations and policy change:

> Consider a country where major structural changes are under way. These will, in general, create winners and losers, in the short run and in the long run. If the poor are all winners, or if there are some poor winners and no poor losers, poverty will of course decline. But measured poverty may also decline even if a significant number of the losers are poor, because their losses are outweighed by the gains of the other poor. The anguish of increasing poverty among some, perhaps a sizable number, of the poor, will not be captured by the national level of decline in poverty. There will be a disconnect between those who focus on these official statistics, and those whose focus is on poor losers.

The churning that our study reveals and emphasizes shows just how important these considerations are empirically. Across the study regions, on average, for each person who moved out of poverty there were three people who moved either up or down. And even in cases like Bangladesh, where the focus groups reported a net poverty reduction of 12 percentage points, 7 percent of the initial poor saw their fortunes worsen.

But more important than the consequences for targeting or design of narrowly conceived "poverty" programs are the broader implications for poverty strategies. The broad conceptualization of poverty by the respondents in our study translates into high rates of poverty; at the same time, we found high fluidity of transitions into and out of poverty. This finding has three implications.

First, attempts to characterize "the poor" as different are mostly misconceived. The people who either are in poverty, will be in poverty, or are at risk of an episode of poverty make up a large share of the population. As our study respondents conceive of it, the poor *are* us.

Second, a poverty strategy needs to facilitate what already happens. Rather than attempting to rescue individuals from a poverty trap, poverty strategies need to facilitate the aspirations and initiatives of those now poor so they can escape their condition. Thus, a broader effort to unblock opportunities should substitute for a focus on intensive individual interventions.

Third, vulnerability is a fact of life. Given the massive numbers who fall into poverty, effective poverty reduction strategies cannot focus only on helping the poor move up; they must also help those who are up stay up.

Defining poverty down

The very high level of upward mobility and churning of the poor that our study documents is of course fundamentally related to how one defines poverty. If one insists on more and more penurious standards for poverty, then perhaps one will find less mobility, and a higher fraction of the "poor" at any point in time will be those in long-term episodes of poverty (poverty traps). Moreover, as fewer and fewer people are regarded as "poor," they will in some senses appear more like an identifiable group. But at the levels of poverty that the community focus groups identify, poverty is initially a very large fraction of the population (typically around 70 percent). At these higher levels of poverty, there is more fluidity up, down, and out of poverty.

The levels of poverty that our focus groups report are very different from what might have been obtained in our study regions had we used a US$1 a day standard that the World Bank uses in some global measures of poverty (box 3.1) or other income-based technocratic definitions of pov-

BOX 3.1
Poverty lines and people's perceptions of poverty lines

The present-day idea of a poverty line goes back a century to Charles Booth's work in 1889. Booth developed the first quantitative classification of poverty based on income, with the "line of poverty" set between 18 and 21 shillings per week. However, the measures below and above the line of poverty remained vague. It was Benjamin Seebohm Rowntree (1901), inspired by Booth, who offered more precise income categorizations and who consistently used the term "poverty line" in his study of poverty in York, England. This was the beginning of the tradition of measuring poverty by income and focusing solutions on redistributing or increasing incomes (see Himmelfarb 1992 on the evolution of thinking about the poor and poverty).

Today, the US$1 a day standard, adjusted to local currency using purchasing power parities (PPPs),[10] is widely used to track trends in global poverty. The World Bank's *World Development Report 1990* was the first to employ a universal poverty line to compare and aggregate poverty statistics across countries. Using constant 1985 PPP prices, the report proposed two poverty lines: US$275 per person per year for the extremely poor and $370 per person per year for the poor. The range was chosen to span the poverty lines estimated for a number of countries with low average incomes: Bangladesh, Egypt, India, Indonesia, Kenya, Morocco, and Tanzania. The lower limit of the range coincided with a poverty line commonly used in India. The international poverty line was later revised in 1993 PPP terms and set at US$1.08 a day (Chen and Ravallion 2000). The threshold was set using the median of the 10 lowest poverty lines in the set of countries used by *World Development Report 1990* and Ravallion, Datt, and van de Walle (1991). To gauge the sensitivity of poverty indicators, a line twice this value—US$2.15 per day—was also used.

Since 2000, the World Bank has based its global poverty and inequality measures on these two poverty lines. The poverty rate calculated using the US$1 a day line is usually treated as a conservative estimate because aggregate poverty in the developing world is defined by perceptions of poverty rates in the poorest countries (World Bank 1990; Ravallion, Datt, and van de Walle 1991; Chen and Ravallion 2000). Drawing on new International Comparison Program survey data for 2005 to calculate new PPPs, Ravallion and Chen have just repeated this process, calculating the average poverty line found in the poorest 10 to 20 countries at US$1.25 a day per person. Some national poverty lines are below this line and some are above. For example, the national poverty lines used in both China and India are closer to US$1 a day at 2005 prices. However, better-off countries tend to have higher poverty lines than the frugal US$1.25 standard. In discussing poverty in middle-income countries, the higher US$2 a day standard is more appropriate. This is the median poverty line for all developing countries.

---

erty. As figure 3.5 shows, the focus groups reported that poverty rates were typically 20 to 30 percentage points higher than the $1 a day headcount poverty rates (in making the comparison, we matched as best we could the regions of the country—we used rural estimates only prior to the revision of the poverty level to US$1.25 a day—and time of the survey).

Our focus group perceptions often aligned fairly closely with a standard based on US$2 a day—sometimes higher, sometimes lower, but nearly always closer than to the $1 a day standard.

FIGURE 3.5

$1-a-day international standard appears to underestimate poverty compared to focus group estimates

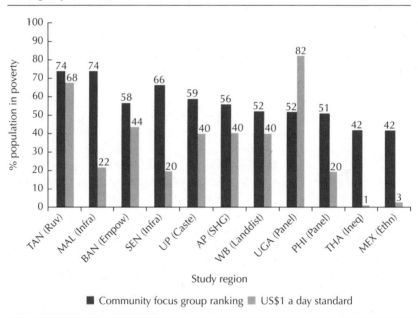

Source: Authors' estimates using ladder of life data and data from PovCal (World Bank); closest match on year and using rural estimates only.

Note:

AP (SHG) = Andhra Pradesh, Self-help groups	TAN (Ruv) = Tanzania, Ruvuma
BAN (Empow) = Bangladesh, Women's empowerment	THAI (Ineq) = Thailand, Inequality
	UGA (Panel) = Uganda, Panel study
MAL (Infra) = Malawi, Infrastructure	UP (Caste) = Uttar Pradesh, Caste
MEX (Ethn) = Mexico, Ethnicity	WB (Landdist) = West Bengal, Land distribution
PHI (Panel) = Philippines, Panel study	reforms
SEN (Infra) = Senegal, Infrastructure	

The point is not to dispute the World Bank's numbers (as our study is not representative), but rather to point out that there is no reason to expect the $1 a day standard and people's everyday notions of poverty to correspond. Any definition of poverty is a social convention, and social conventions are agreements about meanings among the actors involved in a given discourse around a given purpose. The actors involved in the discourse about the $1 a day poverty line are those who are interested in making international comparisons and monitoring global progress toward the first Millennium Development Goal focused on poverty.

Since attempts to define poverty are explicitly and unavoidably social and political, one should not confuse "technical" with "better." There is no neutral, objective, "scientific" definition of poverty that has priority over subjective and qualitative definitions of poverty. The principal difference between the official poverty lines that use technically demanding techniques and the community poverty lines based on the responses of individuals and focus groups is not that one is "subjective" and the other is "objective;" rather, the difference is in where the subjectivity is exercised and by whom. In one case it is exercised by a technocrat who asserts a convention about what is an "appropriate" food basket for the poor to consume—a once and for all assertion that allows the state to "see" poverty reduced to a single administratively controlled measurement (Scott 1998). In the other case, the subjectivity is exercised by the affected individuals in ordering their own reality.

Obviously, this is not meant to argue against the virtues of official global or national poverty lines for some uses. They clearly have their merits, particularly in terms of providing a common poverty criterion for comparisons across countries or across regions within a country, or perhaps for tracking progress over time.[9] But each definition and measure of poverty is appropriate to its own sphere of discourse, and there can be no suggestion that technical measures have exclusive rights—or even primacy—in the conceptualization, definition, or measurement of poverty. Claims about "the poor" or "poverty" based on standards that define poverty down by setting very stringent criteria are no more or less reliable than any other social convention.

How Important Are Local Factors?

We have shown that the large churning in poverty status, as people move up and down the ladder, belies the notion of a fixed and distinctive category of people who are "poor." Let us now ask: How much movement out of poverty is due not just to the country where people live but to the locality within the country? To extend the escalator metaphor, while the country's overall pros-

perity escalator may be fast or slow, people live in localities that have escalators of their own. A key question is how much difference there is between
the speeds of the local escalators. It could be that all are synchronized and
hence the average speed is also very close to the speed in each village, or it
could be that the countrywide average speed masks tremendous variation in
local speeds.

This is another area where tools have determined results. Household
survey sampling does not produce reliable estimates of village-level poverty
because sample sizes are typically far too small. Hence, most of the attention
in poverty research has gone to the change in poverty at the *national* level
(focusing only on net movement) and its relation to overall economic progress, to changes in inequality, and to the correlates of poverty at the *household*
level (as in the standard poverty profiles). Less attention has been paid to the
variation in poverty at the *local* level and its potential determinants.[11]

While our results on the poverty dynamics of individuals add to a growing literature, on the topic of local level variation, our technique is unique
and gives new insights. Since the community mobility matrix ranked the
entire population of a village or neighborhood, we have essentially census-
like estimates of the levels of well-being and their changes for a small locality.
These estimates allow us to examine the extent of difference between the various measures of prosperity and poverty reduction across these localities.

There are two main findings. First, the variation across villages in their
perceived movement out of poverty is much larger than expected. Even within
prosperous economies there are villages that are lagging, and within stagnant
economies there are villages with rapid poverty reduction. Second, while the
poor and nonpoor within villages tend to move together, there is heterogeneity in the extent to which local prosperity is shared.

Prosperity

We begin with an examination of the indexes of "prosperity." Figure 3.6
contains box-whisker plots that illustrate the central tendency and dispersion of the prosperity index (PI, the gross proportion of all households that
moved up), the falling index (FI, the gross proportion of all households
that moved down), and the net prosperity index (NPI, the net proportion
of all households that moved up less households that moved down) across
communities in the study. The box and whisker plot is a graphic device
that shows both the central tendency and dispersion of data. In the graphs
for each study region, the line in the middle of the box is the median (the

50th percentile of the data) while the left edge of the rectangular box is the 25th percentile and the right edge is the 75th percentile.[12] The lines extending from the box (the "whiskers") illustrate the more extreme values. This graphic device shows the order across study regions in their typical value. For example, the box plot on the prosperity index is ordered from top to bottom by the study region median value of PI (so study regions higher had more upward movement). At the same time, one can see the variation across villages/communities within the study regions by the width of the boxes (and "whiskers" from the boxes). (These statistics comparing distribution of outcomes across *communities* are not exactly the same as the corresponding statistics for households in the study region, as the number of households in each community varied.)

There is a wide range of outcomes across the study regions. Net prosperity over a decade varies from only about 3 percent of households in Malawi to more than 60 percent in (the sampled regions of) Mexico.[13] Also interesting is that much of the difference in prosperity is due to the proportion falling, not just the proportion rising. So, for instance, in many African regions with low net prosperity, many households moved up—but many more moved .down. In Malawi, 43 percent of poor households and 21 percent of nonpoor households moved up; these figures were similar, 44 percent and 24 percent, for West Bengal. But net prosperity is only 3.3 percent in Malawi versus 21.6 percent in West Bengal. The difference is entirely in the falling: in West Bengal 8 percent of poor and 28 percent of nonpoor households fell over this period, while in Malawi 25 percent of poor and fully 67 percent of nonpoor households fell.

The advantage of having estimates for each community is that we can show the variation in prosperity across sampled villages. The box plots show that it is enormous: in fact, the variations across communities in the study regions are nearly as large as the cross-region differences. For instance, Thailand is one of the study regions with highest net prosperity—but the bottom 25 percent of Thai villages have an NPI lower than all but six of the study region medians. Conversely, Malawi has the lowest NPI of any country, but the top 75 percent of villages have NPI similar to West Bengal or Senegal (at the cross-region median). So even well-performing countries have lagging communities, and lagging countries have thriving communities.

If one does a simple analysis of variance of NPI (net prosperity), one finds that 73 percent of the variation across villages in the entire study is variation across villages *within* the study regions. This finding suggests that while overall national context is important to poverty reduction, there are

FIGURE 3.6
Rising, falling, and net prosperity indexes show large variations both across study regions and across communities within regions

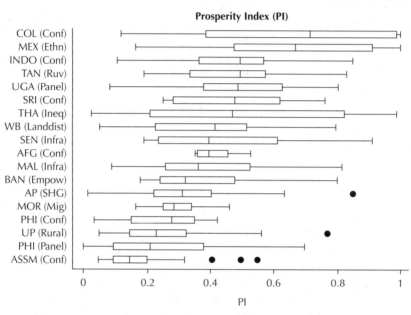

Prosperity Index (PI)

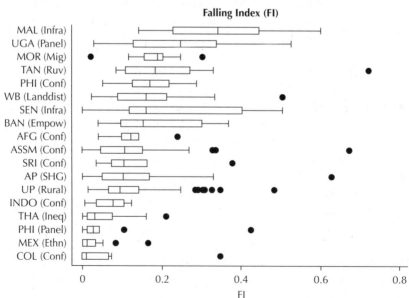

Falling Index (FI)

FIGURE 3.6 continued

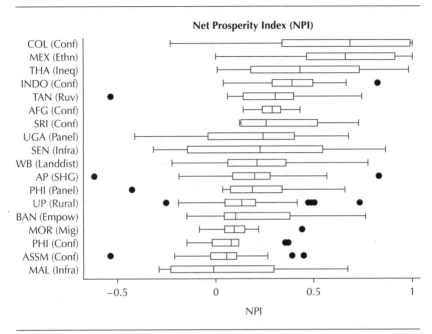

Net Prosperity Index (NPI)

Source: Authors' calculations with ladder of life community mobility matrixes.

also locality-specific trajectories that, over a decade, make a big difference to the individuals in those places.

This is a new finding. While many have emphasized the obvious—that there are rich and poor places within countries—this finding is about the speed of poverty reduction and shows that there are very different paces in local prosperity.

Movement of the poor

What about those who start initially poor in the distribution—the population group of most interest in our study? Figure 3.7 summarizes the MOP (fraction of poor who moved out of poverty) and MPI (fraction of poor who moved up) indexes for all study regions. The box plot on MOP shows large differences across regions: a great deal of movement out of poverty in Mexico, much less in conflict-affected Colombia and Assam.

Again a major finding is the large variability across the villages within each study region. The box plots show that the movement up of the poor

FIGURE 3.7

Movement out of poverty and mobility of the poor indexes show large variations both across study regions and across communities within regions

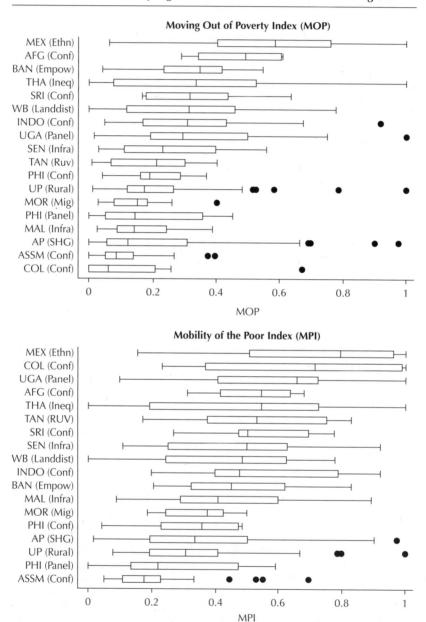

Source: Authors' calculations with ladder of life community mobility matrixes.

is not primarily a "study region phenomenon": that is, a household's likelihood of moving up from poverty was related to its village of residence at
least as much as to the study region the village was in. The simple analysis
of variance finds that 75 percent of upward movement of the initially poor
(MPI) was variation across villages within study regions and only 25 percent
depended on the study region.

The large differences between villages in the *changes* in overall rankings
of perceived household well-being suggest that there may be locality-specific
elements of poverty experiences to be explained. In this sense, these findings set the stage for qualitative exploration—of processes and interactions
among factors that may explain mobility or lack thereof in different contexts.
If all of poverty progress depended either on the characteristics of individuals
or on national characteristics (or on some combination), then studying local
factors would be of little interest.

Co-movement of the nonpoor and poor

How does movement out of poverty relate with net prosperity across study
regions and communities? Do the poor and nonpoor move up together? Do
initial poverty levels matter? This section graphs relationships between some
of the indexes derived from the community mobility matrix to address these
questions and the policy debates they entail. Does growth or net prosperity
matter for movement out of poverty or movement of the poor?

Figure 3.8 shows how the fortunes of the poor and nonpoor moved
together across villages. Each graph (one per study region) shows for each
community the MPI (fraction of people who began poor and moved up)
and the MRI (fraction of people who began nonpoor and moved up). This
comparison allows one to visualize how the fortunes of poor and nonpoor
in the same communities were associated as the graph shows a 45-degree line
(equal movement of poor and rich) and a best-fit line through the villages
(which are sometimes very few). This figure and the accompanying regressions of MPI on MRI village by village suggest three points.

First, as discussed earlier, almost three-quarters of the variance in net
prosperity in the study regions consists of differences between villages in the
same study region. When this village mobility is broken down for poor and
nonpoor within each village, it appears that, *on average*, the poor and nonpoor
moved up together across the study communities (in addition to figure 3.8,
see the regression results in annex 3.1).[14] This is not to suggest that upward
movement of the nonpoor causes upward movement of poorer households.
Rather, the findings suggest that there are large positive and negative village-

FIGURE 3.8
On average, the poor and nonpoor moved up together across study regions

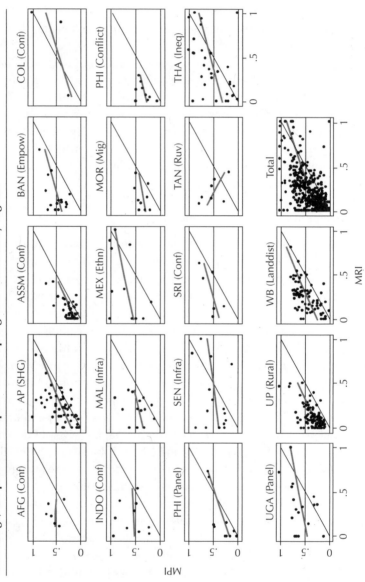

Source: Authors' calculations with ladder of life community mobility matrixes.

specific shocks to prosperity and that these usually affect the movements of both poor and nonpoor households similarly. But in some cases they are affected equally, while in other cases the shocks seem to have benefited either the nonpoor or the poor disproportionately.

This co-movement of the poor and nonpoor across villages is an important background to the entire Moving Out of Poverty study. It suggests that there are large "shocks," positive and negative, that affect the prosperity of villages; these are not specific to households, but neither are they national in scope (or statewide in the case of India). Moreover, these shocks are not specific to the poor but affect poor and nonpoor alike, though to differing degrees. One important agenda of the broader study is to identify the correlates of local prosperity—are they economic conditions, infrastructure, functioning of local democracy, social conditions?

Second, though the increases in well-being of the poor and nonpoor tended to move together across villages, the extent of their co-movement differed across regions. As seen in figure 3.8, in the four Indian states the movement was essentially one for one. However, the other regions display different patterns. Annex 3.1 uses statistical techniques to identify different patterns in the degree to which the prosperity of the poor and nonpoor moved together. The important point is that the relationship itself seems quite different across regions. In the context of the larger Moving Out of Poverty study, this heterogeneity across regions is also of great interest as it suggests that determinants of the upward movement of the nonpoor and poor are not uniform.

Third, the large variation across villages in the extent of movement of the poor and nonpoor is itself of interest. This raises the question of whether these differences across villages in "shared prosperity" result from identifiable features of the economic, political, and social structures of the villages or from positive and negative economic shocks to those villages. At the economic level, different types of shocks will reward different types of assets and have different impacts—to cite just one example, economic changes that increase demand for labor (which is equally shared) will have a different impact than will economic changes that increase returns to land. Exploring and perhaps explaining these differences is an important agenda of the overall MOP study.

Positive and negative shocks are not necessarily symmetric. In fact, the association between falling of the poor (FPI) and falling of the nonpoor (FRI) is much weaker than the association between MPI and MRI. Hence, as illustrated in figure 3.9, the co-movement across villages of *net* prosperity of the poor (NPP) and nonpoor (NPR) is much less than their co-movement of upward mobility.

FIGURE 3.9

Association is much weaker between net upward movements of the poor and nonpoor than between their gross upward movements

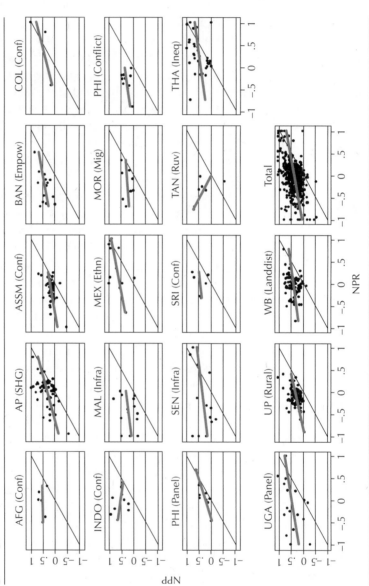

Source: Authors' calculations with ladder of life community mobility matrixes.

This may reveal asymmetries in gains versus losses, but it may also be a mechanical effect of a ladder of life that is "bottom-coded." That is, those on the very bottom step of the ladder of life cannot move further down the ladder, even if their well-being has fallen. Therefore, villages with large proportions of the nonpoor falling may not see similarly large falls among the poor, because many of them began and ended on the bottommost step. For instance, in table 3.2 one sees that in Tanzania, Uganda, and Senegal, the fallers among the initially poor were about 15 percent while the fallers among the nonpoor were about 50 percent (and about 30 to 40 percent of the fallers among the nonpoor fell into poverty). Almost certainly, the "truncation" effect of the ladder of life approach makes it more difficult to observe common falls than common rises: the "top coding" problem is much less severe, given that far fewer people were in the uppermost category in either period.

Examination of Local Determinants of Moving Out of Poverty

Let's start with a poor person who is working hard to build her assets. What helps? What hinders? Our hypothesis, as detailed in the conceptual framework developed in chapter 1, is that her ability to increase her well-being is influenced by the opportunity structure she faces, which, in turn, is defined by the broader institutional, social, and political context of the society where she lives. We are concerned with two main types of institutions at the local level: markets or available economic opportunity on one side and institutions of local democracy on the other side. These institutions influence the rate of return an individual is able to get on her assets as well as the claims on those assets.

Social divisions and social inequality, however, can reinforce inequality in access to political and economic opportunities (Tilly 1999; Rao and Walton 2004b). Hence, when thinking about mobility of the poor, a third set of variables becomes important—and these have to do with agency of the poor.

Agency can operate at the individual or collective level. At the individual level, it is measured by a sense of self-confidence, power, and self-efficacy. The belief that "I can make a difference" can be an important precursor to action (Bandura 1995, 1998). Capacity to aspire also motivates a person to action and can lead to different and better futures (Appadurai 2004). For the most marginalized people, their collective agency in organization, representation, voice, and identity is critical in overcoming social discrimination that leads to economic, social, and political exclusion and inequality. Without this collective capacity to negotiate, control, and bargain, individual initiative on its own may not be sufficient. Taken together, individual and collective agency can modify or create direct access to new economic opportunities, or it can work through democracy, leading to greater mobility.

If we take the example of a rural farmer in Tanzania, any one of the above correlates can influence the channels that lead to a change in income. Economic opportunity and local growth can lead to better prices for her produce, reduced costs of fertilizers, or a new market space that makes it profitable to engage in additional activities (such as livestock rearing, selling milk, etc.). If the farmer knows, however, that local government officials will expropriate the gains from her produce, she will have little incentive to produce. Self-confidence and a sense of "I can do it" can also positively affect her productivity, as can collective action. She will also have more incentive to produce if she receives fair prices on her products or expects to be given credit when applying for a loan.

Examination of local conditions and poverty reduction

We have shown that there are large differences in reported poverty reduction across villages, even within study regions. This raises the question of which local characteristics are associated with the villages that experience more rapid poverty reduction.

Before presenting some multivariate regressions that address this question, we should first mention three reasons we do not put more emphasis on using the cross-village variation to examine effects. First, while we gain benefits from allowing members of each village to define their own steps on the well-being ladder and their own definition of poverty, we also lose direct comparability. This means that even if two villages report the same change in net prosperity in terms of the net proportion of households moving up, we cannot be sure that these are equivalent movements, as the steps could have been set farther apart in one village than in the other. Second, as explained next, we want to emphasize context, which means we do not anticipate that a linear regression pooled across purposively different contexts (e.g., sampling in conflict areas) that forces numerical identical associations among variables will be a particularly fruitful research strategy. Third, regressions cannot answer questions about causal structure, so this study is not designed to test questions about underlying economic models of behavior or economic structure.

All that said, for the villages from the four states of India, we did pool the data and examine the correlations (table 3.3). We did this analysis for

TABLE 3.3
Various measures of well-being dynamics are associated with local (village-level) factors in four states of India

Variable	MOP	MPI	MRI	FPI	FRI	FRIP	NPR
Difficulty of finding private employment	-.031***	-.0266**	-.0208*	-.0013	.0047	.0132	-.0167**
Difficulty of employment × economic access	.0101***	.0102**	.0078**	-.0023	-.0062	-.0072**	.0047*
Improvement of market outlets in the community	.0445***	.0469***	.0241***	-.012**	.0012	-.0157	.0047
Government attention	.0694***	.0527**	.0081	-.0043	-.0012	-.0084	.0276*
Government attention × political participation	-.028***	-.0259***	-.0099**	.005	-.0098	-.0071	-.0085*
Women membership in community council	.0015	.0025**	7.70E-04	-6.90E-04	-.0015*	-.002***	-2.20E-04
Presence of private health center	-.0691	-.1382***	-.0267	.067*	.0664	.0841	-.0244
Private health center × access to social network	.0181	.0418***	.0099	-.0165	-.0123	-.0207	.0078
Educational opportunities	.0033	.008	.0032	.0058	-.0022	7.80E-04	-.0012
Distance from the nearest city	-9.2e-04**	-.0014***	-1.80E-04	6.2e-04**	1.00E-04	4.30E-04	-9.30E-05
Irrigation facility	1.10E-04	.018*	-.0057	.0027	.0222*	.0318***	.0043
Collective action to solve water problem	-.0227**	-.0364***	-.0019	-.0032	-.0143	-.0074	-7.90E-04
Share of initially poor population	-.3426***	-.1578**	-.252***	.0976***	.1426**	.219***	.0425
Andhra Pradesh dummy	-.0259	.0022	-.0294	-.0274*	-.0215	-.0394	-.0424**
Assam dummy	-.1113***	-.1759***	-.135***	-.033*	-.0538	-.051	-.078***
Uttar Pradesh dummy	-.0847***	-.1412***	-.171***	-.0236*	-.0369	-.005	-.0478***
Constant	.4223***	.4366***	.3873***	.0595*	.2287***	.0944	.0566
Observations	288	288	288	288	288	288	288
R^2	.43	.32	.35	.12	.14	.21	.12

Source: Narayan, Petesch, and Paul (2009).

Note: A positive coefficient with MOP, MPI, and MRI means it helps upward movement; a negative coefficient with FPI, FRI, and FRIP means it prevents downward movement.

*$p < .10$ **$p < .05$ ***$p < .01$ (White heteroscedasticity-consistent standard errors)

measures of upward mobility of the poor (such as MOP and MPI) and of the nonpoor, and separately for rises and falls (as there is no reason to impose symmetry to upside and downside factors).

The results are consistent with several narratives. First, reassuringly, availability of employment is associated with greater reductions in poverty. The association of employment expansion and prosperity should not come as a surprise; what is interesting is that the larger poverty-reducing effects are associated with greater equality of opportunity—with the presence of more jobs to which access is relatively uniform.

The results also suggest that greater expansion of markets is associated with moving out of poverty (and moving up of the nonpoor). Clearly, cause and effect could run both ways, as one would expect new markets to open up in prospering villages.

The "attention of the government" seems to be associated with upward movement for the poor, but not for the nonpoor.

At the same time, there are puzzling correlations. Having a private health center is associated with less upward movement of the poor. *More* collective action to solve water problems also, curiously, is associated with less upward movement of the poor. We discuss these negative signs in chapter 7 on collective action.

Overall, the simple regressions are consistent with the view of large differences in outcomes across villages. Some village characteristics raise the mobility of both the poor and nonpoor, while others affect poor and nonpoor differently. But regressions do not identify causal links or economic structure and must be interpreted simply as identifying patterns that need to be explained.

Context is important in understanding local influences

Like all phenomena, poverty can be usefully viewed from many different angles and through many different lenses. We can view a forest from an airplane 10,000 feet up, and each leaf will meld into a green blur; or we can examine a tree with the naked eye and see many individual leaves; or we can put one leaf under a microscope so powerful that the forest, the tree, and the leaf all disappear and only the underlying cells are visible. As one moves closer, aspects that seemed the same are revealed to be full of specificity and texture.

So too, villages that appear exactly alike on a census or poverty map turn out to be full of local texture when scrutinized up close. The appropriate lens for viewing depends on the question being asked. In this study, we use empirical analysis like the regressions in table 3.3 to examine broad patterns, but we keep in mind that these regressions necessarily smooth over local texture and context.

Consider the cases of Dhampur and Malkapur, two villages located in the Adilabad district of Andhra Pradesh. Both communities share a history of economic shocks caused by persistent droughts and unexpected rainstorms that have adversely affected agriculture, the main source of livelihood. Both communities report multiple additional factors contributing to their poverty, including family feuds leading to land division, irregular work opportunities leading to indebtedness, lack of proper roads and transport leading to problems of communication, and irregular power supply leading to failure of electric irrigation pumps. Both villages have had a similar sequence of infrastructure development and delivery of basic services. Collective action is a significant feature of both: Dhampur has 22 self-help groups and Malkapur 18. Yet the two communities diverge in their accounts of who gained and who lost the most in the face of crises and opportunities.

Over the past 10 years, social stratification seems to have declined sharply in Malkapur, and at the time of data collection the community was characterized by solidarity and unity. People attribute this change to the efforts made by the state-sponsored Janmabhoomi program in 1997, which encouraged greater community participation.[15] In the decade between 1995 and 2005, access of lower-caste groups to temples and schools in Malkapur improved, leading to feelings of cohesion. Self-help groups in Malkapur engaged people from different socioeconomic backgrounds, bridging distances between groups. In addition, people believed that their ability to contact government officials and leaders had increased, with the political environment in 2005 conducive to active participation in decision making.

In contrast, social stratification is pervasive in Dhampur. Groups are demarcated strictly on the basis of their caste membership (untouchables, lower castes, backward castes, and upper castes) as well as their religious identity and education levels. "We are not treated properly," complained a discussion group of men and women from lower castes. "They [higher caste people] do not even give us water as they consider us untouchables. We have to drink water with our hands only. We are not allowed into the temples. Even if we push ourselves into the temples, we have to pay a fine in the panchayat."

Caste inequalities run parallel to economic inequalities in Dhampur, with the higher castes also occupying higher positions on the ladder and the untouchables ranked the poorest. These inequalities translate further into political differences in rights to contest elections or speak in matters of local governance. The lower castes said, "All of us never participate in the decision taking process of the village. Lambadis [upper castes] are the rulers in the village. They have more land. They alone contest in the elections and they forbid others to participate in the elections. We can never compare ourselves with them. They have economic strength and manpower as well."

Worse, state action to distribute land to lower castes in Dhampur has resulted in garrisoning among the better-off groups against the poor. The upper castes in Dhampur felt threatened and complained about a government law that gave only the lower castes the power to buy and sell land in the community. A discussion group of men from lower castes said, "There is a rule that all of us lower-caste people should obey those from the higher castes. We cannot deny them. If we do so, we are not given any work, without which we cannot live. If we see anyone belonging to the higher caste in the bazaar, we have to take our slippers in our hand and walk. Even now, if they get to know that we are talking about such things to strangers, we would be punished."

While self-help groups in both Malkapur and Dhampur function in a similar manner, groups in Dhampur have begun to dwindle. Members attributed the decline to the higher monthly saving commitment fixed by the economically better off in their groups, with no thought given to the economic capabilities of poorer members.

The indicators for mobility among both the poor and rich are indicative of the social context of the two villages. Although both communities had an identical share of poor people moving up (MPI of 41 percent), Malkapur had a higher percentage of people moving out of poverty (MOP of 29 percent compared to Dhampur's 17 percent). Moreover, prosperity seemed to be unequally shared in Dhampur, with nearly 44 percent of the nonpoor experiencing upward movement (MRI) and no decline.

The experience of Dhampur suggests that inequalities embedded in social structures may prevent poor people from gaining access to opportunities. On the other hand, as the case of Malkapur suggests, a good local democratic structure, cooperative local leaders, and active self-help groups may help ameliorate caste differences and open up opportunities to all.

These case studies show that pro-poor government policies and growth in economic opportunities can have different impacts on poor people depending on the way these policies and opportunities interact with other features in the local environment—inequalities based on wealth, social class divisions, political connections, and responsiveness of local government, among others.

Conclusion

The Moving Out of Poverty study, by looking at the phenomenon of poverty with several different tools, is able to illuminate different aspects of transitions out of poverty.

First, we find that poverty is a transitory condition and that there is enormous fluidity of households into and out of poverty. Speaking of "the poor" as if they constituted a distinct set of people is just not a fruitful approach to poverty reduction in poor countries. Poverty is a condition, not a characteristic. This then frames the question: How does one facilitate transitions by households out of the condition of poverty?

Second, by using rankings of entire communities, we can rank the importance of local conditions for poverty reduction. We find that although national (or regional) differences are certainly important, empirically more important are locally specific changes that affect both poor and nonpoor.

Third, we used our village-level data to launch an empirical analysis of the conditions that determined changes in poverty. This motivates much of the subsequent study, as we examine the local conditions in both economics (chapter 5) and politics (chapter 6) that are associated with greater local prosperity and movements out of poverty.

Annex 3.1   Associations in the Upward Mobility of Poor and Nonpoor across the Study Regions

Table A3.4 shows the results of regressing the net upward movement of the poor (MPI) on the net upward movement of the nonpoor, first across all villages (first row) and then for each study region.

The ordinary least squares (OLS) results show that there is a strong association but that it appears to be well less than one for one. But before concluding that growth is typically not shared and before discussing the heterogeneity of results across countries, we should note that measurement error in MRI would bias downward the regression estimate of the association between MPI and MRI results (an attenuation bias toward zero). When we adjust for the potential bias from measurement error, we find that the data typically are consistent with one-for-one co-movement of the poor and nonpoor.[16]

Examining the country-by-country results, table A3.4 shows a set of five study regions. In the first group, the Indian states show roughly one-for-one movement of poor and nonpoor.

The second group (Thailand, Bangladesh, Mexico, Philippines, Sri Lanka) statistically rejects that the association of MPI and MRI is zero across villages, but it also estimates the association to be significantly less than one for one. In the villages of these regions, as the proportion of nonpoor households moving up increased, the proportion of poor households moving up increased by less, presumably resulting in an increase in inequality. However, if one examines the "reverse regression" results, the lack of one-for-one association in these cases could be the result of measurement error.

In the third group (Uganda, Senegal, Indonesia, Morocco), the co-movement of poor and nonpoor appears to be quite small, as OLS regressions using this data cannot reject the hypothesis that the association is zero (but can reject that it is one for one).

In the fourth group (Malawi, Tanzania, Afghanistan, Colombia), the number of villages was too small for the analysis to have any statistical power. For instance, the point estimate for Malawi is 0.43, but the precision of the estimate is so low that neither zero nor one can be statistically rejected.

TABLE A3.4

On average, the poor and nonpoor in the same villages moved up together across study regions

Study region	N	OLS coefficient	Std. error	R^2	1/coeff from reverse regression	t-test H0: $\beta = 0$	t-test H0: $\beta = 1$
Pooled (with fixed)	471	0.54	0.05	0.32[a]	2.26	11.93	10.29
Regions that reject zero association and fail to reject a one-for-one association							
Uttar Pradesh	111	0.84	0.15	0.36	2.35	5.77	1.13
West Bengal[b]	81	0.76	0.11	0.35	2.20	6.94	2.16
Andhra Pradesh	57	0.79	0.13	0.29	2.72	6.10	1.65
Assam	51	0.83	0.21	0.40	2.06	3.88	0.81
Regions that reject zero association but reject a one-for-one association							
Thailand	33	0.49	0.21	0.24	2.08	2.39	2.45
Bangladesh	17	0.50	0.12	0.38	1.31	4.14	4.12
Mexico	13	0.39	0.18	0.27	1.44	2.17	3.42
Philippines	11	0.60	0.08	0.60	1.00	7.55	5.01
Sri Lanka— conflict	7	0.50	0.23	0.50	1.02	2.20	2.17
Regions that fail to reject zero association but reject a one-for-one association							
Uganda	18	0.27	0.18	0.11	2.46	1.55	4.10
Senegal	16	0.32	0.23	0.15	2.20	1.42	2.98
Indonesia	11	−0.18	0.44	0.01	−12.99	−0.41	2.68
Morocco	10	0.29	0.25	0.14	2.11	1.14	2.87
Regions that fail to reject either zero association or a one-for-one association							
Malawi	9	0.43	0.37	0.08	5.68	1.17	1.56
Tanzania	7	0.07	0.79	0.00	67.11	0.08	1.18
Afghanistan	7	−0.10	0.65	0.00	−14.71	−0.15	−0.14
Colombia	4	0.57	0.29	0.52	1.11	1.96	1.46

Source: Authors' calculations with ladder of life community mobility matrixes.

a. This is the R^2 of the bivariate regression of MPI on MRI excluding the study region fixed effects. With fixed effects, the R^2 increases to .422.

b. West Bengal is included in this category even though the *t*-test using OLS rejects one for one on the basis of the instrumental variable results in which the association is one for one for West Bengal (see note 16).

Notes

1. If *exactly* the same survey is conducted, the household survey can also be used to compare changes in poverty—but a major lesson of the past two decades of poverty research is just how hard it is to conduct *exactly* the same survey and how even small changes in questionnaire design or survey technique can lead to large changes in measured poverty.
2. This is an exercise in "poverty mapping" that attempts to use a combination of census data and household surveys to produce very fine-grained estimates of poverty.
3. We refer to a "village" even though in some urban areas it was a neighborhood, and in cases of a large village, it may have been a smaller unit of the village. In the latter case, the subunit does not necessarily correspond to the political or administrative jurisdiction called a village, but it is often closer to what people think of as their "village" in a social and spatial sense.
4. It should be kept in mind that because the mobility matrixes are not comparable across villages, we do not know whether two steps in one village represents a smaller or larger movement than one step in another village. One methodological concern is that some amount of the differences between villages or study regions in measured churning may be due to these differences between villages in numbers of well-being categories. If one took the same underlying mobility in consumption expenditures and divided it up into smaller and smaller categories (e.g., quartiles to deciles), then for exactly the same mobility in expenditures, one would observe more mobility across categories. However, careful examination of the data from the four states of India, which have larger numbers of villages than the other study regions, did not suggest this was the case. The measured mobility index was not systematically higher for villages with more ladder of life categories (with the possible exception of certain villages in Uttar Pradesh that had only four or five steps on their ladders and showed lower mobility).
5. The "poverty gap" measures can measure movements within poverty—for example, an increase in the poverty gap implies that those who are poor are further from the poverty line. But they are also net measures and cannot distinguish uniform moves of households from churning.
6. These include studies by Grootaert and Kanbur (1995) on Côte d'Ivoire; Pritchett, Suryahadi, and Sumarto (2000) on Indonesia; Carter and May (2001) on South Africa; Baulch and McCulloch (2002) on Pakistan; Deininger and Okidi (2003) on Uganda; and B. Sen (2003) on Bangladesh. Studies of vulnerability, poverty transitions, and income mobility using short-run panels include Pritchett, Suryahadi, and Sumarto (2000) in Indonesia; Dercon (2004) in Ethiopia; Glewwe and Hall (1998) in Peru; and Carter and May (2001) in South Africa.
7. Of particular note are the multiround surveys that cover long periods with multiple observations on each household (and its splits), such as the Indonesia Family Life Survey (IFLS), the NCAER India panel used by Bhide and Mehta (2004) and Munshi and Rosenzweig (2005), the China panel used by Jalan and Ravallion (2002), and a panel data set from Kagera, Tanzania, used by Beegle, de Weerdt, and Dercon (2006). Baulch and McCulloch (2002). They show that while transient poverty can be addressed through income-smoothing measures,

addressing chronic poverty may require more income-growth policies such as investment in households' productive earning capacity. Some of the earliest work on panel surveys of households, the work on Côte d'Ivoire in the 1980s, concluded that measurement error in income in rural settings was so large as to make the estimates of income changes virtually meaningless. Even with a switch to the use of consumption expenditures as a proxy for long-run income, the measurement error problem remains serious.

8. For a good discussion of horizontal inequality, see Stewart (2001).

9. We do not dwell on the many methodological difficulties in doing these tasks reasonably well. Other studies (e.g., Deaton 2004) have examined discrepancies in their calculation due to the infrequent updating of PPP exchange rates; some recent very large shifts in cross-national measures of poverty are due exclusively to these adjustments. Other difficulties involve correctly adjusting for regional price differentials and maintaining comparability of poverty lines over time given changes in relative prices.

10. PPP estimates are necessary to make international comparisons of income/consumption welfare. PPP is a conversion rate for a given currency into a reference currency (such as US$) that aims to ensure parity in terms of purchasing power of commodities—both traded and untraded—between countries.

11. The emergence of the "poverty mapping" agenda (e.g., Lanjouw et al. 2007) has to some extent changed this view, because it links household survey data (which tend to have less than 20 household observations per primary sampling unit) to census data (which have complete household observations and detail at the community level).

12. Not all data is symmetric, so there is nothing that dictates that 25th and 75th percentiles would be equidistant (many people assume this because they are used to having mean plus/minus a standard deviation, which assumes symmetry).

13. Again, because the samples are not representative of the country and there are only 12 study villages in Mexico, some of the cross-country differences represent sampling phenomena rather than countrywide phenomena.

14. The pooled regression across all villages (with fixed effects for each study region) shows a coefficient of .54 and an incremental R^2 of .32 (not including the fixed effects).

15. The Janmabhoomi program was a government initiative that dealt with issues of caste inequality, encouraged participation in local governance by empowering the gram sabhas (village assemblies), and promoted formation of more self-help groups. Some observers of local government feel that the program bypassed the local panchayats, thus weakening them.

16. A second technique for addressing measurement error is to use an instrumental variable. Fortunately, the male and female focus groups in India ranked the households independently, so we have a classic instrumental variable of repeated measurement. If one performs the same regressions using the women's estimates of MRI as the instrument for the men's estimates of MRI, one gets estimates that for each of the Indian states are very close to 1, as the estimates are higher by a magnitude that suggests measurement error is 10 to 20 percent of the total observed variation in MRI.

I Believe I Can

If you fall 10 times, you have to stand up 10 times, no matter what happens.

—GRACIELA, A 53-YEAR-OLD DISPLACED WOMAN,
El Mirador, Colombia

I think I can face anything; it is just a matter of self-discipline.

—LOIDA, A 35-YEAR-OLD FEMALE MOVER,
Kilaluna, Philippines

A strong breeze can break branches. A whirlpool in the ocean waters can sink boats. But a strong willpower can give you courage, and even if your destination is a thousand miles away, you can be successful.

—AMIT, A YOUNG MAN,
Jigna, Uttar Pradesh

As our field team approaches, Oy looks up from her cassavas. The researchers introduce themselves and mention the purpose of the visit. She smiles and says, "My life has changed for the better over the past 13 years. We are able to have things we never had; we are very proud and happy."

Thirty-nine years old and a native of Klong Pud, a small farming community in Thailand, Oy is identified as a mover out of poverty. She has two young children in school and a loving, hardworking, and supportive husband with a steady job. The family lives in a proper house and farms their own land, selling the produce in the market.

Conditions were not always so good for Oy and her family. Born to a family of laborers and married to a craftsman, she worked under harsh conditions from a young age, at one point migrating to another village to work on a ginger farm. She and her husband lived in a small shack with walls of woven bamboo and grass on a piece of land belonging to their relatives. Their fortunes began to improve in 1991, when Oy started selling vegetables at a nearby market that was also close to Bangkok. She began sales with a traditional Thai melon that her uncle cultivated. "I did not buy them," she says of the melons. "I just took them at first, put them in a cart that could be attached to a motorcycle, and sold them in the city." The response was encouraging, and Oy started selling other vegetables as well. She gathered them from people, sold them in the market, and split the proceeds with the producers. "I was the only person who would buy the vegetables and sell them outside. I would get up at 2 or 3 a.m. each morning. Wholesale trade started in the market around 2 or 3 a.m. with retail trade at 4 a.m. I had to be there until 8 a.m. each day."

The business gradually picked up. Saving bit by bit over the years, Oy bought land, a pickup truck to transport the vegetables, and a car. She also built a proper house for the family. "Our house was a shack earlier. This gave me more willpower. I would wake up very early. I was committed to building a permanent house like other people." Her husband's fortunes changed, too, when he landed a job in the highway department. Oy now cultivates corn, cassavas, bananas, and fruit on her land and has bought additional land as an asset for her children.

Movement up has not been without sacrifice. Oy recalled her early days in the business: "My husband had to get up early to take the vegetables and me to the market, and later in the day he would pick me up and take me home. I had to leave my children with my relatives. I was sleep deprived and tired each day. Truthfully speaking, I felt ashamed selling in the market. But when things were difficult, the shame just disappeared."

Asked about the secret to her success, she says, "All we had was perseverance and physical labor. Being poor gave us the perseverance to better ourselves. The changing point was selling vegetables. It was as if we had found the right channel. Everything we touched made money. From having nothing at all, we were able to have everything that we wanted. This was possible because of our commitment, ability to economize, and knowing how to save. I thought only that this is what I have to do today, and I did it. It is we who cause change." She recalls, now with tears in her eyes, "When we were still poor, when we were living in a shack, people looked down on us. They would not talk to us at all. They would talk badly of us to other people. Some committee members, when they had news, would not tell us. Nowadays they talk to us."

Oy concludes, "I have more confidence. When I put my heart into doing something and think that I can do it, and then am able to do it, there is more confidence. I was able to build up my status so my confidence gradually increased." She shares her wisdom with our team: "Don't do things halfway or in between. When you are committed to doing something, do it. Some people do trade half-heartedly and quit. To be in trade, one needs determination, concentration, perseverance. If there is no perseverance, there will be nothing left. You cannot stop. Another thing that helps is confidence in children. They should be better than us." She glances at her children who are playing nearby, a wistful look in her eyes.

Halfway around the world from Thailand, Santa María is an urban, crime-infested informal settlement on the outskirts of Cartagena, Colombia. The crowded shantytown is home to many people displaced by internal conflict. The settlers typically survive on activities like informal vending, bricklaying, and casual labor; a fortunate few own and run small businesses.

A small agricultural group called the Ambarema Peasants Association helps people find work on nearby farms to supplement their income from informal sales and labor.

Our team walks through the settlement looking for Pedro, a 32-year-old man who lives in poverty. They find him laying bricks. One of the first things that he speaks of is how much he misses his home in the countryside, from which he was displaced. "That was a good time," he reminisces. "We were never hungry. There was always food—raising a pig, raising a hen, and eating it. Here even if we have money, we do not eat." Pedro has been laying bricks since the age of 17, and this work has given him an additional source of income besides farming. He learned the skill from his brother-in-law. "I had to learn. The masters in the work taught me. I learned thanks to others. But I set my own goals."

Upon arriving in Santa María, Pedro engaged in petty vending, the only work immediately available. He thinks this work helped him face a difficult period of his life, although he says his economic recovery would have been easier if he had had a formal job. "That was the one giving me the rice," he says of informal vending. "But for me there is no bad job. There are only desires and dreams."

His bricklaying skills came to his aid when he received an offer to become assistant to a neighborhood engineer. "The engineer saw that I knew how to do things, and he promoted me to the post of an officer. That is how I got some contacts and started meeting people." Since 2001, he has been connected to the Ambarema Peasants Association. "When I run out of work, I go looking for *maraña* [casual labor]. In the time that I don't have to harvest, I go out and sell or look for any way to find some rice. The work in the [land] parcel has been there since 2001. They gave me the terrain because people know I like agriculture." For Pedro, working on the farm represents a connection to the activity he grew up with and lost because of the displacement. "There is no possibility of going back to the place where I had my lands," he says. "But I feel confident, because I like setting goals for myself. I like moving on, overcoming obstacles."

Belief in Self

The stories of Oy and Pedro resonate with their belief in themselves, with the confidence to set goals and pursue them relentlessly, overcoming obstacles. Noted scholars and thousands of grassroots practitioners have argued the importance of putting people and their agency at the center of development.[1] Amartya Sen argues that agency—a person's ability to act on behalf of what he or she values—is both intrinsically valuable and instrumentally effective in reducing poverty. Policies supporting poor people's agency call for an expansion in their capabilities, which Sen defines as the freedom to achieve valuable "beings and doings" (1985, 1992, 1993). This capability set, according to Sen, is much wider than the traditional utilitarian or asset space and consists of material, human, social, and political assets and even a psychological sense of self-efficacy (confidence, imagination, aspirations). These capabilities allow every human the freedom to function as she wishes.

In chapters 1 and 2, we argued that poor people are capable of being agents on their own behalf and that they have high aspirations for themselves and for their children. In this chapter, we dig deeper in our data to show how the flow of household effort and initiative depends first and foremost on the individual's personal agency, empowerment, aspirations, and sense of control over his or her own destiny. Our focus is to understand how power within a person can help in the movement out of poverty.

We start our analysis by examining poor people's own definitions and understandings of power. These reflect Lukes' (1974) classic division of power into "power to" and "power over." Poor people also talk about what feminist scholars have called "power with." Poor people have tremendous belief in themselves, but they also have a deep understanding of the prevailing inequality in distribution of resources and power. This inequality negatively affects relations between the poor and the rich, because people respond with jealousy, resentment, and "weapons of the weak," and also the relations among poor people themselves.

Against this backdrop of inequality, people in our study repeatedly stressed the importance of personal agency. Over and over, they said that self-confidence, a sense of control over one's own decisions, and a sense of "I can do it" are what allows a person to move up.

This sense of personal agency appears to precede the acquisition of other valuable assets, such as education, money, or a house. People see these as reinforcing their internal efficacy, which has to come first. Oy says simply, "If there is no perseverance, there will be nothing left." In other words, poor women and men agree with what psychologists have long said—that external conditions or resources are necessary for empowerment but not sufficient (Diener and Diener 2005). A discussion group of women in Satgailijhara, Bangladesh, put it this way: "What if a woman has a lot of money and education but she doesn't have the capacity to use it? How can she get empowered? The poor have power too. They have enthusiasm. The rich, who have money, sometimes don't have enthusiasm."

Another psychological dimension, the capacity to aspire, to imagine a better future for oneself and for one's children, is importantly linked to moving out of poverty. The dreams and aspirations of young people do not seem to be limited by their parents' occupations.

If these psychological capabilities are so important, what can help or hinder them? We focus particularly on personal agency and end the chapter by looking at several factors that can increase personal agency—material assets, education, and political connections—and an important factor that decreases it, namely health and death shocks. This sets the stage for the following chapters that discuss how personal agency, assets, and capabilities interact with the broader opportunity structure to affect movement out of poverty.

What Is Power?

Power is in having and being. Some people see power as only having. Some people see power as something internal: my values; my abilities.
> —Ernesto, a 20-year-old man, El Mirador, Colombia

Power is nothing but to go ahead in life with courage.
> —Discussion with men, Khatara, Assam

Men and women interviewed for the study define power using simple terms and language from their everyday lives.[2] Yet their definitions echo definitions of power also found in the social, psychological, and political literature.[3] People describe power first and foremost as "power to"—as the capacity to act on their own behalf, to take initiative, to be autonomous, to influence their environment. They feel that the main sources of such power are confidence and determination within themselves and support from their families. "Power with" is the power that comes from associating with others, both within the family and in groups. Poor women in particular emphasize the importance of associating with one another; they see this as helping them overcome many barriers that they could not possibly scale as individuals.

People also understand another form of power, "power over," meaning control over people and resources. Like sociologists, people in the study speak of this kind of power in relational terms: certain people in their communities have more power while others have less. At times, these definitions mirror J. K. Galbraith's (1983) in the way they distinguish between power achieved through use of various resources (usually money) and power based on force. Akin to the ideas of Lukes (1974) is people's belief that power over others is

TABLE 4.1
Poor people distinguish four different types of power

Type of power	Who	Sources	Scope of control	
			Resources: education, assets, money	Opportunities, rules, and laws
Power to	Poor people	Self, family	No	No
Power with	Poor people	Self, family, groups	No	No
Power over (positive)	Well-off people, government, civil society, local leaders	Love, authority, social respect, morals	Yes	Yes
Power over (negative)	Goons, elite, local leaders, law enforcement	Authority, fear, force, coercion, money	Yes	Yes

exercised not only through the formal institutions of the state, but also through the informal influences of social, cultural, and religious norms and beliefs.

"Power over" is further broken down into good power and bad power. Power over someone can conceivably be used for the individual or common good. But it can also be used to oppress others, and we encountered innumerably more instances of bad power than good power in our data. Inequality of resources is always at the root of such bad power. Table 4.1 summarizes poor people's perspectives on each of several different types of power—who wields it, its sources, and the scope of control that it confers.

"Power to"

> I never say, "I can't." I say, "I can, but I just don't know how."
> —Jainer, a 29-year-old man, El Gorrión, Colombia

Confidence in one's own abilities and a determination to improve conditions for oneself and one's family together lead to the power to do things. This capacity to act on one's own behalf—by managing a small business, farming, migrating, or sending one's children to school, for example—is important to poor people in all the study regions. Men in Nelutanga, Sri Lanka, defined power as "our personal strength." Raghubir, a young man in Booti, Uttar Pradesh, said, "Our hands are our power because we can do labor and earn money from them." In Kagera, Tanzania, power is "to execute your decisions and targets that you have put for yourself." In several Cambodian communities, people defined power as the "power to act independently, the power to manage and control one's family, and the power to earn a living." For women in Kagera, Tanzania, and in Manivali, Sri Lanka, power lies in "the ability to execute thoughts, decisions, and targets." And for women in Choudhuri Pum, a village affected by conflict in Assam, power means "doing work without fear."

For poor people like Oy and Pedro, their determination to persist without giving up hope is often the most important dimension of their power. Such persistence is especially emphasized in certain places like the barrios where internally displaced people live in Colombia. Evicted from their homes by armed conflict, people relied on their self-confidence and determination to move ahead. When asked about power, Alfonso, another displaced man in Santa María, said, "Power is in suffering. We have to hang on, resist, work, and move on." Liz, a young woman in El Mirador, Colombia, thought that it is possible to be powerful even if one is poor because "you can be powerful in your actions and decisions."

"Power with"

My family is my power, you know.
                    —Usman, a 60-year-old man, Patobako, Indonesia

In addition to drawing on their own internal qualities, poor people gain power in their associations with others, particularly their families and, to some extent, other members of their communities. The power that derives from such bonds can be called "power with." Many people said that power lies in the love, unity, and comfort that families offer. "No matter if we are poor, if we have the love of our family, we are powerful," commented Julio, a 19-year-old in Villa Rosa, Colombia.

In the South Asian context, large joint families are commonly seen as sources of power. Parveen, a woman in Satgailijhara, Bangladesh, explained, "Suppose I have five children; they will protect me if someone tries to hit me. I have no power if they are not behind me."

In addition to their families, poor women and men sought power in the unity of their communities, friends, neighbors, and social groups. Several poor people in the barrios of Colombia described community solidarity as a critical resource that gave them the power to survive. "Real power comes from poverty, united people," exclaimed Wilson, a young man in El Mirador, Colombia. Roshan, a man in Ashikabad, in rural Uttar Pradesh, concurred. "The meaning of power is unity. If there is a single stick, anyone can break it. But if the sticks are tied in a bundle, then nobody can break the bundle."

A single poor woman's voice drowns in silence. Although women within households are generally seen as having less power than men, they can sometimes gain power when they join hands with other poor women in groups. This was particularly evident in Bangladesh and in Andhra Pradesh, where microcredit and self-help groups are strong. In these villages, not surprisingly, women relate power to working together in groups. But such change can also lead to tensions within households because men have to adjust to women's empowerment.

Microfinance organizations have been active for decades in Bangladesh, organizing women into credit groups. Unlike many women in the other study regions, who said that they felt powerless, inferior, or trapped, women in the Bangladesh study villages often appeared confident and assured. They dressed well, spoke up, participated in household decisions, and stepped out of the house to markets. Some felt confident enough to enter the public sphere, marching to local politicians to speak out against injustice. These changes in women also forced the men in their communities to change. Some applauded women's empowerment, but others appeared anxious and resentful. They longed for bygone times when the rules were simple and women did what they were told (box 4.1).

"Power over"

> To be powerful means to be a tyrant, to be oppressive in the way you are ruling. It also means that people do things under pressure; they don't have freedom. All they need to do is just obey and do whatsoever whether they want it or not.
>
> —Discussion with men, Matdombo, Malawi

People also equated power with having control or authority over someone or something. Youths in Butmuli, Uganda, defined power as amaani, meaning having authority over something. In Ferjama, Morocco, youths described power as lakham, meaning authority or the one who takes irrevocable decisions. In Chikwanje, Malawi, power usually meant "authority where you have people that you can control." In Lumyana, Malawi, youths equated power with "the boss, because he has got some people that he controls. If he says do this, they do it, and so he has power over them."

Even within families, there are obvious hierarchies of power and authority. Usually the elder adults, in particular the parents, command more respect and have more power than younger family members. According to Ngagane in Ndagiel, Senegal, "You can be rich and live in the same house

BOX 4.1
Changes in women unsettle men in Bangladesh

In Bangladesh, we used a tool called the ladder of empowerment to explore with women and men the steps in women's empowerment. Men's and women's discussion groups in each community created their own ladders, with women at the bottom step having the least power and women at the top step having the most. Men and women sometimes differed dramatically in their descriptions of women's status. Indeed, the ladders drawn by men's and women's groups in the villages of Mirabari and Nurpur, summarized next, were so dissimilar that it was hard to imagine that they described the same women. In general, men described women at the top step as clever but also as quarrelsome, interfering, and disobedient. Women described this same top category of women as intelligent, as behaving well, and as respected by others.

Men expressed deep ambivalence about women's empowerment. The men in Nurpur, for example, are proud and supportive of the intelligent women at step 3, yet they feel that there is less harmony between a couple when the woman is at this level. In Mirabari, a man named Osman summed up: "I think the ordinary women are the best. They don't need to become clever women. The clever women have more power, but they command less prestige from us."

Men's discussion group, Mirabari
Step 3 (clever women): They demand good saris. They take whatever they need from the husband. If there is a dispute between two parties, they get involved, and they often quarrel with people. They don't follow the codes of Islam: they go out without a veil, and they wear short saris in a way that shows the belly. They hold jobs or do income-generating activities. They do the shopping themselves. Some have gone through secondary school. They don't listen to their husbands and can even physically assault men. They don't obey the judgments of the village court. They are not scared of anything.

Step 2 (ordinary women): They remain neutral during any dispute. They give people good suggestions and protest against any injustice. They know the difference between good and bad. Some wear the veil and some don't. They develop the family. They help the husband cultivate vegetables; they are skilled at handicrafts and teach others. They have studied up to class 8 or 9.

Step 1 (simple women): They don't do any harm to others even if someone does harm to them. Some of them are educated, but some are not and can only sign their names. They wear the veil when they go out, but they don't go out much. They do handicrafts and raise poultry. They have more peace in the family.

Women's discussion group, Mirabari
Step 3 (intelligent women): They educate their children. They dress well and live well even during famines. They provide good advice to the husband and

(continued)

BOX 4.1 continued

keep financial accounts properly. They behave well with the husband, in-laws, and other relatives. Most people appreciate their good qualities. They can count up to 100.

Step 2 (somewhat knowledgeable women): They have little educa-tion. They try to earn money, but what they earn is not very much. They can run the family satisfactorily. When their husbands become angry, they also become angry.

Step 1 (foolish women): They do not earn any income because they do not have the intelligence to do any work. They sit around idle. They cannot keep accounts of expenditures. People call them foolish.

Men's discussion group, Nurpur

Step 3 (intelligent women): They have education, know how to earn money, and give intelligent advice to the husband on how to earn money. Husbands follow their advice. They educate their children and make their families sol-vent. But there is less agreement between the husband and wife. The wife says, "Do I understand less?"

Step 2 (moderately intelligent women): Their education is up to the primary level, and they are eager to educate their children. They can manage their fami-lies well and understand accounts of income and expenditure. They earn some income and give their husbands good advice. Their courage is moderate; they are shy. They do not want to go to marriages and other parties because they do not want to be seen by other men. They enjoy life very little, have little entertain-ment. They say, "The husband supplies food; he earns money. I shall obey his words." The relationship between husband and wife is very close and intimate.

Step 1 (unintelligent/foolish women): They have no education or knowl-edge. They cannot bring up their children properly because they cannot con-trol them. They cannot make themselves understood when speaking; they do not know how to behave with others; they have no sociable qualities. They do not even understand that there is a profit in making a fan by investing 10 taka. The family survives on what the husband brings in.

Women's discussion group, Nurpur

Step 3 (self-reliant women): They have money, jobs, education. They are active; they have full power and freedom. They are not punished if they do wrong. They do not care about anything, even if society speaks ill of them.

Step 2 (moderately powerful women): They have education but they do not hold full-time jobs; their husbands prevent them because of religious orthodoxy. They depend on the man; they cannot do everything indepen-dently. They look after their families and children. They get respect.

Step 1 (powerless women): They have no freedom and are weak physi-cally. They have no education. They are idle. They have no land.

as your elder brother; you can also meet all the needs of your household; but you cannot take any decision without his permission." In communities like Ndagiel, the traditional laws of primogeniture (right of the first-born son to inherit) specifically give older family members positions of power. In Indonesia, cultural norms of showing respect for parents place mothers like 32-year-old Sanah in positions of power. She said, "In the house, I have power and authority to manage my own household, because in the house the mother has power."

Like Weber (1947, 1968), our respondents distinguished between coercive power and the authority that is based on charisma, social traditions, values, and laws. In Colombia, even though the rich have more resources and the guerrillas have weapons, poor women and men value the authority gained through social respect above the coercive power wielded by those groups. Mónica, a 16-year-old girl in Villa Rosa, said, "There are some rich people who have no power. Some things cannot be bought with money, for example, love and respect." Because social respect conveys power, it is possible for even poor people to be powerful. Pablo, a young man in Villa Blanca, said that a while a rich man's money gives him power, "for us, power is the humility and respect we earn through our actions."

Power and authority based on morality, ethics, and social traditions is seen as more acceptable than power based on coercion and force. When it comes to power over others, people make a sharp distinction between "good power" and "bad power."

Good power

Across contexts, people spoke of three qualities that allow a person to gain "good power." These are love, respect, and moral leadership. In the community context, people show their love through a spirit of altruism, by being available and willing to help others. In Satgailijhara, a flood-prone village in Bangladesh, a men's discussion group described the powerful as those who are "affectionate to the poor and help them in times of need." In Laskarpur, West Bengal, Tilak said, "There are a few households that are powerful in our village because of their good work. They help the villagers with money at the time of marriage of their daughters. This is power."

The second way to earn good power is by being respectful, showing a willingness to consult and listen to others. "If you are going to lead a group and you don't have respect for your people, then there is a tendency that your power will weaken," reasoned a group of youths in Aludonay, Philippines. "Eventually your followers will go against you if you lead them without respect." Youths in Klong Pud, Thailand, said, "Power is not browbeating other people and speaking to others nicely."

Finally, people stressed the importance of exercising moral leadership and setting a good example. Parents and traditional or religious leaders typically gain power and authority in this way. In Thailand, parents have power because they act as a "good model for the family" and because children are "grateful and loyal to parents." Similarly, men in Lupotogo, Indonesia, referred to power as "having honor and being respected by one's children." In many communities in Africa, community elders and religious leaders enforce moral codes. "The elderly people have a lot of knowledge," said Agatha, a 65-year-old farmer in Gogoba, Uganda. "They give advice to their family members and also guide and direct the youth in the village to restrain them from bad behavior and maintain the value and norms of the community." In Mbassina, Senegal, youths described power as "the ability [of imams] to heal illness thanks to the Koran." Priests are the most powerful in some communities in Kagera, Tanzania, because "they can listen to your sins and have God-given powers." In Banjoydup, Bangladesh, religious leaders called matbors are placed at the top of the community ladder because even "millionaires come to them for justice."

Bad power

While such "good power" was praised, poor people talked even more about "bad power"—power over others as a means to repress and oppress. It doesn't matter much how such power is acquired, whether through wealth, education, political connections, social membership, or sheer force. What matters is the total control over others, often exercised arbitrarily. Women in Mpusola, Malawi, said, "The powerful people are called chiphanzi [big foot]. The term is taken from a popular song that talks of a person in authority who oppresses those below him. It means stepping on them." Such oppressive power is sometimes exercised in defiance of the law, but often the law or at least the police permit or even abet the abuses. In Kdadaum, Cambodia, young women said that the rich people who control the logging business work hand in glove with the police, who have the "power and authority to cut and carry wood and make others pay."

Kesarbai, a woman in Nagara, Uttar Pradesh, gave a graphic description of bad power in her community. "The powerful can suppress others, beat them, and bully them," she said. "It is like a lion tasting blood after which he eats only flesh." So feared are the holders of bad power that even a gesture or a glance is often sufficient to make others obey. In Lomamoli, Philippines, men and women defined power as "mala ayka gus, meaning a certain eye or hand movement that can make people follow and show respect." In Kadonga, Assam, men spoke of powerful people as "those who can make others go up and down by the signal of the finger." And in Batamara, another study village in Assam, power is exercised by "talking down, pointing fingers at someone else's eyes."

Different people are powerful in different local contexts. While landlords are the most feared in several of the study villages in Andhra Pradesh, it is government officials in the Philippines, who in enforcing laws have "the power to create and to destroy." What remains consistent is the use of power to dominate others. Juan Pablo, a 62-year-old man in San Feliz, Colombia, said, "To exercise power correctly, we have to [act] the same as if we had nothing. Money damages the heart and the reason." Mercedes, a woman in Los Rincones, Colombia, concurred. "You know, in our environment it is not good to be powerful," she remarked to our field team. "It is not something to be proud of."

Sources of power

A man without money is like a bird without feathers.
> —Ibrahim, a 70-year-old man, Lomamoli, Philippines

Run, hit, and kill—that is power
> —Discussion with young men, Pittupur, Uttar Pradesh

Power, good or bad, derives from various sources, according to the people in our study. Two of the most important are money and brute force.

Money is perhaps the most ubiquitous and universally recognized source of power. Money allows one to get what one wants through purchase or bribery. "With money, one can buy people," said Alaka, a young woman in Gangua, West Bengal. In Satgailijhara, Bangladesh, young men said, "If you entertain 10 persons with 10 cups of tea, they will be in your favor. Then you can be a powerful man. But that means if someone wants to entertain 10 people with tea, he must be a rich man. A poor man cannot afford this." Money also enables people to control other resources and thus make even more money. Speaking in local proverbs, youths in Riah Khillaw, Afghanistan, stated, "Money makes money and the lack of money makes a headache." In Kdadaum, Cambodia, the rich control forest resources and profit through logging. "The poor work for the rich and do not have power as they dare not argue against or bargain for good remuneration," lamented young men in Kdadaum. "The rich control the loans to the poor."

Those with money can voice their opinions and command social respect, even claim political leadership. "If the powerful speak, people abide by it without any judgment," said a men's group in Kadonga, Assam. In Ibrahimpur, Uttar Pradesh, young men voiced similar sentiments. "No one cares for a poor person in society. The people with money consider a poor man no more than a pest." Moral judgments are often suspended for rich people. In Malkapur, Andhra Pradesh, rich landlords wield such power that no one can question their immorality and ill-doings. "If a rich man falls on the road in a drunken state, people say that he must have fallen down because he hit something. But if a poor man falls on the road, everyone will call him a drunkard," complained men in a discussion with our field team. And in the village of Sapsa, Uttar Pradesh, men said, "Brother, power is obtained through money. Everyone worships the rising sun, but no one worships the setting sun."

An extreme form of domination is the use of physical coercion. On a disquieting note, men, women, and youths in some of our study regions spoke at length about the power of brute force. Not surprisingly, this understanding of power is more evident in the study regions affected by conflict. In Barangay Tucampo in the southern Philippines, Japar said, "Power for me is the capacity to arm oneself. During my time, the armed men easily beat the defenseless. You are powerful when you carry guns." Men and women in the conflict-affected villages of Assam and in the barrios of Colombia also spoke of the power of weapons. In Assam, the army and the local militant groups are seen as the most powerful, while in Colombia it is gang members and guerrillas. Adolfo, a man in La Soledad, Colombia, gave an example of how the power of weapons is abused. "When the guerrillas were here they said, 'there is a meeting,' and we had to be there if we did not want to be shot, no matter if we were sick."

Inequalities in power

Inequality is carrying a sack of sugar throughout the whole year without tasting it.
                    —Men's discussion group, Chanpasha, Bangladesh

Poor people know that they live in an unequal world. They have deep knowledge of the structural and social factors that lead to "durable inequalities" (Tilly 1999).[4] Across the study regions, poor people define inequality as restricting their opportunities and choices. Whether it is the opportunity to participate in markets, to access government aid, or to speak up in community decision making, poor women and men face unequal terms of engagement. The dice are loaded particularly heavily against poor women.

Poor people lack clout in the marketplace, often because of the small scale of their transactions (see chapter 5). They must buy high and sell low. Cory, a woman in Baroygor, Philippines, remarked, "If we are going to buy fertilizers, we will find it very hard on our pocket, but if it is our turn to sell our products, they are sold at low prices." Added Ling, "As corn owners, we cannot say that our corn will be sold at 10 pesos a kilo. No, we cannot do that. Instead, we are the ones asking the buyers, 'How much is the current price of our product?' There seems to be no equality. The farmers depend on the traders." Like the farmers in Baroygor, the fishermen of Kismopara, Bangladesh, depend on the powerful few who own ponds in the community. "The canal belongs to them," said Rahima, a woman in the village. "No one can fish there or bathe cattle."

In some of the African study contexts where government and donor aid is a crucial form of support, there are stark differences between those villages and households that can access aid and those that cannot (see chapter 6). This form of inequality is acute in Malawi. Men in the village of Mzaponda described inequality as "denying others from getting any type of fortune or luck. When donors give assistance to organizations but no assistance comes to the village, that is inequality."

Besides leading to lost opportunities, inequalities result in poor women and men losing voice and control. "A rich man can fool you the way he wants," said a group of women in Kodola, Uganda. "You can dig for him, and he can tell you to come tomorrow for money. He has the money, but when you go tomorrow, he can again tell you to come the next day. As a poor man, you will have nothing to do but to follow what he tells you. The poor are always looked down on and despised." And in Shantakalia, Bangladesh, women remarked, "Those who are powerful scold us when we talk to them because we are powerless."

Even among poor people themselves, opportunity sets differ for men and women. Women across our sample often reported that their husbands restrict them to the kitchen, where they exhaust themselves in menial household chores. "We have less energy because we do quite a lot," said a group of women in Kagera, Tanzania. "In fact, it is not that we have less energy, but our energy is finished due to a lot of work that we do during the day and at night. Many men do not appreciate this and what they do at the end of it all is to beat you up." The women who managed to step out of the house spoke of receiving far lower wages than men despite bone-grinding labor. In addition, they have no freedom to spend these wages. "We cannot spend our earnings as we like," said Sarola, a woman in Khetaswar, Assam. "The men rebuke us.

We cannot even buy a sari of our choice." Women in Surjana, a village in Uttar Pradesh, agreed. "If we want to get training for stitching work or embroidery, the men scold us and ask us to stay in the house. If we insist on getting trained, they avoid us, saying they cannot afford it, whereas they themselves waste our money on their paan" (a betel leaf mixture for chewing and smoking).

Everyday resistance

When poor people are unable to confront unequal power directly, they often resort to what Scott (1985) calls "weapons of the weak," using tactics such as sarcasm to cope with their situation and subtly rebel. People often used metaphors to talk about their lives indirectly. In some villages in West Bengal, poor youths laughingly compared their situation to that of a weak football (soccer) team. "Two teams are playing football and only one team can win," said Kaushik, a young boy in Ranigar. "Players on one team are powerful so they won. The less powerful have less opportunity to score because they cannot run fast enough."

In a village in Kagera, Tanzania, at the end of an animated discussion on the ladder of life, the researchers introduced the official poverty line. At first there was total silence, and then people erupted with sarcastic comments amid great laughter. "Is that a baby you mean to have live on that much money?" "When you give a person that much, prepare a prison for him, because after a few hours he will start stealing!" "The person with so little is already dead." "If you are old, yes, you can live on less because your stomach has wrinkles on it." "Those people [officials who set the poverty line] look down on us. Why should they think that we should live on less than that, while they themselves live on a lot more?"

Resistance sometimes goes beyond words to actions. In several villages in Tanzania and Uganda, poor people reported withholding their participation in the political process and in meetings to protest the abuses of political leaders.

Jealousy of others' gains

If a rich person becomes arrogant and happy, this will make neighbors and other members of the community resentful, emotional, and spiteful.
                    —Men's discussion group, Barumangga, Indonesia

While belief in self is important, poor people can also turn on each other in the fight for limited resources in an unequal world. One person's rise is assumed to be at the expense of others, and people not infrequently attempt to thwart their neighbors' efforts to get ahead. A beer brewer and seller in Kiwgazi, Uganda, related his story: "A man came to my home and expressed surprise when he asked for beer and I gave it to him. He said he had met a friend who told him that there was no beer at my place. Clearly this man [the friend] did not wish that I sell my beer. He was envious that if I sold my beer, I would improve at a faster speed than him."

While jealous actions usually amount to no more than slights, in some cases, jealousy motivates petty theft, destruction of property, and even murder. The victims, as described by the study participants, are not just the rich but also poor people who are beginning to accumulate assets. In Malawi, for instance, people often sleep with their livestock so no one can harm their animals. "Just yesterday, someone killed my two goats by giving them a poisonous substance," lamented a man in Madkumba village. "They are trying to reduce what I have, but I can say that they will fail and I will still continue to improve."

Destruction of private property, such as the burning of houses and poisoning of wells, was reported in a few places. A slightly better-off man in a village in Assam reported that someone had poisoned his fish. "I have two fisheries—one is near the house; the other is on the hillside. In the fishery on the hillside, somebody gave poison in jealousy. I have lost about 30,000 rupees of fish." In the fishing community of Kramrrak, Indonesia, some fishermen reportedly threatened their more successful peers. "One of them threatened to burn my house," said a fisherman our team met. "I said please do. I'll give you the gasoline. But if you want to do it, do it after terawih [night prayer in a fasting month], so nobody can see you. Turned out they didn't have the guts." Destruction of public property was occasionally mentioned as well. In Sirkona, Uganda, a women's discussion group reported the sabotage of drinking water pipes. "One rich man was bringing water, but the pipes were cut by the community members. Consequently, there is no safe water in the whole village, which exposes people to high health risks."

In some African and Indonesian communities, people who had suffered sudden misfortunes sometimes attributed them to acts of witchcraft carried out by jealous parties. A comparatively well-off woman in Kagera, Tanzania, told the field team, "In 2002, I suffered a strange disease. I later realized that my neighbor had bewitched me. I cannot tell you more than this, but it is all due to people being jealous of what we and our children have achieved." The killings of successful individuals were reported in a few places, although it was unclear who the guilty parties were. In Welumbe, Sri Lanka, a woman said that her father had been targeted and killed by those who were jealous of him. "We were doing really well in those days. People couldn't stand that at all."

Resentment against the successful has been observed and explained in different ways. Hirschman and Rothschild (1973) speak of the tunnel effect. When cars are stuck in a multilane tunnel, any movement in the next lane leads to initial happiness as drivers assume that their lane is about to move as well. But if movement continues in the next lane while traffic remains stuck in their own lane, drivers quickly become frustrated—even more frustrated than if no lanes were moving at all. So, too, in the economic sphere. Failure to fulfill one's own aspirations is surely a frustrating experience (Ray 2006), and it may become even more frustrating when others are seen to be enjoying success. Such jealousy can eventually give rise to conflicts.

Social mores also come into play. In parts of Africa, a successful person may be criticized if he or she fails to redistribute resources to others, particularly the extended family. For those who would move up, this change creates a fundamental tension. To get ahead, they need to accumulate, save, and reinvest, but doing so violates traditional social norms that call for sharing (Ashforth 2005; Ferguson 1999; Pottier 1988). Those who appear to be leaving others behind have been the targets of accusations and even attacks.

Rich people also jealously guard their monopoly position and are not above sabotaging the efforts of poor people to move out of poverty. In the village of Ibrahimpur, Uttar Pradesh, a lower-caste farmer explained, "The small farmers do not have any engines so they take water from the big farmers. Therefore, they can grow only one crop. If some farmers try to cultivate another crop, then the [upper-caste] Thakurs let their animals loose in their fields [to eat the crops]." Youths in Chamgotia, Bangladesh, said, "The upper-class people always resist the poor if they want to attain their prosperity through good jobs. Say, for example, if a rickshaw puller wants to purchase an auto-rickshaw [small taxi], the richer section of people, being jealous, misguide him."

Power, Personal Agency, and Mobility

When someone comes out of poverty, people start respecting him. He is considered powerful.
                    — Ibrahim, a 56-year-old man, Shazimir, Afghanistan

Poverty winds around people like a python so much so that they are unable to breathe properly.
                    —Men's discussion group, Gobordia, Assam

Poor men and women make a direct link between power and moving out of poverty on the one hand and between powerlessness and stagnation on the other. Poor women and men can see that their agency is restricted by social, political, and economic structures that limit their control over resources and opportunities. The rich hold all the aces: they use their political and social connections, their education, and their assets to climb even higher on the ladder. As Dyrberg states in his Circular Structure of Power (1997, 28), "The ability to make a difference is itself constituted by the making of differences."

For those stuck in unequal power relations, unable to breathe, it may seem ludicrous to suggest that belief in oneself is a powerful weapon for getting ahead. Yet, that is precisely what many poor people in our study suggested. Their only hope for escaping poverty is to hold onto their spirit and not give up, come what may. "The most important thing is the family union and the desire to keep on living, moving on, will. Without that, there is nothing," summed up Adriana, a woman in San Feliz, Colombia.

Psychologist Albert Bandura (1995) has demonstrated experimentally that when beliefs about self-efficacy are manipulated independent of performance or external conditions, they affect future performance. Thus a person's internal sense of efficacy plays an independent causal role. Reviewing the psychological literature, Bandura (1998) concluded: "People's beliefs that they can produce desired effects by their actions influence the choices they make, their aspirations, level of effort and perseverance, resilience to adversity, and vulnerability to stress and depression." Hoff and Pandey's (2004) experimental study with middle-school children in India reveals the power of identity labels in reducing self-confidence and reproducing inequality in an environment that is expected to be prejudicial. Among children in mixed-caste groups that were given the task of solving mazes, the performance of the "untouchable" children dropped dramatically when their low-caste status was identified publicly.

Quantifying personal agency

In our study, we use two quantifiable measures to understand the role of personal agency. One is a measure of internal power and rights based on how an individual rates herself or himself on a 10-step ladder of power and rights 10 years ago, at the beginning of the study reference period (1995). The second is a measure of a person's sense of control based on whether she or he experienced any change over time in control over everyday decision making.

The movers in nearly all study regions on average self-identified themselves at a modestly higher position on the ladder of power and rights 10 years ago compared to the chronic poor (figure 4.1). It is interesting to note that both movers and chronic poor (together making up the initial poor set) in the African study regions placed themselves slightly higher on the ladder of power and

FIGURE 4.1

Movers place themselves modestly higher on power and rights 10 years ago compared to the chronic poor

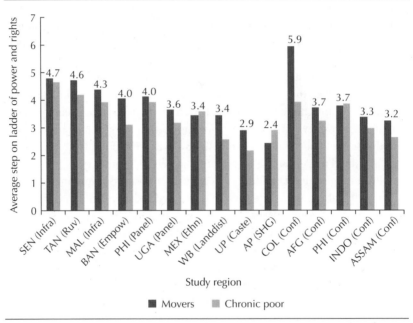

Study region

■ Movers   ■ Chronic poor

Source: Authors' analysis using data from household survey; all study regions where data were available; *N* = 7,916.

Note:

AFG (Conf) = Afghanistan, Conflict	PHI (Conf) = Philippines, Conflict
AP (SHG) = Andhra Pradesh, Self-help groups	PHI (Panel) = Philippines, Panel study
ASSAM (Conf)= Assam, Conflict	SEN (Infra) = Senegal, Infrastructure
BAN (Empow) = Bangladesh, Women's	TAN (Ruv) = Tanzania, Ruvuma
empowerment	UGA (Panel) = Uganda, Panel study
COL (Conf) = Colombia, Conflict	UP (Caste) = Uttar Pradesh, Caste
INDO (Conf) = Indonesia, Conflict	WB (Landdist) = West Bengal, Land distribution
MAL (Infra) = Malawi, Infrastructure	reforms
MEX (Ethn) = Mexico, Ethnicity	

rights than their counterparts elsewhere. We can speculate that poor people in our African communities may emphasize self-belief because they have little else to rely on. It is also notable that perceptions of power and rights appear to peak in conflict-affected Colombia.[5] Our Colombian respondents emphasized that one needs strong belief in oneself to survive destruction and displacement. "Yes, it has risen," said Alejandra, a woman in Villa Rosa, referring to her self-confidence. "I have done things I did not know I was going to do. I did not know I was going to develop, coming to an office, explaining to someone my rights as a displaced person and fighting for them." Graciela explained, "We, the displaced, have been moving up step by step. We are barely standing up and if we fall, we will not be able to stand up again."

Except in a few study regions, people who had fallen into poverty reported that they had started lower on the ladder of power and rights compared to those who had not fallen (the never poor). Starting with more self-belief thus seems to help people move up *and* to avoid falling down (figure 4.2).

On the second measure, control over everyday decision making, most movers (nearly 74 percent) thought that they currently had control over all or most of the decisions in their daily lives. Less than half (46 percent) of those stuck in poverty believed they had such control (figure 4.3). Success in moving out of poverty, it seems, strengthens self-confidence and inner efficacy.

FIGURE 4.2

Fallers place themselves modestly lower on power and rights 10 years ago compared to the never poor

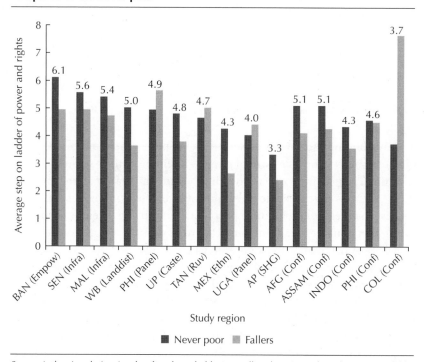

Source: Authors' analysis using data from household survey; all study regions where data were available; $N = 7,916$.

FIGURE 4.3

Movers report control over all or most decisions, while chronic poor and fallers report less control

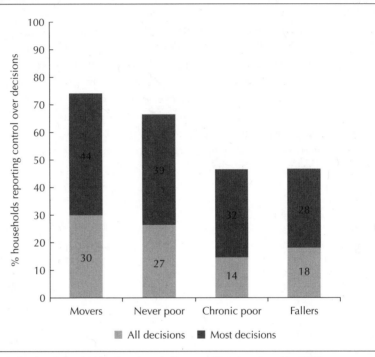

Source: Authors' analysis using data from household survey; all study regions; $N = 8,945$.

This finding should not be surprising. As poor people manage to accumulate resources and move out of poverty, it reinforces their self-respect and wins them respect from others. Men in Boodanpur, Uttar Pradesh, summed up the virtuous cycle: "People feel more powerful after coming out of poverty because their relations with other people start improving. There is a common saying that a hungry man only invites further drought and is not welcome anywhere. A rich man is welcome everywhere."

A couple of words of caution. One, it is possible that movers, basking in the glow of their success, may recall themselves as more confident 10 years ago than they really were. Two, it is possible that in telling their life stories to interviewers, respondents attributed success to their own agency while blaming failures on external factors. In an early methodology workshop for the study, the late Charles Tilly, an adviser to the project, cautioned that we should interpret life stories with these caveats in mind. "Every life history is a retrospective moral tale which has an account of self in it," he said. "[People emphasize their] own agency and frustration at what restricted them from exercising it. Detect these moral accounts." Anthropologists, ethnographers, and sociologists, including Tilly and others, have warned of the biases inherent in such self-eulogies. In his book titled *Why?* (2006), Tilly shows that social relations shape the accounts that people give to others to explain particular events. In particular, he argues that people have the tendency to limit the number of actors and actions in their narratives, situating all causes in the consciousness of the actors and elevating the personal over the institutional.

In our study, the fact that mobility status is not self-assessed but assessed by the community reduces the potential for these biases. The designation of households as movers, chronic poor, never poor, or fallers is based on the community mobility matrixes, which are derived, in turn, from focus group rankings of households on the ladder of life. It is striking, then, to see people who were independently identified as movers *by their peers* also self-identify themselves as having been at a higher position on the ladder of power and rights 10 years ago.

Association with upward mobility

To test the association between these subjective factors and an individual household's ability to move out of poverty, we ran multivariate linear regressions on our quantitative data from the household surveys. We used individual household mobility as the dependent variable and examined its partial association with several other independent variables. As noted, our measure of a household's movement out of poverty is constructed from community perceptions, not from the household's own recall or ranking of its mobility. This approach was to reduce potential bias arising from regressing own perception of mobility against own perception of a host of factors, including subjective well-being. People who ranked themselves as having moved out of poverty might also be more likely to say they were more self-confident, just because they have generally positive attitudes.

Our dependent variable is whether or not members of a household moved out of poverty (MOP) over the 10-year study period or, at times, whether they moved up at all (MPI), irrespective of whether they crossed the poverty line. This approach limits the sample to those who began in poverty, and hence the regressions show the association between several variables and whether one was a mover or remained stuck in poverty (chronic poor).

Although our dependent variable is binary and there are more sophisticated estimators that are statistically more efficient, we use a linear probability model. This method has the advantage that the coefficients are easy to interpret, as the difference in probability of being a mover versus chronic poor associated with the factors included as independent variables (conditional on all of the independent variables).

We used roughly the same specification for all study regions. Although we could have improved the fit by adding or dropping variables for each region, we were interested as much in the heterogeneity of the results across regions as in creating the statistically "best" model. This also limits the scope for data mining to search for "statistically significant" associations.

The specification includes a range of variables that we feel represent various elements of our framework, mainly economic, social, and political institutions as well as several standard household characteristics. All of the results reported in subsequent chapters are based on the same regressions with a full set of co-variates (we do not do regressions for each variable); the results are integrated into the respective thematic chapters. The full specification and results are reported in appendix 6.

We often had several items in a questionnaire that plausibly measured the phenomenon of interest (such as personal agency). Rather than run "horse race" analysis to see which measure fit best with the dependent variable, we used principal components to combine the variables into a single measure. We did the principal components analysis (PCA) region by region with the same variables (when available) but allowing the weights to differ. Although there are many limitations to principal components analysis as a data reduction technique, it has the advantage of not referring to the dependent variable in the construction of the measure of the independent variable and hence is not data mining.

The results are reported based on coefficient standard errors that are robust to within-cluster correlation. Although we have many household observations, we have relatively few communities, and hence we should expect rather large standard errors on the community variables. Also, some of the community variables are based on "key respondents" who were selected to answer the community survey (based on the community classification) but were not necessarily representative of the village. Hence, the pure measurement error in assessing community-level variables is likely to be large.

Finally, we want to emphasize that we see the regressions as a data summary tool—not as the "test" of a model, nor as estimates of "coefficients" or "parameters," nor as indicating causality in any way. But regressions are useful in pointing to partial associations, and we use them as just another technique to grapple with the masses of data and information to understand the complex reality at hand. We hope the reader will take them in that spirit.

We created a personal agency index using principal components analysis. The index is based on our two questions mapping subjective well-being or internal power/self-efficacy: position on the ladder of power and rights 10 years ago and change experienced in control over everyday decision making.

Figure 4.4 reports the association between the personal agency index and household movement out of poverty. The single dots represent the coefficients: the higher they are, the higher the magnitude of the estimated association. The bars around the coefficient represent the one and two standard error bounds. The more tightly clustered the bounds, the lower the standard error and, for any given magnitude of the estimated association, the more likely a test that the association is zero would be rejected. We report the data in this way because given the data descriptive nature of the exercise, we do not want to become *t*-statistic fetishists and confuse low-powered and high-powered failures to reject. So we show the magnitude of all estimated associations and their standard errors so that readers can see for themselves the general

FIGURE 4.4
Personal agency has an association with moving out of poverty

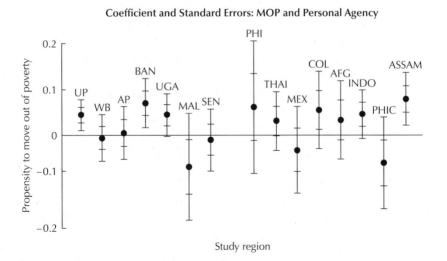

Source: Multivariate linear regression analysis using data from household survey and community questionnaire (see appendix 6).

tendencies in terms of sign and magnitude as well as infer the likely p-levels associated with the coefficients. In all the graphs reporting regression results, we follow the same order of study regions: India, South Asia, Africa, East Asia, Mexico, and conflict-affected regions.

Figure 4.4 shows that feelings of self-efficacy, power, and control have a significant association with movement out of poverty in Uttar Pradesh and Assam and in Bangladesh, Uganda, and Indonesia (the standard error bounds are much tighter around the coefficient). This finding means that people who had a higher sense of power in 1995 and who perceived an increase in their control over everyday decision making over the 10-year period in these regions were also those who moved out of poverty. Interestingly, when we ran the same specification with FRI (when the rich fell by one or more steps) as the dependent variable, we found that the association between our personal agency index and falling was mostly negative. In fact, it was significantly negative in Uttar Pradesh, Assam, and Bangladesh, suggesting that starting with a higher sense of power is associated with lower chances of falling. While we do not claim causality, it is striking that there is an association between individuals ranked by their community as fallers and the fallers' own ranking of their initial power and rights.

It is illustrative to look at the relative magnitudes of association in a couple of countries. In Bangladesh, where this association is significant, a 2-unit increase in the control that an individual exercised over her everyday decisions (1 = less control, 3 = more control) is associated with a 15.5 percent increase in the probability of moving out of poverty. This is higher than the effect that a unit increase in the index of assets or owning a house could have: each increased the likelihood of mobility from an initial state of poverty significantly by 12 percent.

Uganda is another study region where the index has a significant association with mobility from poverty. Breaking it down into its component variables, we find that a 2-unit increase in control over decision making is associated with a 9 percent increase in the exit rate from poverty. In comparison, the association with assets in influencing chances of escape is lower (7 percent) and insignificant. This is not to argue that assets are not important. They play a significant role in enhancing capabilities, including psychological capabilities such as internal power and self-confidence to take action. However, in their own self-assessments, movers seem to place more importance on internal empowerment than on assets. The former, as our qualitative evidence suggests, has to come first, although clearly internal power and control increase with success in moving out of poverty.

Capacity to Aspire

I was obliged to work as a farm laborer to augment the income of my husband. When he died, my motivation doubled because I had to feed my family and send my children to school.
                          —Gloria, a 57-year-old widow, Kilaluna, Philippines

The capacity to imagine a future that is different and better is an important motivator to overcome the difficulties of the present. People across the study regions expressed strong aspirations to secure a better future for themselves and their children. As reported in chapter 1, nearly 77 percent of households hoped that their children would be better off in the future. Gloria, a widow in Kilaluna, Philippines, recalled, "Even though my husband left us a farm, I still work as a farm laborer, especially during off seasons and while waiting for our harvest." When our team met her, Gloria was described as someone who had successfully moved out of poverty, overcoming all odds.

Success in achieving one's aspirations leads to even greater faith and confidence in oneself. Not surprisingly, movers out of poverty exhibited higher aspirations for their own future than did the chronic poor. On average, 80 percent of the movers felt that they would be better off in the future, compared to 56 percent of those stuck in poverty. Still, 56 percent reflects considerable optimism, given the obstacles that the chronic poor face. Moreover, when it came to aspirations for their children, an astonishingly high 70 percent of the chronic poor across study regions expected their children to be better off. While they had modest aspirations for themselves, they held high hopes for the next generation.

Figure 4.5 shows the differences in aspirations of the movers and the chronic poor for their own future by study region. In all but two regions, movers had higher aspirations than did the chronic poor. The exceptions are the households interviewed in Bangladesh and Colombia. In the former, a sense of empowerment through microcredit groups had spread through the ranks of those in poverty, raising their aspirations. In Colombia, our sample was specific to very poor communities largely occupied by displaced people who had lost everything. These people could only look up in hope of better times. "My desire to improve my situation is the biggest desire I have," said Humberto, a poor man in the El Gorrión barrio. "I set a goal for myself every day. When I got here, I thought how difficult it would be for me to move on. Before, I used to ride a bicycle, but I had the hope and goal of having a motorcycle and now I have one. The idea is setting goals."

FIGURE 4.5
Movers had higher hopes for their own future than did the chronic poor

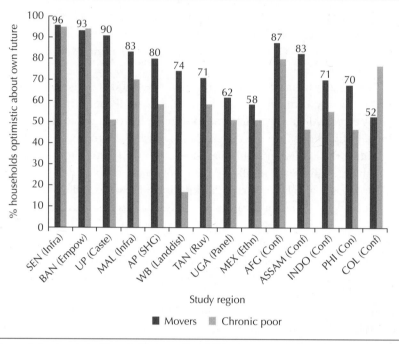

Source: Authors' analysis of household survey; N = 5,260 (movers = 2,431; chronic poor = 2,829).

To test whether aspirations are associated with an individual household's ability to move out of poverty, we created an index of aspirations that included questions about aspirations for self and for children.[6] The index was then included along with other independent variables driven by our conceptual framework in a multivariate linear regression model with household movement out of poverty as the dependent variable. Even more than personal agency, aspirations on the whole tended to have a positive association with the likelihood of moving out of poverty—significantly so in three Indian states, in Uganda, and in Afghanistan (figure 4.6). When we ran the same specification with falling as the dependent variable, we found that higher aspirations were also significantly associated with lower chances of falling, especially in the Indian states.

Take the case of West Bengal, where aspirations have a significant association with an initially poor household's ability to move out of poverty 10 years later. Considering the individual components of the aspirations index, we find that a 2-unit increase in beliefs about one's own future (1 = worse off; 3 = better off) corresponds to a 35 percent increase in exiting poverty. A

FIGURE 4.6
Individual aspirations are a robust correlate of moving out of poverty

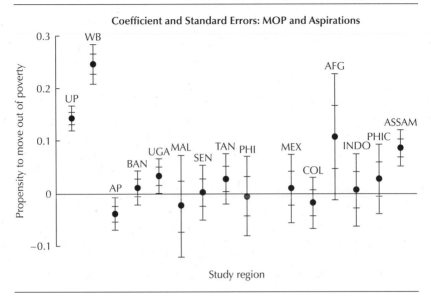

Coefficient and Standard Errors: MOP and Aspirations

Source: Multivariate linear regression analysis using data from household survey and community questionnaire (see appendix 6).

corresponding 2-unit increase in aspirations for the future of one's children (1 = worse off; 3 = better off) is associated with an even higher probability of exiting poverty, 38 percent. In orders of magnitude, the association between aspirations—both for oneself and for one's children—and moving out of poverty is higher than the effect of assets. A 1-unit increase on the assets index increases the chances of escaping poverty in West Bengal by only 5 percent.

Similarly, in communities torn by war and death in Afghanistan, a strong belief that the future will be better has a striking association with mobility, more so than assets, education, and ownership of livestock, all of which emerge as insignificant in our multivariate linear regressions for the study region. A 2-unit increase in beliefs about one's own future increases the likelihood of escape from poverty by 21 percent; a concomitant 2-unit increase in aspirations for one's children nearly doubles the probability of exit to 42 percent.

Our findings build on the work of scholars like Appadurai (2004), who shows the importance of "capacity to aspire." Poor people's aspirations do not seem to be confined to their own reference group.[7] Where aspirations are lacking, generating this capacity to envision a different future should become an integral part of poverty interventions and solidarity movements among poor people.

Aspirations and dreams of youth

My professors tell me: Abdul Kalam was also a village boy. Now he has served as the president of India. His genius was not suppressed within the village. You should also try your best in the same way, so that you may achieve your goal.

—Sutunu, a young boy, Kantipur, West Bengal

Whenever our teams traveled to the field, they came back highly energized on the days that they engaged with youth. Across study regions, young people were eager to talk. They gave inspiring accounts of their future plans and provided the most frank insights into the way social relations, democratic structures, and economic opportunities actually worked in their communities.

Young men and women have visions for themselves that often go far beyond the occupations of their parents. This is true especially for youths whose parents are engaged in agriculture or informal work. Table 4.2 reports the occupations desired by youth (boys and girls together), broken down by the primary source of income of their parents. In both mover and the chronic poor families, children of parents engaged in casual labor, sale of livestock or forest products, and

TABLE 4.2
Path deviation in youth: Youths whose parents are in agriculture or the informal sector want to do something else (start a business, get a job)

Parental source of income	Youth aspirations (percentages)			
	Regular employment	Business	Agriculture and allied activities	Informal work
Mover parents				
Regular employment	69.7	26.9	3.0	0.4
Business	36.1	56.7	6.3	1.0
Agriculture and allied activities	47.8	48.5	3.3	0.4
Informal work	39.8	44.5	14.8	0.8
Chronic poor parents				
Regular employment	66.9	27.3	4.3	1.4
Business	38.8	57.4	1.9	1.9
Agriculture and allied activities	44.8	49.4	3.7	2.1
Informal work	43.8	37.2	15.6	3.5

Source: Authors' analysis of household survey (a section of which was conducted with youth in the household); all study regions; N = 2,113 (children of movers = 1,070; children of chronic poor = 1,043).

other nonagricultural sources of income wanted to do something else; most wanted to start their own business or get a job. However, there was path dependence if parents already held a regular job or had a business.

Among chronic poor households where the parents were engaged in farming, half of the children wanted to open small businesses such as copy machine centers, telephone kiosks, and clinics. Another 45 percent aspired to salaried jobs in government or the private sector. Only 4 percent wanted to work in agriculture. Youths in Dapi Toube, Senegal, explained why: "Our parents have always practiced agriculture, and yet they are still poor."

As in Senegal, youths in West Bengal complained that agriculture was stagnant. Even if they planned to continue farming, they hoped to have an additional, nonagricultural source of income such as a business. "I would like to start wholesale business of potato because I know that in this business profit is good," said the son of a farmer in Anakha. Unemployed and the son of a casual laborer, Mohammed in Bhuinadi wanted to start a business of "bringing readymade clothes from the city to sell them in the village market." Young people apparently realized very early the importance of diversification, which the field research in West Bengal found was crucial for mobility.

Salaried jobs, particularly government jobs, were prized for the regular income and pension benefits they afforded. Utpal, a young woman in the village of Leteku Gaon, a community affected by the separatist insurgency in Assam, summed up the majority view. "In the future, I want to do a government job for its security. After my death, at least my dependent will get a pension or other facilities. Besides, it will ensure a regular monthly income." But most youths found themselves incapable of pulling the necessary strings or bribing their way to secure a job. A higher proportion of children whose parents were already in a salaried job aspired to one, perhaps believing that their parents might be able to afford the bribe or make the necessary connections. Frustration with the slim prospects of finding a job sometimes led youth to turn their sights to business. According to 21-year-old Lucky from Barbakara, Assam, "Now we do not get any government jobs. I do not want to lose time in searching for one. I think I will profit more by investing that amount of time in business. I want to be a construction contractor. I am presently working as a temporary worker for a construction company. With this experience, I will certainly be successful in business."

Some youths did want to engage in farming. "It is wrong if anybody thinks that one can earn only by getting educated," said a group of young boys in Andhra Pradesh. "We can earn by doing agriculture also. This is also God's grace. We should be gifted enough to serve Mother Earth. I want to serve the people by supplying food grains." Interestingly, wherever youth opted for farming or associated activities like fish breeding, they also spoke of adding value to agriculture by purchasing equipment like tillers, irrigation pumps, and fishing equipment.

Hardly anyone aspired to work in the temporary informal sector. Those who did not choose salaried employment, business, or farming mentioned a variety of other occupations. Some young boys, especially in the African study regions, spoke of joining the army. Damson, who was in secondary school in Chiksisi, Malawi, wanted to become a soldier "to maintain peace in the country, to go on peacekeeping missions for the United Nations, and to get a lot of money in retirement benefits and a special respect, which I badly want."

The occupational choices of many youths were driven by a desire to do social good. Being a nurse was a preferred occupation for the girls in Damson's village. "There are few nurses in our country, and this is causing many deaths in hospitals," said a group of girls. "We would therefore like to work as nurses and assist the country in saving people's lives. We'll also be able to assist our families." Erupakshi, a young boy in Appilepalle, Andhra Pradesh, held an ambition of becoming a lawyer. "So I am studying well," he said. "I want to become an advocate and help poor people fight for justice." Padma, a girl in Virupapuram, Andhra Pradesh, was studying to "become a good doctor who could serve the poor free of cost. Serving the people is equal to serving God."

For women though, the choices were often restricted. Most young girls opted for home-based occupations like sewing or for jobs where they could return home early, such as teaching. Several said they expected only to be good mothers and good wives. "What does the future mean for us?" asked a group of girls in Dayabhara, Bangladesh. "The responsibility of thinking rests on our male counterparts. They think of everything. To be married means the end of all hopes and aspirations."

Youths across study contexts worked hard to achieve their dreams, as did their parents. Some children went to night school while working as day laborers. Parents often sold off their assets to finance their children's education. Poverty, however, remained the most important obstacle to realizing these dreams. Some youths like Sattar in Chanpasha, Bangladesh, simply gave up. "I had great hopes in life, but none of them have been fulfilled," he said. "I was studying in a madrassa [a religious school], but I had to discontinue the studies. It was my hope to become an established *moulovi* [religious teacher], but I could not become so. It is now out of fear that I do not nurture any hope. Whatever Allah wishes, I shall be so." Some youths persevered. Narasimha, a young man from Gopepalle, Andhra Pradesh, was one of them.

He said, "Where there is a will, there is a way. I am now studying for a bachelor degree in science. I want to become a lecturer in organic chemistry. My parents encourage me by saying not to worry about the expenses incurred on education. So, I want to study well and reach my goal. I believe that anything can be achieved if we have confidence in ourselves."

What Facilitates and Hinders Personal Agency?

Because psychological dimensions are so important, it is useful to understand the factors that strengthen these dimensions. We focus here on the individual assets and capabilities that strengthen a person's agency to take action on his or her own behalf. Our quantitative data combined with the stories we heard from people suggest several factors that can either help or hinder poor men and women in their efforts to become effective agents in moving out of poverty. Quantitatively, we tried to do this by using multivariate regression techniques. Our measure of individual agency (the personal agency index) became the dependent variable. On the right-hand side, we used independent variables that we believed could explain higher or lower personal agency. The framework and variables used for the exercise are listed in annex 4.1, followed by the results in annex 4.2.

In this section, we highlight a few key factors that either facilitate or hinder personal agency—ones that were most frequently mentioned in the qualitative data or that emerged in the quantitative data. On the positive side, we examine ownership of assets, education, and political activism and connections. On the negative side, we focus particularly on the effects of health and death shocks.

Assets and education

Although he is uneducated, 55-year-old Mir is one of the successful few who has been able to move out of poverty in Afghanistan. In 1981, he moved with his family and his parents to Shazimir, close to Kabul. Together father and son set up a small shop and built a house. "At that time, the markets were good, and we were able to save some money in three to four years." In 1993, with the fighting raging between mujahideen groups, Mir's business collapsed. At around the same time, his father fell sick and died. Since then, however, Mir has been able to reopen his shop, and his two sons have also started a carpet-weaving business. The family now lives comfortably. Mir still wonders what his situation would have been had he not had the advantage of having a house and shop as assets to build on.

Across study contexts, people are unequivocal about the importance of starting out with or acquiring some assets. In India, land is of paramount significance: those who began in poverty and later moved out of it almost always made investments in land, both for income generation and as an asset that could be sold should the family suffer a shock in the future. In the East Asian study regions, people invest in assets that can help them in farming or small business, like *carabaos* (water buffalo) for tilling in the Philippines, or motorcycles that could be used as *kepaks* (small taxis) in Indonesia. Those who started out with some assets, perhaps bequeathed by parents, found it easier to acquire more assets than those who started out with nothing.

In some Cambodian villages, people see assets as making the crucial difference between transitory poverty and permanent destitution. A discussion group in Salvia Prey explained, "The destitute have no assets, no lands or draft animals—nothing except their unskilled labor. [Destitute households] are often headed by a widow with small children and a disabled husband. They live in cottages made of palm leaves and rely on collecting morning glory, insects, and so on. Unlike the merely poor, the destitute cannot go fishing because they do not have fishing equipment."

Besides providing an economic foundation on which to build, poor women and men said that assets give them confidence to move ahead. This association between asset ownership and confidence was confirmed in our quantitative data: our measure of initial asset ownership was positively and significantly associated with our personal agency index in several study contexts (annex 4.2).[8] Those with more control over their decisions were also more likely to report a higher average asset score. In figure 4.7, the y-axis plots the *difference* between the current mean asset index score for households with control over all decisions and that of households with control over no or few decisions. Notice the responses of the never poor: those who reported control over all decisions on average had a considerably higher mean asset score (1 unit higher) than those who had control over no or few decisions. Even among the chronic poor and the fallers, those with more control were likely to have a higher asset score.

Similarly, households that experienced a higher increase in their position on the 10-step ladder of power and rights were also more likely to report acquisition of a house. In figure 4.8, those who reported more increase in power (tercile 3) also experienced a greater increase in house ownership compared to those who reported a lower increase in power (tercile 1).

Besides assets, education is a significant confidence booster. Again, in our regression analysis, we find a positive association between education and

FIGURE 4.7
Households with more control over decisions report ownership of more assets

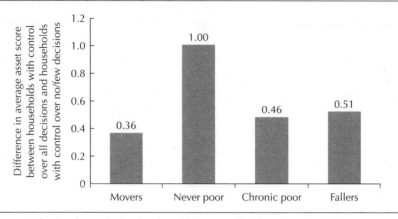

Source: Authors' analysis using data from household survey; all study regions; *N* = 8,973.

FIGURE 4.8
Households with greater increase in power are more likely to have acquired a house

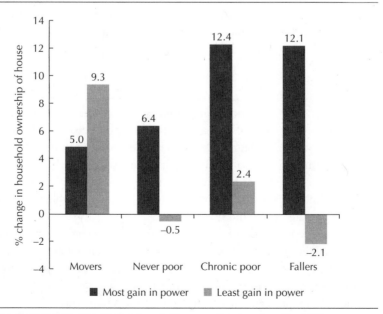

Source: Authors' analysis using data from household survey; all study regions; *N* = 8,822.

personal agency, significantly so in Andhra Pradesh, Mexico, Indonesia, and Thailand. In the qualitative data, too, both adults and youths spoke of the importance of being educated. When asked what was the most important thing she had ever bought, Aklima, a 27-year-old mover from Bakimati, Philippines, replied, "My education, which was given to me by my parents. If my parents did not spend for my education, then maybe I would not have been able to finish my studies. This is the only wealth that was given to me by my parents, which could not be taken from me or sold. My life has become better because of the education that I have. If I was not able to finish my studies, I could have been working as a laundry woman or a farm laborer." Young women in Cambodia remarked, "Education is the most important asset of people in this world. Being well educated, one can find a good job with a high standard of living. With good education, one can manage to have a better life or set a clear goal. The educated person never fears facing financial insecurity because he or she has a permanent well-paid job. For example, a literate adult woman is able to find a good job in the garment factory. Those who have no education cannot find such fortune and become mobile laborers, a more risky job."

Political connections

> To gain success in business, political favor is needed. To export eggs, chicken, and meat, or to import seedlings, you need a good connection with politicians to get permission and to get the legal documents ready.
> —Mohammed, a 25-year-old man, Banjoydup, Bangladesh

Knowing a political figure is often as important for building self-confidence and power as owning assets or even being educated. We found a significant association between our measure of political connectedness—whether a household had met a local politician—and personal agency, as shown in annex 4.2. Figure 4.9 shows how our study respondents related the two. With the exception of the movers, households that had experienced greater increase in power (tercile 3) were more likely than households that had experienced less increase in power (tercile 1) to report that they had met a local politician during the study period.

Connections with political leaders are seen to be particularly useful in the South Asia region. In West Bengal, joining the ruling party cadre is seen as the surest way to acquire power and move out of poverty. In the town of Masaru, youths without such connections lamented their inability to start a business. Shyamal, who wanted to be a businessman, said, "Only the people who are close to the panchayat get permissions. So poor people cannot

FIGURE 4.9
Households with greater increase in power are more likely to have met a local politician

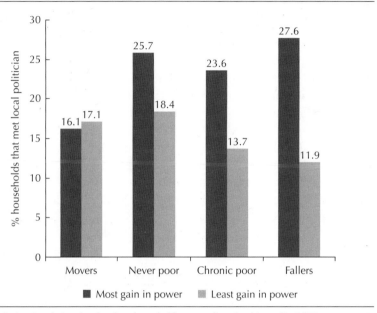

Source: Authors' analysis using data from household survey; all study regions; N = 8,822.

acquire power. However, if poor people can save some money and be engaged in politics, they can acquire power."[9]

People routinely use "political privileges" as a means to gain power and move ahead. Often such connections are acquired through relatives or friends. Lily, age 30, was employed in the municipal offices of Bakimati, a community in Lanao de Sur, a conflict-affected region in the Philippines. A university graduate, she offered a role model to young women in the village. However, an interview with Lily revealed that the key trigger to her upward movement was help she received from the mayor, who happened to be Lily's sister-in-law. Immediately after graduating in 2000, Lily joined the mayor as her campaign manager. She also doubled up as a maid in the mayor's office, a job she described as humiliating. "I was living in their house at that time, and I even had to do the household chores. I didn't like what I was doing because I felt like a maid and that was not the job that I was applying for. I was earning only 500 pesos a month, but I had to do that because she [the mayor] promised me that I would have a position in the municipal office."

Lily was finally accepted as a municipal clerk in 2001, a position she held at the time of the survey. She felt she could ask the mayor for assistance at any time. "There were times that I was able to ask for some personal favor from her, considering that she is my husband's sister."

Besides moving up through connections, bribing government officials is a useful strategy. Lily studied for a year at Shariff Kabunsuan College, but then decided to transfer to a different college "because a friend told me that I could pass all my subjects if I would pay the instructor." In Philippines-conflict, respondents associated corruption in local government with an increase in their power. In Uganda, Senegal, and Colombia, too, we found a positive and significant association between corruption and our personal agency index.

People typically initiate contacts with political leaders to seek individual favors rather than to press collective requests. However, in some places where people's organizations have become strong—some communities in the Colombian barrios, or villages in Andhra Pradesh where women's self-help groups are thriving—these organizations have been able to get the attention of politicians to address community-wide issues. In some cases, this has improved both the targeting and implementation of government programs.

Death and illness: Putting lives on a downward spiral

My situation has worsened. I am ill; my shop business has collapsed and I have no income. He who does not move forward moves backward.
—Samba, a 43-year-old man in chronic poverty,
Maurikoube, Senegal

You can assist a bird only when it still has some strength.
—Discussion group in Chubaka, Kagera, Tanzania

One of the biggest obstacles poor households face when they attempt to improve their well-being is the serious illness or death of someone in the family. Health and death shocks are a primary reason for falls into poverty, and indeed the incidence of health shocks was higher among fallers and chronic poor than among movers in virtually all the study regions (figure 4.10).[10] The only exception is Mexico, where more movers than fallers reported experiencing an illness. The association of health shocks with falling is strikingly high in the African study regions. Nearly 85 percent of fallers in Uganda, 79 percent in Malawi, and 73 percent in Ruvuma, Tanzania, had experienced a health shock in the decade prior to the survey.

FIGURE 4.10
Fallers and chronic poor report more health shocks than movers

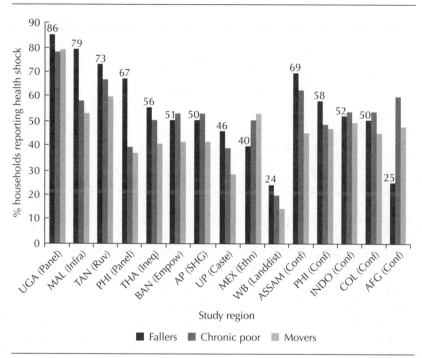

Source: Authors' analysis using data from household survey; *N* = 8,058.

Sometimes treatment is available, and poor households cannot afford it. Just as often, there is a complete lack of health services or the services that exist are too far away or are of extremely poor quality. This is a common situation in the African study regions: health services are either too remote to access or are captured by corrupt practitioners. In Zokwaza, Malawi, the nearest hospital is 65 kilometers away. "We have to pay high fares in order to get there," said women and men in the community. "Otherwise, we have to cycle from three o'clock in the morning and arrive there in the afternoon." But cycling is not an option if one has to transport a sick person or a woman in labor. "Women in labor can force you to sell your land and animals to get a taxi," said a discussion group in Bukwaime, Uganda. "This inevitably interferes in one's plans to invest his money into development projects which could have made an improvement in one's well-being." In Bamlozi, Malawi, people could go to a government hospital, but they reported that at the hospital "there are no essential drugs, while the same drugs bearing Malawi government marks can be found in abundance in private hospitals."

In such circumstances, many poor people go to quacks or traditional healers or simply die in pain. In Leteku Gaon, Assam, a state that recorded the highest incidence of health shocks among the four Indian states in our sample, a teacher reported that malaria had ravaged the village in the absence of proper health facilities. "In 2004, our village was badly affected by malaria and cerebral malaria. About 12 people died. Before cremating one body, we had to prepare for another." The ladder of life discussion with women confirmed the epidemic and its effects: "A shadow of sorrow prevailed in the village. Even those who did not die became angry and mentally disturbed. The villagers lost interest in work."

In the Malawi study communities, people described falling ill because of hunger. Women in Madkumba said, "The men had swelling in their legs because of too much walking in search of food. The women were consuming wild roots at home, waiting for food to be found." Besides hunger, the threat of HIV/AIDS is a daily reality for a majority of respondents in Malawi and in some other African regions in our sample. People in Chikluzi, a village in Malawi with high HIV prevalence, described how the pandemic had affected them. "Intelligent people are dying. When so many people die, development declines," said one. "I left for one week in 2003, and by the time I came back eight people had died. The day I arrived, another person died. Sometimes you go to the graveyard to bury someone, but before you come back, you just hear that someone else has died." In Kamlondo, Uganda, nearly every household had lost a member to HIV/AIDS. Young people were dying at the highest rate, depriving the community of their strength. "This has greatly led to the loss of productive people," said men in the community. "If they were still around, we would have been very developed."

People identified four types of shocks caused by death or illness. First, the death or disappearance of a family member, particularly the breadwinner, can set entire households on a downward spiral into poverty. Across study sites, widows and orphans are placed at the bottommost step on the well-being ladder. Miriam is a 50-year-old chronically poor woman in Riah Khillaw, Afghanistan. Her husband migrated to Iran in 1997 during the Taliban's rule, and by 2005 she had had no news of whether he was alive or dead. Miriam and her four children had been living off handouts from neighbors and relatives. Her eldest son worked as a laborer, and her second son, 12 years old, was contemplating doing so as well. Miriam herself tried tailoring, but anxiety about her husband gradually weakened her. "I do not have good health," she told the field team. "My nerves are weak, and my eyes do not work well. I have a stomachache. I cannot sleep without medicines. We do not have our own house; we live in my husband's sister's house. They are in Iran at present, and when they return to Afghanistan, we will be shelterless and our life will get worse. I worry about my children. They live with hardship and humility. I have no hope for their future."

Second, deaths, illnesses, and accidents typically force big expenditures that result in dissaving. People have to sell off precious assets to cope with medical treatment or funeral expenses and often go deeply into debt. Jahangir, a chronic poor man in Uttar Pradesh, had labored for years to accumulate three assets that he believed would enable him to move out of poverty: a bicycle, land for farming, and a permanent house instead of the flimsy *kutcha* hut that sheltered his family. Juggling work as a daily wage laborer and a vegetable seller, Jahangir had saved bit by bit for these assets, and he did manage to buy a bicycle. But the untimely death of both his parents in 1990 threw Jahangir, then 25 years old, off the saving track. He had to borrow from a village moneylender to finance the funeral expenses. Eight years later, Jahangir's family still lived in the hut; his wife and two young boys had joined him as wage laborers to pay the loan from the moneylender. In 1998, just when he had saved enough to construct a proper house, the wall of his kutcha hut fell down, breaking Jahangir's hands and legs. "I had to give up my job as a vegetable seller. I spent about 10,000 rupees [approximately $250] for my treatment, which I took from a moneylender in the market. I still haven't paid this back. Both my sons and my wife do labor and organize to get some provisions back home. I took another loan to construct the house because after the accident, we put up a temporary polythene roof. We were constantly attacked by monkeys. I had to take a loan from a village moneylender to construct a room where we could all stay."

Buried under debt, Jahangir tried to work as a laborer, but with his disability, he was paid less than others. The third shock occasioned by illness and accidents, as in this case, is the loss of earning power. For the chronic poor, many of whom are daily wage laborers, their bodies and hands are precious assets, and disabilities and sickness spell devastation. Moreover, having a sick or injured person in the family to care for can reduce the earning power of other household members. In Zokwaza, Malawi, a key informant described HIV/AIDS as one of the most important factors in the community's decline. "People are spending more time attending to patients and funerals instead of working in the fields or doing other income-generating activities." Youths in Kabkore, Uganda, added, "Once one is infected with AIDS, she or he becomes very weak and can't dig much land to move out of poverty."

Finally, and perhaps most importantly, encounters with death and illness can kill confidence in oneself and dreams for the future. Jahangir, in Uttar Pradesh, summed up the impact of his misfortunes: "Now I am losing trust." Adults spoke of severe anxiety and mental illnesses like depression after the death of their spouses or children. Peter, a 22-year-old stuck in chronic poverty in Tulma, Philippines, resorted to drinking when his first child died. "It was a big blow," he said to our field team. "I was always drunk. I lost my interest to work. It seemed that I had gone insane in my thoughts." Zamada, a woman in poverty in Glikati, Philippines, had a similar experience when her three children died. Seven days after the last death, Zamada herself fell ill. She said it was primarily because she was not able to express her feelings. "I got so sick after the deaths. My relatives would tell me that I should talk about them because they had seen that all through, I had been awfully quiet." The final blow came with the death of her mother in 2006, the year our team interviewed her. Zamada also became sick then and lost the confidence to work.

Heartbreakingly, children often gave up their hopes and aspirations to do better when their parents died. In Kibtuntula, Uganda, several youths we met were grieving parents lost to HIV/AIDS. As orphans, they had no money to finance their school fees and had given up hope for the future.

Simple cross-tabulations between the incidence of health shocks and one of our measures of personal agency—control over everyday decision making—revealed that households that reported less control over their everyday decisions compared to 10 years ago were also more likely to report a health shock during the survey period (figure 4.11). For instance, only 35 percent of movers who said they had more control now than earlier also said they had suffered a health shock over the 10-year period. In comparison, 44 percent of movers with less control had experienced such a shock. Similarly, those who suggested that they had control over *all* their decisions also ranked themselves higher on a four-step scale corresponding to their current health (4 = excellent health; 1 = very bad health).

Households with lower aspirations for their children were also more likely to report experiences with sickness or illness (figure 4.12). Only about 35 percent of movers who expect their children to be better off said that they had experienced a health shock. However, nearly 57 percent of those who expect their children to be worse off cited a brush with illness. That health

FIGURE 4.11

Households with less control over decisions report more health shocks and poorer current state of health

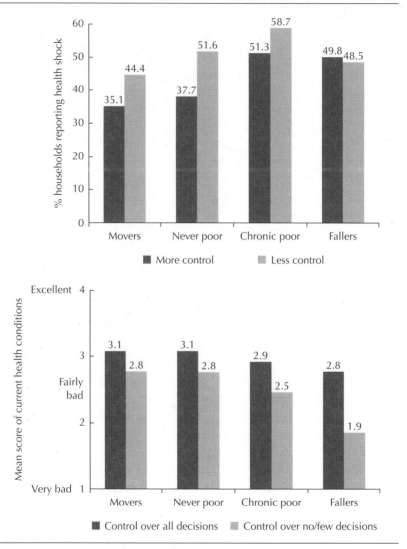

Source: Authors' analysis using data from household survey; all study regions; $N = 8,973$.

FIGURE 4.12

Households with lower aspirations for their children report more health shocks

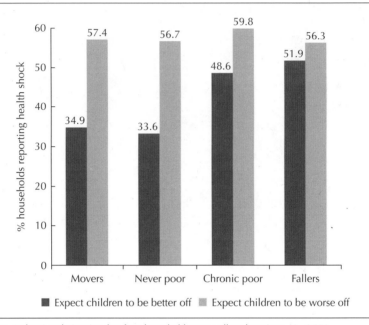

Source: Authors' analysis using data from household survey; all study regions; N = 8,058.

shocks lower confidence and personal agency across study contexts was reaffirmed by the negative association between health shocks and our personal agency index in virtually all study regions in our model (annex 4.2).

It isn't surprising, then, that poor people greatly fear illness. Julieta, a woman in El Mirador, Colombia, remarked, "God give us some health for moving on, to keep on fighting. I do not want to get sick." In the remote village of Katugende, Uganda, Ruth, a widow in chronic poverty agreed: "Unless sickness strikes, there is always a chance of developing further if I work hard." And when asked if anyone in her community was safe from falling into poverty, Miro, a farmer in Ramili Qali, Afghanistan, replied in the negative and added, "Not if a bad incident takes place, for example, death or an incurable disease. We have a proverb which says that if both arms break, a person may be able to work, but if the heart breaks, he will not be able to work." For poor, vulnerable women and men, one incurable disease or one death is often the thin line that divides their ability to work and move out of poverty from their giving up hope and heart.

Conclusion

Poor people have a deep and immediate understanding of power and power relationships. They know their own powerlessness in the context of deep-rooted inequalities in economic, social, and political structures. Despite the strangulation they sometimes feel, or perhaps because of it, poor people display a strong internal sense of power, self-confidence, and will to persist, no matter what.

Our evidence clearly indicates that poor men and women can act as agents on their own behalf. With few assets, limited or no education, and few if any social or political connections, they still aspire and strive to move out of poverty. The life stories suggest that psychological self-efficacy is often the most important precursor to action, and the magnitude of effects reflected in our quantitative data confirms the importance of personal agency and aspirations in poverty escapes. Yet these psychological dimensions have been ignored almost completely in international development programs, which rarely transcend the vague rhetoric of "putting people at the center of development."

These results obviously do not mean that we need self-esteem schools for the poor. They do call for a change in *how* development is done. Development programs and strategies must be designed and carried out in ways that uphold people's dignity and reinforce their sense of self-respect; this is true even in conflict contexts where people are frightened and have lost everything and in the most impoverished communities where they may be nearly starving. This change can be done through participatory development programs in which participation does not become another tax, but instead generates positive returns to participants.

Deeply entrenched gender inequalities can be addressed by focusing on "power with," through investment in collective action by poor women. The success of the microcredit movement in Bangladesh and of women's self-help groups in Andhra Pradesh has shown that forming groups of socially marginalized women can help. Over time, as these spread and become social movements, they can change deeply entrenched social norms. In Andhra Pradesh, for example, meetings start with rituals, songs, and prayers to help women break through old barriers and begin to recognize their self-worth. The focus is on addressing priority needs first through collective strength. In both programs, when women are asked about the most important difference in their lives, they most often first talk about the loss of fear.

Steps to increase material assets, particularly permanent housing, can go a long way in reinforcing poor people's self-confidence and giving them an economic foundation to build on.

Health shocks bleed people's resources and destroy their hopes and dreams. No matter which data we examine, whether from life stories, group discussions, or questionnaires, the critical role of health shocks as a cause of destitution emerges with heartbreaking regularity. Provision of affordable, quality health care is one of the most important things that can be done to save lives and livelihoods.

As important as personal agency is, it is only one side of the equation. Strategies to boost self-efficacy cannot succeed as long as skewed opportunity structures thwart poor people's initiatives. Economic, social, and political inequalities in their environments keep poor people down even though they dream of rising. Thus, two people with the same level of confidence and aspirations may end up with different levels of power, depending on their individual capabilities and on the economic, social, and political opportunity structure within which they pursue their interests (Kabeer 1999; Narayan 2002b, 2005; Petesch, Smulovitz, and Walton 2005; World Bank 2006; Rao and Walton 2004b).[11] This opportunity structure is embedded in institutions, and in the next three chapters we tackle the three main types of institutions with which poor women and men interact: markets, local democracies, and their own collective groups.

Annex 4.1   Factors Associated with Personal Agency

Asset index, 10 years ago
• PCA index of assets owned with current weights (10 years ago, rh201 i–xiiib)

Social assets

Personal access to networks and associations
• Number of groups household belonged to (10 years ago, h406Tb)
• Extent of linking social capital (currently, h410)

Community access to networks and associations
• Change in access to networks and associations (rc919: focus group discussion)

Participation in local government
• Change in participation in community (over 10 years, rc916)

Political assets
• Voting in state/national elections (currently, rh508)
• Meeting local politicians (over 10 years, rh503iii)

Education
• Education of household head (currently, h106)

Health shocks
• Health shocks (over 10 years, rh305)

Violence against women
• Violence against women within households (10 years ago, h609b)

Household access to information
• Trend in access to information about local government (over 10 years, rh515b)

PCA index of corruption
• Corruption in government officials in village (c506b)

Elite capture
• Officials act in their own or public interest (over 10 years, h507)

Extent of social divisions
• Differences between people based on ethnicity, caste, etc. (c414b)

PCA index of ethnic/religious/gender discrimination in schools
• Trend in ethnic/religious discrimination in schools (over 10 years, c305b)
• Trend in gender discrimination in schools (over 10 years, c304b)

PERSONAL AGENCY INDEX

PCA index of current personal agency using household-level data
• Current position on ladder of power and rights (h707)
• Current control over everyday decisions (rh501a)

Note: See appendix 4 for explanation of codes.

Annex 4.2 Full OLS Regression Results with Personal Agency as Dependent Variable

	UP Caste	WB Landdist	ASSAM Conf	AP SHG	BAN Empow	UGA Panel	MAL Infra
Asset index, 10 years ago (PCA rh201 (i–xiii)b, with current weights)	0.324 [10.77]***	0.216 [5.11]***	0.284 [6.03]***	0.232 [5.76]***	0.512 [4.51]***	0.215 [2.75]***	0.144 [1.53]
Number of groups household belonged to, 10 years ago (h406Tb)	0.069 [2.98]***	0.032 [0.78]	0.145 [2.56]**	0.003 [0.10]	0.063 [2.32]**		
Extent of linking social capital (h410)	0.387 [2.99]***	0.26 [2.74]***	0.037 [0.31]	−0.161 [1.47]	−0.152 [2.69]***		0.084 [0.24]
Change in access to networks (rc919)	−0.042 [1.35]	0.078 [1.19]	−0.017 [0.43]				
Change in participation in community (rc916)	−0.067 [1.93]*	−0.057 [0.80]	−0.043 [1.00]	0.027 [0.27]	0.119 [1.36]		
Voting in elections (rh508)	−0.029 [0.16]	−0.014 [0.10]	0.473 [1.78]*	0.858 [2.49]**	0.137 [1.76]*	0.258 [1.60]	−0.196 [0.79]
Meeting local politicians (rh503iii)	0.067 [5.45]***	0 [0.01]	0.072 [2.62]***	0.09 [4.77]***	0.14 [8.93]***	0.103 [2.54]**	0.183 [3.41]***
Education of household head (h106)	0.008 [1.83]*	−0.013 [0.72]	0.012 [1.95]*	0.106 [4.34]***			0.024 [0.35]
Health shocks, over 10 years (rh305)	−0.21 [3.78]***	−0.186 [2.28]**	−0.438 [5.01]***	−0.138 [1.74]*	−0.159 [2.71]***	−0.131 [1.25]	−0.48 [1.67]*
Violence against women, 10 years ago (h609b)	0.106 [2.22]**	−0.101 [1.38]	−0.002 [0.03]	0.398 [3.29]***			−0.148 [0.79]
Access to information on government programs (rh515b)	0.036 [0.80]	0.452 [5.84]***	0.038 [0.86]	0.166 [1.62]	0.06 [0.90]		0.107 [0.46]

Note: Blank cells mean that either the variable was not available or had to be dropped because of high multicollinearity with other variables. School inequality included only for India regressions.

SEN Infra	TAN Ruv	AFG Conf	INDO Conf	PHI Conf	COL Conf	MEX Ethn	PHI Panel	THAI Ineq
0.069	0.047	0.278	0.098	0.104	0.12	0.146	0.056	0.238
[0.70]	[0.67]	[3.10]***	[1.01]	[1.53]	[2.28]**	[1.88]*	[0.40]	[5.88]***
	0.201		0.055	0.034	−0.05	0.012		0.029
	[2.70]***		[0.77]	[0.72]	[0.83]	[0.17]		[0.74]
	0.256	0.653	−0.023	0.281	0.281	−0.085		0.224
	[2.27]**	[0.85]	[0.17]	[3.03]***	[1.44]	[0.44]		[2.50]**
0.163	0.211	−0.063	0.007	−0.095	0.252	0.2		
[0.76]	[1.85]*	[0.25]	[0.09]	[2.13]**	[1.20]	[1.24]		
−0.03	0.206	−0.111	0.202	0.31	0.149	−0.151	0.155	−0.003
[0.12]	[1.17]	[0.18]	[0.42]	[1.59]	[1.27]	[0.85]	[0.29]	[0.01]
0.028	0.035	−0.177	0.073	0.066	0.041	0.076	0.04	0.023
[1.31]	[0.95]	[1.65]*	[1.39]	[1.82]*	[1.01]	[1.41]	[1.16]	[0.75]
	0		0.076			0.157		0.103
	[0.08]		[2.69]***			[3.41]***		[2.11]**
	−0.106	−0.022	−0.008	−0.024	−0.283	−0.015	−0.45	0.075
	[0.61]	[0.17]	[0.08]	[0.37]	[2.67]***	[0.12]	[3.44]***	[0.73]
0.215	0.071	0.24	0.005	0.175	−0.083	−0.036	−0.21	−0.085
[1.55]	[1.44]	[2.42]**	[0.04]	[1.30]	[1.27]	[0.62]	[1.02]	[0.96]
0.044	0.022	0.179	0.385	0.016	0.151	0.146	0.061	0.012
[0.33]	[0.23]	[0.72]	[4.47]***	[0.13]	[1.44]	[2.42]**	[0.40]	[0.15]

(continued)

	UP Caste	WB Landdist	ASSAM Conf	AP SHG	BAN Empow	UGA Panel	MAL Infra
Corruption in local government, 10 years ago (c506b)	−0.015 [0.61]	−0.01 [0.25]	0.01 [0.24]	0.025 [0.48]	0.036 [1.14]	0.063 [1.85]*	−0.19 [2.60]***
Household perception of change in elite capture (h507)	0.054 [1.69]*	−0.277 [3.17]***	−0.158 [1.76]*	0.001 [0.01]	−0.004 [0.07]	0.152 [3.57]***	−0.355 [3.57]***
Extent of social inequality in community (c414b)	0.064 [2.44]**	0.038 [1.03]	−0.08 [2.13]**	0.152 [2.23]**	0.143 [2.61]***	0.088 [1.90]*	0.181 [1.70]*
Extent of discrimination in schools (PCA c304b, c305b)		0.038 [1.14]	0.007 [0.23]	−0.089 [1.83]*			
Constant	−0.165 [0.61]	−0.424 [1.15]	0.235 [0.66]	−2.287 [4.58]***	−0.949 [4.52]***	−0.63 [2.57]**	0.736 [1.31]
Observations	1635	1192	746	839	862	683	106
R^2	0.18	0.19	0.23	0.22	0.16	0.15	0.21

Note: Cluster-robust t-statistics in brackets. Blank cells mean that either the variable was not available or had to be dropped because of high multicollinearity with other variables. School inequality included only for India regressions.

*p < .10 **p < .05 ***p < .01 (White heteroscedasticity-consistent standard errors)

For key on codes and abbreviations, see appendixes 2 and 4.

SEN Infra	TAN Ruv	AFG Conf	INDO Conf	PHI Conf	COL Conf	MEX Ethn	PHI Panel	THAI Ineq
0.227	0.017	−0.05	−0.062	0.061	0.248	0.106	0.009	0.018
[2.39]**	[0.39]	[0.17]	[2.25]**	[1.88]*	[2.31]**	[0.94]	[0.17]	[0.24]
0.042	−0.045	−0.007	0.192	0.056	−0.119	0.017	−0.29	−0.029
[0.35]	[0.56]	[0.05]	[1.40]	[1.09]	[0.88]	[0.18]	[2.71]***	[0.22]
0.536		−0.008	−0.015	−0.22	0.164	−0.363	−0.12	0.101
[2.26]**		[0.06]	[0.24]	[2.62]***	[1.39]	[1.48]	[1.51]	[1.70]*
−1.45	−0.97	−0.62	−2.012	−0.22	−0.959	−0.39	1.05	−0.36
[1.61]	[2.02]**	[1.35]	[2.82]***	[0.58]	[2.40]**	[0.88]	[1.37]	[0.52]
263	292	83	315	300	218	291	163	497
0.12	0.13	0.22	0.16	0.1	0.19	0.12	0.07	0.1

Notes

1. See, for example, A. Sen (1985, 1993, 1999), Nussbaum (2000), and Alkire (2008). The roots of community development, participatory development, cooperatives, and the "people first" concept all are based on the premise that poor people's active agency is central in their movement out of poverty.

2. This response was to a question in a focus group exercise on livelihoods, freedom, power, and democracy that was conducted separately with women, men, and youth in each community. The participants in each group were asked, "What does power mean? What does it mean to have power? What does it mean to be powerful? What are the local definitions, terms, or sayings that capture the concept of power?" The question was left open ended, although the word used to introduce power was predetermined in training workshops before the investigators went out into the field.

3. There is a vast social science literature on power, starting with Weber and Marx. Some of the most influential works include those of Steven Lukes, James Scott, Anthony Giddens, Antonio Gramsci, Charles Tilly, J. K. Galbraith, and Alvin Toffler, and from the grassroots perspective Robert Chambers, Naila Kabeer, John Gaventa, and Ainsur Rahman, among many others.

4. In *Durable Inequality*, Charles Tilly argues that much of the inequality previously attributed to differences in individual ability and characteristics is instead a consequence of factors that generate *categorical* inequalities. These systematic inequalities between categories of people give certain types of people advantages from the start, allowing the persistence of categorical divisions in the future. Categorical inequalities are usually established through exploitation and opportunity hoarding. Over time, however, emulation and adaptation to social inequalities exacerbate social divisions, contributing to their persistence in the long run.

5. The difference in African observations (more power and rights than elsewhere) may also reflect the fact that within many African countries, some societies are historically less hierarchical than those in other parts of the world. The other study region where power levels were high among the poor is Bangladesh. This probably reflects the considerable increase in women's empowerment due to interventions by NGOs (box 4.1).

6. The technique of principal components analysis was used to create the index.

7. Boudon (1973) postulated that most individuals evaluate their performance against some "reference group" that they are part of. People belonging to a lower class have a lower reference point and, therefore, are prone to being easily satisfied and less motivated to reach positions in the upper class.

8. The asset index was created using the technique of principal components over all assets.

9. Interestingly, our measure of political activities in West Bengal showed an insignificant association with personal agency in the regressions (annex 4.2).

10. There is an extensive body of literature that suggests that illness and death are the most common triggers for declines into poverty. For more details, see Anirudh Krishna's studies on reasons for upward movement out of and decline into poverty in the Indian states of Rajasthan, Andhra Pradesh, and Gujarat (Krishna 2004, 2006; Krishna et al. 2005).

11. See Rao and Walton (2004b) for an excellent discussion on inequality of agency and the role of culture. For issues in measuring empowerment, see Ibrahim and Alkire (2007), Alsop and Heinsohn (2005), Narayan (2005), Kabeer (2001), and Mayoux (2003).

The Dream of Equal Opportunity

There is a ditch in front of us and a well behind us.

—WOMEN'S DISCUSSION GROUP,
Govindapalle, Andhra Pradesh

Lot owners need water for their lots, and farmers also need water for their farms. Hundreds of hectares of rice farms rely on one lake. Our good government never shouts at the lot owners, who usually drain water from the lake to their lots. But they very often shout at us.

—DISCUSSION WITH YOUTHS FROM POOR FAMILIES,
Preysath, Cambodia

Getting a permit is tough. You must have contacts and money.

—DISCUSSION WITH WOMEN,
Villa Rosa, Colombia

There is no problem in doing business. All can do it. But where there is no light, no bridge, and no roads, what business will you do?

—DISCUSSION WITH WOMEN,
Biralipara, Assam

F or the most part, women and men in poverty are willing to work hard, take initiative, and persevere to realize their aspirations. But it is by no means ensured that hard work and initiative will translate into upward mobility. This chapter examines how national and local conditions, particularly market conditions, can constrict or expand opportunities to move out of poverty.

If all individuals were born with equal life chances, and if there truly were equal opportunity for everyone, then the just desserts of a free market really would be just. But we all know that the world we live in is not a world of equal opportunity. Some of us are born in rich countries, some in poor countries. Within countries, some people are born in booming regions and some in regions suffering long-run decline. Some are born male, some female; some are born into the favored social class, racial group, or caste, and some are not. Some are born to wealthy parents and some to parents with few assets.

These multiple, often interacting, layers of geographic, social, and economic inequalities create unequal access to markets and opportunities. Our study found that most poor women and men would be more than happy to participate in markets on fair terms, but when they try to do business, they often lose out in state-regulated or collusion-dominated markets that are anything but free. The opportunity sets they face for obtaining credit, for purchasing inputs, for selling outputs, and for meeting the tax and regulatory requirements of the state are very different from those that the well-off enjoy. Thus the "invisible hand" of the free market is instead a very visible hand of markets that are rigged against the poor. What poor people in our study mainly asked for is a level playing field, where they would have equal opportunities to use their assets and initiative to get ahead.

The conventional approach to poverty consists of national policies to promote rapid growth along with safety net or targeted programs to mitigate

181

the consequences of poverty, combined with some measure of investments in human capital for future generations. We would argue that expanding poor women's and men's economic opportunity sets requires more. National policies, including those to promote overall economic growth, undoubtedly play an enormous role in the reduction of aggregate poverty, and we review that evidence. However, local conditions significantly shape the opportunities available within communities. Even when a country is on a rising tide, local conditions will affect whether households are able to sail out of poverty or confront choppy seas. Government interventions to improve opportunity sets within communities—by building infrastructure, connecting producers to new markets, facilitating more and better credit, and ensuring a favorable climate for small business—can go far in allowing people to use their assets and initiative to move up.

Economic Growth: The Rising Tide

Growth may be everything, but it's not the only thing.
—Joseph Stiglitz, *Foreign Affairs*, November/December 2005

Although our study was not framed to contribute to debates about the relationship between national economic growth and poverty reduction, the topic is too important to ignore. Let us start with a clear question: How is growth in measured aggregate consumption expenditures (ACE) related to reductions in the headcount measure of absolute consumption expenditure (HACE) poverty?[1]

This question can be reduced arithmetically to growth and a distributional adjustment, which itself has two components. First is the growth in aggregate consumption. The distribution effect is both whether the poor got more or less proportionally of the increase/decrease than their initial share in the total and how many people were near the ACE poverty threshold to start with. The relative magnitude of the two effects (growth and distribution) in the proximate explanation of poverty reduction is an entirely empirical question. If differences in (distribution-adjusted) growth across countries are large and changes in distribution over time are small, then differences across countries in poverty reduction will be mostly attributed to differences between countries in their growth. Moreover, if the distribution of income changes a great deal over time and differences in medium or long-term growth rates are small, then the opposite conclusion—that distribution mattered most—could emerge.

Kraay (2006) uses household data sets covering medium- to long-run spells of 5 to 10 years and finds that around 90 percent of the variation across 80 countries in the pace of HACE poverty reduction in the 1980s and 1990s can be attributed to growth (figure 5.1). Many other studies, such those by Ravallion (1995, 2001), Ravallion and Chen (1997), and Fields (2001), also confirm the strong correlation between poverty reduction and aggregate economic growth. In addition, the review by Cord (2005) of the experiences of 14 countries during the 1990s shows that more rapid growth is strongly associated with more rapid poverty reduction.

Understanding three stylized facts can help us both grasp Kraay's results and understand what the findings do and do not imply. The first stylized fact is that the differences across countries in economic growth are enormous. If we examine the growth rate of gross domestic product per capita across all developing countries over a decade and compare high performers (those in the top 10 percent) to low performers (those in the bottom 10 percent), the difference is around 6.5 percent per year. The second simple fact is that while countries differ in their level of consumption and income inequality—for example, South Africa and Brazil are very unequal and Hungary is very equal—*changes* in inequality tend to be small. When Deininger and Squire (1996) first assembled data that allow an investigation of changes in inequality, they found that with a few exceptions (notably China), equal countries stayed equal and unequal countries stayed unequal. A third stylized fact is that, at least in recent data, the pace of economic growth and the changes in inequality are roughly uncorrelated. It is not the case that countries growing more rapidly tend to have bigger increases in inequality (Ravallion 2004).

If you combine the three basic facts—that growth rates differ greatly across countries, that changes in the distribution of consumption within countries over time tend to be small, and that these changes are unrelated to growth—it arithmetically must be the case that most of the cross-national differences in poverty reduction can be attributed to differences in growth.

One common confusion in the debates about growth and poverty is about the role of inequality. If, for the same increase in total growth, the measures of inequality worsen because of changes in the lower tail of the distribution, then it is possible that poverty reduction will be less than it would have been otherwise. But this change does not mean that "increased inequality is bad for poverty reduction" in a causal (not arithmetic) sense. From 1978 to 2000, China experienced the most impressive reduction in absolute poverty in the history of mankind. At the same time, it experienced the largest recorded increase in inequality. The growth in China was sufficiently rapid

FIGURE 5.1

Comparison of spells of growth and poverty reduction shows that the pace of poverty reduction is strongly associated with growth, but with variation around this pattern

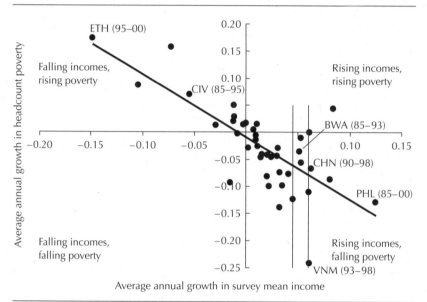

Average annual growth in survey mean income

Source: Adapted from Kraay 2006.

Note: ETH = Ethiopia; CIV = Côte d'Ivoire; BWA = Botswana; CHN = China; PHL = Philippines; VNM = Vietnam.

that those at the bottom of the distribution, getting a smaller and smaller share of a larger and larger pie, ended up with much more pie. The question of whether increased inequality was "bad" for poverty reduction in China depends on whether the same rapid economic growth could have been produced without the increasing income inequality. Perhaps yes, perhaps no, but this is a counterfactual question. One can compute what poverty reduction "would have been" if growth had stayed the same while inequality increased less, but just because one can compute a counterfactual does not mean that the assumed levels of growth and inequality would have been feasible.

Cord (2005) separated poverty reduction into a growth component and a distribution component in 10 countries for which data were available. She found that sometimes growth and redistribution worked together (e.g., in Brazil and Bolivia); sometimes growth was positive, but increases in inequality led to less poverty reduction than would have occurred had (counterfactually)

FIGURE 5.2

Although inequality may help or hinder poverty reduction, its contribution to poverty reduction over long episodes tends to be less than that of growth

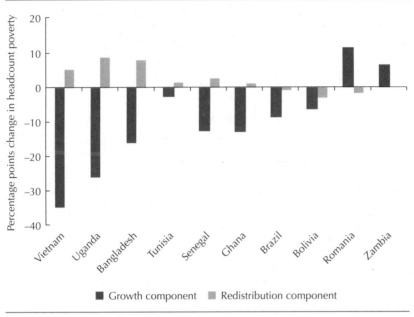

Source: Cord 2005.

the growth been distribution-neutral (e.g., in Vietnam and Bangladesh); and sometimes growth was negative, but distribution improved (e.g., in Romania). But Cord's data, shown in figure 5.2, are striking in two respects. First, the differences in poverty reduction due to the growth component were typically much larger than those due to the distribution component, even for episodes shorter than a decade. Second, in these 10 countries, one sees that in the five countries with the most rapid poverty reduction, *inequality increased* (Vietnam, Uganda, Bangladesh, Senegal, and Ghana). In the two countries where poverty increased (Romania and Zambia), *inequality decreased* or stayed the same.

Growth is good. A sufficiently large rise in the tide will lift nearly all boats. This change implies that if national policies are able to speed up economic growth significantly, this will almost certainly facilitate rapid poverty reduction. Our study acknowledges this important role, and it is not designed to provide new information on either the role of growth or on what policies, if any, might succeed in accelerating economic growth.

But, as discussed in chapter 3, poverty reduction is about much more than the upward speed of the national economic escalator. First, the extent to which growth provides opportunities for individuals to improve their income—through new jobs, new crops, or new business initiatives—varies greatly, depending on the sources of growth but also on how economic opportunities are either facilitated or limited by policy. Second, the national picture does not reveal the dynamics of localities, and these can easily get lost in national aggregates.

The Geography of Opportunity

If you want to get information on your pension or receive medical services, you have to first walk for 4 kilometers.
—Discussion with men, Chakax, Mexico

Policy makers increasingly recognize that location and geography are important for development. There has been a revival in the branches of economic thinking concerned with which economic activities and opportunities are located where, and why. The impact of "location, location, location" is visible in our data. In the two study regions in Tanzania (Kagera and Ruvuma) and in Malawi, where the subsampling was done based on distance to markets or roads, the results show most clearly that proximity to towns and access to markets over roads improve economic opportunity.

For instance, the Kagera study found that a household's initial endowments of assets (like land and education) matter much more for upward mobility in communities that are isolated and remote than in those that are well connected. The difference lies in the opportunities available. In remote villages, agriculture is the only route out of poverty, so starting with sufficient land matters much more. By contrast, in economically well-connected villages, households can engage in trade and business, and even those with small amounts of initial wealth can move up.

This importance of economic remoteness emerged in both the quantitative and qualitative data gathered by the study team. Quantitatively, the Kagera study was based on revisiting a set of households, spread over 51 villages in the region, that were surveyed in 1993 and again in 2004. Regression analysis was used to explain household outcomes in 2004 using characteristics measured in 1993, including age, sex, education, health, characteristics of the household head, household demographic characteristics, network characteristics, initial assets position, and community fixed effects. The results were striking. The model predicted falling down much better than it predicted moving up and out of poverty. Seventy-eight percent of the people whose assets were predicted to drop did in fact see their assets drop. In other words, for nearly four-fifths of the households that fell, this drop was predictable in 1993 based purely on observed characteristics. Upwardly mobile households were much harder to pinpoint: only about half the households that were predicted to rise did in fact do so. This finding suggests that the processes that keep people in poverty were relatively well captured by the regressions, but not the processes by which they move out of poverty.[2]

Next, the team turned to the qualitative data to examine the variation in upward mobility unexplained by the regressions. To do so, it picked life stories of individuals with similar predicted outcomes but different actual outcomes.[3] A key conclusion of this "matching" analysis was that the *interaction* of locality connectedness with an individual's starting position (land, education, etc.) was strongly associated with the different paths. In remote communities, 71 percent of "surprise risers" (those who were predicted to fall, but in fact rose) had better initial *household* conditions. But in communities that were well located and connected (close to the border, connected with roads, etc.), the household's initial conditions added little to explaining the surprise risers, accounting for only 31 percent of unexpected movement of the matched households.

Two examples from Kagera, Tanzania, illustrate the point. Located in the northern part of Kagera, Kamsoni is close to the Tanzania–Uganda border and is a major center of trade. A high-quality tarmac road, built in 2003, links the village to the regional capital of Kagera on one side and to the Ugandan border and Kampala on the other. Public transportation is available at least 10 times a day in both directions. Residents of Kamsoni engaged in various businesses, exporting agricultural produce, loading trucks, changing currency, and so on. A woman in the village spoke of the expanded set of choices that her community's location offered her. "During the harvest, I can sell crops to either country. Things like clothes and other assorted goods are cheaper here compared to other areas in Bukoba Rural District. A lot of people are seen coming here to purchase these goods. This gives me the feeling that in other places such goods are expensive, though I have never been there to compare."

As the crow flies, Ntogo is not far away from Kamsoni. It is by Lake Victoria, also close to the Ugandan border. The location offers residents some advantages: a large majority of them depend on fishing as a source of income and also engage in cross-border trade. However, residents have mixed opinions on the benefits of being so close to the lake. A man explained, "We get fish from the lake, which is delicious food. But the lake is also hindering our progress, because Ugandan leaders are not visiting us regularly. Tanzanian leaders do not care about us, because for them we are at a location in Uganda."

Unlike the good tarmac road serving Kamsoni, a dirt road leads to Ntogo. It ends abruptly at a swampy area prone to flooding, near the outlet of the Kagera river into Lake Victoria. From there the only way to travel on to Uganda is in small boats. A respondent from the village lamented, "If the road connected us to Uganda directly, say in the absence of the lake, transport and business with Uganda would be easier. Now traveling to Uganda involves engine and rowboats to cross the lake, but crossing the lake in a rowboat is risky."

The importance of roads is reflected in the growth and mobility patterns of the two clusters. In Kamsoni, it was possible to move up even from the bottom step on the ladder by dint of one's initiative and hard work. "You do not need capital to grow; being trustworthy is more important," commented one respondent in Kamsoni. The influx of money through trade created opportunities for new income-generating occupations such as brewing and distilling, running small shops, and changing money, which in turn reduced dependence on agriculture and initial wealth. Traders brought in new ideas, exposing people to life outside the village.

In contrast, agriculture was the only way out of poverty in Ntogo. Those with insufficient land, occupying the bottom three steps of the village ladder in 1993, found it difficult to move up. Most people who had been at step 1 in 1993 were reported to have died. The few who survived had stayed at the bottom step over the past 10 years. The discussion group stated that the only reason these step 1 people were even alive was that they had been helped by a charitable organization. Of those who had been at step 2 in 1993, most were reported to have either fallen further down or stagnated. It was only at step 3 and up that some people—although a minority—had risen through their own efforts, combined with support from the government.

The important effect of location for moving out of poverty emerges in many other study regions as well. Poor women and men with low initial wealth in India, for instance, find it difficult to access markets, get information on government programs, and move up if they live in communities far from the district headquarters. Displaced households in Colombia find it doubly hard to move out of poverty if they ended up in a remote barrio, far removed from jobs and services in the city centers. Those who resettled in the El Gorrión barrio, for instance, rued their inability to find work there. Given the scant employment opportunities, a job applicant's characteristics like age, appearance, and lack of references become cause for discrimination.

Job training sessions take place in the city center, making it difficult for El Gorrión residents to participate.[4]

In sum, we found that initial household conditions matter less when communities are well connected and when economic opportunity sets expand. When the economy is booming and buzzing, who you are and where you start becomes less important. We also found that there is less discrimination and greater tolerance in more connected regions (see chapter 6).

Rich and Poor in the Marketplace

The rich have more power. They have power to control the local market price.

—Discussion group in Somrampi, Cambodia

Even in favorable locations where people have physical access to markets and livelihood opportunities, it can be very difficult for poor people to use these opportunities to move up.

In the village of Somrampi, Cambodia, a majority of households grow rice for their own consumption. But the soil is not very fertile, the crop is entirely rainfed, and less than 10 percent of growers can produce enough rice to feed their families. As a result, about 85 percent of the households in the village also engage in ocean fishing for fish, shrimp, crabs, and small marine creatures such as snail eggs. The export market for these products has been expanding since the 1990s. Our team met with a group of elderly people in the village who served as key informants about livelihoods in Somrampi. Of fishing, they said, "It is our breath of life here."

But poor fisherwomen and fishermen in Somrampi are not able to exploit the potential of fishing as readily as the richer ones, some of whom are the big fish traders in the village. Poor villagers recognize the success of those who have used fishing to move out of poverty, and they long to emulate them. But they face many obstacles, beginning with their lack of assets. Most poor households do not have boats or the necessary fishing equipment or the money to buy them. Some work for those who do have boats, earning just enough for daily survival. Others collect crabs along the shore. A few poor people, especially in households where no male adult is present, buy crabs from the village market and pick them at home so they can sell the crabmeat.

Even when they have products to sell, poorer households in the village face hurdles in markets and those imposed by the government, a function of the power structures in Somrampi. Those who manage to overcome these obstacles usually have a personal connection to the traders or to the government officials who control fishing. A group of households that had fallen into poverty explained their disadvantage:

> Rich middlemen who buy crabmeat and sell it at the Kampot market are also people who have the ability to control economic opportunity in this village. As of now, there are three middlemen in Somrampi village, and all of them are classified rich and have multiple business activities. The price of crab depends on these middlemen. If they give us 10,000 riels per kilogram of crab meat, it's okay, and if they give us only 8,000 riels for the same weight it's also okay. They can help us, and they can also cause us problems by reducing the price. We are so poor, and we don't have enough productive assets such as fishing tools, agriculture tools, and so forth; hence we have to borrow money from them to buy all these instruments. Because we borrow money from them, when we get something from the sea such as marine fish, crabs, and shrimp, we have to sell to them at locally set prices. There is no choice for us to select our buyers according to what we want.

They add as an afterthought, "If we think deeply, prices are different between those offered by middlemen in the village and prices in the market. But the difference is acceptable because we earn very little output from time to time, so if we go to sell it in the market, we have to spend for motor taxi and time of selling there."

Those who have escaped poverty in Somrampi have often been able to exploit their personal connections to negotiate a better deal for themselves. A group of women told one person's story:

> Mr. Kounn was poor 10 or 12 years ago, but now he is one of the best off in the village. He dared to take risks in raising crabs, though he did not have any money in the beginning. Around the early 1990s, he contacted some traders whom he knew in Phnom Penh and borrowed thousands of dollars for this business. He also had another job: renting other people's lands for collecting oyster skin for pearls. He would sell a sack of such skin for a dollar. For a piece of land that he rented for 3 damloeung of gold, he could make 20–30 damloeung of gold from oyster skin. He could do that because he knew some traders and where to sell the oyster skins. How can poor people like us do the same thing as him? We do not know any traders or persons whom we can make a deal with like Kounn or high-ranking officials that can help facilitate such businesses. We are too small to do things like Kounn. That's why our living conditions remained the same over the past 10 years.

Corruption on the part of local authorities also favors the rich and thwarts the efforts of the poor. Some fishermen in the village use *kraleng tang*, a very fine fishing net, to catch small marine creatures. The use of the net is illegal and carries harsh penalties, but well-connected households manage to avoid the fine. Even though staff members of the government fisheries department monitor the village once or twice a month, "Those engaged in the illegal practices have good connections with the fishing authority . . . and can, therefore, continue to operate without any concern." If poor people try to use the illegal net, the hand of the law comes down hard. "If the fishery authorities arrest us, we dare not argue against them, but just pay the money according to what they demand," said a discussion group of women. "If we do not pay them, we cannot get our nets back. It's difficult to make any complaint to the court without any corruption."

The police apparently work hand in glove with the more powerful, restricting opportunities for the powerless. "The police demand money at many checkpoints along the road," continued the women. "People have no power to make any complaint. Even if they do, no one listens to them." A female trader in the village confirms, "They say they are the police and/or fishing authority, but when there are marine robberies and then we report to them for intervention, they say it is beyond their responsibility and try not to listen to us. We don't know what their roles really are."

The women concluded by reflecting on how some people in their community and not others had been able to use fishing to move out of poverty. "The poor are normally the followers. They have no savings, so they have to take time to carefully observe others' success first. But when they step in, then there are many people already in the business while demand has not increased. In 1993 we were not so different. At that time, we all had around 5 plonn [half a hectare] of rice land that was given by the government. We were about the same. There is now a huge difference. The rich are reaching for the clouds, and the poor are deepening under the earthworms' shelter. The haves lend out money and make a profit, whereas the have-nots get worse off and sooner or later sell out all their land."

This narrative from Cambodia is just one story, but it resonates with the message that emerged from countless visits to all the countries in our sample: poor people are not able to access markets on an equal footing with the rich.

Economic inequality is the most predominant axis of difference. Poor people are aware that they get unfair prices for their produce, but given their small scale of operations and neediness, they have little bargaining power.

They remain dependent on rich traders, who bail them out in times of distress but also exploit them. Poor rice farmers in Chakboeng, Cambodia, reported, "They [rich traders] purchase rice from us farmers at the same low price. We have limited options to sell our produce. It is hard to say that they put pressure on us, because many of us normally seek their help to buy farm inputs on credit. We can sell our rice to whomever we prefer, but in the end they will not listen to us when we need help from them."

Besides inequality due to wealth, our study respondents also perceive inequalities based on political connections and caste membership. In our sampled communities in India, for instance, one needs to pull strings in order to gain access to government employment programs and licenses. Evidence from communities in Uttar Pradesh suggests that political leaders manipulate government economic schemes to benefit households from their own caste or religious affiliation. In the village of Darogapur, Uttar Pradesh, the lower-caste groups are stuck in low-wage occupations like hand-rolling cigarettes and doing manual labor. The rich often do not pay them for work performed in their fields. Religious and caste divisions also affect business opportunities in the village. According to a focus group of young girls, "If a Muslim opens a shop of edibles, then the Hindus do not eat anything at that shop. Among Hindus too, if a Harijan [Dalit or untouchable] opens a shop, then the Muslims, Brahmins, and people of other castes do not eat anything at that shop."

Ethnic and religious identities are also important for accessing opportunities during or after civil conflicts. The conflict between Christians and Muslims in Lupotogo, a community in North Maluku, Indonesia, meant that Basrum, a Muslim resident of the village, could not work any longer in the nearby port area because many of the laborers working there were Christians.

Fair Access to Markets: Is the Hand Really Invisible?

In *The Wealth of Nations*, Adam Smith (1776) famously alluded to the power of the market as the "invisible hand":

> Every individual . . . neither intends to promote the public interest, nor knows how much he is promoting it. . . . He intends only his own gain, and he is in this, as in many other cases, led by an invisible hand to promote an end which was no part of his intention. Nor is it always the worse for the society that it was no part of it. By pursuing his own interest he frequently promotes that of the society more effectually than when he really intends to promote it.

Smith's invisible hand, in modern contexts, roughly translates into decentralized market economies where markets are free from government controls and where private buyers and sellers can participate on a fair and equal footing. Fair prices are supposed to be set purely by the impartial forces of demand and supply.

But Adam Smith also knew that participants in real markets would organize with a visible hand to grab whatever they could: *"People of the same trade seldom meet together, even for merriment and diversion, but the conversation ends in a conspiracy against the public, or in some contrivance to raise prices."* Our data suggest exactly such elite collusion. Poor producers and consumers in these countries lament that liberalization, rather than bringing fair prices set by supply and demand, has created rigged markets where the rich use their power to tilt both prices and scales in their favor. Poor people find themselves disproportionately affected by market changes, whether an increase in fertilizer costs in Senegal or Malawi or a fall in the price of coffee in Tanzania or tobacco in Indonesia. Moreover, even in liberalized and supposedly free markets, poor people find their efforts to participate further hampered by government intrusion that often seems to end up reinforcing the unfair market advantage of the rich and well connected.

Poor people in free markets: Problems of scale, influence, and resilience

> *Competition from big shops such as supermarkets that are able to produce on large scale and at lower cost means that a small retailer is not able to offer the customer attractive prices.*
> —Discussion with men, El Mirador, Colombia

> *If a rich person sees one of his businesses fail, there are still others that can help him bounce back.*
> —Sotero, a 51-year-old man, Newsib, Philippines

Consider a small farmer in Malawi—let us call him Charles—who has a maize farm. Let us assume that his annual production of maize is about 500 kilograms. The production requires about 50 kg of fertilizer. Assume now that Charles sells his maize for MK5 (5 Malawi kwacha) per kilogram for a total of MK2,500, and the fertilizer costs him MK750, resulting in a profit of MK1,750. Now consider Richard, a large landowner who lives in the same village as Charles. Richard's annual maize production is 5,000 kg. Because he has links with big traders in the market, he can sell his maize for MK7 per kilogram. Richard makes MK35,000 in sales and spends MK7,500 on fertilizer, resulting in a profit of MK27,500.

Let us now suppose that over the next two years, fertilizer prices increase from MK750 to MK1,500 for a 50 kg bag. Charles's profit drops to MK1,000 and Richard's to MK20,000, as long as the price of maize and the productive of their farms remain unchanged. In another two years, fertilizer prices rise still more to MK3,500 per bag. Charles is now deep into losses, but Richard is still solvent, although just barely.

The example illustrates three problems that poor producers and consumers face while selling or buying in free markets. The first is a problem of scale. Poor people buy and sell in small quantities. Thus even a small change in fixed costs—in the price of inputs, say, or the cost of transportation—has a much higher impact on them. If the charges of commuting between the village and an outlying market double, a small farmer will think twice about taking her one basket of bananas and traveling to the market, even though she knows her bananas would fetch a better price there than in the village. Her neighbor, who has a huge banana farm and can afford to hire a truck to take his produce to the market, and who expects to sell many baskets of bananas while there, may still make the trip.

Small scale, in turn, leads to the other two problems—those of influence and resilience. In the above example, Richard is able to charge MK7 per kilogram for his maize, 2 kwacha more than the price charged by Charles. Why? Because Richard produces 10 times more maize than Charles and consequently has the influence and bargaining position to negotiate for a higher price with maize buyers. Richard also has resilience. Even after fertilizer prices increase fivefold, he is able to avoid losses without increasing the rate he charges for his maize. Charles, a smaller farmer, is disproportionately affected by the change in fertilizer prices and goes under relatively quickly.

The exorbitant price and unavailability of fertilizer was cited as a common reason for falling down or being unable to move out of poverty in our sample sites in Malawi. At the time of the survey, some communities reported that fertilizer cost as much as MK4,000 for a 50 kg bag on the black market. "Our soils are disabled. They need fertilizer," said a discussion group of men in Bamlozi. "People really worked hard in their gardens, but what they harvested was so little that they could not afford fertilizer."

Poor people's lack of influence in the marketplace was also evident in Ruvuma, Tanzania, where the coffee industry was in distress. After liberalization of the coffee market, the selling price of coffee was usually set by wholesale traders. The price of coffee fell while the price of fertilizer increased

more than fourfold between 1995 and 2005. Across our study of communities in the region, small coffee producers spoke of their lack of control over
coffee prices. In Chiwolo, farmer Jyazint declared, "Do we see a free market
after liberalization or a disorganized market? The traders and buyers have
killed the coffee industry in our community. Traders are not for the interest of
farmers, nor do they think of committing some of their resources to improve
the quality of coffee so that they will be able to buy good coffee during the
successive crop seasons." The plight of small coffee producers was similar in
other communities in Ruvuma. In Ngimyoni, where 75 percent of all households cultivated coffee, liberalization led to an initial increase in coffee prices
but also to increased price volatility. Smaller farmers, who had been protected
from a rise in the price of inputs by state subsidies, were no longer shielded,
as the private traders offered no protective mechanism in times when fertilizer prices rose or coffee prices dropped.

To make matters worse, the big coffee traders in Ngimyoni reportedly
used unfair practices like fraudulent scales that helped them buy more coffee
for less money. They engaged in a practice known locally as *masomba*, meaning
sunflower (because the coffee became as weightless as a sunflower). A plastic
container known as a *dumla*, which when full contains 2 kg of dried coffee
beans, was equated to only 1 kg of coffee by the agents. Using the dumla,
traders would overfill a 50 kg bag of coffee so much that it weighed at least
60 kg. The farmer was paid for only 50 kg, while the agent got 10 kg free.

Even though the government abolished masomba in 2001, better-off villagers still exploit poor women and men by making loans to them, in cash
or in kind. Before handing over the money or goods, the lender may force
the borrower to sign an agreement attesting that he or she has borrowed
more money or materials than is actually the case. For instance, for a loan
of 10,000 Tanzanian shillings (T Sh), the borrower may be forced to attest
that she or he had borrowed T Sh 30,000—three times the actual amount.
Yokim, a 48-year-old man, spoke of his experience. "I borrowed a bull worth
T Sh 50,000 for the ceremony to end the mourning period of my late mother,
but I had to pay T Sh 80,000 three months later." Yokim had been above the
community's perception of a poverty line, but he fell into poverty during the
study period.

Some of the communities in Kagera, Tanzania, have given up coffee
farming entirely. The fall in the price of coffee was dramatic over the five
years between 1995 and 2000, as much as 90 percent in some communities.
In Nyakahora in Kagera, women said they could no longer plan for their
income. "Much as we sell coffee, we are not happy. And then coffee until

when? After all, it is a men's business. We need alternatives for women too!" At this point our field investigator asked what would happen if the prices of coffee did not go up in the next 10 years. "Nothing," the women replied. "Actually, we have even uprooted a good number of coffee plants."

Poor cultivators across study regions—with their one bag of coffee, tobacco, groundnuts, or maize—find themselves in no position to negotiate with bigger buyers. In Biralipara, Assam, a group of men pointed out, "The number of farmers has increased, and there is only one market. There are more people who come to the market to sell than to buy. Knowing this, traders buy the goods at low prices." Women in Afghanistan have few options for selling dresses that they have stitched at home. They cannot go to the local bazaar and have to rely on traders to collect and sell their products. Khori Gul, a tailor in Nasher Khan, Nangarhar, reasoned, "The price we get for one dress is not very fair. We make one dress in three or four days, and the price we get is around 300 Afghanis [about US$6]. But when it goes to market, the shopkeepers sell that dress for 1,800 Afghanis [US$36]."

Farmers know that their produce might fetch a better price if they take it to market themselves, but they have to consider the high costs of transportation. Even small increases in charges to transport produce to markets hurt small producers. Dorothea, a village farmer in Ruvuma, explained, "Farmers fail to trade in Mbinga town because of lack of reliable transport. One trip to Mbinga per person is 6,000 shillings plus 2,000 shillings per bag of maize of 90–100 kilograms. Farmers fear the expenses involved and the unreliability and uncertainty of the market. If you take your maize to Mbinga and find the selling price is low or there are no customers, what would you do?"

Another problem lies in competing with large-scale manufacturers or imported goods sold in the supermarkets. "If the government bans the import of fruits and cereals from Iran, Pakistan, and China, farmers can move up, because right now all kinds of fruit come from Iran and we cannot compete with them," said Sher Ahmad, a farmer in Zakwak Ulya, Herat, Afghanistan. For fruits and vegetables, the competition from foreign countries also depends on the exchange rate. Several farmers our field team met in Herat complained that they have to sell their products at an unprofitable price. A few farmers have started adding value to the products to close the gap; for instance, women in Zakwak Ulya turn figs into jam. But among small producers, such value addition is typically done on too small a scale to yield significant returns.

As in Afghanistan, small shopkeepers in the barrios of Colombia cannot keep pace with the products introduced in local supermarkets. In El Mirador, a local supermarket called El Potrerillo has been a source of employment in the community, but it has also displaced many small businesses. The closure of businesses is also attributed to the influx of foreign goods that have replaced domestically produced goods, a problem that at least one respondent blamed on globalization. On the other hand, in El Gorrión, where there is no supermarket, a focus group of men acknowledged that buyers go outside the community to find supermarkets "in order to save that little bit, even if it is just 50 pesos." Some small shopkeepers in the community have been forced to close down as they can no longer afford to sell cheaply.

Disadvantaged by their small scale and lack of market clout, poor producers often spiral downward into economic distress that they are ill equipped to weather. Botisi, a 55-year-old man in Matdombo, Malawi, stared at his empty granary with grief. "Look at my harvest," he told our investigator. "It is only four bags—just enough for me and my family. When I get fertilizer, I split the bag into two—half for the maize garden and the other half for the tobacco garden. It is not enough. I don't have any livestock, not even chickens. My granary is empty, and this is just the beginning of the year."

Botisi and several other Malawian farmers who had fallen into poverty over the study period blamed the rise in fertilizer prices in large part for their downfall. Some took desperate measures to remain solvent. They begged their friends for fertilizer, tried growing other crops that were not fertilizer-intensive, even undertook *ganyu* (daily wage labor) to feed their hungry children. Yet these measures were seldom enough.

In Guluteza, Malawi, men described how those who are better off want to lend fertilizers to their friends. "But then another person tells them, 'Do not dare give him fertilizer; he is a crook and he will not give it back.'" Some households have shifted from maize to other crops like vegetables or groundnuts that require less fertilizer. In Zokwaza, women started cultivating groundnuts as a cash crop. Local people noticed that the women were making more money, and soon a majority of households in the village started farming groundnuts. Due to the increase in the number of people going to sell groundnuts in the nearby market, bus services to the market at first improved. Eventually, however, the government-operated bus services stopped, and more private transporters entered the area, wanting to cash in. A woman farming groundnuts in the village explained how this change had affected her margins. "Now, if one is using the *matola* [private transport], they are more expensive. People pay 250 kwacha for transporting a bag of groundnuts. In the past, on the government buses, we could even get *katundu* boys who would assist passengers loading and off-loading their goods on the bus.

But now people have to incur all these costs, even paying those who assist them in putting their luggage on the bus."

Stretched thin, several small farmers in our study communities in Malawi have taken up ganyu. But with the rise in the number of households willing to do ganyu, not many people are actually able to find work. In the community of Lumyana, a men's discussion group said, "Poverty is just rampant here. People who can afford to hire ganyu workers are just three. Yet there are over a hundred people who are looking for ganyu."

It doesn't help small farmers that prices of other essential goods in Malawi have increased with devaluation of the currency over the years. "Necessary commodities are becoming more and more expensive," said one participant in a discussion group in Bamlozi. "It is as though you keep a certain amount of money to buy an item the following day, but then you are told that the money is not sufficient to buy that commodity because its price has increased." Food prices are the most severely affected. As in Bamlozi, households in Matdombo were facing food scarcity at the time of the field team's visit. "A farmer struggles to grow crops like tobacco amidst high prices of fertilizer. But when it comes to selling these crops, he finds that the prices have gone down. People depend on these businesses to buy food, soap, salt, and sugar. *And because they are small, they easily suffocate.* It is very easy to eat up the little capital you have due to food insecurity at home."

This is not to say that currency devaluation or ending general fertilizer subsidies are not at times necessary measures in difficult macroeconomic situations—only that the *transitions* are so much more difficult for the poor to accommodate. When relative prices change, this eliminates some opportunities and opens others. But people must be able to take advantage of these new opportunities if they are to avoid pain. When people are already on the margins, as poor women and men often are, the resilience necessary for reallocation isn't there.

How government rules and regulations restrict opportunity

> *When people think of investing their money, they see only annoyances and hassles ahead.*
>
> —Discussion group in Kagera, Tanzania

Even in supposedly the freest of markets, our study found, governments intervene in various ways seemingly designed to appease and reward the more powerful interest groups. We discuss here three primary ways in which government intervention in markets can restrict economic opportunities for the poor: through licensing of livelihoods and occupations, through rules and regulations around use of common property resources, and through allocation of benefits like jobs, credit, and inputs for agriculture.

Licensing. Governments can interfere in households' ability to expand their portfolio of activities into business. According to the World Bank's *Doing Business* report for 2008, acquiring licenses for a business in India is not easy. It takes 20 procedures and 224 days on average—and costs over five times the annual income per capita (World Bank 2007).

In the Colombian barrios, small business owners have to pay a *vacuna*, an illegal but ubiquitous tax. Poor people there and in other study sites complained that even small-scale activities like hawking and peddling require licenses from the local government—licenses that are selectively awarded. In the barrios the field teams visited in Colombia, for example, there are restrictions on permits for vending in the city center. "Getting a permit is tough," said a group of women in Villa Rosa. "You must have contacts and money. For fruit vendors, it is not a problem in the barrio, but they [the local government] don't let them sell in the city center. The vendors need a permit to sell, and to get the permit one has to speak to the syndicate of vendors and the municipality and have 200,000 pesos to give for the permit. We need the freedom to work." Permits for small businesses are also reportedly difficult to come by in some barangays in the Bukidnon region of Philippines. In Kitlong, the women reported that the *zubirri*, a local leader, distributes permits and loans "only to those who already have big businesses. That's unfair to those like us who want to put up a business."

Barriers around use of common property resources. Many poor people live by selling firewood that they gather from a nearby forest or fish they catch in a nearby lake. They thus depend for their survival on common property resources to which they have no secure access or tenure rights. Especially with respect to forest resources, government policies and regulatory frameworks often create barriers for poor women and men who live from these resources (Molnar, White, and Khare 2008). In Central and West Africa, large areas have been designated as community forest but only a fraction of this land has been allocated to communities for their use (CIFOR 2005).

In our study, we found that communities in poor rural areas of Cambodia and Africa experience such barriers intensely. Villagers in Kdadaum and Koh Phong, Cambodia, are afraid of forestry authorities for the fines they charge. "Sometimes we meet them while carrying wood and we have to spend 200,000 riels [US$50] to not be arrested. If we don't, then our cart is kept at the provincial office, and we are put in custody." In Lumyana, Malawi, a recent ban on charcoal burning along with restrictions on access to a nearby forest reserve has hurt the livelihoods of the poorest villagers. And in Kamsoni, Kagera, Tanzania, poor households that had regularly visited a nearby forest to gather firewood, timber, and materials for weaving mats lost their livelihoods when the government closed the forest to prevent deforestation. A man in the village said, "It is now scary that all guys who were laborers in the forest are turning into bandits. Those who owned the timber-cutting projects are now competing for money changing."

Rigged distribution of jobs and government schemes. Finally, governments can intervene positively by offering poor women and men credit and other inputs at subsidized rates, which can give them the initial impetus to produce and compete in markets. Or they can offer them employment opportunities in public work programs and elsewhere that guarantee precious regular income. While we found evidence of both types of assistance, it didn't always result in the desired outcomes. Stratification along social and economic lines in communities usually led to distribution of economic opportunities offered by local governments among a privileged few.

Though no longer a concern at the time of the survey, households in Indonesia reported that government jobs during President Suharto's regime had been allocated along party lines. "At that time if you were looking for work, you were questioned. If you were an NU person [supporting the opposition party], you weren't hired, but if you were a Golkar person [a ruling party supporter], you were," reported a woman in Patobako, East Java. In some communities in Malawi, it was possible to receive inputs such as seeds and fertilizers on loan from the government. But our respondents spoke of considerable inequality in access. "We can register our names with the agricultural adviser in order to get fertilizers and maize seeds on loan," said a group of men in Matdombo. "But after the exercise someone can sneak around and influence the adviser to delete some of our names, saying that we are very poor and would not pay back the loan at the end of the growing season. This causes inequality since some people can get more fertilizer while others like the poor cannot get anything and remain in poverty."

Discretionary behavior on the part of the local government was commonly seen in the Indian study communities that are divided along caste, religious, and political lines. Benefits of government schemes for credit, jobs, and housing are perceived to accrue to those who belong to the ruling party's caste or religion. Even so-called public goods are not entirely free from capture. Infrastructure projects, for example, are reportedly allotted to contractors close to the local panchayat, often resulting in poor construction quality. A group of women our team interviewed in Langpuria, Assam, spoke of bribe taking in their village. "The contractors pocket 95 percent of the amount sanctioned for such works and spend only 5 percent of the amount for development," they said. "They construct bamboo bridges in place of concrete roads."

Programs that do help are usually either those that result in the provision of some quasi-public goods, like roads or irrigation works, that can benefit everyone, or programs that are specifically targeted toward poor people. But even targeted subsidies and transfers are often distributed discriminately—and not necessarily to those most in need.

In sum, our evidence suggests a very *visible* distortion of the market in favor of dominant groups and against poor people. Sometimes there is a deliberate attempt by the elite to capture a larger share of the gains available, for example through the practice of masomba. Poor people often lack the scale, influence, and resilience needed to get a toehold in markets and to negotiate a better return for their produce. In some cases, this problem has been an inadvertent outcome of efforts by governments to open up markets, as these efforts sometimes result in markets with little competition and greater volatility of input and output prices.

How Does One Expand Opportunities and Unrig Markets?

Markets and government rules about markets *could* be unrigged and opportunity sets expanded for all. Although each local situation is different and requires different interventions, poor people in our study suggested five general approaches that could help: construction of roads; promotion of access to new markets; investments in inputs like water, electricity, and telecommunications; provision of more credit; and easing of access to land, land titles, and business licenses. In all these cases, the manner in which government services are delivered—whether the government is responsive and fair to all, or corrupt and captured by a few—can either enhance opportunities or curb them. Economic organizations of poor people, whether self-help groups or associations, also can help them boost their bargaining power in markets. This important issue is discussed in detail in chapter 7.

Roads: Making crucial connections

> *Earlier, people would cross the river with their vegetables by a ferry boat.*
> *The bridge has been very helpful for them. Now a truck can directly go to*
> *the gardens. There has been a vegetable revolution in the village.*
> —Discussion with key informants, Chamgotia, Bangladesh

In his bestseller *The Tipping Point*, Malcolm Gladwell (2000) spoke of the pivotal role of "connectors": individuals who "act as conduits . . . helping to engender connections, relationships and 'cross-fertilization' that otherwise might not have occurred." Although Gladwell was talking about human connectors, our data suggest that roads are among the few policy tools that can serve as connectors in regions where poor people live. They create links between people in remote rural areas and the outside world, and between small farmers and traders looking for a good crop. They promote cross-fertilization of ideas— about planting new seeds, using new technologies, producing new products to meet new demands. Moreover, unlike Gladwell's connectors, roads require no prior knowledge or personal relationship for change to spread. Roads are the most *impersonal* mechanism that makes a difference, and almost universally so, across our sample of communities in different study contexts.

Roads serve as catalysts for new occupations. Villages in the study sites in Cambodia with good roads are generally more dynamic, with thriving small businesses. In Chakboeng, a village that received a road in 2000, a group of young men described the change: "The number of village shops selling groceries, secondhand or new dresses, and household commodities has increased remarkably since 2000." In Chamgotia, Bangladesh, a newly constructed bridge on a nearby river and an 11-kilometer tarmac road have changed the lives of about 120 families in the village who used to depend on daily wage labor for a living. They now work as van drivers and rickshaw pullers, earning much more than before. Lower transport costs have also considerably lowered the costs of selling for those cultivating rice and vegetables in the village. As in Kagera, Tanzania, farmers in Chamgotia can easily transport their produce to nearby towns on the road instead of carrying it on their heads or ferrying it by boat across the river.

Finally, roads save time on travel. This time can then be spent on other economic activities, leading to diversification of income sources and mobility. In Shazimir, a community near Kabul in Afghanistan, our respondents discussed how the newly constructed road was helping them. "You know what they say: Time is gold. Shopkeepers very frequently lost time on the way to the city center. Thanks to this road, they save at least half an hour to go to the bazaar. It took usually one hour; now it takes 30 minutes."

Communities not connected to passable roads face severe challenges. In Langpuria, Assam, people spoke of destroying their own crops because buyers cannot reach them. Women in the village lamented, "*Vyaparis* [businessmen] from nearby towns do not come to buy our produce because of the bad communication system. As a result we are not getting the expected price for our produce. Some cultivators are forced to damage their produce themselves because of nonavailability of customers. No one is ready to buy vegetables even at 20 paisa [less than 1 cent] per kilogram." In an isolated village in Kagera, Tanzania, a bunch of bananas sells for half as much as it would fetch in a nearby trading center. But the only way to reach the trading center is on foot. Our respondents noted, "Although this trading center is only 4 kilometers away, the path going there is very steep and traverses a cliff, making transport of bunches of banana on foot very difficult."

In addition to facilitating economic opportunities, roads are also seen to be agents of small but definite social changes. They make it easier to reach hospitals and schools. Young girls who were earlier wary of traveling long distances to learn said they are now enrolling in school. Women in communities with roads spoke of how they can now frequent markets and return home in a timely manner. A 32-year-old woman in Kamsoni, Kagera, praised the new tarmac road as she can now "go to town without informing my husband because I am sure of coming back and cooking, even before the children return from school." At times, the very presence of a road elevates the status of those living in the village. A group of men in Rahamat, a village in rural Uttar Pradesh, noted that cars can now easily reach their village for social ceremonies like marriages. "Having a road has improved the social status of the villagers," they said.

In addition to roads connecting communities to the outside world, paved roads within villages are also important. In India, our respondents described how muddy earthen tracks in their villages are health hazards and barriers to movement. Interviewees in Darogapur felt that the brick soling of tracks within the village has helped. "[Earlier] there was mud in the rainy season. It was difficult for the animals to move. People had to carry their crops and fodder for animals on their heads, and they were always fearful of slipping. After brick soling, the road has become wider and the streets of the village are now dry. Now motorbikes, bicycles, and jeeps can easily come into the village. People can easily carry their can of milk on their bicycle and go to the market. There is prosperity in the village."

Markets: Engines of change

During the season we sell our fruits at a very cheap price and in a very short time because we don't have cold storage to keep them and we can't reach different cities in Afghanistan. The lack of access to market will cause [farmers] to fail.

— Discussion with men, Zakwak Ulya, Herat, Afghanistan

In today's seamless, borderless world markets, competition from all parts of the world determines metal, bullion, and stock prices. But in small, rural communities such as those in our sample, the physical marketplace remains the focus of exchange. In his *Principles of Economics*, Alfred Marshall (1890) argued that small neighborhood markets were best suited to certain types of trade—"things which must be made to order to suit particular individuals, such as well-fitting clothes; and perishable and bulky goods, such as fresh vegetables, which can seldom be profitably carried long distances." Men and women in our communities in some ways justify Marshall's rationale for the local market. They can barely carry crops like bananas profitably over long distances to a big, wholesale market, so they depend on their local market to sustain sales.

The establishment of a new marketplace, however small, is considered a harbinger of increased economic opportunities within a community. Across our sample, nearly 28 percent of communities where people believed that economic opportunities had improved over the study period also reported the presence of a daily or weekly market. In contrast, only about 9 percent of communities where economic opportunities had supposedly contracted over the same period had a market. Having a market within a community implies multiple benefits. It provides space for people to set up their own shops, allowing them to diversify and increase their sources of income. It usually leads to better returns for farmers and small traders, who no longer have to bear the heavy costs of transportation to distant markets. And it spurs consumer dynamism within the community, creating virtuous circles in which new shops open to satisfy increasing demand.

In Purani village, Uttar Pradesh, a weekly market was set up in 1995. It functions every Wednesday and Saturday, and traders looking to buy agricultural produce from farmers in Purani visit the market on those two days. Farmers who previously were forced to carry their produce long distances to district markets now only need to display samples of their wares. Only when satisfied with the price do they invite the traders to collect the crop from their fields. A men's discussion group on livelihoods explained, "The difference is that earlier [when they took their crop to distant markets], the traders paid us as per their choice. As we had to carry the crop all the way, we did not want to carry it back, so we sold it at whatever price we received. Now there are traders in the village itself. We show a sample of the yield to them, and if we like the rates we sell it to them and they carry the product from our houses."

Support to production: Water, electricity, telephones, and farm inputs

Now we can keep the vegetables we buy at the weekly souk [market] for the entire week. We can prepare fresh salads, as they do in cities. We have now begun to live as human beings instead of living to the rhythm of the hens—going to bed early and rising early.
—A man in Lamraab, Morocco, on benefits of receiving electricity

Farming is still our main source of income. But we recently added another income-generating business like e-load and cell phone charging. It helped us a lot because it is where we get the money to buy formula milk for our only child. My wife also helped by selling cooked food in the school.
—Mohama, a 30-year-old chronic poor man, Glikati, Philippines

Besides roads and markets, creation of infrastructure such as assured water supply, electricity, and telephone networks can greatly enhance economic opportunities within communities. Equally important is the provision of affordable inputs and technical support for farming.

Water. Water is a crucial resource, especially since agriculture is the main source of livelihood in nearly 94 percent of the communities where we could gather community-level data. Communities that depend on the rains for farming are at a disadvantage compared to communities where permanent irrigation structures ensure a year-round water supply. Fifty-nine percent of communities that reported an improvement in economic opportunities also reported improved availability of irrigation inputs. In comparison, only 32 percent of communities where economic opportunities had narrowed over the study period reported an improvement in irrigation facilities.

Two communities in West Bengal illustrate the difference. A majority of the population of both villages is engaged in the cultivation of rice. However, in one village, Parasya, water is available all year through canals from a nearby dam. These canals were dug in 1998 through the combined efforts of the West Bengal irrigation division and the local district council. They were designed to channel water from the dam to as large an area as possible, and they have greatly boosted the community's production of rice, a water-intensive crop. The constant water supply has also helped farmers grow vegetables. Our team met farmers in the village who identified the system of canals as the main reason for their prosperity.

Compare this to the scenario in Gutri village. Also dependent on rice farming, Gutri has the advantage of being close to a river. Yet that does farmers no good, because no working canals exist to bring water from the river to their fields. In 1998, people in Gutri asked their local authorities to repair and further excavate an old canal that had linked fields in the village to the river and also helped reduce the overflow of water during the rainy season. The canal had not been reexcavated for a long time and was practically unusable. Despite their pleas, at the time of the survey in 2005, the canal was yet to be repaired.

Men and women in Gutri described their plight: "Earlier, agriculture was the way to development. But now it depends on rainwater. Farmers are able to manage only one crop a year, while years ago we could cultivate two. Farmers are now facing losses due to low yields, as are the agricultural laborers, because their work is now confined mainly to the sowing and harvesting period. They get work for only two months in a year. For the rest of the time, they sit idle. If floods occur in the river, the situation becomes worse. Then there is no work for even these two months. Moreover, the extra rainwater does not pass due to blockages in the canal." The village has four primary schools and received electricity a year before the survey, but as one of our respondents said, "For people who cannot afford even two square meals a day, education means nothing at all. Electricity is of no use to them. The first important thing for them is to perform work from which they can earn and get food. The people from the labor class are now almost dying and the panchayat has not paid any attention to the repair of the canal."

In Ramili Qali, Afghanistan, a grape-farming community that lost its irrigation structures in the war, villagers judged the reconstruction of the irrigation siphon in 2005 to be the most positive recent event for the prosperity of the community. Key informants noted, "When the intake was rebuilt, all our fields started being irrigated again. Of course, the grapevines did not immediately regrow and produce, but it allowed our farmers to grow other things, like wheat, maize, and poppy. Nowadays, the grapevines are growing again. It might take up to seven years to get back to the level of production we had before the war."

In contrast, the village of Namdenye in Ruvuma, Tanzania, was suffering a severe water crisis that villagers described as one of the most important factors causing a decline in their well-being. The village never had access to tap water, depending instead on water from shallow wells, most of which were nonoperational at the time of the study team's visit. The closest river is 27 kilometers away. The government took steps to address the problem by constructing three shallow wells, but these only worked for two months. Villagers blamed the failure of the project on poor workmanship: the wells apparently were dug during the rains when the water table was high, and when the rains ended, they went dry.

Lack of water constrains prosperity in Namdenye in several ways. Villagers remain dependent on the rains to grow their crops. They cannot build more permanent, burned-brick houses, as such construction requires a significant amount of water. With no local water supply even for drinking, people risk their lives to fetch water from ponds in a nearby wild game reserve. Women and girls waste precious productive hours searching for water. When found, it is often not safe for human use, and the village has seen an increase in waterborne diseases such as cholera, typhoid, and dysentery.

Electricity. Although less vital for survival than water, electricity is a precious resource for poor women and men. It helps even the poorest set up small cottage industries at home, something especially useful for women. Women across our study regions—especially in East Asia, where more villages are electrified—spoke of how they can make pickles, jams, and other foods at night and sell them in the market the next day.

San Dogon, a barangay in Bukidnon, Philippines, is a good example of how electricity can have multidimensional impacts on prosperity. Households in the barangay said that the arrival of electricity has opened a number of new livelihood opportunities for them, such as selling ice candy, which they stored in their electric refrigerators. Women with electric sewing machines can earn money sewing at home. Farming, too, received a boost as residents now operate electric irrigation pumps that ensure a regular supply of water. One person said, "The residents were overjoyed to see an abundant supply of water. Our forefathers did not have that opportunity before. It spells the difference in our lives. Some people are into backyard gardening. They were able to plant vegetables and flowers even during the dry season because we are assured of water supply."

In other study sites too, women spoke of how electricity had eased their lives. In the remote community of Rancho San Juan, Oaxaca, Mexico, where livelihood choices are limited, women can weave sombreros at night and earn some additional money. They exclaimed with delight that they can now get news over radio and television and grind corn in electric grinders to make tortillas.

Finally, well-lit streets after sunset contribute to better law and order in a community. Women find it easier to step out of their homes at night. So do older people, who can walk without fear of falling into ditches or being bitten by animals and snakes.

Telephones. While electricity is bringing change to barangays in the Philippines, rural villages in Bangladesh are being transformed by cell phones. Satgailijhara is one of the villages in our study sample that gained from the construction of a Grameen Phone telephone and telegraph tower. Although the tower was only built in 2003, the benefits are already plain to see. Those who have gained most are small traders looking to start a new business in the community. Abdul explained the advantages of having a cell phone. "Earlier, one had to travel a long distance and carry rice and pulses for either selling or personal consumption. Now one need not travel with goods. Earlier people spent 200 taka for carrying goods; now they only need to spend 10 taka for making two phone calls. Those who have poultry farms, for example, need to make only a few phone calls. The parties would rush to them to take the delivery of poultry birds."

A few people in Satgailijhara have opened shops selling mobile phones and are making good profits. Women have started operating cell phones on a hire basis, bringing in additional income to their families. For some poor people, the phones have allowed seamless flows of credit and finance that were previously difficult to access. Mohammed said, "The Grameen tower has contributed a lot. When I urgently need money for purchasing land, I telephone my brother who is working in the city. What a big advantage!" The brother then wires money via his cell phone to the local bank, which Mohammed can collect the next morning. Mohammed's experience corroborates the benefits of mobile banking innovations under way in other developing countries, such as South Africa's "virtual bank" and Kenya's M-PESA. The reduction in transaction costs for wiring money through cell phones—as Mohammed's brother did—is dramatic.

In our study, communities that reported an increase in economic opportunities over the study period were also ones where the presence of public phone networks had more than quadrupled since 1995. By contrast, in the communities where opportunities had decreased, phone connectivity was only 1.5 times greater than it had been a decade earlier.

Inputs and technical support for farming. Better agricultural techniques and access to affordable inputs can make a big difference to agricultural productivity. In 66 percent of the communities that reported an improvement in economic opportunities, respondents also reported improvement in access to agricultural inputs. Access to such inputs improved in only 39 percent of communities where economic opportunities had reportedly decreased.

In villages in Kagera, Tanzania, government officials are credited for improvements in farming skills and for a shift to production of crops like tomatoes. Households that have moved out of poverty in both villages are thankful for the training provided by agricultural extension officers. A mover in Kamsoni said, "I got advice from a government farmer extension worker in 1994 on how to produce tomatoes. Afterwards, I have been cultivating tomatoes which have contributed to my income. I have managed to keep my family and build a house."

The importance of agricultural innovation is evident in our sampled communities in Uttar Pradesh, West Bengal, and Bangladesh. In the latter two regions, cultivation of high-yielding varieties of rice has brought dividends for farmers. The harvest period for these varieties is much smaller, and their yield is higher.[5] In Uttar Pradesh, cultivation of cash crops such as sugarcane and peppermint is reported to have improved the fortunes of entire villages. In Shekhapur village in Sitapur district, moving out of poverty is seen to be a process of gradual accumulation through investment in cultivation of sugarcane. This investment includes purchase of higher-yielding varieties of seeds and agricultural equipment. Most movers in sugarcane-growing areas attempted to add value to their commercial crop by purchasing equipment (threshers, tractors, and cane crushers) and by sowing high-yielding varieties of cane.

Credit: Boost to initiative

The organizations themselves are the main obstacles for expanding business activities, because they provide lower amounts of loans. That is why many people do not become members, though they need the loan. They need bigger loans.

—Discussion with men, Pirjadi, Bangladesh

While roads, irrigation networks, and markets help open opportunities, obtaining affordable credit is often the key that allows people to take advantage of these opportunities to start a business or improve their farming. In Galalolo, a community in North Maluku, Indonesia, farmers who had benefited from lower interest on formal credit provided under the Kecamatan Development Program summed up: "Having capital means having no difficulties."

The importance of credit is reflected in our quantitative data. Communities that rated their economies as strong or very strong at the time of the survey were also more likely to rely on government banks as a source of credit. Almost 40 percent of the economically strong communities, but only about a quarter of the economically weak communities, said that government banks were among the top two sources of credit in their area. Households in local economies rated weak or very weak were more likely to rely on friends, relatives, and moneylenders than on banks for their financial needs.

The mere presence of formal credit facilities, however, isn't enough. For several reasons, poor people in many communities find it difficult or impossible to obtain adequate loans on good terms from these sources. Figure 5.3 sums up the hurdles poor people face in accessing credit.

One of the first constraints identified by poor people across communities is that the loans offered by different organizations—civil society or the government—are simply not large enough to be transformative. Despite the popularity of microfinance, tiny loans seldom allow people to build more productive, permanent assets, so they remain trapped in low-total-return activities. Alam, a man in the village of Digbari, Bangladesh, expressed discontent with the size of loans granted by microfinance institutions in his community. "I think NGOs have been the beneficiaries. What has happened to the millions they have collected? This is our money. Yet we get only 3,000 taka as loans while they earn millions of taka."

FIGURE 5.3

Poor entrepreneurs face obstacles in gaining access to credit

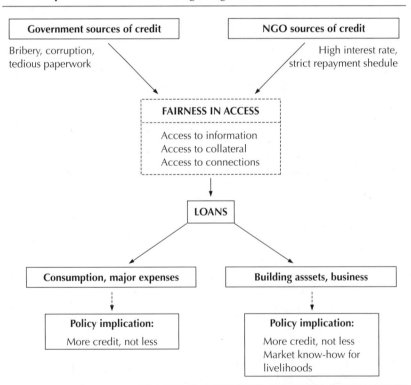

The tendency is for these small loans to be used not for production but for daily consumption and pressing household needs. A sudden expense such as a marriage in the family, a funeral, an illness, or even abject hunger can force a poor family to use a loan toward nonproductive ends. Across study regions, households stuck in chronic poverty were far more likely than movers to borrow for regular consumption purposes (figure 5.4).

Under such circumstances, servicing loans becomes a financial drain on households. In Chanpasha, one of the Bangladesh communities that has witnessed a surge in microcredit, men admitted, "Loan facilities have become easier than in the past. However, many are taking loans for business but spending them in unproductive sectors of the family. So they are unable to repay their loan installments in due time. Loan repayment, therefore, is playing a major role in the increase of their expenditure."

In Korrapadu, Andhra Pradesh, men and women recognized that the state-led initiative on self-help groups is providing them with valuable credit.

FIGURE 5.4

A majority of chronic poor borrow for regular consumption purposes

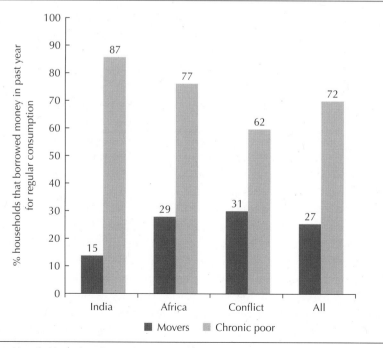

Source: Household questionnaire.

But they added that the loans only help them cope. "We continue to work hard. But if an unplanned event happens, we are left with a big problem. We seek loans for weddings, constructing houses, treatment, and deliveries." In Mzaponda, Malawi, women agreed: "Our businesses are failing to expand just because the operating capital is very minimal. [We overuse credit] in trying to solve our own problems like buying food and other things that may need money to be addressed. . . . If our capital had been big, then this would not have been happening."

The second constraint poor people face in the credit market is fair access. Even in communities where formal loan facilities are present, poor men and women find themselves excluded for three reasons: they lack information about credit; they are unable to offer collateral demanded by formal lending organizations; and they lack the political connections to be approved for loans or, alternatively, the wherewithal to bribe loan officers.

"We hear from other places like Mbinga that there are credit facilities," said Yusta, a woman in Chiwolo, a village in Ruvuma, Tanzania. "But we do not know how to access them, and nobody has come to explain this to us." Households in Maguli, another community in Ruvuma, also cited lack of information as the primary reason for their inability to tap credit schemes. Alex, a 50-year-old farmer and fisherman our team met in Maguli, said people are organizing savings and credit cooperative societies as an alternative to more formal credit sources. But it is difficult for people to join the societies, he said, because they have not been trained in how to use financial services.

At other times, getting credit is hard because of poor women's and men's inability to offer collateral. Not all farmers in Abzif, Morocco, have benefited from the local agricultural credit bank. A discussion group in the community explained why. "The majority of the inheritance here is nonconsigned, that is, without deeds. The farmers therefore lack legal title of ownership and cannot guarantee a repayment to the bank." This problem is particularly intense for the displaced households our team interviewed in Colombia, who have no land, no property, and no guarantee from anyone to offer as collateral. A discussion group with women in Villa Rosa, a barrio of displaced people, said, "The local credit organization lends money at 2 percent. But you have to have a small business for more than a year, and bring documents showing you own a property that is in good condition. If you don't have that, you must have a guarantor and bring an account of expenses and an inventory." The displaced people in El Mirador, Colombia, face a similar dilemma. "Banks demand papers showing property rights to a building," said a discussion group of men. "Credit organizations demand licenses and guarantors, which the people cannot produce, and if they get money, it is only a fifth of what they had asked for."

The constraint of political patronage and corruption is particularly strong in the South Asian context. Women in Hasanbagh, Bangladesh, reported that "no loan can be obtained without giving money to the officers of the local bank. . . . The officers receive both an official salary and a bribe." In Donekal, Andhra Pradesh, women agreed: "If we go to the banks for loans, they ask us to bring this paper and that paper. If we go to the mandal [block] office for statements, it is difficult. They talk in a careless manner. Things do not work out properly. We incur a lot of expenditure. Bribes have increased, and work is delayed."

The third constraint consists of high interest rates and strict installment schedules enforced by organizations offering loans. This is particularly true of civil society organizations. In Kamlondo, Uganda, people fear taking loans from NGOs after a poor experience with an organization that offered short-term loans at 25 percent interest with a seven-day repayment period. Several borrowers have had their properties attached because of failure to repay. Many communities in Bangladesh also complained of the high interest rates and frequent installments they have to pay to microfinance institutions. Men in Shantakalia said, "If we take a loan of 15,000 taka, we have to pay back 30,000 within nine months. If we fail to repay, then we have to sell our land for repayment."

Lending organizations in some communities restrict credit to certain types of production, effectively constraining poor people from following the livelihood of their choice. In Guluteza, Malawi, Andrea, a 52-year-old chronic poor man, was forced into farming tobacco as no organization in his village would provide fertilizer on credit to farmers who grow any other crop. "I had a very bad experience with joining these groups," said Andrea in his life story interview. "I started tobacco farming, and at that time, I joined the tobacco farmers club through which I could get fertilizer loans. But after realizing very little from my tobacco sales, I still had to pay about 9,000 kwacha for fertilizer and another 8,000 kwacha for some club charges and credits, and I only got 11,000 kwacha from my tobacco sales. This was a very bad experience for me, and from then on, I made up my mind never to join any group dealing with monetary issues. I realized that credit is very painful."

Finally, even where credit is available, many poor entrepreneurs feel they lack the skills to make productive use of the loan. In Hasanbagh, Bangladesh, Barku said, "The societies give loans for small grocery shops, vegetable business, purchase of rickshaws, etc. But then, after giving loans, they do not monitor the ways the loans are used. Even if someone throws the money into the pond, they would not care. People are using the loans for family purposes. Some are constructing houses, buying cows, and repaying debts with the loan money." In Aludonay, Philippines, getting a loan is "not a guarantee that one would succeed, especially if you don't know how to run a business." Residents of the community long for comprehensive livelihood programs. "They should come up with livelihood projects for farmers so that they will no longer take loans," suggested a discussion group of men. "Loans would only add to debts for farmers."

Land titling and business licensing

> *Authorizations are not distributed fairly, but are based on corruption and clientelism. If you give money, you will receive your permit in two days. If you don't, you'll be sent from one department to another until you give up your project or pay the bribe.*
> —Discussion with women, Izrane, Morocco

Legal and financial reforms undertaken by governments can bolster people's ability to take economic initiative in several ways. For farmers, opportunities for land titling can be key facilitators of greater success. For traders, reasonable legal requirements for starting a business, obtaining licenses, employing workers, registering property, getting credit, trading across borders, and paying taxes can aid profitability.

Land reform and land titling. For poor people, gaining legal title to their land is crucial on two counts: it gives the household some semblance of food security and permanence, and it opens doors to other opportunities, including access to credit. Our study found that even in communities where credit sources are present, having a land title is usually the only way to qualify to receive loans from banks. This is a particular problem in communities that consist mainly of immigrants or people resettled from other places. In the Colombia sample, for instance, most communities reported that banks demand papers proving land ownership, which the displaced are unable to produce. In other study regions too—Kagera in Tanzania, rural communities in Afghanistan, and·the states in India, among others—documents showing ownership of land are a necessary condition for obtaining loans.

Moreover, people without title can be booted off their land. Households in Biralipara, Assam, for instance, live each day under the threat of eviction. Located on the border of another Indian state, Nagaland, and a forest reserve, the land and all the houses in the village are the property of the forest department. "People are insecure because anytime they could be asked to leave this place, as they do not have ownership over this land," remarked a discussion group. "One week earlier we heard that the entire village would be taken over by the government. We feel very insecure and helpless. We cannot imagine what our condition will be if we have to leave our houses. We do not have any idea where we will go with our little children." A few other communities in Assam are in a similar position; more than 80 percent of households in some of them do not have land titles in their name.

One-time land reforms initiated by local governments in some communities have reduced initial inequalities in ownership of assets and spurred individual initiative in farming and business. Land titles also provide poor people with valuable collateral against which they can access credit. Nearly 30 percent of communities where opportunities had expanded over the study period also witnessed a land reform program during this time, whereas land reform had taken place in only 13 percent of communities where opportunities had become fewer. The association between land titling and strength of the local economy in our communities is revealing. In communities with strong or very strong local economies in 2005, nearly 86 percent of households reported holding legal title to land, but in communities with weak or very weak economies, only 58 percent did (figure 5.5).

FIGURE 5.5
Land titling is strongly associated with perceived strength of local economy

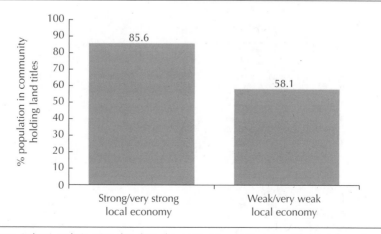

Source: Authors' analysis using data from the community questionnaire with key informants and responses to the question "How strong is the local economy at the present time? Very strong, strong, medium, weak, or very weak?" *N* = 452 communities.

Although there is evidence that public works projects can help local prosperity, the association of public works with local economic strength is not as marked. There is only a slight difference between communities with stronger and weaker local economies in the incidence of public works projects (figure 5.6). If public works are well targeted, there should be more of them in less prosperous communities.

Licensing. Abzif, a community in Beni Mellal province in Morocco, was among those in our sample where economic opportunities had improved considerably over the study period. In large part, this improvement was due to the ease with which the local government in Abzif provided licenses to start projects and small businesses. A discussion group of women in the community said, "The authorizations are easily given. The small activities have proceeded without problems: phone boutiques, sewing shops, hairdresser shops, and electricians. Ten years ago people didn't have the same odds of accessing economic opportunities. The authorizations for projects were the privilege of some categories of the community: big rich families who were close to politicians. People were also not safe or immune from

FIGURE 5.6
Public works projects are not strongly associated with perceived strength of local economy

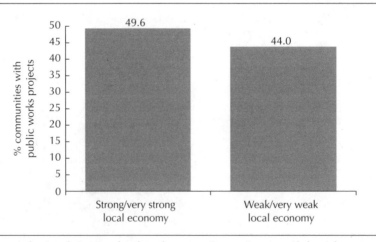

Source: Authors' analysis using data from the community questionnaire with key informants and responses to the question "How strong is the local economy at the present time? Very strong, strong, medium, weak, or very weak?" N = 452 communities.

some injustices. Now the situation has improved a little: the authorizations are accessible, and the concerned authorities support the people who have projects in agriculture, cooperatives, handicrafts, shops, or sewing."

As in Abzif, it seems that local governments elsewhere, if they wanted, could make the process of setting up businesses easy. In fact, the ease with which local governments make business licenses available was an important factor distinguishing high-performing communities from those where the local economy was considered weak. But it was disheartening to find that in most communities, people seeking licenses had resigned themselves to a long and costly process.

In India, where acquiring a license often takes seven months and costs five times the annual income per capita (World Bank 2007), poor entrepreneurs seem to take the process for granted. For our respondents in Uttar Pradesh—a state where bribe taking and corruption are more widespread than in any of the other Indian states in the sample—the practice of giving bribes to get a license is a way of life. In Rahamat, a prospering community in the state that has benefited from roads and improved irrigation structures, people spoke of being forced to give bribes to start any business. "You need a license to start a big business. The licenses are distributed at the district level, and middlemen make money for giving the license. This is common. For example, meat shops, poultry rearing—all need a license," said Shabbir, a village resident. In Doola Mau, corruption is so widespread that nothing can be done without giving a bribe. "Those who pay more can get their work done faster," women said. "Because the poor don't have money to give bribes, their work is never done." Nor can poor people in most communities rely on law enforcement to deter bribe taking. The police in Dinapur, a farming community in Uttar Pradesh, are reported to collect levies regularly. Women spoke of how "the police inspector comes every month and people have to give to him . . . whatever you call it, tax or expenses."

Worse, our quantitative data suggest that corruption around procedures is more prevalent in communities where the opportunity sets have reportedly expanded. Those trying to take advantage of new opportunities find themselves swimming against a current of increasing corruption rather than propelled along by a pro-business stream (figure 5.7). At the time of our survey, in 2005, 50 percent of such communities reported that "most or almost all" local government officials are corrupt; only about 21 percent recalled this extent of corruption at the start of the study period 10 years earlier. In comparison, only 42 percent of communities where opportunities decreased over

FIGURE 5.7
Big increases in corruption were reported in communities where opportunities have expanded

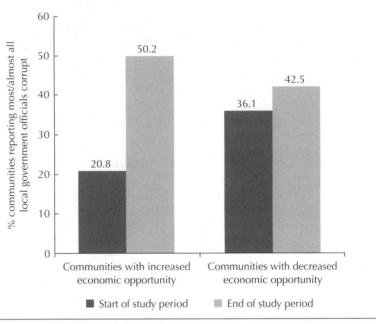

Source: Authors' analysis using data from the community questionnaire with focus group discussions and responses to the question "Compared to 10 years ago, do people in the community have more, about the same, or fewer economic opportunities?" *N* = 450 communities.

the study period reported that a majority of local government officials are corrupt, not much higher than the 36 percent that thought so 10 years ago. Thus the perceived jump in corruption was markedly higher in communities where more opportunities had become available.

Our qualitative data suggest that as communities gradually climb the ladder of prosperity, they create spaces for more rules and regulations around licensing and other processes that can be twisted to serve the interests of local officials. Households in our sampled villages give in to bribery because they believe that giving eventually means receiving.

Conclusion and Policy Recommendations

People in poverty want economic opportunity. When opportunity sets expand in a dynamic local economy, people can take initiative and move up or out of poverty. All too often, however, people find channels of upward movement blocked and their initiatives thwarted. There is nothing in our study to gainsay the key role of rapid economic growth in creating the conditions for poverty reduction, but there is clearly more that can be done—in environments of slow or rapid growth—to expand opportunity and unblock paths to mobility for poor people.

Location matters, and so does connectedness. Within national economies, there are large variations between localities in the rate of progress. One important reason is disparities in infrastructure and in ease of connection to the outside world. Thus, a powerful lever for increasing economic dynamism and opportunity is the provision of quasi-public goods like permanent roads, physical market spaces, irrigation waterways, telephone networks, electricity, and cheap, reliable transport. Roads, in particular, improve villages' access to markets, credit sources, schools, and health services. Remote communities not reached by passable roads are at a large disadvantage, unable to tap markets and attract service providers. Connecting communities with roads also has positive spillover effects in the social domain. Our evidence suggests that as communities get connected with the larger society, the hold of the traditional elite usually weakens and patron-client relations become less important for survival.

Fair access to markets is key. Conversations with chronic poor and movers in the various study sites reveal the many ways in which equal opportunity at the local level remains a myth. Rather than being guided by an invisible hand, markets are often rigged by visible hands in ways that disfavor poor producers and consumers. Poor people typically lack both the scale and the expertise needed to overcome these obstacles. At the mercy of big players in the formal marketplace, poor producers often operate on the fringes, in an informal economy of petty trading, micro-agriculture, and sharecropping. A focus on expanding opportunities for poor people requires analysis of the business climate not just for large, formal producers but for tiny and small entrepreneurs at the bottom and for those moving up.

Our study highlights the potential of *liberalization from below*.[6] Even where the opening up of markets has had an initial positive impact, as in some communities in Tanzania, this effect quickly wanes, because poor people must deal with high prices for inputs and low prices for their produce. Liberalization from below is different from liberalization that helps only the rich or middle class. In China, for example, the big surge in poverty reduction came soon after agricultural markets were liberalized in such a way that even poor, small farmers could buy and sell surpluses on their own terms. In rural communities, opening up procurement chains and markets, increasing local grain storage capacity, and improving access to information on prices are some measures that can usher in better returns to poor people. Economic organization of poor people can play a critical role. The initiative to bring about change can come from any institution—government, civil society, or the private sector.

ITC, a private sector company in India, is placing computers in villages to facilitate its agribusiness. In less than five years, the program has connected more than 3 million medium farmers in India to markets through village-based Internet kiosks called *e-choupals*.[7] After checking prices at no charge on the ITC computers, farmers can choose to buy or sell through ITC or go to local markets instead. Efficiency improvements in transactions have led to increased revenues both for farmers and for ITC. Only 10 percent of the farmers using e-choupals are poor, however, and ITC is now setting up part-nerships with poor people's organizations to increase coverage. Collective action and economic organizations of poor people are very important and are discussed in chapter 7.

Poor entrepreneurs need more and better finance. Poor people often cannot access formal credit facilities or do not have the collateral to obtain loans. Many depend on moneylenders for credit. Even when poor households man-age to access formal credit, they typically receive small loans at high rates of interest. These are used relatively quickly for everyday consumption and do little to improve a household's productive capacity. Debt repayment itself becomes a major part of household expenditure. Poor people need larger loans, new and innovative financing arrangements for small enterprise, and support in making best use of credit.

Local governments can either block or spur economic dynamism. Strong local democracies that ensure property rights and a positive business environment are critical for ensuring that the benefits of opening up markets are more equally shared. However, land titling, business licensing, and other economic policies adopted by local democracies often help only the socially dominant, wealthier class. Corruption in local institutions affects poor people more negatively than rich people, who have the capacity to either control or bypass such institutions. Hence, attempts to help poor women and men improve their economic lives have to take into account the local dynamics of social and political power.

In sum, when our lens shifts to conditions at the local level, we can better understand how to expand opportunity sets for poor people and help facili-tate their own initiatives to improve their lives.

Notes

1. The usual question about the relationship between "growth" and "poverty" leads to methodological debates, because growth is typically measured with national accounts data whereas poverty is typically measured with household data. Under such circumstances at least some of the divergence between growth and poverty in the data will have nothing to do with income distribution, but will simply reflect the fact that these two data sources disagree on the magnitude of the change, even in conceptually equivalent measures.

2. For more details, see the Kagera synthesis report by Joachim De Weerdt on the Moving Out of Poverty Web site.

3. The methodology was close in spirit to propensity score matching.

4. Proximity to borders and cities did not necessarily help in all conflict-affected regions. In the Indian state of Assam, for instance, communities bordering other states exhibited higher levels of violence due to problems of infiltration.

5. High-yielding varieties of rice were introduced in the early 1970s in West Bengal. However, the benefits from their cultivation were waning by the time of the survey. Our respondents spoke more about agricultural diversification and expansion into nonfarming business activities as a means to move out of poverty.

6. This term was first used almost a decade ago by Ela Bhatt, founder of the Self Employed Women's Association (SEWA) in India. SEWA has over 700,000 members working in more than 70 trades in seven states across India. It fights to build assets for its members by seeking fair wages and benefits and upgrading their skills.

7. *Choupal* is the Hindi word for a rural gathering place where people can sit down together to talk.

All Politics Is Local:
How Better Governance
Helps the Poor

When people have freedom, the community is practicing democracy. Democracy and freedom are the same because we cannot experience freedom if there is no democracy. Without democracy there is chaos. How can a community prosper in that case?

—DISCUSSION WITH WOMEN,
San Dogon, Philippines

When you have no power, stop dreaming; you will have no freedom, no equality, and democracy will remain a story to you.

—DISCUSSION WITH MEN AND WOMEN,
Kijuronga, Kagera, Tanzania

The rich man in the village is the head of the village; the poor man is the head of the burial ground.

—MEN'S DISCUSSION GROUP,
Govindapalle, Andhra Pradesh

C onsider two communities in two different countries. Let us call them, for the moment, country A and country B.

In country A, the village of Tindyata is poor and is perched on a mountain slope, where it is prone to flooding. Despite its precarious location and its poverty, the village enjoys what appears to be an idyllic political climate. Elections in 2003 were a turning point. "The elections were equitable and open, everybody participated, and the result was our will," said women in the village. "Currently, there is more freedom of speech, so the viewpoints of the officials are beginning to change. Now they are asking for our opinions in matters concerning our interest." The men agreed: "The elections were a very important victory for our community. People are proud to be represented at the local council. They are happy to have somebody who helps them obtain administrative forms and documents. The elected official is our spokesman. He has brought us hope." Women praised the official for being "always willing to lend a sympathetic ear to our problems," and both women and men affirmed that people participate more in decision making than they did 10 years ago. Women noted that the official had actively participated in the creation of an association for community development, which acts as a watchdog on government activities. Besides the association, improved access to information through the media has helped strengthen official accountability.

By most accounts, these improvements in people's ability to contact and influence the local government have not brought any concrete benefits to the community. Tindyata remains what people called a "forgotten city." Residents blame centrally designed laws and rules that disregard local realities and hamper people's efforts to improve their situation. Regulations regarding the construction industry are a case in point. The rules permit construction only on presentation of a clear construction plan to the municipality. Local people said that the rule is bizarre, given that there are no architects locally available to approve such plans. One of the men in a discussion group admitted, "The elected official is with us, but he can't do anything."

Even so, most people our team met in Tindyata cherished their newfound democracy and sense of liberty. They felt it was intrinsically valuable to be able to make their voices heard through their elected official. And they felt a sense of liberty and security. A woman in a discussion group exclaimed, "Now you can sleep in the street forever without anybody disturbing you."

Far away in country B, Anakha is an agricultural village of rice and potato farmers where nearly 70 percent of the population was stuck in chronic poverty in 2005. While Anakha's poverty is roughly on par with Tindyata's, it seems to be politically illiberal. A single political party rules through fear and dominates the economic, social, and political lives of poor people in the community. Unlike in Tindyata, elections in Anakha are alleged to be rigged.

"When one party makes any mistake, other parties used to protest against it. But now the ruling party has all the power. There are not many people here to speak against them. They fear for their lives," reported men in the village. Villagers described the "muscle power" of local politicians and the power of the gun that could "stop mouths." The ruling party is said to ignore people's opinions in decision making. "People appear in the meeting only as a show," a woman lamented. "All decisions are taken by party leaders. Those who are party supporters get more benefit than the common people." Even a 20-year-old woman was ironic in describing local politics: "We are enjoying the mockery of our party leaders. We are enjoying the mockery of democracy."

A person's ability to climb the economic ladder in Anakha is said to be entirely a function of political contacts and membership in the ruling party. Those without such affiliations are considered doomed. All economic strategies to move out of poverty—by getting a job, obtaining credit to set up a small business, or improving agricultural productivity—are only available to party members. Distribution of benefits from government programs for the poor and elderly are either misused or distributed along party lines. Men said matter-of-factly, "To get benefit here, people have to join the ruling party after leaving opposition parties." Party members can access credit without mortgaging their land, get plots of land allotted to them without documentation, even secure government jobs. "Since 1996, most of the people who have been getting land have not been worthy of it. The list was made by our village head and some party members. The government officers had even rejected the names of several people who got land. The really needy people are, therefore, getting deceived from getting land."

Party membership improves social rank in the village as well. A young woman spoke candidly of the differences. "Common people who are not party supporters do not get much importance during social occasions. They are treated in a way as if they were not people of this society." Social alienation extends to the youth. Young men who are party supporters get to participate in festivals and sports. Even in youth clubs, party supporters are regarded as having more power.

Poor people aspire to join the party, but most cannot. Forced to work in the fields every day to survive, most cannot spare the time to attend party meetings or afford monthly donations. Observing the party's stranglehold on opportunities—and the fact that over the past decade, only 5 percent of poor villagers in Anakha have moved out of poverty—many young people conclude that the only way to get ahead is to become a politician. A 24-year-old was clear about his goals: "I would like to join the party in the future because one can improve his condition here after joining the party. My father is a cultivator, and my mother a local cigarette maker. They cannot improve their condition. So I have a future plan to live differently." Others concur: "If one is to get freedom and money, party support is more important than education."

Country A is Morocco; the village of Tindyata is in the province of Chichaoua. Country B is India, and the village of Anakha is in the state of West Bengal. These contrasting community stories remind us that to understand how democracy plays out in the lives of poor people, we need to look beneath broad national labels to examine specific local realities.

Morocco's movement toward a more open system started in the 1990s. The reforms, guided by King Hassan II and his son Mohammed VI, included greater respect for human rights, more opportunities to form civil society associations that could openly discuss issues like corruption in government, and introduction of a new family code that gave women more rights. The reforms also opened up the Moroccan parliament to universal suffrage and gave elected members more power to question the executive. Despite these advances, political scientists think Morocco exemplifies a "competitive electoral authoritarian" regime. Experts of this democratization have criticized it as a top-down process that reflects the monarchy's attempt to appear modern. The king remains the executive head of state, military chief, and religious leader; he can veto parliament decisions and hire and fire entire government bodies. In that sense, the reforms appear to be "a quest for modernization, not for popular participation and government accountability" (Ottaway and Riley 2006). But realities on the ground appear more nuanced. Although not all communities in Morocco reflect the same degree of satisfaction in their young democracy as Tindyata, people in most villages we visited are satisfied with their local elected representatives.

The state of West Bengal is widely acknowledged as among the first in India to have successfully created democratic structures at the local level. Its experience of nearly 25 years of electing village panchayats is evidence of the state's commitment to grassroots democracy. A stable, leftist state government has held office for more than three decades, with an absolute majority. Scholars have attributed the party's continued electoral success to its actions to reduce rural poverty through measures such as land reform. Given this long track record of local democracy, one would expect considerable engagement of local populations in community-level decision making in West Bengal. The discussions in Anakha, however, suggest otherwise. Although there are many communities in West Bengal where people praised their local leaders, in 21 percent of the communities visited in the state, people complained of "muscle men and goons." Clearly, even in the largest democracy in the world, India, the intrinsic freedom that democracy supposedly brings is not guaranteed.

These experiences in Morocco and India are emblematic of what we found in the other countries visited for the Moving Out of Poverty study. Democratic functioning in local communities varies widely and does not always reflect the national image or label. Across our sample, we found that 93 percent of the variation in the extent to which local political leaders pay attention to citizens is explained by within-country variation. In considering the effects of democracy on poverty, therefore, we should keep in mind the well-worn precept that "all politics is local."

Food or Freedom: A False Dilemma

In Morocco and in villages across Africa, South Asia, East Asia, and Latin America, poor men and women engaged in deep discussions about the nature of democracy and freedom. They debated the effectiveness of democracy as practiced in their communities—what democracy does and does not deliver, and how it could be improved. They attached intrinsic value to the practice of democracy, no matter its flaws. Even in Morocco, with its recent and incomplete democracy, a group of men told the field team, "With democracy, we have become aware of many things. We have left our caves and have become more open to the world." People spoke of the intrinsic worth of freedom: freedom to think, to speak, to protest, to dream, to live with dignity and respect. At the same time, they attached an instrumental importance to freedoms that allow them to work, to move around, and to choose occupations and assets that can help them bring food to the table.

We found very little evidence to suggest that poor people want to trade off democracy and freedom for food. They feel they have a right to both. Nor do poor men and women believe they must fulfill their basic needs before they can meaningfully exercise democratic rights and freedoms.[1] In *Development as Freedom*, Amartya Sen (1999) critiques the tendency of those in privileged positions to create a hierarchy of needs for those who have less. The oft-repeated but misleading question, according to Sen, is "What should come first—removing poverty and misery, or guaranteeing political liberty and civil rights, for which poor people have little use anyway?" To this question, he replies:

> Is this a sensible way of approaching the problems of economic needs and political freedoms—in terms of a basic dichotomy that appears to undermine the relevance of political freedoms because the economic needs are so urgent? I would argue, no, this is altogether the wrong way to see the force of economic needs, or to understand the salience of political freedoms. The real issues . . . involve taking note of extensive interconnections between political freedoms and the understanding and fulfillment of economic needs. The connections are not only instrumental . . . but also constructive. Our conceptualization of economic needs depends crucially on open public debates and discussions, the guaranteeing of which requires insistence on basic political liberty and civil rights. (147–48)

The notion that freedom and liberal democracy are luxuries that should be considered only after basic needs such as food have been met has its origins in Western history. In Western Europe, democracy emerged after the Industrial Revolution had already brought growth in incomes and basic education, and this history still informs thinking about the correct sequencing of economic growth and democracy. Some suggest that poor countries should "grow first," gain from "development dictatorships," and later embrace democracy (Huntington and Nelson 1976). This concept is reflected in the celebration of the East Asian miracle, in which Korea, Indonesia, Singapore, and Taiwan suppressed human freedoms but achieved spectacular economic growth accompanied by poverty reduction (Barro 1994; Przeworski et al. 2000). This thinking is also captured in the India–China debates. Some observers believe that democracy, with its endless debates and need for political consensus on policy reform, has slowed India's growth, while others make a case for a long-term democracy dividend, with democratic India being "a tortoise to China's hare" (Varshney 2007).[2]

The survival of democracy in India challenges the basic assumptions of many political scientists that literacy and middle-income levels are necessary preconditions for democracy. Defying democratic theory, India's lower classes have participated in elections at a higher rate than its middle and upper classes since the early 1990s. In fact, the "lower the caste, income, and education of an Indian, the greater the odds that he will vote" (Varshney 2007). Although the fact that poor people vote to a greater extent than rich people could be interpreted as a sign of desperation among the poor to make their voices heard, the fact that they do vote is an indicator of a healthy electoral democracy.[3]

India is not alone. By the end of the twentieth century, democracy became the preferred way of organizing political systems. There is still wide variation in types of democracy, ranging from liberal democracies to illiberal pseudo-democracies to electoral authoritarian regimes (Diamond 2002, 2005). Nonetheless, most political scientists agree that the essence of democracy is competitive politics through free and fair elections and a responsive government that is accountable to all its citizens—in brief, contestation and participation (Dahl 1989; Varshney 2005). Democracies encompass civil liberties to different degrees. These liberties include the right to vote, the right to information, the right to protest and form associations, the right to own property (still weakly defined in many polities), and the right to participate in politics and in society.

Most of the debate about democracy is at the national level; in fact, there has been an obsession with formal national elections. Although they are an important precondition for democracy, the presence of elected representatives at the national level does not guarantee a functional democracy, nor does it guarantee freedoms for poor people in their communities.

We concentrate, therefore, on understanding people's interactions with democracy at the local level. We focus on the demand side and not on factors that affect the supply side, such as rules that govern political parties and election finance. We are particularly interested in the interactions between local people and their elected officials and in the responsiveness and accountability of politicians to citizens, especially poor people.[4] Clearly, variations in the history, age, and depth of political democracy across countries matter, and this detail should be kept in mind in examining the country-specific results.[5] We do not seek to evaluate the impact of decentralization per se, but we do examine the relationship between local political structures and the likelihood of moving out of poverty.[6]

We start with poor people's own definitions of democracy, its constituent elements, and its functioning at the local level. We consider associations between local democracy and community prosperity and gains at the household level to examine who benefits from local democracy, looking in particular at two phenomena—corruption and elite capture—that can serve to channel the benefits of democracy to a few. Finally, we examine the factors that can lead to local democracy becoming more pro-poor.

What Does Democracy Mean to Poor People?

Democracy means to appreciate opinions. It means musyawarah mufakat *[deliberations to reach consensus].*
  —Discussion with young women, Kacokerre, East Java, Indonesia

No democracy exists in this country, or fair judgment in the court. Those who have money, the judgment is in favor of them.
  —Discussion with men, Shantakalia, Bangladesh

Most poor people in our sample associate democracy first and foremost with the freedom to control their own lives, to do whatever they wish as long as it does not hurt others.[7] Democracy is an aspiration. In Afghanistan, for example, democracy means "entire freedom: shaving your beard, wearing any kind of clothes you want, listening to a radio cassette, and swimming in the warm weather." Freedom of expression and of worship were also mentioned across study sites. In conflict-affected countries, people value freedom from fear and freedom of physical movement. For women everywhere, democracy connotes freedom in both the domestic and public spheres (see chapter 2 for a discussion of people's views on freedom).

Table 6.1 summarizes the definitions of democracy from one study region, Malawi. Like people in other regions, the study participants in Malawi went far beyond the common, limited understanding of democracy as centered on elections. Although multiparty politics were mentioned, freedoms of various types topped the list.

Nowhere is the identification of democracy with freedom more evident than in Afghanistan, where the nascent democracy, with all its uncertainties, is associated with release from the restrictions the Taliban imposed. In 2006, when field work was conducted, the end of Taliban rule and the beginning of democracy had improved security, which in turn allowed greater freedom of movement, especially for women and children. Omra, a 50-year-old woman in the community of Morlaw Ghano in Nangarhar province, described the change: "Democracy is working better now than in the past. All our children can go to school—even girls—and everyone feels freer to look for a job, to go to Jalalabad."

TABLE 6.1
People in study communities in Malawi associate democracy first and foremost with freedom

Understanding of democracy	No. of times mentioned
Freedoms (of expression, worship, association, etc.)	22
Having power or being given a chance to lead for development	9
Multiparty politics (ruling and opposition parties)	8
Participatory decision making	5
Everybody ruling/ability to elect and remove people in power	3
Security	2
Working together (e.g., the chief and his people)	1
Gender equality	1
Living in harmony, without discrimination	1

Source: Focus group discussions on livelihoods, freedom, power, and democracy.

In Shazimir, near Kabul, women relished the freedom to go to the bazaar and to work outside the home as teachers and office workers. For a woman in Zakwak Ulya, Herat, the improved security brought simple pleasures to be cherished: "Everyone wants to have democracy, to pray, and to go to the cinema."

Deliberative versus representative democracy

For democracy to function there must be freedom to appreciate the aspirations and opinions of every person.
—Young woman, Yasapira, North Maluku, Indonesia

Across study regions, the right to vote was cited as an important dimension of democracy. When asked to define democracy, poor men and women in Uttar Pradesh, the Indian state with the largest population and parliamentary seat share, summed it up in two words: "our rule."[8] But people across study sites defined democracy as going beyond voting, a right they often seemed to take for granted. They identified three features they considered essential: voice, participation, and justice.

In this sense, poor people in our sample seem to support scholars who conceptualize democracy as participative, deliberative, and direct, rather than as merely representative. The essential distinction, according to Cohen and Sabel (1997, 321), "is not the level of participation, but the topic of agenda: direct democracy requires decisions on substance, whereas representative democracy involves choice on legislators who decide on substance" (see also R. Chambers 2003; Fung and Wright 2003).

People across study regions said that meaningful democratic participation is not possible without voice, the freedom to express themselves both individually and collectively. They value discussion and consensus building. Young women in the village of Yasapira, North Maluku, Indonesia, interpreted democracy as the "freedom to express all aspirations without being restricted by norms or regulations. For democracy to function, there must be freedom to appreciate the aspirations and opinions of every person. Opinions will emerge if people are free to express them. But without this freedom of expression, a discussion will not reach mutual agreement." People in Afghanistan also recognize the importance of voice. "It means that one can freely give their opinions," said Tahir, a young farmer in Morlaw Ghano, Nangarhar. "If you cannot express your ideas, how can you be free?"

Freedom of expression includes the freedom to protest. Zair, another villager in Morlaw Ghano, noted, "Freedom of speech is more important than other types of freedom because one can express one's ideas about injustices and violation of rights in the government or in the community." In Delapong, Philippines, people defined democracy as the right to organize an antigovernment rally. Young women in Tulma, also in the Philippines, said democracy gives people "the right to vote; you have the right to choose." But they added, "You also have the right to protest the laws or policies passed for implementation. You can go for a rally or a signature campaign."

Poor people's discussions of voice and participation reflect two important theoretical and empirical insights. First, discussion groups and our quantitative data suggest that underlying norms of trust, solidarity, unity, and tolerance provide the essential foundation for participation and voice in decision making. Nearly 45 percent of those who said that their local democracy now pays *more* attention to their concerns also reported improvement in trust levels in their village or neighborhood. Only 22 percent said that trust levels had deteriorated. In Sri Lanka, a women's discussion group said that participation entails a spirit of "unity, togetherness, and participation of each and every one." In the village of Appilepalle, Andhra Pradesh, people concurred: "Democracy means all of us living together. We do our own work, but we live together. We are friendly with our neighbors and we live happily."

Second, the most important participation is collective, and participation itself reinforces norms of belonging and unity. Participation in collective efforts generates what economist Vijayendra Rao (2008) calls symbolic public goods (see also Mosse 1997; Turner 1982).[9] Communities in Andhra

Pradesh, a state with large numbers of women's self-help groups, defined democracy "as a system whereby people participate collectively, with unity and in harmony, for village development and for collective problem solving." "Democracy means to join with people to rule ourselves," concluded a discussion group in the village of Bestharapalle. "It is to achieve what is required for the village through groups."

The emphasis on norms of trust, unity, and participation in discussions of democracy partly reflects the deep inequalities in our study regions and communities. Poor people, women, and other marginalized groups confront many barriers to making their voices heard in decision making (Fung and Wright 2003; Kaufman 1968).[10] Thus, the third essential feature of democracy is justice. In discussions about democracy, poor people spoke about the importance of equal rights, equality before law, equality between men and women, and equality between different ethnicities, castes, and religions. They emphasized the need for protection of individual rights under law even when they did not expect to be able immediately to *claim* all their rights.

In the community of Izrane, Morocco, justice is considered to be the most important feature of democracy, even more than liberty and equality. People emphasized that justice must be impartial and independent. A discussion group of men stated, "The judge must not receive telephone calls that dictate to him what he must do. Without pressure, he must fully apply the law. The oppressor must be judged, and the innocent must be acquitted. There must be liberty of speech. I declare, I denounce, or I write to newspapers what I observe as anomalies. The liberty of critique must be protected by law."

Concepts of equality and justice differ depending on the local context. Participants in Afghanistan stressed gender equality; they hoped that the turn to democracy would mean that women could move around more freely than they could under the Taliban. The importance of economic equality was mentioned frequently in West Bengal, perhaps reflecting the state's four decades of communist rule. Finally, in caste-stratified Andhra Pradesh, people focused on the ideal of equality between different caste groups. Male youths in Bestharapalle, for example, defined democracy as a state where "people of different castes and religions are treated equally, and equal justice is done to all people. Then we can say that there is democracy in our village."

How Local Democracy Makes a Difference

Democracy means an easier life [yombalal] or progress [yokoute].
—Discussion group, Geona, Senegal

Democracy brings development to the community. When there is democracy, things like water, schools, and hospitals will be available to the village, which are otherwise hard to get.
                        —Men in a discussion group, Kabtito, Uganda

Democracy can bring development, but at present it does not do so. Our democracy is made up of the politics of promises. Democracy wastes time. People go on talking about politics endlessly, and there is no more time for work.
                        —Men in a discussion group, Bugokela, Kagera, Tanzania

We encountered several forms of local democracy in the countries we visited. In Afghanistan, the local democratic structure is the shura, a council of elders responsible for resolving disputes in the community. It is headed by a *malek*, a title that traditionally was passed from father to son; in the post-Taliban era, the malek is elected by the people. In the Indian context, local democratic bodies include the *gram sabha*, or village assembly, and the *panchayat*, an executive body whose five members are chosen by the gram sabha. The panchayat implements government schemes in the community and oversees provision of basic services like local roads, drinking water, electricity, and sanitation. A similar role is played by the village executive committee in Tanzania and the barangay in the Philippines. What interests us is not the form of local democracy, but how well these democratic structures are functioning.

Democracy as an ideal is cherished, but the practice of democracy in any particular setting may be deeply flawed, in part as a result of deep social divisions. In theory, local elections, competitive politics, and equality under the law *should* lead to responsive local governance. Whether they do so is an empirical question. We developed a measure of responsiveness based on four indicators: people's ratings of the extent to which local elected officials take into account citizen concerns, their ratings of whether they have any influence on the actions of local officials, their ratings of the extent to which they trust these officials, and finally whether they are satisfied with the way democracy works in their local government.

We first test whether there is any relationship between our measure of responsiveness and improved community-level outcomes, including delivery and quality of basic services, presence of roads, and public safety. We then turn to benefits to individuals across our sample of countries. Finally, we pose the question of whether individual gains for some may imply costs to others in the same community.

Community outcomes

Because of electricity, now we are watching TV, we are getting news of our own country and abroad, and we are living our life happily. Because of street lights, females can go anywhere at night. There is electricity in the mass education center, so everyone is studying as well.
                    —Men's discussion group, Khalsi, West Bengal

Security has started improving, maybe it is a change in the government. . . . Nowadays when a person is taken to jail, you don't see that person coming back and giving you a greeting.
                    —A woman in a mixed discussion group, Bamlozi, Malawi

Djatick is a Wolof village of 654 inhabitants in a rural district of Senegal. Life has been tough in this isolated, agriculture-dependent community over the past few years. Drought and devastating locust invasions have slashed yields of the main commercial crop, groundnuts. Lack of rain has resulted in culling of cattle herds, and people move for days looking for pasture. As a result, more people have fallen into poverty than have escaped it. Since 1995, 70 percent of the nonpoor have plunged into poverty and 43 percent of those who were already in poverty have fallen further down. Only a few have managed to move out of poverty. Most people in Djatick still live in mud-brick huts with no electricity, relying on kerosene lanterns for light. Many households survive only by sending their children to work in a nearby town.

Our team was surprised, then, to find when they arrived in Djatick that its people were optimistic. Lamine Top, a successful son of the village, had put his job in the Ministry of Education on hold and returned to be elected president of the local rural council. People sang his praises. Since his election in 2002, he had raised the council budget and invested heavily in basic infrastructure, which included drilling a borehole as part of the national rural infrastructure program. Previously, women had walked to a well six hours away, spent the night there, and come back in the morning with water. So excited were the villagers about the borehole that they contributed 180,000 CFA francs toward the project, and the transparent management of the borehole led to the repayment of a CFAF 350,000 loan. Other improvements included the reopening of a health post built in 1990 and the addition of classrooms to a primary school. Meetings involving representatives of all 25 villages in the local council area are sometimes held in Djatick, easing feelings of marginalization and isolation among residents. Although they remain poor, people were proud of their leader and of their role in electing him. A men's discussion group noted, "If a local representative does not perform well, we can get rid of him through the ballot box."

Provision of basic services and infrastructure. The experience of Djatick does not appear to be unique. We asked people across study sites a variety of questions about local services and much later in the discussion switched to the quality of their interaction with local government. We specifically asked whether local government paid more or less attention to their concerns today compared to 10 years ago. Overall, one-third of the communities experienced some improvement in local government responsiveness by this measure.

We then compared these responses to changes in community services. When we look at our results across countries, the pattern is striking. Communities where local governments had become more responsive had better access to clean water, schools, doctors, nurses, and public health clinics than communities where responsiveness had decreased. The quality of education and health services also showed more improvement (figure 6.1).[11]

FIGURE 6.1

Quality of health and education improved more where governments became more responsive

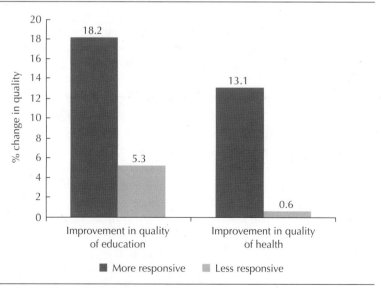

Source: Authors' analysis using data from the community questionnaire with key informants and responses to the question: "Compared to 10 years ago, does the local government now pay more, about the same, or less attention to what people like you think when it decides what to do?" *N* = 412 communities.

The presence of roads, too, is closely associated with changes in local government responsiveness (figure 6.2). Communities where responsiveness had increased were much more likely to have a passable road to the nearest urban center than those where responsiveness had decreased (81 percent compared to 58 percent). A new road in the village of Kabtito, Uganda, was built on the direct initiative of the district local government. Similarly, in Changsari, Assam, a village road was built using grants made by a local member of the legislative assembly. Both roads had improved market access and employment options for village residents.

Maintenance of law and order. We were also interested in whether greater government responsiveness was associated with better security in communities. At minimum, people expect their local elected officials to maintain law and order. We found that improvement in levels of peace and safety was greater in communities where local governments are more responsive (figure 6.3). Communities with a more responsive local government reported a 16 percent improvement in peace levels, compared to a 10 percent increase reported by communities where responsiveness had worsened over the study period.

Individual outcomes

> *When, in our village, a [housing] colony was made in 1986 and we got a house [from the government], I was really happy. I felt the same happiness as a hungry man gets on eating food or a naked man on getting clothes.*
> —Prem, a young poor woman, Sapsa, Uttar Pradesh

In the village of Sapsa, Uttar Pradesh, Prem's life changed when she benefited from a centrally sponsored but locally delivered government program called Indira Vikas Yojna that gives land to poor households. Prem was the youngest of 12 children and the only girl. She received no formal education and was married at the age of 12. As our team sat on the floor of her immaculate home, she said, "We were so poor that we lived in a small hut, and when it rained, the roof used to leak. When, in our village, a [housing] colony was made in 1986 and we got a house, I was really happy. Exactly two years later under the Indira Vikas Yojna, we got land. Now instead of working for other people, I can make a small living. I can farm on my land and earn for myself. Earlier we were landless; now we are called farmers." She supplements her farm income with money her husband earns selling fruit in Delhi. "In 2003, we converted our hut into a proper house. This change created much happiness too. Because the money that you have earned is in your hand, [you can] do whatever you want."

FIGURE 6.2
Roads were more likely to be present in communities where governments became more responsive

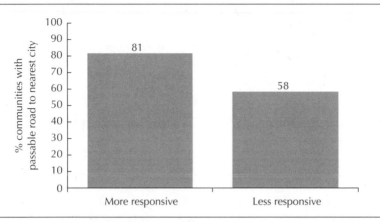

Source: Authors' analysis using data from the community questionnaire with key informants and responses to the question: "Compared to 10 years ago, does the local government now pay more, about the same, or less attention to what people like you think when it decides what to do?" *N* = 412 communities.

FIGURE 6.3
Communities where governments became more responsive were more likely to report an increase in levels of safety and peace

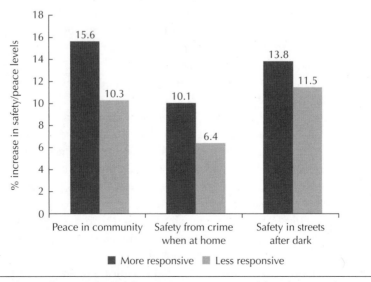

Source: Authors' analysis using data from the community questionnaire with key informants and responses to the question: "Compared to 10 years ago, does the local government now pay more, about the same, or less attention to what people like you think when it decides what to do? *N* = 420 communities.

When we first started discussing the study with political scientists, some wondered why we expected any relationship between local democracy and moving out of poverty. Fortunately, the data collection had already started. The presence of basic infrastructure—water, roads, electricity, health facilities, and schools—clearly facilitates livelihoods and often prevents disease, a major drain on incomes. But as Prem's life story shows, a responsive local government can do much more beyond provision of infrastructure to assist livelihoods.

In the hundreds of life stories we studied, local government plays positive roles in poor people's lives in many small and big ways: by providing farming inputs, loans, training, land, and housing and by providing disaster relief. In Kabtito, Uganda, besides constructing a road, the local government distributes improved varieties of seeds that have helped farmers increase their income. In Delapong, Philippines, people spoke about a well-administered scholarship program for poor children and about loans to start small businesses. In Thailand, local self-government bodies called Tambon Administrative Organizations (TAOs) provide support in building feeder canals for irrigation, enabling farmers to produce two rice crops a year. The TAOs also help communities manage the Baht Village Fund, which provides credit to buy agricultural machines such as seed planters and crop harvesters.

Local governments played a particularly valuable role in supporting livelihoods in conflict-affected areas. Lupotogo, a community in North Maluku, Indonesia, was hit by conflict between Christians and Muslims in 1999. Residents credit the local government's help in large part for their recovery. "After the conflict, there was government assistance in the form of *katinting* [motorboat], handicraft tools, cooking tools, and so forth," said Umi. "If it wasn't for that assistance, what work would we do? Because everything was destroyed during the conflict." In a katinting, fishermen can go farther out to sea and bring back a bigger catch, increasing their profits.

As a check on our qualitative data, we once again performed multilinear regression analyses to see whether there is a statistical association between the probability of moving out of poverty and local government responsiveness. At the household level, we combined four questions into one. Our measure includes indicators of the level of trust people have in their local government officials, whether they are satisfied with democracy in their local government, whether their local government takes into account citizen concerns, and their ability to contact local government and influence its actions.[12] We control for the effect of other factors such as economic prosperity, collective action, corruption, individual empowerment, social stratification, and the usual individual factors such as assets and education.

FIGURE 6.4

Responsiveness of local democracy has a significant association with moving out of poverty, particularly in South Asian study regions

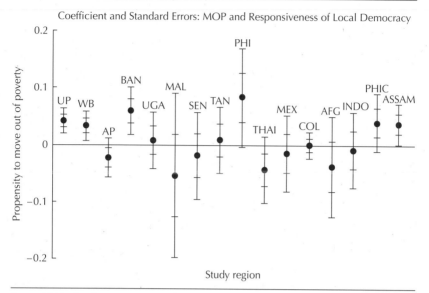

Source: Multivariate linear regression analysis using data from household survey and community questionnaire (see appendix 6).

Figure 6.4 reports the association between our measure of "responsiveness of local democracy" and household movement out of poverty. As in other box plots, the single dots represent the coefficients: the greater their height, the higher the value of the coefficient. The bars around the coefficient represent the one and two standard error bounds. The more tightly clustered the bounds, the smaller the standard error and the more significant the association between responsiveness and moving out of poverty (MOP).

As figure 6.4 illustrates, the evidence is mixed. There is a positive association between a responsive local democracy and moving out of poverty in some regions, the association being strongest in the Indian states (with the exception of Andhra Pradesh) and in Bangladesh.

For illustrative purposes only, let us take the case of Uttar Pradesh, where responsiveness of the local panchayats has a significant influence on poor households' ability to improve their well-being. A change in the local government's ability to pay attention to citizen concerns from a minimum score of "less attention" to a maximum score of "more attention" increases the likelihood of moving out of poverty by 6.6 percent. Compare this to the influence of a unit change in the household head's education level, from illiteracy to primary schooling or from primary schooling to secondary schooling. This change affects MOP by 3.4 percent.[13] An increase of 1 hectare in the amount of land owned by the household at the start of the study period only pushes up the household's likelihood of moving out of poverty by 1.3 percent. Similarly, each of the other component variables—satisfaction with local democracy, trust in local government, and ability to influence government actions—has a greater influence on MOP than land or education.

In the African and some conflict study regions, however, responsiveness of local democracy is insignificant for MOP. In the conflict regions, in fact, there is usually a negative association between responsiveness and MOP. The exceptions are the conflict-affected communities in Assam and the Philippines, where increased responsiveness of the local democratic structure is associated with an increase in MOP (positive sign). In the Philippines, this phenomenon may be because of a generally positive perception of local democracy and the many government-financed programs at the local level. In India, it may reflect the important role that local panchayats play, at least in service delivery and in implementing centrally sponsored programs for poor families.

There are two ways of looking at these results. On the positive side, one can marvel at this evidence of strong and significant positive association between local democracy—despite all its real-life messiness—and moving out of poverty. These results remain *after controlling for other factors*. All this in general bears out poor people's faith in local democracy.

On the negative side, one can point out the variations and the negative associations in some countries. And finally, the results do not tell us anything about the cost of moving out of poverty or whether one person's success may hurt the efforts of others.

Benefits to some, costs to others

> *There are people who get jealous of you and wish you to fail. [A person]*
> *might pay somebody to steal your working animals or your crops.*
> —Men's discussion group, Paitatu, Philippines

In communities where resources are limited, if I gain access to some resources, you may have even less. In other words, if I win, you lose. We do find evidence of poor people fighting over limited resources. Thus, the question of whether a responsive local democracy benefits some people at the expense of others is a serious one for our study.

We approach this question using a technique called the leave-out mean (LOM), which averages the response of all households in the village *excluding* a given household (let us call it household X). It could well be that household X's perceptions of government responsiveness are influenced by the benefits it derives from the local public works program, but that its participation in the program serves to exclude others. In that case, the overall social impact of the program could be negative. The leave-out mean for X is the average of all responses on responsiveness of local government *less* X's own response. This helps differentiate private effects from purely social effects.

In earlier research in Tanzania, we applied the leave-out mean technique to measure the impact of social capital (group membership) on an individual's well-being and on the well-being of the rest of the community where the individual lives (Narayan and Pritchett 1997). We found that even if an individual does not belong to any groups, he or she gains by living in a village where many people belong to groups—a pure social benefit. Later, a study in Indonesia used the technique to disentangle the private and social effects of household participation in local government. It found that one household's participation has a strong crowding-out or chilling effect on the voice and participation of other households in the same village (Alatas, Pritchett, and Wetterberg 2007).

In the present study, we constructed a similar leave-out mean variable for our measure of responsiveness of local democracy. Figure 6.5 captures the association between this variable and household MOP using multivariate linear regressions, as reported in appendix 6.

In many of the South Asian study contexts where this variable was significant, we observe negative spillover effects.[14] This finding is reflected in the negative coefficient on the leave-out mean variable in Uttar Pradesh and significantly so in West Bengal, Assam, Bangladesh, Malawi, and Senegal. This observation suggests that there is considerable crowding out among poor households in their fight over the very limited goods—fertilizer packets, water, scholarships, houses, and so on—distributed by their local governments. In Indonesia, the Philippines, and Andhra Pradesh, however, the association is positive and significant, which seems to be related to three factors. First, in middle-income contexts, governments have focused much more on improving community-wide facilities used by everyone, primarily infrastructure such as roads, bridges, electricity, and schools. Second, it is possible that when limited goods are distributed, this is done in a way that is widely perceived to be fair. Finally, it may be that in wealthier contexts, targeted programs are so well endowed so that all who qualify benefit equally.

FIGURE 6.5
Responsiveness of local democracy to some has negative spillovers on others

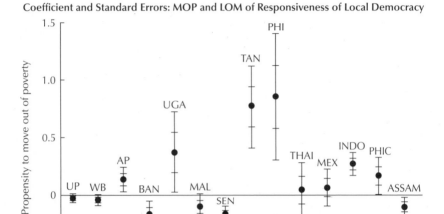

Coefficient and Standard Errors: MOP and LOM of Responsiveness of Local Democracy

Source: Multivariate linear regression analysis using data from household survey and community questionnaire (see appendix 6).

Why Isn't Local Democracy More Effective?

Although poor people in poor environments turn to their local governments with hope, their hopes are often dashed. Across communities, we found three factors that block democratic structures from being more responsive and playing positive roles. They are rules and regulations, especially those governing micro and small businesses; corruption; and elite capture of resources and power by particular groups. The extent of elite capture appears to be closely linked to the extent to which the community is divided by caste, ethnicity, and religion—that is, the level of social stratification.

Restrictive rules and regulations

When you are looking for a license to do business, sometimes you are told to come tomorrow. If you go back to the office the following day, you are told again to come tomorrow. Hence, you have to put your hands in your pocket to ensure that fast service is delivered to you.
        —Discussion with women, Kaludoma, Ruvuma, Tanzania

You see this young man, this executive officer? He is tiny. If I push him,
he would fall. He cannot even carry a jerry can of water. But touch [him]
and see what he will do. They have powers hidden in the rules they design.
Their powers are hidden in papers.

—Discussion groups with men and women
in a village in Kagera, Tanzania

Over and over again, in the communities we visited, we found that rules
and regulations discriminate against poor women and men. Discretion and
lack of accountability at the local level lead to pervasive informal levies that
are a net drain on any poor person who ventures to be entrepreneurial.[15]
Poor people might find their livelihoods shut down or strictly curtailed by
regulations supposedly intended to protect the environment or the common
good, with no provision made for alternative livelihoods. And in some cases,
the rules imposed by higher levels were just plain silly.

Despite economic liberalization at the national level, poor people at the
local level remain subject to complex rules around licensing, ownership of
assets, and livelihoods. Across contexts, local government officials have devised
informal regulations that sometimes appear to have no purpose other than to
create a hidden or not-so-hidden flow of private revenue. Women in Surjana,
Bahraich, Uttar Pradesh, reported, "The hawkers or vegetable vendors in the
market have to pay a tax of 3–4 rupees [about 10 cents] per day. If they want to
open a regular shop in the market, then a license is necessary. For the license, the
expenditure is around 4,000–5,000 rupees [US$100–US$125]." A fisherman
in Chakboeng, Cambodia, found himself paying huge fines. "One day I put a
broul [bamboo trap] to catch fish in the open fishing area of the river. But then
a number of fishery inspectors approached and forced me to take the broul out
of the river unless I paid them US$600. On behalf of the village fishery com-
munity, I spent almost a morning bargaining for a reasonable fee of US$400, or
1,600,000 riels. Finally, the inspectors agreed to this amount. I then had to borrow money from a Vietnamese fisherman I knew to pay them. Although I was
fishing in the open area, I could not claim my rights because they had guns."

Authorities frequently impose a flat tax on all businesses irrespective of
their size, which penalizes small businesses and favors large ones. In Chiwolo,
Ruvuma, Tanzania, the village government imposed levies on households
with micro businesses such as shops, fishmonger stalls, and mini-restaurants
known as *migahawa*. Kevin, a small businessman, complained, "The local
government has been very active in collection of levies from petty businesses.
Unfortunately, there are no clear rules and regulations when it comes to

imposing levies." People said the rules are designed to favor certain local government officials who themselves own businesses in the community.

In many communities by lakes or coastal waters, fishing in shallow waters has been banned to protect dwindling fisheries. Poor fishermen do not have the necessary equipment to fish safely in deeper waters, with their currents and storms. In Maguli, Ruvuma, Tanzania, such a change in the law led to the death of four poor fishermen who ventured into deep waters in their small canoes.

In Afghanistan, the ban against growing poppy has imposed great hardships in the absence of other viable livelihood choices. Many people told us that when they returned to their lands with nothing and started rebuilding their houses and farms, the only way to survive was to cultivate poppy. In one community, people said, "There was no hope for us in Pakistan, and we were only waiting to see our country achieve independence and to return. We were finally able to come back in 2002. We were very happy but also afraid to see what had become of our village. Once we were back, poppy cultivation was the only way we had to improve our damaged economy." In another village, the groups said, "People have lost everything—their tools, their houses, their properties, and even their families. Poppy was the only income for us, first, because poppy does not need a lot of water to grow, and second because the income we get when we sell it is five times higher than for other common crops, wheat or barley." Although few would argue that poppy growing should be legal, it is indisputable that laws against it have penalized poor people. It is imperative to give poor people other attractive livelihood alternatives, for the sake of the antidrug policy's success as well as for sheer fairness.

Corruption

Money, money, money! There is no responsibility or accountability from authorities and government officials.
        —Discussion with men and women, Somrampi, Cambodia

They say first keep money in our hands. Then you will see magic.
        —Discussion with men, Appilepalle, Andhra Pradesh

Corruption appears to be widespread across the study regions. Overall, 70 percent of the communities reported dealing with corrupt government officials, and 50 percent reported that all or almost all local officials are corrupt. The numbers from our household survey are not very different: 60 percent of respondents on average said that bribe taking is omnipresent (figure 6.6). By and large, the never poor report more extensive corruption, which probably reflects their more frequent contacts with local governments as they run their businesses.

FIGURE 6.6

More than half of households across study contexts believe that most or almost all government officials in the country engage in corruption

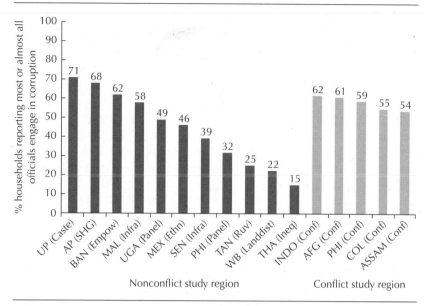

Source: Authors' analysis using household survey; $N = 8{,}215$.

Note:

AFG (Conf) = Afghanistan, Conflict
AP (SHG) = Andhra Pradesh, Self-help groups
ASSAM (Conf)= Assam, Conflict
BAN (Empow) = Bangladesh, Women's
  empowerment
COL (Conf) = Colombia, Conflict
INDO (Conf) = Indonesia, Conflict
MAL (Infra) = Malawi, Infrastructure
MEX (Ethn) = Mexico, Ethnicity

PHI (Conf) = Philippines, Conflict
PHI (Panel) = Philippines, Panel study
SEN (Infra) = Senegal, Infrastructure
TAN (Ruv) = Tanzania, Ruvuma
THAI (Ineq) = Thailand, Inequality
UGA (Panel) = Uganda, Panel study
UP (Caste) = Uttar Pradesh, Caste
WB (Landdist) = West Bengal, Land distribution
  reforms

In Uttar Pradesh, where over 70 percent of households mentioned corruption, discussion group after discussion group complained that bribes are needed to launch any new livelihood. Bribes are demanded for getting a land record signed or obtaining a license to start a business. In the village of Rahamat, women said, "For farming, the big officers close the deals. They don't do any work without taking money. How will we pay money when we can't even fill our stomachs?" Men concurred, "You need a license to start a business. It may be anything—opening a meat shop, rearing hens—all need a license. The licenses are distributed at the district level, and the middlemen make money for giving them. People usually pay up to save themselves from trouble." In Piprawan, Lakhimpur, young women agreed, "You have to first place money in their hands and then they sign." The stories were similar in Andhra Pradesh, where bribes were needed for everything, from participation in food-for-work programs to obtaining caste, income, old age, and even death certificates. Some likened corruption to "water spreading under a mat."

In Bangladesh, young people reported bribe taking as among the most serious constraints to their ability to fulfill their aspirations. Nasima, a young woman, said, "Previously, a word of mouth was enough to get a job. Now it is impossible to get a job without paying a bribe." Young women in Konchala, Bangladesh, commented, "The local leaders take bribes for giving jobs at Eco Cotton Mill. They take 5 taka every day from the girls who are given jobs."

Youth, particularly in the South Asian context, often express a desire to find government jobs, which, once obtained, are held for life. Giving bribes to obtain these jobs is considered part of the process that will later lead to receiving. In Barbakara, Assam, young men said, "Who does not think about giving money these days? If they get a job, it takes only a short time to get back the money."

Across contexts, most people seem more or less resigned to corruption as a way of life. Bribery is seen as a necessary evil if one wants access to government services.[16] In Kaludoma, Ruvuma, Tanzania, bribes are the only way to "ensure fast service being delivered." In a community in Uganda, a man explained, "The leaders in this place are so free that they can even enjoy corruption. We are so enslaved that they can ask us for bribes, and we give them because if we do not do so, they will imprison us. Who wants to go to prison? Why can't I give him 2,000 [shillings] and be free?"

Overall, with the exception of Malawi, bribery appears to be less prevalent in the African communities than in the South Asian or conflict-affected communities. The lowest bribery numbers were in Thailand; these were confirmed by qualitative data in which Thai communities praised their local governments. In West Bengal, relatively low levels of bribe taking may be related to a culture of equality promoted by the socialist government; more likely, distribution of benefits in the state is determined by party affiliation rather than by direct bribes.

Corruption, of course, goes beyond bribe taking to include any misuse of public office and resources for private gain. In some senses, the practice becomes a two-way street: people ask for favors with the expectation that they will have to give something in return. Often this something is money; sometimes it is political support or merely respect. Thus, the lines of callers outside the offices or homes of elected officials are long as people pay their dues. This veneration of politicians is limited strictly to their term in office. People in the village of Chedulla, Andhra Pradesh, noted, "If the wife or some relative of the powerful person dies, everyone will weep. If the powerful person himself dies, no one will visit the family and console them." Once a politician departs, naturally or via the ballot box, allegiance shifts to the next person who "sits in the chair."

In our household survey, we asked respondents whether at any time in the past 10 years they had met, called, or written a letter to a local politician. If the answer was yes, the interviewer asked whether the respondent had done so for a personal matter or a public issue. Across our sample, more than 75 percent of the households surveyed had contacted a local politician for private matters. There were no major differences between those who had moved out of poverty and others on this score. In South Asia (the Indian states, Bangladesh, and Afghanistan), this percentage was as high as 90 percent. Only in some of the African contexts did we see a reverse trend. For instance, in Ruvuma, Tanzania, equal numbers had approached local politicians for public and private matters.

These findings may help explain the variation in the crowding-out effects of local democracy. When people approach politicians only for their self-interest, having their individual problem resolved may lead to others being left out. These effects are more likely to emerge in places with low levels of economic development, where even basic service delivery requires political connections and where the government and politicians have some resources to distribute, as they do in South Asia.

A final excerpt from an animated discussion group with young men in Bangladesh on democracy and corruption:

Noor: *One has to pay for a job.*

Ibrahim: *Not everyone accepts bribes. There are some good people too.*

Noor: *Your brother, Ibrahim, now that he has a government job, will also accept bribes. He got the job by paying 100,000 taka. Doesn't he have to recover the money?*

The group erupted into laughter. The cycle of corruption continues.

Does corruption help or hurt mobility?

Like dogs at burial grounds, they [government officials] look for money for every work.

—Discussion group, Vellamaddi, Andhra Pradesh

Although corruption is clearly a bad thing, we wondered whether the pervasive corruption we encountered might nonetheless have helped some poor people move out of poverty. We therefore tested the association between MOP and corruption using multivariate linear regression analysis (for detailed results, see appendix 6). Our measure captures corruption levels 10 years ago on a four-point scale, ranging from a few to almost all local government officials engaging in bribery and corruption.[17]

We found that corruption mostly has a negative association with MOP, significantly so in Uttar Pradesh, Bangladesh, Senegal, and Mexico (figure 6.7). In other words, the greater the corruption, the harder it is for people in these contexts to move out of poverty. The impact of corruption in Uttar Pradesh is striking. An increase in the incidence of corruption among local government officials from "almost none" to "almost all" is associated with a 10.2 percent decrease in MOP. In other words, it is sufficient to offset the influence that land and education, *together*, have on a household's chances of escaping poverty.

In several study regions, however, there is a positive association between corruption and moving out of poverty. In Tanzania (Ruvuma), and Indonesia, the relationship is strong and statistically significant. In these contexts, even after controlling for other factors including responsiveness, corruption

FIGURE 6.7
Corruption has a mostly negative association with moving out of poverty

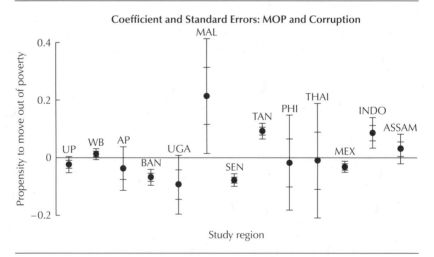

Source: Multivariate linear regression analysis using data from household survey and community questionnaire (see appendix 6).

facilitates movement out of poverty. This finding suggests that poor people who can afford it can bribe their way out of poverty. In Ruvuma, for instance, a change in corruption levels from the minimum (almost no local government officials are corrupt) to the maximum (almost all are corrupt) increases the likelihood of moving out of poverty by 18 percent. Owning assets at the beginning of the study period helps: a unit change in assets is associated with a 7.6 percent increase in MOP. But clearly, assets do not help as much as being able to bribe corrupt local officials.

The widespread practice of bribe taking, although annoying to those forced to pay up, does not appear to detract from the legitimacy of the state. In fact, despite the negative association between corruption in local government and their mobility, respondents in study contexts like South Asia seemed to want more government intervention rather than less. This mirrors the finding of Di Tella and MacCulloch (2007) that people who perceive corruption to be high in their contexts tend to support more government intrusion into economic matters. When corruption is high, left-leaning politicians' rhetoric against corruption finds support and results (paradoxically) in public support for more government intervention. It is also possible that when poor people find markets rigged and impenetrable, they place their faith in government delivery.

Elite capture

After being elected, the chairman and members become blind; they eat up all the aid received from the government.
> —Piara, female farmer and mover, Digbari, Bangladesh

Elite capture is pervasive at the local level. Theory predicts it.[18] Empirics support it.[19] Not surprisingly, we found ample evidence of elite capture in our study villages, where it further diminishes the resources flowing to poor people.

For poor women and men, power and privilege are big obstacles to accessing the programs supposedly targeted to them. In 1997, the farming village of Matdombo in Malawi suffered a prolonged drought that led to great hunger. The government announced that each household in the village would receive 10 kilograms of free fertilizer and 1 kilogram of free maize in what were called "starter packs," handed out under the government's targeted input program. The distribution of these packs, however, was not neutral. A discussion group of men explained, "We registered our names with the village chief, but our names didn't come out each and every time we did so. We didn't get anything while some households got more than three packs. The rule was one pack for each household!" The women added, "The leaders [the village headman and his councilors] made a list of all households. But when they went aside, they removed the names of some people, and in place of them they wrote down the names of their children who do not even stay in the village. Their children then sold fertilizer and maize at a higher rate and made money." Young boys in the village scoffed, "He [the leader] even wrote down the names of his former wives, whom he divorced a long time ago, while many people well qualified for the program received no packs."

"The poorest have nowhere to complain," lamented men and women in another discussion group in Matdombo. "Sometimes they are given things as handouts, but these things do not reach them because those who give out the things deal with the well-to-do, and the things end up in the hands of the well-to-do. Power is desirable because it comes with fringe benefits."

Elite capture affects everything—seeds and fertilizers, jobs and scholarships, credit, land, public services such as health clinics, even cemeteries. Absurdly, the elite have even figured out how to capture pure public goods such as roads. People in Namdenye, a village in Ruvuma, Tanzania, described how a local investor had virtually captured the feeder road linking the village to the main highway. The investor reportedly purchased land that started at the road junction and covered the whole feeder road up to the village, so that the feeder road now passes through his private property. After buying it, he fenced his property and demolished the signage at the road junction. With the feeder road inaccessible, the villagers have to traverse bushy and steep slopes to reach the main road. Mohamedi, a village resident, spoke of the incident bitterly. "We have been cut off from the government. Even if the district education officer wants to visit our school, he will never find it, as there is no sign showing where the school is located." The villagers also fear that crop buyers will be unable to reach the village.

How to acquire power and become an elite

Without money, everything is empty. If you have money, you can even get tiger's milk.

—A young man, Dhamalia, Assam

The upper castes are the dominating people with power. When they speak, they speak with guns in their hands.

—Discussion with women, Jugsana, Uttar Pradesh

Money comes from the party. When a bridge is constructed, money is demanded. Money is extorted at gunpoint. One feels strong when he does politics.

—A man, Hasanbagh, Bangladesh

Elites clearly have many powers and privileges. So we asked our respondents: How do people become elites?

Acquire wealth. Across study regions, everyone was clear that the surest way to acquire power was to acquire money, through legal or illegal means. Money opens the way to education, jobs, and connections; it conveys the power to do good deeds or bad deeds. In the village of Nasher Khan, Afghanistan, people quoted a proverb: "If the hand is full, it does not matter if it is full of bees." In Bangladesh and India, where tigers have become rare, "the milk of the tigress is available if one has money."

In a Bangladeshi village, young Masum said, "Money is everything. If you spend money, you can buy the police and the administration, and people will be afraid of you." In Digbari, young men told us, "Being rich is the easiest route to acquiring power. Many things can be done if one has money. You can roam around with followers and speak in a loud voice."

One can gradually acquire a measure of power by getting out of poverty. A youth in Hathina, Uttar Pradesh, described the process, "It is akin to drops of water collecting gradually to fill in a pot. As a person slowly moves up and out of poverty, he starts gaining power. Then there is everything at your disposal."

Be born into the right family. In many places, people spoke about the continuity of elite status across generations and about the importance of having "ancestral property" or other inherited wealth. In Mechiri, Andhra Pradesh, men explained, "Yes, there are economically well-off people in the community who are very powerful. But none of these people have become powerful recently. We have only those who have been powerful from generations, as they own ancestral properties." In Kodola, Uganda, men and women defined inherited power as power obtained "when one is born in a rich and powerful family. That person will always have power over others."

Belong to the right social group. The genesis of economic and political power often lies in social power, and those with the good fortune to be born into the privileged caste, ethnicity, or religion have a huge head start. In many of our study communities, "horizontal inequalities" (Stewart 2001) between socially constructed groups are important in determining the distribution of power and privilege.

In India, caste continues to be a great divider, even as changes are reported in many places. A woman from the village of Ibrahimpur, Uttar Pradesh, spoke of how the lower-caste villagers live in constant fear of their Thakur (upper-caste) landlords. "We live here as if a tongue between the teeth. The Thakurs are the teeth and the lower castes are the tongue. If they [the lower castes] commit a mistake, then the tongue will be cut off." In the village of Jugsana in Agra district, the upper castes are doubly powerful because of their money and weapons. Our findings from Uttar Pradesh suggest that scheduled caste households are significantly less likely to move out of poverty than other social groups.

In communities affected by conflict in eastern Sri Lanka, ethnicity is an important criterion influencing access to government programs. Young girls in the community of Thambulla in Ampara asserted that local government programs reach only the dominant social group in each locality. "If there is a program in the village with a majority of Muslims, they benefit more compared to other ethnic groups. In a village with a majority of Tamil families, the Tamils get more benefits than other groups. There is no equal distribution among the village."

In communities in Afghanistan, people belonging to different tribes within the same ethnic group have different levels of power. A discussion group in Shazimir said, "The Hazaras coming from Turkmen are not as free and powerful because they are strict. This comes from their low education level. They do not allow their daughters to get education and never let their women go out for work. The people from Ghazni are more broad minded. Although they are Hazara, they are educated, have awareness and money, and also have more freedom."

Over time, social definitions of which group is elite may change through migration (Gupta and Sharma 1991), conflict, or electoral success. In Uttar Pradesh, government policies on land distribution and the reservation of some panchayat seats for lower castes have combined with electoral trends to shift some power from the upper-caste Thakurs to the other backward castes (OBC) and even the Dalits.[20] In the village of Nagara, where the village head comes from the Lodhi caste, only households belonging to the Yadav and Lodhi (OBC) community have access to Kisan credit cards for buying agricultural equipment. The electoral sweep by the Bahujan Samaj Party, a political party of traditionally excluded caste groups, in state elections in Uttar Pradesh in 2007 suggests that they may now have a greater chance of catching up with other caste groups.

Join a political party. Acquiring wealth can take years, and birth into the right family and social group is under no one's control. Joining a political party and becoming associated with political leaders—the bigger the better—is another, perhaps faster way to power and elite status.

It is in South Asia, especially West Bengal and Bangladesh, that acquiring power via politics was mentioned most frequently. In part this may reflect the existence of large government transfer programs in the region, many of them targeted to the poor. In West Bengal villages, people reported that government benefits and jobs are distributed only to party members, including poor members. A women's discussion group in Anakha said, "If common men want to acquire power, the easiest way is to join politics. After joining politics, government money helps to start a business. Through the party, one can easily acquire power. Here there are some people who do not work much, but they work for the panchayat leader and other party leaders. Thus, from the party they get financial benefit. They get loans and below-poverty-line cards [entitling them to targeted benefits], and they do not have to think much about their income."

Across the border in Bangladesh, discussion groups described how one could rise by starting as a party worker, moving up to the *thana* and then the district level, and finally becoming connected with ministers in the central government. Manikjan explained, "After finishing studies, many learn politics through close association with the leaders of the Awami League or the Bangladesh Nationalist Party. After becoming chairmen or members, they rise to prominence through good comportment with people, distribution of cards, old age pension, widows' allowance, relief goods, etc. They earn the heart of the people and slowly move up." Not everyone was so sanguine. As in West Bengal, many people in Bangladesh also reported that government programs targeted to poor households were distributed instead to "boot lickers and party cadres."

How to become a politician

You need money to engage in politics. If you do not have money, how can you hold campaigns? How will you buy people something to drink?
                                —A man, Bugokela, Kagera, Tanzania

A local politician must engage personally: be honest, be polite, be correct, and show love and concern for the village good.
                                —Discussion with women, Koldiaye, Senegal

Only those who have money and goons with them are in politics. They eat other people's money and don't even belch.
                                —Discussion with young women, Pittupur, Uttar Pradesh

Someone who climbs steadily through the party ranks may in time become a politician. People identified three attributes that could help a person rise to elite status this way: money, personal character and good deeds, and finally muscle and guns.

Money. Not all politicians start out rich, but all successful politicians have to tap into financial resources from somewhere. It is easiest when they start with their own wealth. In Kagera, Tanzania, and elsewhere, some of the local government officials also own large businesses. The necessity to spend money on campaigns in democratic systems and the culture of favor mongering it generates have led to a worldwide clamoring for campaign finance reform, with relatively little success.[21] In Andhra Pradesh, people described traffic jams caused by politicians visiting villages at election time. In the village of Kotham, groups said, "At the time of elections, it is like a small festival, as everyone is bribing people with alcohol and money. Contestants pay money to the voters for getting votes." Men in the village of Dhampur noted, "On the day of the festival of votes [election], the politicians make many promises like giving us wages, and they take us in autos and make us vote for them. They give us money, as if only the rich should rule."

In Afghanistan, candidates distributed free mobile handsets to poor people. In the village of Mpusola, Malawi, rich political aspirants provided free coffins whenever someone died. They attended different church services and donated substantial amounts of money during the offerings. Men and women in the community acknowledged that such practices do not always lead to wise voting. "Before we vote, we assess the candidates' homes to see what they own. This is the reason we are having problems—we are choosing people based on their wealth and not because they can help us. We look at their car and we think that they are going to give us a ride in it, not knowing that all we are ever going to get is dust after they pass us on the road."

Personal characteristics and good deeds. Despite the shenanigans at election time, people want their local politicians to have desirable human qualities and to help their communities prosper. The qualities mentioned most frequently were being friendly and approachable, being concerned about the welfare of the community, and bringing in government projects to the community. Trust, honesty, and integrity were high on the agenda. Some people also called for education and knowledge and the ability to lead.

In Indonesia, women's groups in Tattantok said that politicians should be honest, wise, friendly, and united with the people. In Delapong, Philippines, the politician "must show a pleasant personality. He should know how to get along with people. He should be easily approached, especially in times of emergency." Women in Barumangga, Indonesia, suggested that politicians "win people's hearts by doing positive things—by giving food to people, and so on." Respondents in Thailand were the most demanding, perhaps reflecting the Buddhist value of being self-effacing. In Nong Tong, a youth group said that a local politician "should not be conceited or arrogant, should be personable, should not defame others, and should not use his power to bully the villagers. When the local politician gets elected, he should seek funds for village development activities."

In most regions, people acknowledged that it is possible to be elected without being rich. In Kamlondo, Uganda, a men's discussion group expected the local politician to "be sincere, come from a good family, and deliver what he promises." They added, "Our chairman was elected by us. He never gave us sugar or soap. We elected him on merit." In several communities in Andhra Pradesh, people reported that poor men from the lowest caste had been elected because of their reputation, without spending much money on elections, although they were probably aided by the system of reserved seats.[22] However, the ability to win elections without wealth is rare. People in Baroygor, Philippines, went so far as to say that candidates without money have "zero chance of winning."

Muscle and guns. With disheartening frequency, people in many South Asian communities report that the way to political power is through threats and guns. In Tihuliya, Uttar Pradesh, young men described a powerful person as one "who has tons of money, the size of their family is large, there is unity in the family. He has criminal habits, keeps a dagger and a gun, and two to four followers are always with him." In another village, Kursi, young men stated, "If one wants to become a leader, he must have four to six criminal cases against him." Across at least half of the villages visited in the state, getting into politics required *goondagardi* (hooliganism) and guns. In some villages, people reported that the goons wait with crossed arms at polling booths and openly say, "If you don't vote for the pradhan [village head], we will make life difficult for you." Our respondents added, "We want to stay alive. Who wants to be beaten up? We want to live in peace, so we vote as they say." A popular local proverb, *jiski lathi uski bhains*, which roughly translates as "whoever has the stick owns the buffalo," has been modified to "whoever has the gun owns the buffalo."[23] In Alampur, another village in Uttar Pradesh, a women's group affirmed, "Power means to create chaos and thrash people. Power means to beat someone till the blood flows."

Reminiscent of Chicago in the 1920s, people spoke about the importance of "muscle power," the enforcers surrounding a politician. In Anakha,

West Bengal, a men's discussion group said, "Those who are sitting on the top post of the party, they have bodyguards for their safety. And these people save politicians when they face danger. Here people cannot speak against these politicians because of their muscle power." In Gangua, also in West Bengal, a young women's group said, "A gun is the source of all power. With a gun, one can scare others, and rob the power from others' clutches. The politicians in this community do have such power."

In Bangladesh, politicians were described as *dacoits* or bandits. For aspiring politicians, committing crimes and even going to prison can be a good career move. "Someone can become a leader out of anger, murder, and imprisonment. While [he is] in prison, there are posters all around with political writings about [him]. This way a politician captures the eyes of all."

When power is absolute and misused, people sometimes respond with the "weapons of the weak," notably humor and sarcasm. Irshad related the following during a men's discussion group in Chanpasha, Bangladesh:

> My mother had died on Sunday, 10 September. Five months later, when I went to the polling booth to cast my vote, I learned that my mother had already voted. I kept on weeping. My mother had descended from heaven, voted and had left without even meeting me! The army people threw me out after giving me a good bashing. I had a good education about the definition of power on election day.

Is There Any Hope: Can Local Democracy Be Uncaptured?

Rich people are buying politicians to enjoy opportunity.
—Discussion with women, Baintala, West Bengal

They do not call the poor for opinions. Only the wealthy ones are invited.
—A woman, Digbari, Bangladesh

Now people in the community are being consulted. We are more aware of what is happening during the meetings. Promises are being kept. Local leaders have become more modest and more easily accessible than before.
—Discussion group, Lamraab, Morocco

It may seem naïve to be optimistic about the power of local democracy to do any good for poor people, but despite guns and goons, it is already doing good in some places. Indeed, in some places, ratings of government responsiveness have changed for the better over the last 10 years, sometimes quite dramatically. Even deeply corrupt local democracies are not immutable. Chicago changed. There is hope.

Overall, nearly half of the communities across the study regions experienced no changes in their local democracies or in the way they functioned. But there was some improvement. One-third of the communities visited reported that their local government now pays more attention to their concerns, suggesting that change is possible. Moreover, the communities where such a positive shift took place outnumbered by nearly two to one the communities where local democracies' attention to citizen concerns had declined over time (32 percent compared to 17 percent).

In this section, we examine the question of what makes local governments more responsive. We have already described some of the positive associations between responsiveness, improved infrastructure for communities, and improved livelihoods for poor people. Our data reveal one other important finding about responsiveness: communities that rated their local government as highly responsive also had remarkably lower corruption. Sixty-eight percent of communities where people rated local government as highly responsive had no or almost no corruption. By contrast, 68 percent of communities where government was unresponsive reported that most or almost all local government officials were corrupt and took bribes.

In *The Burden of Democracy*, political scientist Pratap Bhanu Mehta (2003) writes that chronic poverty coupled with a lack of accountability has kept Indian democracy from fulfilling its main function, which is to increase the self-respect of all individuals. The "burden of democracy," then, is to find a way to recover a sense of morality and responsibility.

Although guided by theory, we remain empiricists about what makes local democracy work in practice. Given low levels of literacy, high levels of poverty, and many forms of "illiberal electoral democracy" in contexts of deeply embedded social inequality, we do not take for granted that local elections or people's participation necessarily create responsive democracies. Once again, we gave primacy to people's own narratives as we combed through hundreds of pages of notes from communities and combined this qualitative data with some quantitative data.[24] We came up with five factors that appear to be important in unlocking local democracy so that it works more effectively for poor women and men. These are good leaders; local elections; information, particularly about local government; participation; and people's organizations. The mechanisms that make these factors effective are context-specific and difficult to unravel in our cross-country sweep.

Give me a great local leader

What interests us about our leaders is not wealth but humility, integrity, and putting forward the public benefit.
—Discussion with men, Djatick, Senegal

It is difficult to talk to those high, literate officials. Probably some of them have no knowledge of our lives and are afraid to come near us because we smell.
—Discussion group, Salvia Prey, Cambodia

The farming village of Tattantok in East Java, Indonesia, is one of the communities in which responsiveness ratings of local democracy changed from negative to positive during the decade. A relatively prosperous Muslim community, it has an active and educated youth population, but there have been problems with internal conflict, gambling, and theft of animals and crops. The turning point in the community's prosperity was identified as a change in local leadership in 2003. Discussion groups explained, "Before 2003, theft and gambling happened all over the place. Since 2003, gambling has been eradicated. . . . Because of the village head's initiative, there was a meeting that asked the village representatives to help stop gambling." A discussion group of women reported, "The 2003 election of the current *klebun* [village head] was the turning point. We were not happy with the former klebun because he could not fight for people. He only helped those who were close to him. The current klebun fights for us." Participation levels and service delivery in the community improved with the arrival of the new village head. The men continued, "Before, the green cards [for health insurance] existed, but they didn't reach the people. The cards were distributed to those who were closest to the former village head." The women were pleased that they were now encouraged to participate in village meetings. One said, "The building of the current primary school is an example. I made the suggestion that it should be made in an L-shape. They agreed with the idea, and now it is being built in an L-shape."

A majority of communities where democracy ratings improved over the study period identified good leadership as the most important reason for the change. A selfless leader who has "a heart for the community"—as the people of Bukwaime, Uganda, put it—can set a community on a path of development. In Kabtito, Uganda, good local leadership has brought some community development programs into the village and has led to improvement in peace and security. A group of men and women in the village said they can now approach the local village council directly on any matter.

For study communities in Afghanistan, the malek plays a crucial role in bringing improvements to his people. Bibi, a 60-year-old woman in Riah Khillaw, Herat province, praised the leader of the newly elected provincial council in her village, "Mohammed Nasir is a member of the Welayati shura. He is from our community and is now living in Kabul, but he helped the community get electricity and water." In Ramili Qali, Parwan, the malek, who is also head of the local agricultural cooperative, took the initiative to seek out help for his community. During our field team's interview with him, he asked if we could mention the community to a particular person working for a French agricultural cooperative in the area in order to secure the cooperative's help.

By the same token, a corrupt head who works with his coterie of supporters, ignoring the voice of the majority, can prove disastrous for a community. We heard many reports of corrupt, venal leaders who mostly used the local democracy and its programs for their own good or as a vehicle for political patronage—what Bardhan (2002) calls "jobs for the boys."

Free and fair elections increase accountability and responsiveness

The leaders know that if they do not give us attention, especially about problems we face in our area, we will not reelect them. As a result, they make sure that they take keen interest in community affairs.
        —Mukyala, a farmer, Lulyunka, Uganda

We do not know who our representatives are or how to get them. We know only that they come in a vehicle that belongs to the government.
        —Women's discussion group, Mpusola, Malawi

In their research on the success of gram panchayats in implementing land reforms in West Bengal, Bardhan and Mookherjee (2004, 2006) found that greater effort went into land reform in places where local elections were strongly contested by the two rival political parties in the state, the Left Front and the Congress Party. Reform efforts were less intense in areas that were leftist voting strongholds. Bardhan and Mookherjee conclude that the level of political contestation and vote share has a critical effect on responsiveness, a perspective shared by other political scientists. A guaranteed constituency and slack political competition means that ruling parties have less need to satisfy voter demands.

Across our study contexts, people referred to elections as a powerful tool for holding their local politicians accountable. This was reaffirmed by the positive and significant association between voting and the measure of responsiveness of local democracy in virtually all study regions in our model (see annex 6.2).

Afghanistan is a case in point. In the Afghan study communities, people said that the election of community development councils under the auspices of the National Solidarity Program (NSP) has brought local leadership closer to the people.[25] Each council includes 15 male members and 15 female members who deliberate separately and share their decisions. Once elected, the council organizes village consultations on projects to be financed by an NSP grant. Communities are involved in decision making about project design and implementation.

The council in Ramili Qali, a community close to Kabul, was a typically well-functioning one. Elections to the council had reportedly been open and fair. "All the people voted on their own choices," said a group of youths. "They voted with a special zeal and without fear for their favorite candidates." The council heard from women and youth and was open to fresh ideas and opinions from them. A women's discussion group said the district officer could no longer "do everything by his own wish. He is now consulting with the general public and accepts their ideas." The women's council voted to equip the village with two 40-kilowatt generators that provide about four hours of electricity at night to all the houses in the village. The men's council voted for the rehabilitation of culverts and small irrigation structures that help farmers regrow the grapevines burned during the conflict.

While elections in Afghanistan are a means to establish a democratic structure after the anarchy of war, in other contexts they are seen as a way to motivate local politicians to deliver on their promises. In Rahamat, Uttar Pradesh, a discussion group of men explained, "The focus in democracy is on the people. Work is done at a fast pace, and now with election time, the politicians get work done soon to woo the public. Last year, a school was built in our village. A road was made as well, and this has left a good impact on the people."

But the mere ability to vote is not sufficient. Elections are not always free and fair. While elections in some contexts tend to be transparent—particularly in the East Asian study regions, in Morocco, and in Afghanistan—in other places, respondents complained about the conduct of elections. A discussion group of women in Mpusola, Malawi, asserted, "We do not choose politicians. We are asked only to vote. The district officials just come here and say that we have chosen this person to be your councilor or member of parliament, so you should vote for him during elections. So we vote for a person whom we do not know because we don't have a choice." Men and women in Chakboeng, Cambodia, told a similar story. "We did go to vote, but we do not know or even care about whether the electoral process was free and fair. We just think and care about how to make a living. We got nothing from the election except the black paint on our finger" (the ink used to show that someone has voted).

Even fairly elected leaders, of course, can disappoint. In almost all the study regions, there were reports of elected officials and politicians reneging on their mandates. In Yasapira, North Maluku, Indonesia, women spoke of the "rubber promises" of politicians. Politics is all about "telling lies" for one of the villages in Kagera, Tanzania. A discussion group said, "You just have to know how to speak a lot, make people laugh and forget what you said, so that when you come back, they do not ask you what you had promised." In Troula Trav, Cambodia, a discussion group put it this way, "Before the elections we are like small babies who are taken care of. But after . . . when they win . . . they are like stars in the sky. They do not care about us anymore." In Nasher Khan, Nangarhar, Afghanistan, a young girl reported that the local politician had quite literally taken back what he had promised, "We remember one candidate. He came here before the elections and gave us several sewing machines. But when he lost, he came and took all of them back." Universal suffrage is clearly not enough to ensure good leadership and policies that benefit poor people.

Information is power

> *Newspapers nowadays differ greatly from newspapers in the 1970s and even the 1990s. TV has changed as well. They have unraveled many hidden truths. Nowadays, nothing can be veiled. Every day, we read things in the newspaper we couldn't even imagine reading before.*
> —Men's discussion group, Tindyata, Morocco

Two-way information flows between citizens and their representatives are critical for responsible citizenship and a responsive and accountable democracy. Informed citizens are better equipped to take advantage of opportunities, access services, exercise their rights, negotiate effectively, and hold state actors accountable. Without timely information that is presented in forms that can be understood, it is impossible for poor people to take effective action (Narayan 2002b).

Several studies of decentralized governance have underscored the role that easily accessible information can play in ensuring responsiveness. In the city of Bangalore, India, for instance, citizen report cards are revolutionizing the manner in which city residents relate to service providers (Paul 2007).[26] In a panel study of major Indian states, Besley and Burgess (2002) document the role local newspapers have played in increasing the responsiveness of state governments to natural disasters. Reinikka and Svensson (2005) describe the impact of a media campaign informing local communities of their entitlement to school funds from the central government in Uganda. The campaign, along with an increase in central government monitoring, reduced diversion of funds for the project by provincial governments from 80 to 20 percent.

Our quantitative and qualitative evidence affirms the importance of information. Our two measures, newspaper readership and access to information about local government programs, show a significant, positive association with our government responsiveness measure in several study contexts. In fact, access to information about the local government is the single most important factor out of 11 explanatory variables we hypothesized to be associated with responsiveness (annex 6.2).

Improved access to information is helping people monitor their local governments in our study sites in Morocco. In Abzif, for example, a discussion group said, "Before, people didn't feel protected against injustice. People could not protest about what they had to put up with. Before, we couldn't bring up the wrongs committed by governmental representatives in front of a court. But today we can. We are supported by lawyers, newspapers."

In Senegal, the study communities have witnessed a considerable shift in information sources. Independent small private radio stations provide news about government and development projects, allowing the population to monitor their government's performance. Discussions with men in the village of Djatick revealed the changes. "Thanks to private radios, we can now express our dissatisfaction if an elected official doesn't do his job properly, and we can sanction him/her in the next election. Our community now really believes that it's possible to remove a leader who doesn't fulfill our demand." Women in Dapi Toube, Senegal, agreed, "We can denounce certain unfairness thanks to the proliferation of media [private radio stations, mobile phones, etc.]. Formerly, food that was intended for people used to be embezzled and no one talked about it, but that is impossible now because of the media."

Democracy is participation

> *In the past, we did not dare to get in touch with the civil servants. When we talked to them, we were already shaking. But today we do not have to be afraid at all.*
>
> —Men's discussion group, Nong Tong, Thailand

The strong link between democracy and participation, underscored decades ago by the liberation theologian Paulo Freire (1974), was reaffirmed both in group discussions and in our quantitative data. Communities where local government had become more responsive over time also had much higher participation rates than those where responsiveness had decreased (62 percent versus 39 percent). In our regression analysis as well, we find positive association between people's participation in community decision making and our measure of responsiveness of local democracy in most of the study contexts, significantly so in some of them (annex 6.2). When participation in decision making is real and translates into local government decisions, democracies function for the benefit of all, as seen in the positive spillover in our leave-out mean exercise reported earlier (figure 6.5). We found this to be true in three contexts: Mexico, Thailand, and Andhra Pradesh.

In the state of Oaxaca, Mexico, where all the study communities are indigenous, people's participation is rooted in a traditional form of self-governance called *usos y costumbres* (literally, practices and customs). Under this system, citizens have the right and obligation to vote in public assemblies on governance issues. In the community of Guapa del Mar, a woman described how the system works, "Any decision or problem is communicated to the citizens, and it is not just the president who decides but the entire village." A young man praised the system as free from the danger of elite capture. "There is no relation between political and economic power because the decisions are taken by the community and are not taken by the persons who have economic or political power here in the community." A 60-year-old man in the community proclaimed with much pride, "There is no corruption or bribery here; never has been."

Study communities in Thailand reported a rise in what are called "village civil society gatherings." Eighty-four percent of all household survey respondents said that they participate more in consultation meetings now than in the past. More than 60 percent reported that the Tambon Administrative Organizations take into account their concerns and listen to their needs. The village of Nong Tong is typical. A small hamlet of 52 households engaged in paddy and vegetable farming, it has a village headman and a village committee that also elect a representative to the next-higher administrative level of the tambon. The TAO and its members were generally reported to be responsive. It has built roads, formed different types of groups, and encouraged people to participate in community affairs. Access to information through a recently installed public broadcast tower has helped people demand accountability from their local government and "more distribution of authority to the villagers." Homjun, a paddy farmer in the village, said, "Satisfaction is to see the people participating in activities." Another man added, "There is freedom and no abuse."

Not all communities are as fortunate in having meaningful participation. In Upper Deuri, Assam, the village leaders are said to exclude ordinary people. "The villagers cannot affect the decisions of the panchayat. Actually, the panchayat does not give us a chance to speak about any decision. Every decision is taken by a meeting in the *gaon bura's* [village head's] house or in the drawing room of the president. We have nothing to do there," reported a discussion group of men. Discussion groups in Salvia Prey, Cambodia, spoke of exclusion based on wealth: "The officials are too high and costly for us to contact, too far to reach and not always available to talk to. We are down-to-earth, illiterate, and dirty."

People's organizations and self-help groups

> *Before I was just one person; now I am 10. And so I feel I would dare to go up to any government official.*
> —Venkatlakshmi, member of a women's self-help group,
> Chedulla, Andhra Pradesh

As with the findings on participation, we find mostly a positive association between the numbers of groups in communities and responsiveness levels in almost all study contexts (annex 6.2). The strongest findings emerge from Bangladesh, known for large numbers of women's groups formed through well-established NGOs such as Grameen Bank, BRAC, ASHA, and Proshika. Over time, the presence of the collective—just the fact that women get together to undertake some activity—eventually spills over into local government performance.[27]

In Andhra Pradesh, there has been an explosion of women's self-help groups (SHGs) across the state. Ironically, these groups, formed under a statewide government-run program, are now challenging corrupt and inept government and elected officials. Illiterate women are getting organized, running groups, managing savings and credit, and launching new income-generating activities. In many communities, they have become a political force through their sheer numbers.

In one incident, SHG members brought to account a corrupt teacher working at the government school in the village. The teacher had demanded Rs 200 (approximately US$5) extra from each student, causing one SHG member to stop sending her child to school. The other women went to the school to make inquiries. This situation rapidly turned into a confrontation, at which point the SHG set a date for a formal meeting and informed the teacher that she would be required to submit details of her expenditures on that date to the groups. "She, the teacher, then got nervous and returned all the money, and soon after that had herself transferred to another district," recounted our respondents with glee. They added, "Now we're being called for school functions and are invited to attend functions even by officials!"

As women's self-help groups have become a social force in some areas, local leaders have started to pay attention to women's needs and women's votes. This attention, in turn, may have helped reduce levels of domestic violence in these communities. We found some evidence that communities with low levels of domestic violence also have more responsive local democracies. The association was significant in Uttar Pradesh, Senegal, Ruvuma (Tanzania), and Mexico (annex 6.2). To remove problems of endogeneity, violence levels 10 years ago were considered; lower domestic violence then seems to be associated with higher current responsiveness of local governments in some study contexts. The mediating variable was civil society activism that over time changed the norms around domestic violence, drinking, and respect for women. This change, in turn, encouraged government to show greater responsiveness toward women, treating them with respect and including them in local decision making. In Andhra Pradesh, for instance, several of the study communities with well-organized women's self-help groups had been successful in reducing the consumption of *arak* (locally brewed alcohol) among men and the domestic abuse that often followed.

A Tale of Two Communities

> *De landlord is landlord, de politician is landlord, de judge is landlord, de shurf [sheriff] is landlord, ever'body is landlord, en we ain' got nothing.*
> —A Mississippi sharecropper's testimony in 1936,
> cited by Schulman (1994: 16)

As long as poor people are competing with richer groups who control their livelihoods—and who also happen to be the political leaders and magistrates in their community—poor people are likely to lose. Whether in Mississippi or in Kagera, Tanzania, economic and political forms of power inevitably converge to defy all policy attempts at change. Redistribution schemes must be carefully designed if they are to overcome the self-interest of powerful intermediaries and reach poor people. Interventions that improve the functioning of local democracy, discussed above, improve poor people's chances of benefiting from targeted government programs.

However, there is another, less-explored way to achieve the same end, which is to expand the economic pie at the local level rather than focusing only on redistribution.[28] Benjamin Friedman, in *The Moral Consequences of Economic Growth* (2005: 4), argues that across the Western world, a period of economic growth, with rising incomes for the *clear majority* of citizens, "more often than not fosters greater opportunity, tolerance of diversity, social mobility, commitment to fairness and dedication to democracy." When living standards stagnate or decline, most societies make little progress on these goals and may indeed go backward.[29]

There are strong parallels in our community-level study. But we also find that the extent of social stratification affects who benefits from economic growth or opportunities at the local level. Let us look at two case studies of village development from West Bengal.

Baral: Expanded opportunities for all

When our teams arrived in Baral, in the district of Purulia, West Bengal, the village had been facing drought conditions for several years. Conditions were so dire that the government of West Bengal had declared Purulia to be a "dry district." Most households in Baral depend on cultivation of rice, a crop that is water intensive. With the failure of the rains, one would expect a substantial proportion of people in Baral to have slipped into destitution.

In 1995, at the start of the study period, 72 percent of households sampled for the ladder of life exercise in the village were classified poor. Basic infrastructure in Baral was primitive. The road connecting the village to the district center was nonmetaled and muddy, making for a long, treacherous commute to the local market. Though situated on the banks of a river, the village had no proper system of canals to bring river water to the fields. Dependent on the rains, people could harvest only one rice crop a year. Migration out of the village was common. "Earlier, people of our village went to other places to do daily labor," recounted Padmalochan, a man participating in a discussion group. "We cultivated our land only once and people went outside and worked, even for a low wage."

But a series of infrastructural and livelihood initiatives undertaken by the state, district government, and local panchayat in Baral changed all that. In 1995, the state government, working in coordination with the local panchayat, implemented a Comprehensive Area Development Program that focused on agriculture. The centerpiece was efforts to improve productivity of rice by creating seed banks of new high-yielding varieties and training local farmers to grow them. The difference in productivity when compared to native rice was substantial. "Earlier, we produced 10–12 *mon* of paddy from 1 bigha [of land]. But now we are getting 22–26 mon paddy," explained women in a discussion group.[30] The program also helped households diversify their livelihood portfolios by training them in activities such as dairy farming, fish farming, and cultivation of new crops. It made available seeds and saplings of vegetables and flowers and particularly encouraged women to grow them.

In addition to providing agricultural training, the local panchayat in Baral, with funds from the zilla parishad (the district council), was instrumental in the construction of a dam on the river and a network of canals. Canal irrigation had brought multiple benefits to the farmers. About a third of them had shifted to cultivating wheat. "They cultivate wheat in the winters and sell it in the summer. They can get wheat seeds from the panchayat." In addition, the dam enabled people to take up fish farming, bringing in extra income of at least Rs 35–45 per day.

Finally, the local panchayat had built a new metaled road connecting the village to the local market and to the highway leading to the district center. "There is a big market in Balrampur," explained a discussion group of men. "Businessmen come there from Jamshedpur [a prosperous industrial center in West Bengal]. People who are cultivating fish sell it at 1–2 rupees profit per kilogram. Those who cultivate wheat sell it at 1–2 rupees profit per kilogram." This price was more than what producers had earned for their produce in the village market. The additional income rippled through the village economy. Some households had opened small kiosks selling food and other items along the road. Women reported, "The purchasing power of people has increased. They are now buying things from the market for their family. For instance, there are more grocery and sweet shops."

Even villagers who survived on daily wage labor had benefited from the building of the road and dam. They were employed by the panchayat on the construction projects and were paid in both rice and money.

The result of all these initiatives was a substantial increase in income. By 2005, 50 percent of the households sampled for the ladder of life discussion had moved out of poverty over the preceding decade. "We now have goddess Lakshmi in our house," exclaimed one of our key informants, referring to the Hindu goddess of wealth.

Even more remarkable was the reported decrease in social and political inequalities in the village. The opening up of markets reduced the stranglehold of the upper-caste elite. Bihari, an upper-caste man our team met, spoke of the change. "We are Brahmins. Earlier our predecessors felt unsociable toward the lower castes, so all the work in the village was done by lower-caste people. But now even we are working and cultivating along with them." Badal added, "People of higher castes are now going to the houses of the lower castes. They do not insult lower-caste people now."

The improvements also transformed the villagers' relationship with the panchayat. With expanded opportunities, daily wage laborers and small cultivators gained the courage to question their local officials on the workings of local government. Most respondents agreed that there was no corruption or bribe taking in the village, and elections were free and fair. Each time the panchayat received an order to do any public work, it discussed the work in a village assembly where everyone, including women, could give their opinions. If labor contractors refused to pay laborers after work was completed, the laborers could go to the panchayat, which heard their grievances and took action. Jagannath described the shift: "Earlier, the panchayat took one-sided decisions. They did not consult with everyone. Now the opinion of the village people is taken into consideration. They can tell their discomfort and problems. Because of the increase of work and wages, common people have improved their position." Over and over again, people said with great confidence, "We vote for a candidate who will work for us."

Khalsi: Stagnation and discrimination

Life in Khalsi, another village in Purulia, presents a stark contrast. This village also suffered from lack of proper roads and irrigation facilities in 1995—and still does today. Lack of water has made it impossible for farmers to shift to hybrid and higher-yielding varieties of rice. Aloka, a woman in the village, described their plight: "Hybrid crops need sufficient water. Otherwise they need manure. We cannot provide manure due to want of money, and the irrigation system of our village is pathetic. We are dependent on rain." Without a passable road, villagers cannot take their produce in vehicles to markets and the district center. Women said, "If anybody wants to come to our village or go from here, he has to walk on foot through a muddy road because no vehicles want to enter through this road. But we have no other alternative. The road is an obstacle in the path of improvement of our village. If we had a metaled road leading from the main road to our village, then everyone in the village would have benefited in every sphere."

Ten years ago, just as in Baral, 71 percent of the population in Khalsi was in poverty. But by 2005, only 15 percent of Khalsi households had moved out of poverty. With limited options, many poor people migrated to nearby cities for work—a tradition that had stopped in Baral.

The lack of opportunities in the village has left the social and political dynamics unchanged. Young people described the many deeply embedded discriminatory practices. "When a higher-caste person visits a lower-caste person, he has to bathe afterward [to wash off the pollution]. If a lower-caste person drinks water or tea, you have to wash the utensils. The people of the lower caste do not sit in the same row as the higher caste."

Unlike the panchayat members in Baral, local officials in Khalsi were consistently described as corrupt, full of tricks, and uninterested in working for the good of the community. Benefits were channeled along party lines. A men's discussion group said, "Only those involved in the party are recipients of goats, cows, and bullock carts for plowing. We get nothing. The panchayat members and party leaders attend the meeting, and they take decisions about what kind of work, where, when, and how they will do it. They also decide whom they will pay. More than half the government aid is misappropriated by the party leaders and members of the panchayat. The money is divided as booty among the party members and the party bosses. There are no statements of accounts. Whatever the panchayat says is right. It doesn't matter if it is good or bad. Whatever they say, we have to agree with them. Everything they pay is to the party members who are engaged with the party. For others, they always ring the bell 'not available.'"

A sense of frustration was evident across Khalsi. Men said, "We used to visit the panchayat office earlier. But we visit the office only occasionally now because they do nothing for us. They are busy looking after their own benefits and the people close to them." Young girls in the community had the final word. "We don't blame the CPM [ruling leftist party]. [But] we shall have to bring new faces, leaving the old ones; only then improvement will be possible. As they have been ruling for a long time, there is more corruption. There will be no change in the coming days."

Looking beyond the two cases

The contrasting stories of Baral and Khalsi show how the expansion of economic opportunity sets can help open up closed social systems and change political dynamics in a community. To test whether this was true for other communities as well, we return to our leave-out means on local democracy. When the sign is positive, it means that all in the community gain. When the sign is negative, it means that democracy is still functioning to benefit a few at the expense of others.

We wanted to know whether an expansion in economic opportunities in any way lessens the crowding-out effects of local democracy (the negative sign). We constructed leave-out means for responsiveness of local democracy (our indicator for crowding out) separately for communities that experienced rising prosperity over the study period. We then compared them to the leave-out means for villages where prosperity declined.[31] The results, reported in table 6.2, reflect the variation in the depth of social stratification by caste in

TABLE 6.2
Economic opportunities can create positive spillovers

	LOM for responsiveness of local democracy	
State	Bottom 33% of villages ranked on net prosperity	Top 33% of villages ranked on net prosperity
Uttar Pradesh	Significantly negative	Significantly more negative
West Bengal	Significantly negative	Positive
Assam	Significantly negative	Significantly more negative
Andhra Pradesh	Positive	Significantly more positive

the communities in our sample in the four Indian states. We note the pattern of results but do not impute causality.

In West Bengal, in confirmation of our case study findings, the leave-out mean indicator moved from negative to positive with increasing economic prosperity, suggesting a process of "crowding in" rather than crowding out. That is, all gain from local democracy as communities move from less prosperity to more prosperity. Three decades of communist rule in West Bengal has broken the hold of caste; the most important social differentiator is now political party affiliation, something that can be manipulated more easily than the ascribed category of caste.

In Uttar Pradesh and Assam, on the other hand, increases in economic opportunities aggravated exclusion as local democracy concentrated resources in the hands of even fewer people. Uttar Pradesh is deeply stratified along caste lines and has few people's organizations that are not caste affiliated. Assam, affected by protracted conflict and a large influx of people from Bangladesh, is in flux, with ethnic and religious divisions.

Andhra Pradesh has positive signs in communities with low economic opportunity, and the sign even more strikingly becomes more positive in the villages with high economic opportunity. All benefit from responsive local democracies. As mentioned, women's self-help groups have had a strong positive effect on the responsiveness of local democracies.

In conclusion, we believe that an expansion of the economy can have positive "moral consequences" (Friedman 2005), even at the micro level, *provided* that there is some moderating influence on deep social inequalities. These results suggest that democracy and participation of people in governance through poor people's organizations *can* moderate the effect of deeply embedded social inequalities on access to economic opportunities. Growth alone will not automatically increase everyone's access to expanding economic opportunities in an unequal social environment.

The expansion of economic opportunity is important but not sufficient. Inequalities in access can be moderated either by building organizations of poor people, by encouraging civil society activism, or by promoting government ideologies that support equity and dignity for all.

Conclusion: New Roles for Local Democracy—beyond the Zero-Sum Game

Democracy is about something permanent, while politics is something that changes every day.
> —Discussion group, Gabunazi, Kagera, Tanzania

Our micro-level evidence demonstrates that poor people value the ideals of democracy: freedom, rights, equality, participation, and justice. What is striking is that they also see an association between the responsiveness of their local democratic structure—be it the shura in Afghanistan or the village executive committee in Tanzania or the panchayat in India—and their attempts to move out of poverty. While the broad characterizations of democracy as liberal or illiberal may be helpful at the national level, to understand how the functioning of democracy affects poor people's lives, it is critical to focus on the disaggregated level of communities, districts, or provinces within countries. Ninety-three percent of the variation in democratic functioning is within country.

Poverty discourses over the past 60 years have largely ignored political factors and political institutions, despite the recent focus on decentralization of government functions, funds, and functionaries. Our study points to the critical importance of improving local democracy to help people move out of poverty.

Given the existence of "coalitions of power" (Acemoglu and Robinson 2008), local democracy often functions as a zero-sum game. If some poor people gain, others lose. In addition, our evidence suggests that local democracies often become corrupt and co-opted by the elite. The probability of corruption, exclusion, and elite capture is higher in societies that are socially stratified, where lines around social, economic, and political power converge. We put some numbers on the negative effects of corruption to illustrate orders of magnitude. In Uttar Pradesh, a unit increase in corruption decreases the probability of moving out of poverty by 10 percent. It offsets the combined positive effects of increasing ownership of land by 1 hectare and increasing education from illiterate to primary-literate levels. In other places, when they can afford it, poor people are buying their way out of poverty.

Fortunately, there are ways in which local democracy can be uncaptured and kept accountable. They include promoting good leaders, ensuring the right to vote in free and fair elections, providing increased access to information about the local government, and supporting associational life and poor people's participation in community decisions. People's organizations that have legitimacy can play an important role in keeping governments accountable, especially when they achieve scale across localities. A political culture that enshrines values of fairness and equity can also play an equalizing role when economic opportunities expand.

It is important for policy makers to stop treating local government bodies mainly as channels for the distribution of goods and services that come from the central and state governments—as players in a zero-sum game. Well-functioning local governments can be dynamic entities that help liberalize the economy from below. They can do so by bringing in infrastructure, promoting agricultural improvements, encouraging households to diversify their livelihoods, and demystifying rules and regulations that constrain entrepreneurship. As the economic pie expands, there is greater hope of diminishing the importance of social differences in determining economic and political allocations by local democracies.

Local leaders can play a critical role in expanding the economic pie. Our accounts suggest that with the right incentives, local leaders can bring programs to their communities and advance the interests of their constituents at higher levels of government. In South Asia, and to some extent in other regions, a new generation of younger, educated leaders is emerging (Krishna 2002; Powis 2007). In China, local leaders have played a key role in the economic transformation (Qian 2003; Putterman 1995). Mechanisms will need to be developed to track the accountability of such leaders: fair elections and regular state/central government audits (Olken 2004) can prove useful in this regard.

In the end, we conclude that democracy is not a simple concept. Local democracy on the ground has its problems, yet it holds out great hope. In a speech in New York, Adam Michnik, a veteran of the Polish struggle for democracy, captured the ambiguities:

> Democracy is neither black nor red. Democracy is gray. . . . It chooses banality over excellence, shrewdness over nobility, empty promise over true competence. . . . It is eternal imperfection, a mixture of sinfulness, saintliness and monkey business. This is why the seekers of a moral state and of a perfectly just society do not like democracy. Yet only democracy—having the capacity to question itself—also has the capacity to correct its own mistakes.

Michnik is reported to have ended his speech with "Gray is beautiful!"[32]

Annex 6.1   Factors Associated with Responsiveness of Local Democracy

PCA index of voting/elections
• Voting in state/national elections (currently, rh508)

Distance to main center
• Distance to main center (c202bi)

Access to information about local government
• Trend in access to information about local government (over 10 years, rh515b)

Household newspaper readership
• Number of times anyone in household read a newspaper (in past 1 month, h518)

Participation in community decision making
• Participation in community affairs: focus group discussion (over 10 years, rc916)

Collective action (PCA index with current weights)
• Coming together to solve water problems (10 years ago, rc412b)
• Coming together to assist each other (10 years ago, rc413b)

Social capital
• Number of groups household belonged to (10 years ago, h406Tb)

Individual empowerment (PCA index)
• Control over everyday decisions (over 10 years, rh501b)
• Position on ladder of power and rights (10 years ago, h708)

Violence against women in community
• Leave-out mean of violence against girls and women within households (10 years ago, h609b)

Education of household head
• Education of household head (currently, h106)

Extent of social divisions
• Extent of social divisions in community (10 years ago, c414b)

LOCAL DEMOCRACY INDEX

PCA index of current responsiveness of local democracy using household-level data
• Trust in local government officials (rh415a)
• Satisfaction with democracy in local government (rh511)
• Extent to which local government takes into account concerns (rh502a)
• Ability to influence actions of local government (rh504)

Note: For explanation of codes, see appendix 4.

Annex 6.2   Full OLS Regression Results with Responsiveness of Local Democracy as Dependent Variable

	UP Caste	WB Landdist	ASSAM Conf	AP SHG	BAN Empow	UGA Panel
Voting in elections (rh508)	0.094	0.174	0.043	0.019	0.008	0.131
	[3.56]***	[3.16]***	[1.42]	[0.33]	[0.22]	[2.98]***
Distance to main center (c202bi)	0.001	−0.004	0.005	−0.001	0.007	−0.012
	[0.16]	[0.56]	[1.01]	[0.28]	[0.60]	[2.40]**
Household newspaper readership (h518)	0.012	0.009	0.009	0.008	0.003	
	[3.45]***	[2.06]**	[2.42]**	[0.87]	[0.32]	
Access to information about local government (rh515b)	1.08	1.098	0.823	0.567	0.469	
	[20.47]***	[7.62]***	[12.85]***	[5.08]***	[4.67]***	
Participation in community decision making (rc916)	0.057	0.046	0.106	0.006	0.247	0.033
	[0.90]	[0.45]	[1.75]*	[0.04]	[1.38]	[0.40]
Collective action (PCA rc412b, rc413b, with current weights)	0.009	0.007	0.108	0.011	−0.054	−0.094
	[0.18]	[0.11]	[2.91]***	[0.11]	[0.42]	[1.18]
Social capital (h406Tb)	0.025	0.081	0.01	0.001	0.201	−0.127
	[0.44]	[1.52]	[0.24]	[0.03]	[1.98]**	[2.54]**
Individual empowerment (PCA rh501b, h708)	0.156	−0.234	0.294	0.18	−0.09	
	[4.81]***	[5.75]***	[5.98]***	[2.87]***	[1.22]	
Violence against women in community (LOM h609b)	−0.407	−0.084	−0.184	−0.303		
	[3.30]***	[0.35]	[1.45]	[0.96]		
Education of household head (h106)	0.002	0.022	−0.006	−0.015	0.095	
	[0.45]	[1.18]	[1.30]	[0.54]	[2.26]**	
Extent of social divisions (c414b)	0.007	−0.004	0.01	0.15	0.227	0.042
	[0.17]	[0.04]	[0.17]	[1.44]	[2.33]**	[0.78]
Constant	−2.286	−2.496	−1.689	−1.268	−2.445	0.17
	[7.26]***	[5.40]***	[5.99]***	[3.28]***	[4.98]***	[0.90]
Observations	1,635	1,192	746	839	850	714
R^2	0.32	0.34	0.37	0.15	0.11	0.06

Note: Cluster-robust t-statistics in brackets.

*p < .10 **p < .05 ***p < .01 (White heteroscedasticity-consistent standard errors)

For key on codes and abbreviations, see appendixes 2 and 4.

MAL Infra	SEN Infra	TAN Ruv	AFG Conf	INDO Conf	PHI conf	COL Conf	MEX Ethn	PHI Panel
0.15	0.102	0.005	0.442	0.318	0.15	0.146	0.228	0.462
[1.36]	[1.38]	[0.09]	[2.71]***	[5.40]***	[2.54]**	[1.71]*	[2.46]**	[1.92]*
0.001	−0.009	0.001	−0.007	−0.027	0		−0.203	0.011
[0.30]	[1.28]	[0.20]	[1.45]	[0.46]	[0.68]		[1.76]*	[0.98]
0.095	−0.013	0.042	0.043	−0.002	0.007	−0.028	−0.007	0.179
[3.04]***	[3.45]***	[2.34]**	[4.54]***	[0.13]	[0.50]	[1.46]	[0.55]	[2.23]**
0.321	0.34	0.449	0.655	0.279	−0.473	0.556	0.023	−0.44
[2.82]***	[2.09]**	[2.42]**	[1.43]	[3.31]***	[4.96]***	[3.94]***	[4.97]***	[1.37]
0.597	0.294	0.775		−0.146	−0.129	0.154	0.709	0.172
[2.61]***	[1.19]	[1.67]*		[0.55]	[0.50]	[1.66]*	[3.39]***	[1.88]*
−0.757	−0.434	−0.272	−0.441	−0.083	0.133	0.352	0.306	−0.073
[0.72]	[2.16]**	[1.61]	[3.94]***	[0.53]	[0.88]	[2.62]***	[7.60]***	[0.87]
0.012	0.013	−0.027		0.005	0.037	0.105	0.074	0.211
[0.21]	[0.26]	[0.30]		[0.08]	[0.49]	[1.26]	[0.77]	[1.21]
0.02	0.118	0.058	−0.199	0.017	−0.016	0.112	0.051	0.172
[0.13]	[1.24]	[0.70]	[2.33]**	[0.29]	[0.21]	[1.42]	[0.48]	[0.87]
1.728	−0.714	−1.96	0.86	1.275	1.158	0.718	−0.285	−0.55
[2.57]**	[2.44]**	[1.74]*	[5.21]***	[0.68]	[1.31]	[2.49]**	[1.97]**	[0.68]
0.232		−0.077	−0.005	−0.132			0.086	0.058
[1.27]		[1.19]	[0.06]	[0.68]			[1.15]	[0.50]
−0.92	−0.207		0.012	−0.184	0.161	0.093	0.483	0.07
[3.27]***	[0.67]		[0.31]	[0.63]	[1.11]	[2.09]**	[3.06]***	[0.33]
−1.606	1.075	1.698	−3.131	−0.886	−0.726	−3.072	−1.349	0.239
[0.67]	[0.86]	[0.94]	[3.31]***	[0.33]	[0.61]	[3.75]***	[1.82]*	[0.34]
122	287	301	72	368	300	227	294	220
0.26	0.22	0.1	0.35	0.11	0.12	0.17	0.26	0.48

Notes

1. In *Political Liberalism*, John Rawls writes, "The first principle covering the equal basic rights and liberties may easily be preceded by a lexically prior principle requiring that citizens' basic needs be met, at least insofar as their being met is necessary for citizens to understand and to be able fruitfully to exercise those rights and liberties" (1993: 7).
2. It is difficult to sustain the argument that democracy has put a drag on India. Despite contentious coalition politics, India has sustained a growth rate of 8 percent and is expected to grow at 5–7 percent despite the financial crisis.
3. This alternative interpretation of high voter turnout as a sign of voter desperation was suggested by Pratap Bhanu Mehta (personal communication, April 2008).
4. There is a growing literature on accountability, including social and downward accountability. See Bovens (2006); Goetz and Jenkins (2005); Lankina, Hudalla, and Wollmann (2007); Narayan (2002b); Sisk (2001); and Yilmaz, Beris, and Berthet (2008).
5. Country-specific results are available in the country reports, and some will be discussed in detail in forthcoming publications in this series.
6. Decentralization of government is a vastly important and complex subject, but it is not our focus. For an insightful review of some of the issues, see Bardhan (2002), Shah and Thompson (2004), and Crook and Manor (1998).
7. This view emerged in focus group discussions on livelihoods, freedom, power, and democracy that were conducted separately with women, men, and youth in each community. The participants in each group were asked three open-ended questions: "What does democracy mean to you? What are its features or dimensions? Which three features are most important to making democracy work? Why?" In each case, the local-language word used to mean "democracy" was predetermined in training workshops before the investigators went into the field.
8. In his writings on the country-town nexus in India, sociologist Dipankar Gupta contends that the rural political landscape is changing with circular migration. Although lower-caste laborers used to depend on their landed upper-caste benefactors, especially during lean agricultural seasons, they now migrate to cities for work. When they return to their villages, often flush with cash, they seek a new place in the village social and political hierarchy. This trend, together with affirmative action policies such as reserving certain government jobs for lower-caste applicants, has brought more combative politics to rural India (Gupta and Sharma 1991).
9. Focusing on the Indonesian tradition of *gotong royong*, or voluntary communal work, Rao (2008) argues that even though the system initiated by Suharto was coercive, it created over time a collective understanding of what it means to be a good citizen. It helped create a normative desire for citizenship and expectation of democracy, which, in turn, has provided a foundation for community-driven development and decentralized local governance. Looking at the management of common property resources in Tamil Nadu, India, Mosse (1997) argues that water tanks and village temples could serve as public institutions that symbolize social relations, status, prestige, and honor. Turner (1982) suggests that when a

social group celebrates a particular event such as a festival, it "celebrates itself" by "manifesting in symbolic form what it conceives to be its essential life."

10. Fung and Wright (2003, 33–34) focus on how unequal power in society creates problems for the practice of deliberative democracy. Such practice "may pay insufficient attention to the fact that participants in these processes usually face each other from unequal positions of power. Citizens who are advantaged in terms of their wealth, education, income, or membership in dominant racial and ethnic groups participate more frequently and effectively than those who are less well off. If both strong and weak are well represented, the strong may nevertheless use tools at their disposal—material resources, information asymmetries, rhetorical capacities—to advance collective decisions that unreasonably favor their interests." Kaufman (1968) calls this the "paradox of participatory democracy."

11. So we could tease out the variation, responses for communities that experienced no change in responsiveness have not been reported.

12. We used the technique of principal components analysis to aggregate all the variables into a composite index of responsiveness. We test the association quantitatively between our measure of responsiveness of local democracy and an individual household's ability to move out of poverty. Using the multivariate linear regression model reported in appendix 6, we use household MOP as the dependent variable, testing its association with several other independent variables (including responsiveness) that we believe can have an association with mobility.

13. For purposes of our analysis, we have given equal weights to a unit change in education at either level—from illiterate to primary literate or from primary literate to secondary literate. In the real world, this weighting may not hold true. The household head's transition from illiteracy to primary literacy may be more significant in influencing his or her family's chances of escaping poverty than the achievement of a higher level of education.

14. In certain study contexts, the variable had to be dropped because of problems of multicollinearity.

15. According to Prud'homme (1995), decentralization may be accompanied by corruption as it creates more layers of taxes. In his study of Zaire, Prud'homme (1992) estimated that informal taxes at the local level, including payoffs to local authorities, gifts, and donations, were at least eight times more important than formal taxes. Paucity of resources at lower levels of democracies can also open up avenues for rules that conceal corrupt practices. In his study of regional governments in Russia, Zhuravskaya (2000) found that less allocation of resources to local governments weakens their incentive to foster local business development.

16. Using data on bribery of public officials in Uganda and Peru, Hunt (2007) estimates that bribery rates and bribe amounts are higher where clients are frustrated with slow service. Bribery allows clients to avoid the poor service delivered to those who refuse to bribe.

17. It could be that movers out of poverty report lower corruption levels in their community because they have close ties with their local political leader, who has assisted their mobility. Using initial corruption levels and community-assessed mobility as the dependent variable in the regression model reduces room for such halo effects.

18. Schattscheiner (1963) described how multiple interlocking social and economic relationships between local elites act as formidable barriers to progress for others. He famously remarked, "The flaw in the pluralist heaven is that the heavenly chorus sings with a strong upper-class accent." Some theorists consider elite capture as a malaise that is bound to afflict local democracies and/or governments. While political agents at appropriately decentralized levels may have greater incentive to serve voters at large because of their physical and social proximity to them (Seabright 1996; Khemani 2001; Tomassi and Weinschelbaum 1999), this same closeness may facilitate the making and fulfillment of clientelist promises to a few of those voters. This change may be especially true for newly instituted local democracies that try to first serve their political patrons (Keefer 2002). Varshney (2007) calls this the mass-politics constraint.

19. Studies in several countries have attempted to describe the phenomenon of elite capture empirically. Wright (1974) provided some of the first evidence that political factors influence allocation of federal funds across states in the United States. More recent studies that find evidence of elite capture include Bardhan and Mookherjee (2004, 2006) on use of public fiscal grants in 89 panchayats in West Bengal; Olken (2004) on road projects in Indonesia; Lieten (1996), Mathew and Nayak (1996), and Besley, Pande, and Rao (2007) on panchayats in India; and Galasso and Ravallion (2005) on a decentralized food-for-education program in Bangladesh.

20. The caste system in Uttar Pradesh and India as a whole divides the Hindu population into different tiers according to their caste or *varna* (traditional occupation). Castes from the "general category" are engaged in respectable professions such as teaching (Brahmins). At the bottom of the ladder are the untouchables or outcastes. Known today as the Dalits, this category consists of the scheduled castes (SC). After India gained independence, the newly drafted national constitution provided for a separate category of "other backward classes" (OBC). This category consisted of peasant cultivators like the Yadavs and Lodhis, who were not SCs but were as disadvantaged as them in most respects. Although the OBCs did not face historical discrimination, the first Backward Classes Commission in India used caste as an explicit criterion for judging their backwardness. Thus, the OBCs came to be known also as "other backward castes."

21. According to Keefer and Vlaicu (2008), electoral candidates in younger democracies may engage in clientelist practices and corruption to gain credibility and votes. Such patron–client networks often run deep, especially in smaller electorates where "vote buying [is] a cost-effective electoral strategy." However, as democracies age, political reforms that expand the size of the electorate, introduce secret ballots, and impose limits on electoral spending can make elections more issue based.

22. The Indian Constitution (articles 330 and 332) mandates reservations for scheduled castes and scheduled tribes in federal and state legislatures. Scheduled castes have for centuries occupied the bottom of the Hindu caste system, while scheduled tribes are marked by their geographic and cultural isolation.

23. A *lathi*, a long baton, is a traditional weapon that is also used to control domestic animals.

24. We again used multivariate regression techniques. Our measure of responsiveness of local democracy became the dependent variable, and we used independent variables that we believed could explain higher or lower responsiveness. The framework and variables used for the exercise are listed in annex 6.1, with results in annex 6.2.

25. The NSP is a rural development program funded by the World Bank and managed by the Ministry of Rural Rehabilitation and Development. The program provides grants of up to US$60,000 to villages for rehabilitation, reconstruction, and income generation projects.

26. Citizen report cards grade a service provider based on feedback from users. Documenting the success of this innovation in Bangalore, India, Paul (2007) shows that by the third round of report cards, satisfaction with most public services in the city had registered dramatic improvement.

27. This result reaffirms findings in the literature about the positive impact of community participation on service delivery and other governance issues (Isham, Narayan, and Pritchett 1994; Santos 1998; Baiochhi 2005; Foster and Rosenzweig 2001). In a study of 500 villages in South India, Besley, Pande, and Rao (2007) find that gram sabha meetings provide a platform for participation by some of the most disadvantaged groups in the village—the landless and scheduled castes and tribes. Their results show that illiterate households in villages that have held gram sabhas in the past year are more likely to have a below-poverty-line card entitling them to benefits.

28. Knack (2005) presents a similar argument for empowerment policies for poor people. Using the concept of Pareto efficiency, he argues that if the total amount of power available is assumed to be fixed, efforts focused on increasing the power of the poor are likely to face substantial resistance from the nonpoor, who stand to lose. The only politically feasible way to empower the poor, therefore, is to focus on "identifying options for economic and political change that can benefit the poor without necessitating a comparable decline in benefits to the nonpoor," that is, by shifting from what he calls a "zero sum approach" to a "positive sum game."

29. While we are in general agreement with Friedman's main argument, we do not agree with his idea that presumed Western values of hard work and diligence predispose Western societies to economic productivity and growth. The author seems to perpetuate the myth that people in developing countries are morally less advanced than those in the developed world.

30. A *mon* is a traditional measure of weight used in West Bengal and Bangladesh. One mon is roughly the amount of rice that would be harvested from 20 kathas (approximately 1,338 square meters) of land.

31. We used the net prosperity index (NPI) as a measure of prosperity. The index measures the net movement on the ladder of life in a village, that is, all those who moved up less all those who moved down.

32. Reported in the *New Yorker*, December 9, 1996, and quoted by Bardhan (1999).

The Unfulfilled Potential
of Collective Action

*The most important thing is the family
union and the desire to keep on living,
moving on. Without that, there is
nothing.*

—ADRIANA, A 29-YEAR-OLD WOMAN,
El Mirador, Colombia

*We have to organize ourselves for
the journey to the farms. Although
everybody has his own plot, you cannot
go alone.*

—FARMERS IN NAMDENYE, RUVUMA, TANZANIA,
a village menaced by lions

*These people tell us that we have to
contribute for the school, for the police,
and for offices. But we are the ones who
bring stones. We make the bricks and offer
our labor. So where does the money go?*

—MEN'S DISCUSSION GROUP,
Bugokela, Kagera, Tanzania, complaining about
a community-driven development project

Around the world, fables transmit the deepest values of a culture. We start this chapter with a favorite fable from India, "The Talkative Tortoise," probably first recorded sometime in the third to fifth century AD.[1]

Once upon a time, a tortoise lived in a village pond. Two young geese used to visit the pond, and the three became good friends. One year, a severe drought afflicted the region, and all the rivers, lakes, and ponds started drying up. With no water to drink, the birds and animals in the village began to die.

The geese thought of migrating to another lake, but they didn't want to leave their friend, the tortoise, behind. The tortoise came up with an idea. He told the geese, "Why don't you bring a strong stick? You can hold the two ends of the stick in your beaks, and I will grasp the stick in the middle with my mouth. In this way, I can fly with you." The geese agreed, but knowing their friend's talkative nature, they imposed one condition. "You must promise not to open your mouth while we fly."

The tortoise agreed, and the three started on their journey. At one point, they flew over a village. The people in the village were surprised to see the spectacle and started laughing and clapping. Unable to control his anxiety, the tortoise opened his mouth to ask the geese, "Friends—what is this all about?" He fell to his death.

The beauty of fables is that there many lessons and morals that can be drawn. One clear lesson of this fable is to know when to keep your mouth shut! A more central one for us is about collective action, circles of trust, friendship, and the importance of connecting with people unlike oneself to survive and flourish in life.

There is a very extensive literature on collective action, from Mancur Olson (1965) to Elinor Ostrom (1990) to Robert Putnam (1993). Much is already known about collective action in different contexts, but a debate has emerged between those who sing the virtues of collective action and those who see drawbacks. Our findings confirm the importance and potential of grassroots collective action. We suggest strategies to scale up such activities, building on the circles of trust established by groups to increase equitable access to markets and to local democracies.

In this chapter, we highlight four findings and draw out implications for policy. First, across the communities in our sample, the family is the most important context within which collective action takes place. Observing the features of successful families can give us insights that are potentially applicable to other forms of collective action. Second, poor people have a propensity to come together in spontaneous bonding groups, which helps them survive but does not often help them move out of poverty. Third, although there are ways of building on indigenous forms of collective action, outsiders, whether from NGOs or government, often get it wrong. Poor people and formerly poor people our teams spoke with rarely mentioned NGOs as sources of support. Achieving scale in collective economic activities is possible, but it demands radical new thinking, with a strong market orientation and investment in poor people's organizations. Fourth, the most important contributions of collective action may be political, in improving the quality of local democracy and the provision of local public goods. While collective action often substitutes for the failures of governments and markets, there is a need to move from substitution to complementarity between people's organizations and local government performance.

First Site of Collective Action: The Family

What I feel has helped me most is the union of our family. This union is our strength. With unity and agreement, you can do anything.
    —Tomás, a man in chronic poverty, Chakax, Mexico

Across study sites, families stand out as the most important institution in people's lives. Family love and unity provide the moral and psychological support that enables people to survive hard times. Families pool their resources and work together to move out of poverty. People also turn first to their families to cope with shocks, whether financial setbacks, sickness, or displacement by disaster or conflict. But families can also hold people back through demands for sharing (with the risk of free riding), oppressive family traditions (including gender discrimination), and risk aversion.

The centrality of the family emerges in both our quantitative and qualitative data. We used an inductive approach to code 2,700 life stories from India to understand the role of institutions in asset accumulation. People spoke about four sets of institutions that had helped them accumulate assets: public institutions, the private sector, civil society, and the family. Across all mobility groups in India, more than 80 percent of such institutional references were to families. Among the fallers, it was 88 percent; among the chronic poor, 85 percent; among the movers, 82 percent; and among the never poor, 81 percent.[2] This salience of the family was evident in life stories and discussion groups in other country contexts as well.

Trust, loyalty, love, and sacrifice

Since I was a child, my parents loved me so much because I am the fourth and a cute girl. . . . I got married in 1992 and until now I have lived with them. In 1997, my mum got sick and died. All of our relatives came and paid respect and spent money on the funeral. We were all sad and in mourning. Now I live with my old, ill dad. . . . Although we are very poor, there are no arguments or quarrels in the family.
—Chuon, a 40-year-old woman, Kdadaum, Cambodia

Trust, unity, and solidarity provide the foundation on which collective action is built. In discussion after discussion, people reiterated the importance of having these qualities within the family. Often, they see family cohesiveness as a precondition for upward mobility or for maintaining the household's present status.

Families, especially large families, can give people a sense of power. In the village of Nurpur in Bangladesh, Kashem, a woman in a discussion group, said, "To marry into a big house with many brothers and sisters-in-law is power." Tahera added, "The numerical strength of relatives is power. If a man has many children, he has extra power. Other people are afraid of going against him." The young men in the village added, "If the brothers in a family are united, they have power because five brothers are like five sticks [which together cannot be broken]. Other people in the village are afraid of them."

Nasiruddin, a 31-year-old fisherman in Kramrrak, Indonesia, attributed his successful move out of poverty to the love and practical assistance provided by his wife. While he works hard each day to catch and sell fish, his wife sells snacks at a kiosk in the village. He was quick to note that his wife's financial contribution is valuable to the household. "Back then [10 years ago], 10,000 rupiah per day was enough because I had only one child. But today, it is not enough. That's why my wife's kiosk is very helpful to me." Nasiruddin's wife also helps him manage his wealth. "So far I talk only to my wife for management of my assets. Besides her, there's nobody else I turn to for managing my funds. My self-confidence is increasing because my wife understands me. She helps me a lot, like with her kiosk, so I don't feel alone in facing my problems."

Our data reveal the presence of a strong, almost atavistic instinct to sacrifice for the family, especially for one's children and spouse. Parents often struggle throughout their lives to give their children an education (box 7.1). Self-sacrifice may even include leaving one's country and everything one

BOX 7.1
Giving up everything to send children to school

Racman, a 44-year-old woman from Bakimati, Philippines, was rated as chronic poor by her peers in the village. Her husband works on their small farm and on the farms of others. Racman has worked as a waitress, a maid, and a laundry woman, striving to provide two meals a day for her children and to educate them well.

Racman moved to Bakimati with her family in 1998 so that the children could receive an education, as her native village had no school. But the family was forced to leave Bakimati in 2000 because of civil conflict in the Mindanao region. They went to Parang to stay at an evacuation center. Racman served food in a cafeteria in the morning and took in washing at night. "It seemed as if all my energy was drained. There were times that I would ask only for rice instead of money so that I would be assured that my children would have something to eat when I got home. It was so hard, but I had to make some sacrifices so that we would survive. It was better than having nothing for my children."

Racman and her family returned to Bakimati in 2001, after the conflict had subsided. She now sells vegetables and cooked food in the village. It has been hard for the family to acquire property and other fixed assets because they have put everything they have into their children's education. Racman keeps some savings at home in a piggybank, but she says, "I would break my piggybank whenever there are some expenses for my children's schooling." She concludes, smiling, "If my children could finish their studies, then maybe that would be the time that we would experience a better life. That's why I really want all my children to finish college—something I was not able to attain in my life."

knows in order to earn money to send back to the family. Said, a 62-year-old man from the village of Almichi in Morocco, migrated to France to work in a coal mine. His main aim was to earn a pension that would provide financial security to his wife once he was gone. Widows in Morocco lead deplorable lives and were consistently ranked at the very bottom of the ladder of life in our study communities. Said explained, "When I first got my pension, that was a big relief because it will be a security for my wife. If I die before her . . . God knows . . . I don't have any guarantee that my children are going to treat their mother well. Now I can die quietly; my wife is not going to beg to provide for her needs."

Joint portfolios: Farming, business, and migration

Each and every person has to work hard if a family is to reach a higher step. If we simply sit idle and eat, even hills would melt.
—Discussion with women, Govindapalle, Andhra Pradesh

I pray to God that I will never have to return to the United States. Not for fear of work, but for fear of leaving the family. Migration splits the family, and it is not with money that you can cure the effect of separation.
—Adolfo, a 29-year-old man, Guadalamoros, Mexico

Beyond providing psychological support, the family unit plays an extremely important role in the movement out of poverty through its joint and pooled economic activities. Family support for income generation has two important, closely related dimensions. One consists of putting many hands to work, including managing businesses together. The other consists of migrating for employment and sending back remittances. Often these are combined, as when households use remittances from a family member abroad to invest in new livelihood opportunities at home.

Across our study sites, it is common for all members of a household, including women and children, to work. Often, this contribution yields barely enough to meet daily consumption needs. In some cases, though, it enables households to save and move up.

Lal in Kandulimari, Assam, worked as a daily wage laborer and farmed potatoes and chilies on his small plot of land. "The money was enough to fund our expenses for oil and salt," he recalls. With great difficulty, Lal managed to finance the education of his four sons. Rated poor in 1995, Lal's family has since moved out of poverty. His peers attribute his success to the fact that his educated sons have come of age and now contribute to the family pot.

The eldest son has a job in Guwahati. The second one set up a shop that sells electrical equipment in the village. The third works as a decorator for marriage ceremonies, while the youngest sells cigarettes and *paan* (a chewing mixture) at a kiosk in Kandulimari. "No one sits *bekar* [idle] at home," said Lal when asked the secret of his success. "My sons cooperate with each other. In 2003, all of them made this house together. Previously, the house was made of straw and bamboo. Now we have GC sheets [galvanized metal] on the roof, brick walls, and concrete floors." The sons have equipped the house with an electricity connection and furnished it with a sofa, beds, and a television. They have even bought an insurance policy for their father, as well as a pair of cows. "I dream about more progress for my sons in the future," Lal says happily. "That they can progress more is my only wish. If God blesses us, certainly they will prosper."

In putting all hands to work, it is very common for families to send one member to seek employment outside the community, typically in a nearby city or abroad. Remittances sent back by family members who have migrated play pivotal roles in upward mobility. In Morocco and Mexico, migration to Europe and the United States, respectively, are important escape routes out of poverty. Migration is particularly important in conflict-affected communities. The remittances that migrants send back allow their families to cope with the economic shock of conflict and in some cases to save and build assets.

Fasmin, a 25-year-old woman in Kumputhiri, Sri Lanka, is described as a mover by her community. She lives with her child in Kumputhiri while her husband lives and works in Kuwait. Both were born into poor families and initially worked as coolies in the village to earn their daily bread. Fortunately, the husband's mother lived in Kuwait and sent remittances to help the couple cope. In 2003, with the mother's help, Fasmin and her husband migrated to Kuwait as well. While her husband worked as a driver, Fasmin became a housemaid. "After going abroad, both my husband and I earned a lot," said Fasmin. "Earlier, it was difficult to carry on our lives because there were no permanent jobs in this area. We did not have a house to live in. But now my husband earns about 15,000 Sri Lankan rupees per month. We have our own house, and we can do anything we want. So I feel we have a better life now." Although she misses her husband, she thinks it is better that he stay in Kuwait for the time being. "If my husband comes to Sri Lanka, he cannot work here. He has to go back. If the war starts, we would have to move from this place as well." But she adds, "We would eventually want to start our own work here. Being abroad for long is not useful."

Indeed, migration is in some ways a mixed blessing for families. The stress of separation affects both those who migrate and those who stay behind. In our opening story Adolfo from Mexico, recalled the time he spent across the border, in the United States. "It is difficult on the other side. There is a lot of pressure, and I would not like to live this way." Yet Adolfo feels he had no choice but to migrate. "I was helping the family. I was the son. . . ." he shrugged. "There is no money, no work here in Guadalamoros. . . . I pray to God that I will never have to return to the United States. Not for fear of work, but for fear of leaving the family. Migration splits the family."

Investing remittances in new livelihood activities emerges as a clear path to mobility for many households. Shahana, a mover from Dayabhara, Bangladesh, is recognized as one of the empowered women in her village. In 1995, her husband, Haque, was a small farmer in Dayabhara. The family could barely get by. Borrowing money from his relatives to finance the trip, Haque left the village in 1996 to work in Saudi Arabia. The first year was very difficult, as Haque could not send much money home. By 1998, however, he found a secure job in Saudi Arabia and began sending more. The couple soon repaid all their loans and started saving and investing. Shahana used her husband's hard-earned income wisely. She first invested in rearing poultry and cattle. With the profits and additional remittances, she built a brick house with a latrine. She also bought agricultural land and farmed it. She took care that her children never missed school. When our team met her, Shahana was an active member of a saving group and a respected member of her community.

In the study communities in Oaxaca and Yucatán, Mexico, the migration of a family member is a key factor distinguishing those on the higher steps of the ladder of life. The other distinction is diversified family livelihood portfolios, with women earning income and all members working to jointly manage family businesses (table 7.1). In fact, across our study sites in Mexico, a family member finding employment outside the community is a nearly guaranteed route to climbing the ladder. In Yucatán, this endeavor takes the form of commuting to nearby towns to find off-farm employment. In Oaxaca, family members typically migrate to other parts of Mexico or the United States.

Although remittances benefit the receiving families most directly, they can also drive community-wide mobility. In the village of Nurpur, Bangladesh, most residents have at least one family member who has migrated to countries such as Dubai, Pakistan, or Saudi Arabia. People in Nurpur have invested their remittances in local businesses like cell phone sales and furniture. An increase in local supply has enabled people to spend their money within the village rather than in nearby towns. This spending has galvanized the creation of a vibrant market, and the profits, in turn, are leading to more spending in the community.

TABLE 7.1

Migration and multiple hands at work trigger upward movement in Mexico

	Bottom 2 steps	Step where households are no longer considered poor	Top 1–2 steps
Migration	No migration.	*Oaxaca:* Household members have migrated to Mexico City, northern Mexico, or the United States.	*Oaxaca:* Households members have migrated and are often legal U.S. residents with steady jobs.
		Yucatán: Head of household works outside the community in agriculture or construction.	*Yucatán:* Family members have off-farm employment outside the community.
Multiple hands at work	If family members are employed, it is usually as temporary casual labor. Household may grow some food. Wives sell petty handicrafts.	*Oaxaca:* Family grows own food and sells surplus produce. Women make handicrafts, wash clothes, or sell cooked food. *Yucatán:* Women may have salaried work. Many households own small grocery stores and/or raise animals.	Families often own a grocery store, bakery, or tortilla shop in the community. Many still farm on the side or raise and sell animals. More than one member of the household works and wife contributes by selling other produce or services.

Source: Ladder of life focus group discussions, Mexico.

Coping with adversity

In 1986, my house was destroyed, my brother died, and two of my sons were wounded. Airplanes were bombing our village. . . . I was also thinking about killing myself. I didn't have any hope. . . . Now my children are adults and take care of me. I feel more relaxed and confident.

—Naim, a 60-year-old man, Nasher Khan, Afghanistan

An important function of families is to face risks and adversity together. Families pool their resources, both financial and psychological, to confront health shocks, injury, and death. This function of families is especially important in conflict areas. In Afghanistan, we found people using their filial networks to protect their families and to migrate out of the most dangerous zones together (box 7.2).

Across contexts, families use their assets—livestock, land, jewelry—to pay for the expenses of a sick family member. In Tinkata, a coffee-cultivating community in Ruvuma, Tanzania, 44-year-old Analis suffered several miscarriages. After the delivery of her fourth child, who was born with disabilities in 1993, she lost all strength and will to live. Soon thereafter, she became pregnant again and suffered yet another miscarriage. Among the people who

---

BOX 7.2
Solidarity in time of war

Once a beautiful village surrounded by grape vineyards in the Shamali plains of Afghanistan, Ramili Qali now has a haunted look. In 1999, the people of the village lost everything to the intense fighting between the Taliban and the U.S.-supported Northern Alliance. Our team met Abdul, a farmer who recalled the horror of seeing his village burn. "They set fire to our gardens and our grapevines. They blew up the irrigation canal. Of course, the Taliban and the Northern Alliance looted our houses. The Taliban once totally burned some of them. The Northern Alliance soldiers one winter took all the wood, logs, from our houses to make firewood. And both put a lot of landmines in the village." At the time our field team visited Ramili Qali, it was estimated to have 2,000 landmines.

With the village turned into a battleground, families were forced to evacuate to nearby cities like Jalalabad. One man recalled, "The Taliban deported the families: women and children on one side, and men on another side. They were deported to Kabul, then quickly to camps in Jalalabad." The Taliban also put 100 men from the village in a prison in Pul-e-Charkhi. Twenty of the weakest ones died there. The fate of the deported was no better. "The authorities of Jalalabad did not want them. There was news that the Taliban would bring them back to Kabul. It was then that these families decided to leave the country." Pir Mohammad, a farmer in a discussion group, recounted, "Around 500 families migrated together to Kashmir, where some of our villagers were living already. Around 50 families migrated to Panjsher, and another 50 families went together to Iran."

All 500 families that left for Kashmir stuck together. People described with much pride how these families survived until the end of the conflict by taking care of each other in the absence of the men. Even more remarkable was how Pashtuns (the tribe to which the Taliban belong) and Tajiks (of the Northern Alliance) coexisted peacefully upon the villagers' return. "There is no social inequality where we live," men in a discussion group exclaimed proudly. "All people live in the same condition. Since people stopped fighting, they feel unity among each other."

---

helped her was her father-in-law. During her pregnancies, he gave her money so she could go to a hospital that was distant from Tinkata. Other relatives donated blood for transfusion at the time of the miscarriages. "These were my brother, my sister, and my aunt. My husband could not donate because we have different blood groups," she said.

Especially in India, Bangladesh, and Sri Lanka, outlays for dowries and wedding ceremonies often constitute a serious financial shock for a household. Again, families help cushion the blow. Suman, a woman in Kursi, Uttar Pradesh, knew from the time of her daughter's birth that she would eventually need money for a dowry. "I was happy on her birth because she was my first child. But I was also sad because the birth of a girl in a poor family is equivalent to death." Suman's husband fell ill soon after, and the family barely scraped by. "There was no food in the house, and my children and I had to consume *roti* [bread] with salt and vinegar." Suman's mother then sent her some money to run the house. With the money, Suman bought three packets of biscuits, 10 candies, and five packs of cigarettes and set them out for sale. Slowly but steadily, her sales picked up, and eventually she had enough to invest in a small shop. At the time of the interview, Suman had managed to save Rs 2,000 (about US$50) for her daughter's dowry. "I saved every rupee that I had and put it in the bank," Suman told our field team. She cannot think what their fate would have been had her mother not stepped in to help.

Division, desertion, and death: How family breakups can lead to falls

In 1998, my father separated me from the family. It brought me great pain.
The power that exists in unity does not exist when you stay separately.
—Badloo, a 30-year-old man in chronic poverty,
Hathina, Uttar Pradesh

Given the importance of families, losing one's spouse or children through death or desertion or becoming estranged from one's family can trigger a decline into poverty. In a community in the conflict region in the Philippines, men asked, "What if your spouse, whom you depend on, dies? You know that she is good in business and deals well with the customers. [Her death] can be one factor that will push you down. But we cannot really avoid death because that is where all people go."

The problem is particularly acute for women in male-dominated societies. Across study contexts, widows and women abandoned by their husbands occupy the very bottom step of the ladder of life. In Afghanistan and

Morocco, women who are both widowed and fatherless are described as help-less. With little or no income or savings, no insurance, and no social security, many are reduced to begging. A discussion group of women in Tindyata, Morocco, described one such woman in their community. "There is a widow who doesn't have income. She walks around to her neighbors to get what she needs: a little flour, a cup of oil, a little tea, and sugar." Women who lost their husbands during the war in Afghanistan also live in appalling conditions. A group of men in Nasher Khan noted, "Men are like a mountain. Families who have more mountains are more powerful."

A division among siblings that fragments the family inheritance can lead to falling, as can being abandoned by one's adult children. This is par-ticularly striking in the Indian rural context, where it is still common to live in extended or "joint" families. In the village of Khetoosa in Uttar Pradesh, 47-year-old Chander had separated from his brothers and received a meager inheritance. "I only got 8 bighas of land on which it was possible to farm only once a year. Furthermore, because my plot was on the banks of a river, I constantly faced problems of waterlogging. The floods washed away my crops each year." But he didn't lose hope, as he had three sons to rely on. Three years after separating from his brothers, Chander married off his eldest son, taking a loan to pay for the marriage ceremony. "I had little worry about the loan, because I thought that my son would help me in cultivation and we would pay off the loan together. However, this did not happen. My son separated from the family." Chander now feels he is doomed. "Coming out from debt is now difficult. I feel distressed because I have yet to arrange the marriages of two sons and one daughter. It will be difficult for me to come out of poverty. Nobody will come to my help. The rest of the children are small and are unable to do any work. My son's separation has been the great-est cause of our downward mobility. He does not even talk to us, so how can I ask him to repay the loan amount?"

Family as a burden

We can have as many children as we want, like 10 to 15. But then we'll die. How are we going to feed them all? Are we going to feed them maize husks?

> —Discussion with men and women, Bamlozi, Malawi

While large families are a sign of power to many, they can also pose an obstacle to moving up. More people in a family means more hands at work, but it also means more mouths to feed, more bodies to clothe, and more people with conflicting needs and aspirations becoming involved in decisions and plans. It means more sharing and less saving.

Across study regions, families with many children and few working members are placed at the bottom steps of the community ladders. A male discussion group in Riah Khillaw, Afghanistan, described such households in their village. "The poorest usually have big families—on average eight people in the house. They do not own the house they live in, nor any land. This category includes widows, who have a small income and no children of working age, or families where the male head of household is too old to earn a good income." Similarly, a group of men in the fishing village of Mirjakhathi, Bangladesh, thought that smaller families with fewer children are better able to save and invest in livelihood activities. "If they have fewer members in the family, they could even save some money. With that saving, they could buy more fishing nets."

In Malawi, some young people see their large families as an obstacle to achieving their aspirations. "Parents continue having children, but hunger does not go away," said a youth discussion group in Mzaponda. "Being their children, youth fail to speak up to parents to stop this tendency of having more children. There are homes with as many as 15 people. All of them need clothes and other things. So if their parents can get a 500 kwacha note by doing piecework on other people's farms, it ends up on purchase of food. This results in most boys doing farm piecework so they can support themselves."

Especially in African contexts, where norms of sharing are especially strong, kinship networks extend far beyond the immediate nuclear family. Anyone who manages to move up the ladder is expected to extend help to wide circles of kith and kin and even unrelated community members. Deference to this societal norm of sharing can become a net drain on family resources, but failure to provide help is frowned upon and can result in estrangement from the community. Men and women in a discussion group in Mzaponda, Malawi, gave an example: "When they [people in the community] see steam at other houses, that's when they decide to go there and ask for a light, when in actual fact they want to be invited to share the porridge that's being cooked. If you don't invite them, they start saying that you are greedy."

Finally, large families are also seen to be prone to conflicts over sharing of resources and labor. "If several pots are banged together, there will be some noise," argued Ramesh in Kursi, Uttar Pradesh. "When there are more members in a family, the chances of infighting increase. After marriages, divisions are bound to occur as wives influence their husbands. Usually as expenses start rising, it leads to trouble and there is a division in the family."

For some, separation from family can even spell liberation, bringing the freedom to work hard for oneself and not for others. Tarawati, a 45-year-old woman in Bhairo Khurd, Uttar Pradesh, rated separation from her husband's family as the most important positive event in their life. Married at 16 to a poor, illiterate man, Tarawati lived at first with her husband and in-laws, and the entire family worked together on the family farm. Tarawati described her father-in-law as a generous man and the thread that tied everyone together. But after his death, the atmosphere deteriorated. As Tarawati's brothers-in-law married and the family grew, the disputes increased. In 1990, when Tarawati was 31, her husband split from his extended family.

With their own land and a house to live in, Tarawati and her husband could invest in their farm. Working and saving over nearly eight years, they bought a tractor and more land. With these improvements, their farm's productivity increased and their social status rose. Tarawati now lives comfortably in her own house with her husband, sons, daughters-in-law, and grandchildren. "The split was the turning point, because my husband prospered then in his individual capacity," she concluded.

Gender discrimination and violence within families

The only wrong thing I did was to be born as a girl in this society.
—A young girl, Mechiri, Andhra Pradesh

It is the fanaticism of people. They don't like when girls are going to school, and sometimes our families show reaction against schooling, and they say school isn't good for girls.
—Najila, an 18-year-old female student, Ramili Qali, Afghanistan

Not all families are happy collectives, with unity and equity between members. The most potent conflict, although sometimes unexpressed, is between men and women within households. The issues revolve around inequalities and unfairness in decision making, division of labor, distribution of resources, freedom of movement, and respect.

Ndyamuhaki, in Bufkaro, Uganda, said that men in her community hardly consult their wives. "The man will just sell the land without the woman knowing and drink all the money," she said. In Butmuli, another village in Uganda, women indicated that some men in their village had even made decisions to sell off their daughters, typically when they were in an inebriated state at drinking joints. Their wives had no say in the matter.

Like hundreds of researchers before us, we found that members of a family do not necessarily function as a harmonious whole, with similar preferences and spending patterns.[3] Men tend to spend their income on themselves, while women are more likely to purchase goods for children and for general household consumption.

Unequal allocation of resources based on gender is also reflected in the lack of investment in education and health care for girls.[4] When asked what she wanted to do in the future, a young girl in Mechiri, Andhra Pradesh, said, "My parents stopped my education after grade 9. They thought that women shouldn't get more education so they stopped me from going to school. The only wrong thing I did was to be born as a girl in this society. Now I don't have any desires. My parents will take every decision for me." Many girls our research teams met in other contexts remain illiterate and confined to their homes, and can only hope to find good husbands.

Women and girls particularly chafe against restrictions on their physical freedoms—freedom to dress as they wish and go where they please. To women in Uttar Pradesh, freedom means freedom from the veil; in Afghanistan, it means freedom from the chador. In Bangladesh, women long to go to the market without permission from their husbands. According to women in Tecamín, Mexico, while women are hobbled, men freely "come and go and tell their daughters and wives what to do and where to go."

Intra-household inequality frequently gives rise to domestic violence. Across contexts, women report being beaten by their husbands, parents, brothers, and other relatives. In Abzif, Morocco, girls described how their brothers beat them if they stopped on the streets to watch a funeral ceremony pass by. "Even if a man looks at her, to her brother it means they have had illicit relations, and she is assaulted automatically." At other times, women become targets of violence because of small, daily disputes. From villages in Bangladesh to Cambodia, focus groups described how failure to prepare the evening meal on time can invite the wrath of husbands. In Koh Phong, Cambodia, young men said, "Domestic violence results from the fact that the wife does not prepare food in time for the husband who has come back from work in the forest. And sometimes it is because the men are drunk."

A general lack of respect for women is pervasive across study contexts. Demanding dowry (in South Asia) and keeping multiple wives (in Africa) are accepted traditions. The norms of gender inequity are so deeply imbedded in some contexts that men cite religious texts to defend their legitimacy. A man in Kaludoma, Ruvuma, Tanzania, argued, "This is biblical, that men will have power over women. A man is the first one to come in this world. The bride price paid to her parents allows a man to overpower her." In Shantakalia, Bangladesh, men scoffed, "Women's power? What is that? Whatever we say to our mothers, wives, and sisters, they do it." Women who try to oppose such social norms are usually considered aggressive and evaluated negatively, while adherence invites respect (see also box 4.1 in chapter 4).[5]

Melise, a 35-year-old woman in Chiksisi, Malawi, is among those who spoke of earning respect from her husband—but not without initial resistance. Her husband initially refused to let her take a loan for brewing and selling beer. "He said that if I take the loan, I will become promiscuous. He beat me over this issue. What made me determined more than ever was the fact that I was not his only wife. I had discovered that he had another wife from Mozambique whom he married before me." Melise went ahead and took the loan over her husband's objections, using the money to buy a bale of clothes to sell in the local market. The business earned her good money and, eventually, respect from her husband. "He started being nice to me and started telling me that we should sit down and strategize on the way forward."

Amartya Sen (1990) uses the phrase "cooperative conflict" to describe gender tensions within families. He argues that women and men have both congruent and conflicting interests that affect family life. Because of the extensive areas where interests converge, decision making in the family tends to feature the pursuit of cooperation, with some agreed resolution, usually implicit, of the conflicting aspects. Our data mostly support this interpretation. Conflicts are present within families, yet the family still offers the best recourse in the absence of other options available to women.

Markers of successful family collective action

In thinking about what kinds of collective action and entities can help people move out of poverty, it is useful to understand the main characteristics that make families successful settings for collective action. In our data, five such features stand out: underlying norms of trust, loyalty, and solidarity; repeated interactions and relationships over long periods of time; authority and control over decisions and resources; pooling of production and/or joint production; and sharing of both upside gains and downside risks.

These characteristics of successful family collective action are present to a more limited degree in several other types of collective entities, including spontaneous groups of poor people, externally supported community-based organizations, large-scale microcredit schemes, community-driven development programs, and microequity corporations (table 7.2).

The economic literature supports the importance of these features of the family, especially trust. Trust is the foundation of family life: it both derives from and reinforces interactions and relationships built over long periods of time. Such high levels of trust seldom extend to those outside the family. Indeed, some scholars have cited the inability to trust anyone beyond the family as an explanation for why some cultures seem to enjoy greater prosperity than others. Banfield (1958), in his *Moral Basis of a Backward Society*, was one of the first to propose a cultural explanation for underdevelopment. He attributed the backwardness of a village in southern Italy to the inability of villagers to transcend their immediate family interests and come together for the common good. Putnam (1993), also using Italy as an example, discussed the positive impact of a more altruistic, "civic" culture on the quality of political institutions. In *Trust*, Fukuyama (1995) shows how successful family businesses in China are built on high levels of family trust. But this trust does not extend to nonfamily members; hence the difficulties in scaling up family businesses to large corporations.

Our data, too, support the importance of trust outside the family as a basis for cooperative endeavors. On average, nearly 60 percent of respondents across study regions who said they were "very likely" to cooperate to solve common problems—to solve water problems or deal with a crisis—also said that people can be trusted. In contrast, only 40 percent of these likely cooperators said "you can't be too careful" when it comes to trusting others.

In nonfamily settings, especially where parties are unknown to each other, collective economic action may suffer from problems of moral hazard, lack of information, and lack of ability to monitor performance. Arrow (1971) uses the insurance market as a model. Once a client receives a life insurance policy, he has the incentive to engage in discretionary behavior like smoking because he knows that the insurance agent cannot keep an eye on him or that the costs of tracking behavior are too high. Similarly, in the case of joint production, it is difficult to observe everyone's behavior, which gives individuals the incentive to shirk and free ride.

This is seldom the case within families, where repeated interactions and long-term relationships among members reduce the incentive and ability to free ride or cheat.[6] Family members expect to be together for a long time; thus how they treat each other today will matter in the future. People rely on their relatives in running businesses because loyalty to the family fosters a shared commitment to the family firm and its prosperity (Ward 1987; Van den Ber-

TABLE 7.2
Collective entities replicate some but not all characteristics of successful families

Characteristics	Family	Friends	Community-based organizations				
			Spontaneous groups	Organized groups linked to external organizations	Large-scale microcredit schemes	Community-driven development programs	Microequity corporations
Trust, loyalty, solidarity	High	High	High	Low to none	Low/medium	Medium/low	High
Repeated interactions/long-term relationships	High	High	High	Medium	Low/medium	Medium/low	High
Authority and control over decisions and resources	High	Low	Medium	Low	Low	Low/high	High
Pooling/joint production	Both	Pooling	Pooling	Mostly pooling	Pooling	Pooling	Both
Sharing both downside risks and upside gains	Both	Downside	Downside and limited reciprocal upside	Primarily downside; some upside	Downside	Both	Upside

ghe and Carchon 2003). The intimate relations between family members facilitate communication and shared decision making, reduce information asymmetries, and encourage risk taking for the benefit of the firm. Everyone's interests align more easily to growth opportunities, and the costs of reaching, monitoring, and enforcing more formal contracts are practically negligible. The strong social bonds within families withstand many pressures that can tear apart other forms of collective economic action.[7]

Given the difficulty in replicating all the features of families in non-family collective action, joint ownership and production in these settings remains rare. It is more common to find collective action that involves some pooling of activities in the production or marketing chain—for example, a dairy cooperative with individual ownership of cattle but joint marketing of milk.

As noted, families usually face negative shocks together. They also work collectively to get ahead and, most of the time, share the gains. Outside the family, by contrast, it appears that there are more successes in collectively confronting downside shocks than in sharing upside gains. In part, this is because it is easy to verify shocks such as illness, accidents, fires, and death, and there is usually nothing to be gained from hiding the information. Windfall profits are another matter. In this case, the incentive to hide gains is high, because if they are fully disclosed, they will have to be shared.

In the remainder of this chapter, we briefly analyze the successes and failures of the main nonfamily forms of collective action, from the many informal groups of poor people all the way to the few instances of shared equity. We evaluate the extent to which these organizations have been able to reproduce the features of successful family-based collective action. We focus on functional equivalence rather than on form; for example, we consider the extent to which monitoring of behavior has been achieved and do not assume it will always involve face-to-face interaction as in the family.

Friendships Matter

I tried to be a bad boy in school. I liked using drugs. But I had a friend in high school who really affected my life. We treated each other like brothers. I was hooked on drugs; he was not. He became my counselor, and he pointed out the ill effects of my vices. He really influenced me and helped me change. He opened my eyes for me to see all the wrongdoings I had done.

—Noel, a 25-year-old man, never poor, Kilaluna, Philippines

It is not so much our friends' help that helps us as the confident knowledge that they will help us.

—Epicurus

Poor men and women in our study regions universally spoke of the value of having good friends. Friends come to the rescue in times of urgent need with money to buy food or medicine for a sick child. Friends also teach valuable skills—farming, fishing, driving, carpentry, weaving—and provide information on market prices. They may inculcate good habits and encourage quitting bad ones. And in conflict areas, friends guard homes fiercely as if they were their own. When asked whether he felt endangered, Mohtar, a man in Lupotogo, Indonesia, a village affected by Christian–Muslim conflict, said, "When the riot occurred, my house was very sheltered. After all, it was guarded by friendship, wasn't it?" The multiple ways in which friends help each other are illustrated by the story of Richard, a poor man in Tanzania (box 7.3).

Our quantitative data confirm the extent to which people in our communities depend on friends for help. Friends are an important source of borrowing for everyday consumption, second only to relatives. This finding is true for all groups except the fallers, for whom moneylenders are second and friends are third. In the African study contexts, all groups rated friends to be more important than even relatives as a source of credit for consumption.

However, when it comes to bigger loans to finance major household events such as a marriage, an illness, or a funeral, friends fall to third place, after relatives and moneylenders, among all four mobility groups. Poor people's friends are usually poor themselves. Although they can assist in meeting shortfalls in everyday consumption, they often do not have the capacity to help meet major expenses. This is why so many poor people turn to moneylenders for big expenses, and it is also why they attempt to cultivate and connect with richer patrons.

In setting up business activities, the chronic poor and the fallers depend primarily on relatives and moneylenders. In contrast, movers from poverty and the never poor more frequently have access to government banks. Nearly 23 percent of movers and 30 percent of never poor said that they had taken loans from a government bank over the study period to finance their farms and stores. In contrast, only 5 percent of the chronic poor and 18 percent of the fallers were able to access bank loans. While friends may not have helped the poorest finance major events or businesses, all groups considered their friends, along with their relatives, as their most important source of information on government programs.

BOX 7.3
Richard's story: Friends to the rescue

In the remote region of Kagera, Tanzania, our team met Richard, age 43, who had fallen into poverty over the study period. Yet he had retained his faith in life and said that "cooperation with relatives and friends" had helped him pull through.

Richard once earned his living by fishing in Lake Victoria, and he attributed his fishing skills to fishermen he had befriended when he was 18 years old. In 1993, at the age of 31, Richard migrated to a small island in Uganda, also situated on the lake. He stayed there until 1998, catching sardines, a risky and low-paying job. His wife remained at home, taking care of their small family farm. Toward the end of his stay in Uganda, he developed a tumor. His friends there paid his medical expenses. Next, he received the message that one of his children had died. He came home to Tanzania and started mourning.

At the time the field team met him, Richard was cultivating bananas, a skill he had learned from his parents when young. His friends had been an invaluable support for the trade. Whenever he failed to sell his bananas at the local market, he would store them at a friend's house instead of carrying them back to the village. A friend also lent him a bicycle that he still depends on to transport the bananas.

In addition to providing support for his livelihoods, his friends in the village helped him cope with the adversities he faced on returning home. His wife had to be hospitalized, and his child was bitten by a dog. To make matters worse, he was accused of theft. "In 2002, I bought bananas from somebody else and was arrested. I was informed that those three bananas I bought from that guy were stolen one day before." His friends stood by him through all this, and one of them even paid T Sh 10,000 for his bail. "I was about to smell the jail when my friend helped me."

Though he still lives in abject poverty, Richard feels much gratitude. He is saving to cope with emergencies and to buy his own bicycle, and he is an adviser to the village football team. "I still thank God that everything went well. I am on good terms with my community. I feel more confident now than in the past, because my family is more stable, and the society and my friends respect me."

Bonding: Spontaneous Community Organizations

If you do not belong to any group in this village, you cannot survive.
                    —Discussion with men, Bufkaro, Uganda

The most frequent type of collective action our field teams encountered, beyond the family, consists of spontaneous groups of people coming together to pursue common ends. Most people instinctively prefer to associate with those like themselves, and most such groups bring together friends and neighbors who are all poor. In communities with a high degree of social stratification, this tendency to stick with one's own can be problematic. First, it helps keep poor people poor, as they associate with others who also have limited resources, information, and contacts. Second, the elite also bond among themselves, blocking poor people's access to opportunities and sometimes fighting dirty if they feel threatened by poor people in any way.[8] Bonding groups thus reflect and perpetuate these inequalities.[9]

Limitations of poor people's bonding groups: Coping but not prospering

> *There are no formal credit organizations here. One can borrow from friends and relatives if one wants to take a child back to school. You can also borrow from community groups such as Bika Oyeguze and Okusuka [revolving credit groups]. But we don't have sureties, and we are unable to access credit and loans from banks and credit organizations.*
>   —Men's discussion group, Bufkaro, Uganda

In general, our qualitative data show that poor people's groups help them meet important immediate household needs, but seldom more than that.[10] The groups operate on too small a scale and have too little capital to provide the finance, livelihood training, or markets that could help their members move out of poverty. Sustaining small and underfunded bonding groups, in isolation from each other, is often difficult. Without an influx of new ideas, skills, markets, or capital, many such groups dissolve once immediate needs are met—or when they come up against the formidable obstacles posed by the rich, who come together to defend their own interests.

Most often, poor people come together to save. In such groups, sometimes called rotating savings and credit associations, the members meet (usually weekly) to chip in small amounts of money, then take turns drawing the entire pool of savings. A principal purpose of saving groups is to finance immediate household needs.[11] Such groups may be relatively stable, or they may be formed on an ad hoc basis to deal with emerging problems.

On average, we encountered more finance, credit, and saving groups in the study communities than groups formed around livelihood, health, education, politics, religion, or ethnicity, though the presence of political groups is also striking (figure 7.1). On average, more than 2.5 credit groups exist in each community visited.

There are some regional differences. The sampled communities in Bangladesh, Andhra Pradesh, Uganda, and Thailand have more than three credit groups per village (figure 7.2). Conversely, very few credit groups exist in the communities we visited in Colombia, which are home to large numbers of internally displaced people; in these sites, the church and other religious associations play a more important role.

Besides saving groups, funeral and burial groups exist in almost all our study communities in Africa.[12] As in revolving credit groups, members make regular (usually monthly) payments into a common pool, which members can then draw on to meet expenses for burial ceremonies and wakes. A poor man in Ntogo in Kagera, Tanzania, said, "I am a member of the Bushunguru funeral group, and I pay 500 shillings monthly. The group is involved in digging graves, fetching firewood, and contributing 10,000 for buying a shroud.

FIGURE 7.1

Finance/credit/saving groups are more common than livelihood, health, education, religious, or ethnic groups across all study regions

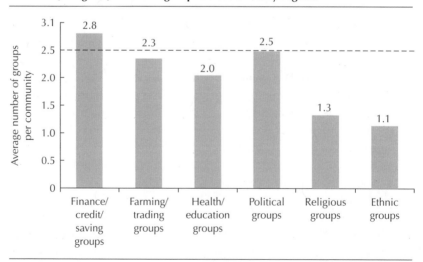

Source: Community questionnaire.

It has never helped me, and I wish it will never help me. Because the group is for funerals, and a funeral is not a good thing."

In the village of Bufkaro, Uganda, women recalled that before the burial groups existed, people sometimes had to sell part of their land to finance funeral ceremonies. "Now, when a member loses someone, the group uses the money that has been raised to buy food for mourners, the coffin, and other requirements for the funeral. Funerals take a lot of money when you have to spend from your own savings." The burial groups in Bufkaro also help when people fall ill. Women in the village recalled how one of them had fallen sick while working in the garden. The chairperson of the group

FIGURE 7.2

Saving and credit groups are more common in Andhra Pradesh, Uganda, Bangladesh, the Philippines, and Thailand

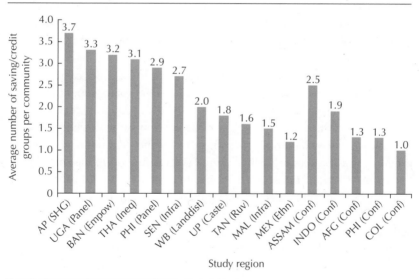

Source: Community questionnaire.

Note:

AFG (Conf) = Afghanistan, Conflict
AP (SHG) = Andhra Pradesh, Self-help groups
ASSAM (Conf)= Assam, Conflict
BAN (Empow) = Bangladesh, Women's
    empowerment
COL (Conf) = Colombia, Conflict
INDO (Conf) = Indonesia, Conflict
MAL (Infra) = Malawi, Infrastructure
MEX (Ethn) = Mexico, Ethnicity

PHI (Conf) = Philippines, Conflict
PHI (Panel) = Philippines, Panel study
SEN (Infra) = Senegal, Infrastructure
TAN (Ruv) = Tanzania, Ruvuma
THAI (Ineq) = Thailand, Inequality
UGA (Panel) = Uganda, Panel study
UP (Caste) = Uttar Pradesh, Caste
WB (Landdist) = West Bengal, Land distribution
    reforms

organized members to carry her to the hospital on an *engozi*, a stretcher made of local materials. The women added with amusement, "We have nicknamed them [engozis] our personal helicopters because they help carry people above someone else's shoulders."

Yet another type of poor people's collective action is the digging society. These groups were reported to involve only women, because "men do not dig." At the start of each agricultural season, the women prepare the land on the farms of relatively well-off households in the community. They use the money to buy household items like saucepans, clothes, mattresses, plates, and cups, as well as books and uniforms for their children in school. However, payment is not always guaranteed, especially when harvests are bad. And because of petty theft in communities, members may need to take extreme measures to protect their money. The treasurer of one digging group resorted to keeping the money "hidden under her bed or in sacks of sorghum or even in a bottle."

Our regression analysis further confirms the finding that collective action rarely help poor people move out of poverty. We use two indicators to measure spontaneous collective action in our data. The first is an index of propensity of collective action constructed through principal components analysis, which includes two questions: (a) the likelihood of cooperation between people in the village in the event of a fire or other calamity, and (b) cooperation in solving common problems like water supply issues in the village.[13] Responses for both were ranked on a four-point scale ranging from very likely to very unlikely. To avoid problems of endogeneity, initial conditions were used for both questions. The second indicator focuses on the extent to which access to networks and associations within the community had increased, remained about the same, or decreased over 10 years (for the detailed specification and results, see appendixes 4 and 6).

Figures 7.3 and 7.4 report the association between the index of collective action and access to networks and household movement out of poverty after controlling for other variables. Study regions where these measures were not consistently available in all communities have been dropped from the graphs. As before, the single dots represent the coefficients: the greater their height, the higher the magnitude of the estimated association. The bars around the coefficient represent the one and two standard error bounds. The more tightly clustered the bounds, the lower the standard error (or error one can expect in the estimation) and the more significant the association between collective action/access to networks and moving out of poverty.

Collective action or change in access to networks is mostly negatively associated with household mobility, except in some regions in Africa

FIGURE 7.3

Community's propensity for collective action has mostly negative association with movement out of poverty

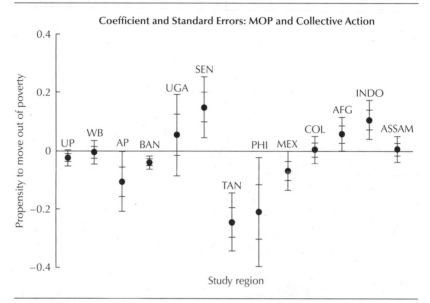

Source: Multivariate linear regression analysis using data from household survey and community questionnaire (see appendix 6).

(Uganda, Senegal) and in Afghanistan and Indonesia. In fact, the association is negatively significant in the study communities in Uttar Pradesh, Andhra Pradesh, Bangladesh, Tanzania (Ruvuma), and Mexico. In purely statistical terms, the negative association implies that propensity for collective action is less among the movers and higher among those stuck in chronic poverty. This is because the chronic poor gravitate to their own bonding groups as a means of coping in the absence of other alternatives. The chronic poor are more likely to engage in collective action precisely *because* they are poor.

In Uganda, the propensity to come together for the collective good has a positive but insignificant association with moving out of poverty. That is, households are more likely to move out of poverty in villages where people are more likely to engage in collective action, but not significantly so. Our qualitative data on groups in Ugandan communities support this finding.

In sum, then, poor people's propensity to come together and cooperate among themselves does not seem to be directly associated with lifting them out of poverty. Poor people's small, spontaneous groups find it difficult to link to

FIGURE 7.4
Change in access to networks has mostly negative association with movement out of poverty

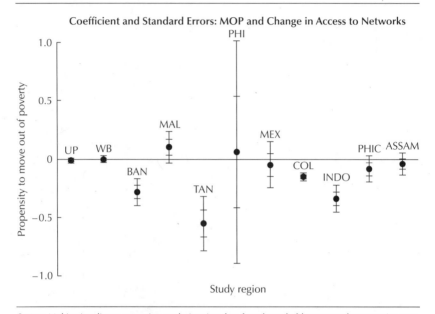

Coefficient and Standard Errors: MOP and Change in Access to Networks

Source: Multivariate linear regression analysis using data from household survey and community questionnaire (see appendix 6).

external funds, organizations, and resources, and they mostly remain excluded from groups of the more prosperous. However, the propensity to cooperate does play a critical role in sheer survival and eases the pain of poverty. Such cooperation also nurtures the trust and self-confidence that can provide a foundation for scaling up collective action and forging external ties so that poor people's groups grow in size and influence. Finally, as we discuss in the last part of this chapter, actions by groups of poor people can improve government performance and the quality of public goods provided by government.

Collective action by those who have the least, then, paradoxically helps society even though it may not lift poor people themselves out of poverty.

Organizing by the rich: Garrisoning against poor people

If anybody catches fish in any private-owned land of the village, he or she needs to share the fish with the ijaradars [private leaseholders]. Catching fish openly in the marshland has been banned for the villagers. The ijaradars arrange to guard the marshland with their own people. They guard

the water. They have 15 or 20 dogs and hire people who possess weapons,
pistols, shields, cutlass, etc.

—Discussion with women, Shantakalia, Bangladesh

Poor people's collective action is deeply affected by social inequality. Deep social divisions result in parallel worlds—and separate bonding groups—for the rich and poor. While poor people's groups lack resources and connections, rich people's groups are powerful precisely because they have these advantages.

Although social divisions appear to be universal in our study communities, caste, ethnicity, and wealth are particularly strong markers of division in the South Asian villages. In Shantakalia, Bangladesh, many poor people live by fishing in the village ponds. But the landlords guard the ponds fiercely, using pistols and packs of guard dogs to keep poor fishermen away. Those who are caught fishing either are punished and sent to prison or are forced to share their catch. Marshlands are guarded as well. According to both women's and men's discussion groups, a local administrative officer ordered the landowners to stop such practices. He also formed a cooperative of the local fisherfolk and leased land to the group. Not surprisingly, the official was soon "transferred." A key informant reported that since the transfer, the problems have started again. He said, "The landowners have now infected the ponds with poison. . . . Many poor people could not tolerate this shock and wanted to commit suicide."

Such extreme behavior seems to be more common during periods of economic stagnation. Growing inequalities may also increase the incidence of crime and cause social networks to deteriorate even further. An elderly woman our team met in Malawi does all her farming herself because she does not trust anyone in her village and fears her crops will be stolen. "I was once a victim of such act. My whole pen of goats was stolen," she said. Her case is an extreme form of what Putnam (2007) calls "hunkering down," that is, people withdrawing into their shells like turtles in economically divided communities.

Organized Groups Linked to External Organizations: Coffee, Dairy, and Pigs

To become a member of cooperatives, one needs to have the means. These
organizations may be a help in moving out of poverty. But in the begin-
ning, it is necessary to have a certain standard of living and a capacity

of financing to pay the "admission fee," to have the cows to be a member
of the cooperative, and to have the guarantees and the money to enter a
system of savings and credit.

—Discussion group on livelihoods with men and women,
Ferjama, Morocco

Poor people's groups are weak in part because all their members are similarly constrained and bring meager resources to the collective. But it is also because these groups are not linked to any outside sources of capital and know-how, such as banks, government agencies, or NGOs. Private sector partnerships are almost totally missing. The absence of such linking organizations in rural areas is striking.

We did find cases of community organizations that bridged social groups and were supported either by NGOs or by the government, unlike the spontaneous bonding groups discussed earlier. But they were few and far between in our data, and they experienced considerable problems in scaling up.

We present three examples of externally supported livelihood groups from our data: from Tanzania, Morocco, and Malawi. All three have been successful in a limited sense. Each, however, is limited to a single community, and scaling up has proved difficult. Using these case studies and others, we identified four types of problems that can hinder the efforts of livelihood groups to be successful and extend their benefits to a wider set of people. First, even when groups are linked to external resources, there often is no attempt to make them self-sustaining in the long run. Second, while external support helps, it also increases the likelihood of corruption, cheating, and elite capture of new resources. Third, groups may experience lack of trust and solidarity among their members. Finally, businesses started by such groups often turn out to be unprofitable because of poor advice or because they quickly saturate local markets.

In Ngimyoni, a village in Ruvuma, Tanzania, 74 of 700 local coffee farmers switched to growing organic coffee in 2002 with the help of TechnoServe, an international NGO. TechnoServe started working with coffee farmers after the government dismantled the state-run coffee cooperatives that had provided farmers with subsidized inputs, credit, savings instruments, markets, and advice. Two years after liberalization, as a new set of middlemen captured the coffee market and international coffee prices fell, the prosperity of coffee farmers dropped dramatically. The only exception was the farmers who had switched to specialty coffee with TechnoServe. These groups boasted, *"Mwe nakulengana na nenga; ne mi mukikundi sa kahawa,"* meaning "You cannot be as well off as I am; I am a member of Specialty Coffee Growers." The normal reply to such boastful words was *"Na ne lasima nyingila mukikundi omo,"* meaning "I will also join the Specialty Coffee Growers Group."

Some specialty coffee farmers in Ngimyoni became part of a new branch of the Association of Kilimanjaro Specialty Coffee Growers. The association consists of groups of 25 farmers, mobilized by TechnoServe, who receive training in best practices for growing specialty coffee. The NGO supplies them with inputs, buys their coffee in cash at good prices, and pays them additional amounts if the coffee fetches better-than-expected prices in the international market. As members of the association supported by TechnoServe, the groups have access to credit to purchase agricultural inputs, and agricultural extension officers from the NGO visit their farms to ensure good practices. TechnoServe has not achieved the scale of the government-run cooperatives, and it has experienced problems including lack of trust, cohesion, and capital among members. Still, the Ngimyoni coffee farmer groups are among the few cases of successful cooperatives we encountered. Not all cooperatives in Ruvuma or other study regions have done as well.

In Morocco, several kinds of formal associations are an important part of community life. These groups range from dairy cooperatives to water user associations to goat breeding associations, some of which are supported by the local government. Membership does entail economic benefits, usually through pooled marketing of products like goat milk. But over time, poor members have complained of losing control over resources to the more powerful, elite members.

The community of Ferjama has the highest level of mobility among both poor and well-off households in our Morocco sample. It has benefited from a range of associations, including a dairy cooperative, a village development and cultural association, and a water users association to manage irrigation. The dairy cooperative in particular has contributed to the mobility of many households in Ferjama. Initiated by the local office of the Ministry of Agriculture, it uses premises provided by a local ruling tribe. The cooperative purchased dairy cattle for its members, deducting payments from their subsequent sale of milk. The cows are individually owned. In addition to collecting the milk and selling it to the central dairy in Casablanca, the association provides fodder for livestock and organizes the breeding process.

The cooperative has expanded over the years as members have invested in more cattle. Women praised the cooperative, noting that the profits have helped people cope with crises in their households. The men were more skeptical. They noted incidents of conflict between members, although, they said,

"We manage to resolve them between us on the basis of our traditions and customs." But fissures were evident. At the time of our study, the members were discussing ways of taking their products themselves to other local and regional markets, bypassing the cooperative. Most important, the cooperative had become less accessible to poorer households in Ferjama. The richer members had raised the membership fee steeply over the years, leaving the poor behind.

A livelihood club of 10 women in the village of Bamlozi, Malawi, was one of the few cases of successful joint production we found, but it also illustrates the serious problems such groups can face. The club was established in 1997 through the efforts of a community development assistant (CDA) who worked for the Ministry of Community Development and Social Welfare. The CDA had approached the village headman to sell him the idea of women's clubs, but people were not interested, having been disappointed in the past by such groups. They said, "We are tired of giving our deposits to the government. The government just wants to steal money from us." After a lot of convincing, finally 10 women who were neighbors came forward to try again.

The first business the women undertook was cooking and selling fritters. They shared the costs of cooking oil and flour and made the fritters at home. By the time our field team visited, the women had expanded their operations into white pig breeding. An initial investment of MK500 was raised collectively by the members and deposited in the government-owned Savings and Credit Cooperatives (SACCO), and the group received a loan of MK34,000 to buy pigs and feed. They also received training in pig rearing and in how to construct a *kraal* (pigsty). The pigs multiplied and the women prospered.

Things started going wrong in 2001, a drought year, when the women had to feed the pigs grass because maize husks had become too expensive. Many piglets died. At the same time, SACCO loan officers started demanding repayment, and the women gave the CDA money to deposit in their account. The CDA told the women that SACCO was misappropriating their money and advised them not to give SACCO any more payments directly. Unfortunately, the CDA—the only man they trusted—then died, and the women were visited by a new CDA. "That new CDA took our SACCO account book to his office. He said they will sort out any differences between them and SACCO." Meanwhile, an outbreak of African swine fever killed many local pigs. Although the pigs reared in the group's kraal were not affected, the new CDA advised the women to sell them and get new pigs.

To this day, the club members don't know what happened to their deposit book or to the savings they used to make payments on the loan. At the time of the field visit, the women were determined to pool their resources and buy two piglets to start over. The 10 women have now worked together for more than 10 years (one new member joined three years ago). All of them are illiterate, but they have joined adult literacy classes so that they can read their deposit books. Despite their problems, the women have prospered somewhat, and they are proud to have contributed to other people's prosperity by selling them piglets. They said, "If you see big white pigs in this village or neighboring villages, they are breeds from our kraal. We sell a four-month piglet at 2,000 kwacha; they sell a full-grown pig for 6,000 kwacha. We really regret that we listened to the CDA boss and sold our pigs for 11,000 kwacha."

Scaling Up Collective Action

Scaling up activities that help improve poor people's livelihoods can yield benefits, but it is difficult to get it right. In this section, we first discuss the surprisingly low profile of NGOs in supporting collective activities in our study sites. We then look more closely at three ways of scaling up collective action: savings and credit, community-driven development, and microequity corporations.

Absence of NGOs

> *I open my thoughts. I can say what I want to say. Right after the conflict, I learned that if I will not air my thoughts, I will continue to struggle. Nobody can say what I can or cannot do [laughs].*
> —Mina, a 20-year-old woman talking about how NGOs helped her in Glikati, a conflict area of the Philippines

Nongovernmental organizations are strikingly absent in people's accounts of the most important factors that helped them move out of poverty in our study sites across countries. Indeed, when movers were asked to name the three main reasons for their escape from poverty, NGO support was hardly mentioned, accounting for just 0.3 percent of the reasons given. It was mentioned just slightly more often than illegal activities (0.1 percent).

This finding does not mean that NGOs are not present or not helping. They are helping in ways that our participants do not directly link to their movement out of poverty. One reason is that direct NGO assistance to households is often small and spread out over time, as is the case with microloans. Often, support for livelihoods is provided without a clear market analysis, leading to quick market saturation or to problems of price and quality.

Second, NGO activity may be linked to provision of infrastructure such as water, schools, and health clinics. Such assistance is critical for survival, but it may or may not be seen as leading to poverty escapes. Third, many NGOs are involved in providing critical humanitarian assistance, assisting orphans or the disabled, or providing relief after humanmade and natural disasters. Finally, some NGOs are involved in activities to "empower" poor women and men, activities that are extremely important but that in themselves may not necessarily translate into economic capital. These qualifications apply to the activities of both national and international NGOs.

In conflict-affected Glikati, Philippines, for example, discussion groups mentioned the local women's association and the international NGO Oxfam. The women's association was a new credit association consisting of 30 women. Perhaps because it was new and small, it was difficult to get much information, even from members, about how the organization operates and which NGO started it. But this is also symptomatic of the problems that affect groups created by outsiders: it is easy to create groups, but difficult to make them function effectively. Oxfam was praised for its many activities, particularly in installing water pumps, which had helped prevent illness in young children. Group participants said, "We didn't realize how dangerous our water here is until Oxfam told us the effect of just dumping human waste into the river." Oxfam also provided relief goods right after the conflict.

In Guluteza and Matdombo, Malawi, several different types of NGOs were mentioned and sometimes praised. The Malawi Council for the Handicapped reaches out to the disabled. Discussion groups reported, "The good part with this organization is that it gives monetary support and also business loans on easy terms to its members once a year in order to do some income-generating activities." Another NGO takes care of orphans. People also mentioned NASFAM, the National Smallholder Farmers' Association of Malawi, which demonstrates modern methods to farmers and buys their produce. People appreciate the support offered by NASFAM, but the success of farmers still depends on exogenous factors, mainly the rains. Malawi suffered from drought in the early 2000s; participants said, "Now the only thing remaining to have is good rain." Marketing remains a problem for some crops. Soyabean farmers said that even when they can produce crops, they have bags sitting in their backyards, unable to find markets. People criticized several credit organizations, saying that they "at times trap people into cycles of loan taking and repayment." Sometimes NGO help is clearly too little. Save the Children distributed 20 blankets once and 11 blankets another time, but "these were not sufficient for the needy."

Despite these problems, civil society has a critical role to play, particularly in helping poor people scale up their economic activities through linked and federated organizations. We encountered a few examples of scaled-up activities, three of which are described below.[14] Two of them are supported by government: the women's self-help group movement in southern India, which reaches millions of poor and often illiterate women, and the Kecamatan Development Program in Indonesia. Grameen Bank is an independent people's organization that includes a bank and several activity-specific companies such as Grameen Telecom.

Microcredit groups

Installment is given weekly, and this is a great problem. If one gets one taka one Tuesday, the next Tuesday they will come and sit for that taka [waiting for repayment]. They will remain seated even at night. They will remain seated for money even if one dies.

—Ziaul, a man in Digbari, Bangladesh

Poor people need more credit, not less (see chapter 5). They are also willing to pay high interest rates, because the alternative of borrowing from a moneylender is usually even more expensive. The Grameen Bank experience and its replication around the world has proven poor people to be bankable, yet we do not see a flow of loans to small entrepreneurs. Banks still hesitate to give poor people loans because of the high costs of monitoring, which raises the probability of default, a classic moral hazard problem (Stiglitz and Weiss 1981; Bester 1985, 1994). Poor people lack collateral with which to signal their willingness to repay.[15] Poor people also borrow small amounts and often live in remote locations, making the transaction costs of serving them high. Recent innovations using "smart cards" are overcoming these constraints and combining microcredit with a broader range of financial services.

According to our data, we report two examples of large-scale programs that deliver microcredit to poor women and a range of services to support poor people's livelihoods. In both cases, despite impressive achievements, it is unclear whether most of their members have moved out of poverty—although it is clear that most are better off than before they participated in these programs. The first example is that of women's self-help groups in Andhra Pradesh, which are sponsored by the state government and now reach millions of poor women. The second is Grameen Bank, a microcredit bank owned by poor women in Bangladesh. Grameen is one of several large-scale microcredit NGOs working in Bangladesh; the others include BRAC, ASA, and Proshika.

Although the SHGs are government-sponsored and Grameen Bank self-financed, the two programs share features in common. Both create solidarity groups of poor women who meet weekly and generally live close to each other. Both start with activities to build self-confidence and trust. Both focus on savings and credit activities. While bringing women together in groups builds solidarity for peer monitoring and ease of transaction with facilitators, loans are given to individuals and are used for individual activities. If one member defaults, all are denied subsequent loans; if all pay promptly, they are entitled to larger loans. This gives incentives for group members to monitor each other and pay promptly. Repayment is made easy with doorstep collection and by splitting the loan amount into small weekly installments, and repayment rates are 90–98 percent. Both programs have started programs to finance and insure against illness and death. Both give loans for children's education and undertake other social protection activities.

Both programs have initiated livelihood activities among members. Grameen's borrowers usually start small businesses, anything from basket weaving to rice cleaning to rickshaw companies. SHG members in Andhra Pradesh have made individual improvements in their livelihoods, from rearing livestock to running shops. Working in groups, they also produce grains, including maize and groundnuts, for the government. The groups have also initiated a rice credit line that has achieved scale quickly and improves food security of all members, who can buy rice in small quantities at lower prices than from the shops.

The Andhra Pradesh SHGs have achieved vertical scale over the past decade by federating across villages into federations at the level of the mandal (second tier of local government) and district. These provide services and loans to members. By March 2007, the state government had helped organize 8.6 million poor women into 688,253 SHGs. These had federated into just over 30,000 village organizations, which, in turn, had federated into 910 organizations at the mandal level, feeding into a smaller number of district-level federations. By 2005, the groups were able to mobilize $250 million in savings every year, receiving $475 million from banks (Aiyar, Narayan, and Raju 2007). Grameen Bank currently extends loans with no collateral to more than 7 million poor people, 97 percent of whom are women. As of October 2007, Grameen had extended loans totaling $6.55 billion, according to the organization's Web site.

It is difficult to obtain precise statistics on the extent to which SHG members or Grameen Bank members have moved out of poverty. From our own study in Andhra Pradesh, we find that belonging to SHGs is associated with moving out of poverty. Grameen Bank estimates that 64 percent of its members have moved out of poverty, though other studies have offered more conservative estimates.[16]

The microcredit model works because the risks are exogenous and non-covariant, which gives people incentives to pool. Social relations become effective substitutes for a failure of the market or the government to provide credit. However, while microcredit through group lending generally helps in sharing the downsides, as people use the small loans to cope with shocks, it has been far less successful in creating upsides by expanding livelihoods.[17] The very practices that microcredit institutions use to enforce repayment discipline may hinder members' ability to use the loans for businesses. For instance, most microfinance institutions (MFIs) give small loans, with repayment beginning immediately. This limits the usefulness of the loans for financing activities like a business, from which returns may only accrue in the medium term. As Roodman and Qureshi (2006) observe, "If a woman takes out a loan to buy and raise a calf, for example, the calf will not start generating income for her a week later, when the first payment is due." Poor borrowers consequently are hesitant to take risks, as they are afraid of business failure.

Some of our study participants from Bangladesh complained that the strict repayment regimen poses obstacles to moving up. In Mirabari, poor people spoke of having to sell their rickshaws to repay their loans. Jibon, a chronic poor woman in Digbari, had to sell off her poultry to repay the installments. She lamented, "I borrowed about 13,000 taka from BRAC and Grameen Bank. Out of that, I have repaid 5,000 taka and I spent the remaining 8,000 idly as my fields at that time were flooded and I could not work. This year, I bought nine chickens. When I could not return the installment amount, I had to repay it by selling the nine chickens." Asiya, a woman in Hasanbagh, wondered, "How good are these loans? We have to repay them in installments each week. The amount they give finishes off quickly."

Community-driven development

People appreciated the fact that even the building of the school is participatory.
—Discussion group talking about the Kecamatan Development
Program, Patobako, East Java, Indonesia

I was asleep. A local guard came in my home and commanded me to go and transport bricks on my head in order to build a school. Am I free? Am I not a slave in my own country and village?
—A poor man in a discussion group about a CDD program,
Bugokela, Kagera, Tanzania

The term community-driven development (CDD) was coined by Hans Binswanger and Deepa Narayan in 1996 at the World Bank to describe programs that give community groups authority and control over development decisions and resources, including finances. Special attempts are made to involve poor people, women, and other marginal groups. Funds generally flow through local governments to community bank accounts. The hallmark of such programs, when they are well done, is transparency: information about rules, budgets, wages, contractors, and bid amounts is widely disseminated in an attempt to reduce the corruption and collusion that have plagued many traditional programs. CDD programs start with solidarity and information meetings among people living in the same village or neighborhood. Community members set priorities, develop proposals, and implement and monitor the programs. Grants are given for communal infrastructure and loans for individual livelihoods. The more successful CDD programs also address downside risks, particularly health risks, either directly or through linkages with existing health care systems.

One of the world's largest and most successful CDD programs is the $1.3 billion Kecamatan Development Program in Indonesia. It reaches about 35,000 villages, half of all villages in Indonesia, with block grants for community infrastructure development. It also supports a variety of entrepreneurial activities through groups. In several of the communities our study teams visited, this program was mentioned as among the top factors contributing to community prosperity. The program taps into local traditions of *gotong royong* (working together to solve problems) and *musyawarah* (public discussion of issues). In conflict-affected communities in North Maluku, both Christians and Muslims credited the program with rebuilding trust across religious groups as they undertook rehabilitation of houses together.[18] The Indonesian experience illustrates the importance of trust, unity, participation, transparency, accountability, and pooling of risks—the features associated with successful families—in making collective action work.

In contrast, the experience with CDD in some villages in Tanzania shows how difficult it is to change existing practices of elite capture and build trust and solidarity. In environments of low trust and elite control over resources, it is likely that external resources will get captured as well. The Tanzania

Social Action Fund is working well in several communities, but in the villages of Gabunazi and Bugokela in Biharamulo district in Kagera, the program is dysfunctional. Both are semi-arid border villages where a constant influx of migrants has resulted in poor social cohesion and low levels of trust. The recent discovery of gold was followed by a surge of gold seekers; this has strained the traditional social fabric and is blamed for a rise in crime. In this context, CDD initiatives are seen as a "development tax," a tool given to leaders and powerful groups in the community to exploit the weak even further. Most decision making about projects is concentrated in the hands of these elites, and poor people see demands to participate and contribute as infringing on their freedom. One poor man in Bugokela said, "Freedom is when you can sleep and nobody comes to disturb you at night, telling you to go and fetch water for building a school."

In both villages in Tanzania, an aura of nepotism and corruption surrounds "development contributions." People try to hide from local officials and policemen so that they will not be forced to hand over what little savings they have. One man commented, "These people tell us that we have to contribute for the school, for the police, and for offices. But we are the ones who bring stones. We make the bricks and offer our labor. So where does the money go? They do not even tell us what they use it for. Of course we understand where it goes. This is the money they use for drinking; this is the money they use to buy more goats; and this is the money they use to pay us when we do casual labor for them."

Poor people's corporations

While there are some efforts to scale up livelihood groups horizontally, across districts, states, and countries, there are hardly any examples of scaling up vertically to create corporations owned and managed by poor people or on their behalf. In our responses from 60,000 people, we found not one example of such corporations. Although hundreds of women were frying fritters, rolling out tortillas, or making cookies, there was no "Mrs. Fields" in our data.

In the United States, Debbie Fields started her business of making cookies for home parties with sales of $50 and $75 on the first and second days. Today, Mrs. Fields Cookies is a vertically integrated company with franchise outlets in malls across America and annual sales of about $70 million. The Indian equivalent of Mrs. Fields is Lijjat Papad, a women's organization manufacturing various products such as baked snacks that are exported around the world. Started by seven women, it is now run like a cooperative, with 40,000 female member-owners who are referred to as "sisters." One of the core values of the corporation is the concept of "mutual family affection, concern, and trust."[19]

The most advanced form of capitalism, shared equity, embodies the norms that are embedded in successful families, notably that of trust. In most cases, corporations accomplish this trust not through face-to-face relationships, but through institutional norms and practices, including financial disclosure and shareholder voting on major decisions. When rules and transparency are violated, trust declines, and even large corporations can sink.

Poor people have the skills, initiative, and trust within their families that can provide a foundation for successful business ventures. What they need to become the next Mrs. Fields or Lijjat Papad are innovative instruments to improve their access to finance, supported by technical guidance. Indeed, what they need are the same financial instruments that are available to the well-off, including equity, and the means to scale up their livelihoods vertically (see box 7.4 for some innovations). The ideal is microequity, where poor people own their businesses. Equity financing reduces risk by sharing it between the microentrepreneur and the financier who gives the grant. It also lowers transaction costs and, most important, gives poor people a stake in their own business (Pretes 2002).

Getting Together for Local Public Goods

Now democracy is working in its full spirit. Compared to the past 10 years, the local government is showing more interest and concern for the public good, as the people's political awareness and comprehension has increased. They are questioning the government on every issue. Meetings are held, public consensus is taken into consideration, and all people are involved in the deliberations. The government's activities and its policies are now people-oriented.

—Discussion with men, Lingatla, Andhra Pradesh

In her now-classic *Governing the Commons* (1990), Elinor Ostrom shows the ability of local groups to cooperate to manage common property resources and avoid overexploitation. Our data are replete with instances of cooperation around local public goods. This cooperation takes two main forms: improving the social environment and improving the physical environment. Unlike group activity around livelihoods, collective action to improve the social and physical environment is generally undertaken by the rich and poor working together to solve problems that affect them all. This is perhaps one of the key reasons for its success.

BOX 7.4
Transforming collective action into corporations of the poor

Corporations "for profit" and "of the poor" are rare and just starting. It is not a surprise, therefore, that we hardly saw any evidence of such corporations in our own data.

Grameen has created a yogurt company as a joint venture with the French Danone company. Sweet yogurt is a traditional food in Bangladesh, hence there is local demand for the product. The factory will produce 3,000 tons of yogurt, employ 1,700 Grameen Bank members, and source milk from 300 microfarms each owning less than four cows. The yogurt will be sold at the affordable price of about 7 cents a cup. Once the French company is paid off, this "social business" will be totally owned by Grameen Bank members, so poor women will have a stake in its success.

Fabindia, a large Indian ethnic wear company, created a number of small producer-owned companies as part of its Artisanal Company Network. Aided by a grant from a private investor, the network has set up community-owned joint ventures in rural areas with artisans and craftspeople as shareholders. Currently sourcing textile and nontextile products from 15,000 artisans across 21 states in India, the network is expected to create 100,000 sustainable jobs for artisan shareholders by 2012. Although the network will ease Fabindia's sourcing supply chain, which is currently overstretched at one location in Delhi, artisans will benefit from inputs, training, access to funding, and sustained demand.

Besides corporations, there are new models of MFIs that are raising finance by investing in public equity markets. Their potential is reflected in the response to the initial public offering of shares in Financiera Compartamos, Latin America's largest microlender. Shares of the Mexico-based microfinance institution (MFI) were oversubscribed 13 times, with prices rising by 22 percent on the first day of trading (CGAP 2007). The pent-up demand for shares is largely a reflection of the high interest rates charged by the MFI, which were at one time in the range of 110 percent per year. Compartamos defends its high-interest, high-earnings strategy as a means to expand the number of people it serves; basically it overcharges existing clients in order to reach out to potential future clients. Despite high interest rates, Compartamos has not at any point lacked clients; poor people are willing to pay very high rates of interest, and the interest rate charged by Compartamos is still lower than the rates charged by moneylenders and other sources (CGAP 2007).[20]

Most collective action around public goods in our sample appears to be a *substitute* for state and market failure. In the absence of basic services such as schools, clinics, or security, or when these services are of poor quality, people come together to provide or improve them. We do find some examples of collective action that *complement* the state. These include people's efforts to share costs and participate in providing public goods and solving community problems in tandem with state efforts. Even when the state is functioning well, groups perform important functions in claiming people's rights and monitoring the performance of the state and markets.[21] In a well-functioning modern state, an informed citizenry, a well-organized civil society, and the threat of losing elections keep governments motivated to perform well.

Improving the social environment

> *Chiefs became tired of thieves, murderers, and those who swear when drunk. They got together and came up with a group that would not be scared to enforce security. People offered themselves, those who were ready to die or kill. They put together weapons such as a bow and arrow, a club, thick rubber bands, a maize flywheel, and a catapult.*
>
> —Discussion group, Bamlozi, Malawi

Almost everyone wants to live in a community and household free from fear, crime, violence, social discrimination, and social tensions. One of the more common forms of cooperation we found is people getting together for self-defense. We also found innumerable cases, particularly in the African contexts, in which community residents have come together to guard themselves.

Village defense parties are common in many African villages we studied, particularly in Malawi and Tanzania. In some villages in Ruvuma, Tanzania, they provide protection against wild animals. In Namdenye, a village located near the Selous Game Reserve, the fear of wildlife is pervasive. Elephants, wild pigs, and baboons destroy crops such as paddy, maize, and bananas that are major sources of income to the community. People are angry that the government seems intent on preserving wildlife at the cost of human life. Several cases of lions hurting and killing people and livestock have been reported to the district authorities, but nothing has been done. The villagers now move together in defense groups. "We have to organize ourselves for the journey to the farms. Although everybody has his own plot, you cannot go alone. If you want to go to the farm while your neighbor has planned another economic activity like brewing, you have to cancel the trip—even if that means staying home idle for the whole day." Although the village defense groups are generally credited with improving security, over time some of these organizations have evolved into local militia, thus threatening the very cause of security for which they were formed (box 7.5).

People's self-defense groups are also common in conflict-affected settings. In several communities in Assam, respondents spoke of how village defense parties had become involved in dispute resolution and had helped young men who had strayed into antisocial activities, sometimes by giving them loans.

BOX 7.5
Community policing in Malawi: From protection to abuse

In the poor farming community of Mzaponda, Malawi, discussion groups spoke of getting together for self-preservation and safety. In 2001, a spell of dry weather caused an epidemic of severe hunger, which in turn led to widespread stealing and violence. "People's maize was being stolen, but the worst affected were the goats. A lot of people lost their livestock," reported a discussion group. A 50-year-old woman continued, "The thieves used to challenge us. They could even take off your clothes if you were found sleeping outside your home. We used to wake up in the morning, see our property, and say 'thank God you really exist!' People were being killed at night while tourists were being robbed. Some were also being murdered."

Despite repeated requests to the authorities, security did not improve. According to discussion groups, the police worked in cahoots with the thieves and released them as soon as they were caught. The villagers then formed what they called Inkatha, a community policing group. The group now provides security in the village. But a discussion group with youths revealed how Inkatha really works. "Inkatha are people who are chosen by people in the village. When they are chosen, they are given powers. When you are caught stealing by the village headman, you can argue, but when you are caught stealing by the Inkatha, you cannot do anything." As our team found out later, Inkatha simply takes the thieves away and beats them. Only then do they hand the thieves over to the police.

Inkatha has helped curb crime and is mostly respected in the community. But there are whispers that the group is becoming yet another evil to contend with. In a discussion on livelihoods, the women in the village had this to say: "Inkatha is causing our businesses to decline. As soon as it is six in the evening, they declare that time is up for business. They come to the place where we sell beer and say that they are going to break the clay pots we are using unless we give them a little bit of something. The money we have been able to generate is already very little. They stop us from making more sales; then they demand money from us for them not to break up our clay pots. Can a person improve [and get ahead] with such acts?"

Such groups are also common in the conflict sites in Indonesia and the Philippines, where at times they are recognized and assisted by the army.

Women in some contexts have organized to improve their own security against violence in their homes. In some villages in Andhra Pradesh, participation in self-help groups gave women the courage to collectively protest the sale of locally brewed alcohol called *arrack*, which they considered a cause of domestic violence. In the village of Malkapur, women came together to close down all liquor shops in the village. "We threw out the storage cans and other vessels filled with liquor," they informed our field team. "This was possible only with the women groups, which gave us collective power." In Dhampur, women revealed how their SHGs fought abuse. "If any injustice is done to our women, we do not keep quiet. Recently, one husband thrashed his wife while he was in a drunken state. Our group came to know about this incident, and we all went to him and abused and threatened him, saying that if it happens again, we will take serious action against him. The power of women's groups is up to that extent."

More broadly, women's voice and organization is challenging deep norms of gender inequality. As they gain confidence, women run up against resistance and sometimes violence. In most cases this gives way to reluctant acceptance, which later turns to admiration as women start bringing new money home. A poor scheduled tribe woman in Pulagampalle, Anantapur, Andhra Pradesh, said that her husband objected to her joining a SHG because the meetings, held outside the village, would cut into her working hours. He beat her, but she joined anyway. She took a loan of Rs 10,000 (about $250) and started a petty shop. Slowly, her husband changed his mind, and he now encourages her to go to group meetings. She is illiterate, but her two daughters are studying medicine. In Dayabhara, Bangladesh, Shehnaz met similar resistance when she joined a group. Her husband beat her, and her mother-in-law called her names. "But now that our family is benefiting from my savings, they don't do this," Shehnaz said. Women in both study sites said they now insist on their names being included on documents like land titles. And they are fearless enough to go to court if abandoned by their husbands.

Overcoming deeply entrenched caste inequalities is another challenge that women's groups in Andhra Pradesh have confronted. Through rituals, songs, and prayers, groups are helping women of different castes break down old barriers. Pedakka, a member of a SHG in the village of Atmakur, said, "When we come together in groups, we realize that the blood in you and me is the same. In the meetings, now everyone sits together. There is no discrimination." In Malkapur, people spoke of how access of the lower-caste groups to temples and schools has improved thanks to women coming together in groups. "Ten years ago, inequalities of caste and religion were predominant in our society. Because of these differences, people belonging to the scheduled caste and tribe communities were not allowed to enter the temple. Now there are no such differences, and even SC and ST people are coming to the temple along with us. They are coming to our houses and sitting beside us." Although caste was specific to the study regions in India, in other sites, too, cooperation in groups is seen as leading to an increased sense of equality. "*Torang*—all of us in the village are equal," said one of our participants in Tattantok, Indonesia. "*Tarada*—there is no difference. The groups taught us that we are together in better or worse."

Improving the physical environment

The community did all this. The school was built with the help of everybody in the community. The families with kids in school had to cooperate, give money.
> —Discussion with women, Guadalamoros, Mexico

People come together to repair or build infrastructure, usually minor. They improve mud roads and paths, clear bush, build schools and places of worship, reclaim ponds and wells. The success of such collective action depends on good leadership and social solidarity, both of which build trust that people's contributions will not be misused. In Guadalamoros, Mexico, where the women were determined to obtain secondary school education for their children, the community built a secondary school, along with a community center and a health clinic. All were financed in part by remittances, and the school eventually received government help as well. In Chiksisi, Malawi, the community started a preschool for young children, coming together to mold bricks for the building. A church-supported relief organization contributed cement and food for the children.

The very act of working together reinforces unity and cooperation. In Senialpara, Assam, people attributed improved social harmony to the coming together of the entire community to build a *namghar* (prayer hall). "We the villagers together dug large ponds and started a fishery last year. By selling fish, we earned about one lakh of rupees, and with this money we constructed a big namghar in our village. This namghar has united the villagers more, and now even people who earlier did not take part in social activities, do; redress of disputes is held in this namghar. Earlier it was very small and could not include all the persons inside, but now it is a lot bigger. This namghar has increased the unity and religious feelings of the people."

Pressing claims and demanding accountability

I have done things I did not know I was going to do. I did not know I was going to develop, coming to an office, explaining to someone my rights as a displaced person and fighting for them.
—Alejandra, a 35-year-old displaced woman, Villa Rosa, Colombia

In addition to improving the physical and social environment, collective community action offers poor people a powerful tool to advance their claims to resources and enhance accountability of government (Heyer, Stewart, and Thorp 2002). We find countless examples of people cooperating to demand better roads, water supply, schools, health clinics, and community halls. Often, they are first denied and succeed only after repeated tries. Our evidence on collective action enforcing accountability is supported by studies that highlight the role of people's collective efforts in working for the benefit of the community at large.[22]

The residents of Shivanoor, Andhra Pradesh, faced a drinking water crisis. Women were compelled to walk 5 kilometers each day to fetch one can of water, which was often insufficient for the entire household. They recalled, "Our bodies pained. Our necks were strained because of holding these heavy water cans. The children who accompanied us had wounds on their feet due to lack of footwear. We used the water only for drinking purposes and bathed only once in 20 days." In 1998, the women together with the rest of the village collectively approached the local leader and sought redress. Their voices were heard, and the community was equipped with a borewell and a water pipeline the following year.

Residents of Barumangga village in Indonesia together decided to request replacement of a civil servant because of his poor performance and corrupt practices. The community was affected by conflict between Christians and Muslims and had received government assistance for evacuees. The civil servant had misappropriated these funds. "In addition, there was a lack of cooperation among his staff, and service to the community was not very good," recalled one of our key informants. Under pressure from the community, the local government finally replaced the bureaucrat.

Most of the examples we found involved people demanding resources or accountability from government. There were very few examples of people demanding accountability or redress from rigged markets, perhaps because cases of joint production and ownership of assets are rare or suffer from free-rider issues, making it difficult for small producers to come together and demand fair prices.

Complementarity and substitution: Interaction between states and social ties

North (1990) and Knack and Keefer (1997) capture in their work this two-way directionality between civic cooperation and the functioning of states. Woolcock (1998) and Narayan (1999) further explore this dynamic interaction between the state and society and argue that different combinations of bridging ties and state functioning can result in different outcomes (figure 7.5).

In the ideal scenario (quadrant I, labeled social and economic well-being), good governance complemented by high levels of cross-cutting ties among social groups leads to positive economic and social outcomes. Informal social groups *complement* the functioning of the state. While people crowd local sports matches, choral groups sing in every church and hall, and neighbors get together to picnic, business clusters produce export-quality goods and government-provided services hum along.

We did see evidence of virtuous circles between local governments and collective action. The village of Mintang in Bukidnon, Philippines, shifted in its democracy ratings from being nonresponsive 10 years ago to being responsive at the end of the study period. This was due to a combination of two factors: election of a village leader who listens and presence of community associations

FIGURE 7.5

Different combinations of bridging ties and state functioning result in different outcomes

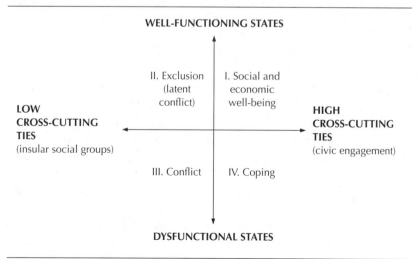

Source: Adapted from Narayan 1999.

that started working with the elected leader. The leader was known to be fair and approachable, and the associations were driven by mutual understanding and respect among community members. The outcome, within a fairly short time, was total transparency in local government budgets.

But all communities are not blessed with the virtues of good leadership or social unity. In such contexts, our evidence suggests that external interventions by government programs such as the National Solidarity Program in Afghanistan and Janmabhoomi in Andhra Pradesh can play a role in engaging communities in development. NSP is a rural development program initiated by the World Bank and managed by the Ministry of Rural Rehabilitation and Development in Afghanistan. The program provides grants to villages for rehabilitation, reconstruction, and income generation projects. In order to benefit from these grants, the communities have to first hold democratic elections of a community development council, which is then engaged in all stages of the project. Similarly, the Janmabhoomi program was initiated by the state government of Andhra Pradesh to engage communities in their own development.

In quadrant II, labeled exclusion, communities have reasonably well-functioning governments but these have been taken over or unduly influenced by the dominant social groups. Exclusion leads to latent conflict. This is visible in many of the villages our teams visited in the South Asian context. The cases of rich landlords poisoning communal ponds to exclude poor fishermen in Shantakalia, Bangladesh, or the upper-caste Lambadis restricting opportunities for the lower castes in Dhampur, Uttar Pradesh, fall into this category.

When such communities degenerate, they land in quadrant III, where conflict, violence, and anarchy prevail, and the state dissolves or collapses. As the state ceases to fulfill its functions, the primary social groups become informal substitutes for the state. Warlords, mafias, guerrilla movements, and other armed groups seize control. We see examples of this in Colombia, where many urban communities have been taken over by different guerilla factions, and community leaders have "disappeared." Some communities in Assam and in the southern Philippines also fall in this category.

However, when societies have cross-cutting ties to a reasonable extent, they can overcome social divisions and cope with poorly functioning governments. This is the situation in quadrant IV, labeled coping. Groups and associations of the poor, such as savings groups and village defense parties, become substitutes for failed or dysfunctional states and provide coping strategies. In Bangladesh, for example, poor men and women wanted to access government loans, but red tape and corruption kept government credit schemes out of reach. People found it much easier to obtain credit from their own groups that were linked to NGOs. Similarly, the Inkatha self-defense groups, which often lead to vigilante justice, start as a system to provide security in communities facing a collapse of law and order.

When formal institutional arrangements fail, whether in providing policing or schooling or credit, people often try to solve their problems themselves, collectively. However, these efforts are substitutes for *failed modernization* and failed formal institutions. Collective action has a cost in time and money, as people must come together for meetings, organize, raise funds, implement plans, manage and repair resources, and solve conflicts. The idea should not be to make citizens fend for themselves in providing basic services, but to guarantee that poor people have access to the basic minimum so they can get on with improving their lives.

When governments and markets do their job, networks and groups of poor people can play a key role in enforcing accountability among the providers of goods and services. They can also enable people to exercise their citizenship rights in the effort to create just societies.[23]

Conclusion

Across our study communities, the most common unit of collective action is the family. It is not indigenous organizations working in isolation, nor is it collective action supported by NGOs, the government, or the private sector. We highlight the features of the family that seem to underlie the success of family collective action: social solidarity, unity, and loyalty; repeat interactions and relationships over time; authority and control over decisions; pooling of resources and/or joint production; and the ability to share both downside risks and upside gains.

All other forms of collective action fall short when they are measured against these criteria. There are some successes, but all have limitations. We draw several important conclusions.

First, in most instances, poor people's collective action in isolated small groups helps them cope and survive but not get ahead. Indeed, in socially stratified societies, poor people's bonding groups reflect and perpetuate social inequality. Poor people bond with other poor people precisely *because* they are poor and find themselves mostly excluded from groups of the rich. This is not to suggest that collective action by poor women and men is unimportant. Spontaneous bonding among poor people provides the essential foundation for scaling up and for creating social movements. Poor people's organizations also have important spillover effects in improving the overall social and political environment.

Second, collective action may not help poor people move out of poverty unless there are outside interventions that help them break the constraints of resources, knowledge, skills, capital, and markets. Interventions like Grameen microcredit and the Andhra Pradesh self-help groups have allowed poor people's groups to link up horizontally and vertically so they can gain sufficient scale to access resources and gradually gain social and political voice in their communities.

Third, creating economic organizations of poor people is very time- and resource-intensive and does not yield immediate results. As a result, there is massive underinvestment by NGOs, the private sector, and governments in organizations of poor people. Without such investment, it will be impossible to scale up poor people's organizations so that they become players with bargaining power in markets. Nor will it be possible for poor people to capture the greater profits higher up the production value chain. Investment in organizations and associations that represent poor people's interests and are not captured by the elite is perhaps the single most important action that NGOs, private corporations, foundations, and the government can take to ensure fairer returns to poor people in market economies.

Fourth, collective action that substitutes for the failure of the state and markets to provide basic services should be viewed as a transitional measure. Collective action traditions are important in all societies and lay the foundations for the emergence of a strong civil society. Their ultimate goals should not be to build schools or fend off lions, but to press demands for equity and to hold governments and markets accountable.

Finally, while there are a few remarkable examples of successful microcredit and community-driven development programs, the challenge ahead is to have many more such large-scale successes. There is a need to create networked organizations of poor people in which they become the owners, hiring managers as needed. Ironically, the only organization that fits this description is the equity corporation. We believe that a big challenge is the creation of corporations and microequity organizations owned by poor people that can help large numbers of poor people move permanently out of poverty and live the lives they choose.

Notes

1. The fable comes from the Panchatantra, a series of five ancient Hindu texts that use analogies from the animal kingdom to teach about life. The books stress five principles pertaining to the value of friendship: *mitra bhedha* (loss of friends); *mitra laabha* (gaining friends); *suhrudbheda* (dissension between friends); *vigraha* (separation); and *sandhi* (union).

2. The fact that family help is most important to fallers and chronic poor may suggest that these groups are less able than others to access other resources (government, NGO, private). This is both a cause and a consequence of their difficult situation.

3. Alderman et al. (1995) recognize conflict within the family as a central element in poverty outcomes. They emphasize that individual household members are likely to have different preferences and that this may affect the impact of transfers made to households to reduce poverty.

4. Using data from Indian hospitals on admissions of girls and boys, Kynch and Sen (1983) showed that girls were typically much more ill before they were taken to a hospital. The families themselves perceived little discrimination in treatment, but there was clearly an earlier recognition of serious ailments among boys.

5. For discussions of gender inequality in the literature, see, among others, Agarwal, Humphries, and Robeyns (2006) and Robeyns (2007). Robeyns argues that social norms are usually gendered, that is, they apply to men and women in different ways. They impose notions of appropriate and normal behavior for men and women, placing clear limits on how assertive a woman can be before she is considered aggressive.

6. Axelrod's *Evolution of Cooperation* (1984) is an important work that led to the recognition of social relationships in economic thinking. In repeated trials of the prisoner's dilemma game, the author found that even when individuals followed tit-for-tat strategies, stable outcomes that were more cooperative could emerge. When they did, these outcomes were usually due to some norms that produced cooperation between individuals.

7. Family-owned enterprises are not completely free from governance issues. Analyzing data from 883 family-owned firms in the United States, Schulze, Lubatkin, and Dino (2003) find problems like free riding and high consumption of perks. Family firms may also be forced to provide employment for family members, which may result in decisions that are suboptimal from a business point of view. See also Gersick et al. (1997) and Daily and Dollinger (1992).

8. For the rich and powerful, bonding social capital enhances opportunities. Bebbington et al. (2006) found that local elites in rural Indonesia were able to consolidate their power through connections to the government and local private companies. O'Brien, Phillips, and Patsiorkovsky (2005) also found evidence of the "restrictive nature" of bonding social capital in communities in the United States and Russia. In extreme cases, social bonding can facilitate violence (the Ku Klux Klan, the Mafia, and Al Qaeda all come to mind). Rubio (1997) shows how high levels of bonding within criminal organizations in Colombia supports illegal activities, with returns exclusively for those involved in the group.

9. The same ties that bind can also exclude entire groups of people. The literature on collective action clearly establishes that bonding only within one's own social group reduces opportunity sets for groups lacking power and wealth. In a famous study, Loury (1977) showed that African American youth are disadvantaged in the labor market in part because their parents lack social connections that would give them information about jobs. Portes (1998) describes how the caste system

in India, with its rigid boundaries, can restrict the lower castes' access to opportunities. Moreover, a history of prejudicial treatment may spill into expectations of poor outcomes. Using controlled experiments, Hoff and Pandey (2006) showed that lower castes in India tend to start believing that as hard as they try, they will get unfair rewards for their efforts. This expectation or belief can further reinforce bonding.

10. Our study's findings are in line with those of previous research by the authors on this topic. In a poverty assessment in Kenya, Narayan and Nyamwaya (1996) found more than 200,000 community groups in rural areas. But these groups rarely helped the poor escape poverty, as they remained disconnected from outside resources. Narayan (2002a) found that members of many indigenous groups in Latin America, while exhibiting high levels of internal social solidarity, remained in poverty. Again, this was because they lacked the resources and power to tilt the rules of the game in their favor.

11. In a study of 70 rotating savings and credit associations in rural Kenya, Gugerty (2007) found that members mostly used group funds to finance immediate expenses such as household items, school fees, food, medical care, and clothes, as well as to pay down debts.

12. Dercon et al. (2006) find funeral groups to be highly prevalent in rural Tanzania and Ethiopia. Such groups, they report, are usually "based on well-defined rules and regulations, often offering premium-based insurance for funeral expenses."

13. Question (a) was "Suppose something unfortunate happened to someone in this village/neighborhood, such as a serious illness, or his house burning down. How likely is it, in your view, that people in the community would get together to help this person? Please rate your answer on a scale of 1 to 4, where 1 is very likely and 4 is very unlikely. Has this changed from 10 years ago? Please rate your assessment of the situation 10 years ago on the same scale." Question (b) was "If there was a problem with getting enough water in this village/neighborhood, how likely is it, in your view, that people would cooperate to try to solve the problem? Please rate your answer on a scale of 1 to 4, where 1 is very likely and 4 is very unlikely. Has this changed from 10 years ago? Please rate your assessment of the situation 10 years ago on the same scale."

14. There are many well-known examples of extremely successful NGOs that have achieved large scale in Asia and Latin America. NGOs also play a critical role in campaigning and lobbying at the national and international levels on such issues as landmine removal, debt cancellation, and increased development support for Africa.

15. Lack of collateral, however, need not be the constraint. In a survey of 1,438 households across six provinces in Indonesia by Johnston and Morduch (2007), only about 10 percent of the households that were creditworthy and not borrowing from banks reported lack of collateral as a deterrent. About half the poor households that were creditworthy reported a strong aversion to taking debt—they simply did not want to borrow and hence did not seek credit. This finding challenges traditional thinking about the potential impacts that giving legal titles to assets like land can have on the poor (de Soto 2000).

16. In a 1998 study, Khandker found that poverty among Grameen Bank members could be reduced by 5 percentage points per year as a result of participation in the program. This participant-level result can be translated into poverty reduction of 2.7 percentage points per year at the village level. However, in a 2005 study using panel data from 1991/92 and 1993/98, Khandker suggests that long-term impacts of microcredit programs are smaller than those obtained from cross-sectional study. That is, a woman's participation in a microcredit program reduces poverty by 1.6 percentage points at the participant level and 1 percentage point at the village level.
17. In a study of 1,438 households in Indonesia, Johnston and Morduch (2007) found that loans taken from microcredit institutions by low-income households served immediate households needs about 30 percent of the time.
18. In a review of the impact of the Kecamatan Development Project, Barron, Diprose, and Woolcock (2007) found that even though the project had little direct impact on mitigating local-level conflict, it indirectly helped change norms, attitudes, and expectations regarding how disputes could be resolved.
19. Information about Mrs. Fields and Lijjat Papad is available on their Web sites, http://www.mrsfields.com/ and http://www.lijjat.com/index1.asp.
20. There are a number of small venture capital funds for micro and small enterprises including Root Capital and Lok Capital, among many others. For descriptions of recent innovations, see the Web sites of the Clinton Global Initiative (www.clintonglobalinitiative.org) and CGAP (Consultative Group to Assist the Poor, www.cgap.org).
21. Heyer, Stewart, and Thorp (2002) distinguish three types of functions that groups perform: overcoming market and state failures (efficiency), improving the position of their members (claim), and distributing resources to the less well-off (equity). They conclude that groups that better regulate within-group relationships (based on rules, intragroup distribution, or other local institutions) are more likely to survive and function effectively.
22. A study of 121 rural water supply projects by Isham, Narayan, and Pritchett (1994) revealed the significant role of participation in keeping the systems functioning. Hammer and Pritchett (2006) find that when water supply projects are redesigned to engage with communities, places with stronger social ties and more cooperation do a better job of creating and maintaining water supply than those with weaker ties. Knack (2000), using data from the United States, finds that in states with more social capital, government performance is rated higher. Our findings also tie in well with Putnam's (1993) work on Italy, which suggested that the density and quality of civic associations was the main factor explaining the quality of regional government performance.
23. One of the main conclusions of the World Bank's *World Development Report 2004: Making Services Work for Poor People* (2003) was that empowering the poor through measures such as increased access to information can allow them to hold politicians more accountable for service delivery.

Concluding Reflections

CHAPTER 8

How do you conclude a study that has taken four years; spanned 21 regions in 15 countries, each with its own country team; used 10 different research instruments, both qualitative and quantitative; and analyzed the responses of over 60,000 individuals? Besides, that is, with relief?

The literature on poverty is old, broad, and deep, and has lately become technically sophisticated as well. Our study adds three new twists. One is that we seek to understand poverty not by finding people who are currently poor and studying them—the usual approach—but by finding those who have *moved out* of poverty and asking them how they did it. After all, if we are interested in reducing poverty, why not ask those who escaped, if only to complement the hundreds of studies that examine those who are still poor? The second twist was that we asked people to tell their own stories. We did this both in individual settings and in a variety of focus group exercises. Rather than conjecturing a theoretical narrative and looking to fill in the details quantitatively, we let people create their own narratives, which we tried to capture. These narratives are not *the* reality or even *their* reality, but they are at least their own public framing of their realities. The third twist is that our study focused on the local realities. While national policies get a great deal of attention in poverty studies, the local conditions in which people live and interact on a daily basis are often overlooked. These local conditions, we would argue, are at the heart of the poverty narrative.

Oscar Lewis's classic *Five Families* (1959) traces the day-to-day experiences and life stories of five poor families in Mexico. With just five narrative arcs, his book, nonetheless, presents a picture of enormous complexity. Imagine, then, our concern about our own study, which uses open-ended research methods to capture tens of thousands of voices and trace thousands of lives. Would anything emerge beyond cacophony and chaos? Perhaps after 60,000 stories, there are no common themes, just 60,000 stories. Or perhaps, faced

333

with the onslaught of data, we would superimpose our own narrative, wittingly or not—after all, "deconstructing" other people's narratives is a popular academic sport.

We tried as best we could to distill from these data a set of common narratives or themes. We do not presume to have identified all the relevant issues, and we are careful not to make specific attributions of causality. Rather, we have tried to construct a set of coherent metanarratives that capture common elements but allow for locally specific variations. Throughout, we have tried to weave together the particular and the general, providing examples from specific regions that illustrate the general themes.

Framing "Poverty"

Two historically persistent metanarratives exist about "the poor": one associated with the political right and the other with the political left. They have played important roles in framing the issue of poverty and poverty reduction.

One metanarrative might be called the Victorian notion of poverty, though it extends further back in time and has had a broader geographic reach than even the empire on which the sun never set. It is that the problem of poverty is the pathology of poor people. If, after all, life is a fair contest, then the problem of losing is the losers themselves. This approach tends to isolate "the poor" as a small, relatively stable group of people whose poverty is the result of either their behavior (drinking, drugs, laziness), their attitudes (fatalism, lack of initiative), their lack of skills (illiterates who cannot learn), or bad luck (mental or physical disability, widowhood). Although few development professionals who work in poor countries share this view, this notion of poverty remains popular among the better-off, in poor and rich countries alike.

Like many persistent ideas, this one has both a small grain of truth and a large dose of self-interest. The grain of truth, on which our study respondents often agree, is that people with serious substance abuse problems or those who do not take initiative are more likely to remain stuck in poverty. However, such individuals account for a minuscule fraction of the millions of people in poverty around the world. This framing of poverty is based on a fundamental fallacy. (All bears have hair, but this doesn't mean that all, or even most, creatures with hair are bears.)

The large dose of self-interest is that if the problem of poverty is a problem of poor people, then it is poor people's problem. This belief justifies either of two unhelpful responses. One is the hard-line approach sanctioning few if any actions to benefit the poor, who are pictured as undeserving. Some even argue that assistance to the poor encourages the bad behaviors that are the cause of poverty (e.g., Murray 1984). The other response consists of charity—identifying the poorest of the poor and giving them just enough to allow them to survive, but not enough to move out of poverty.

The other metanarrative, also from the Victorian era but from a different point on the political spectrum, is that poverty is a systematic and unavoidable result of the operation of market forces and that solving poverty requires mass-based political action. This would have the government in a vanguard role, acting to "save" the poor from the vagaries of an indifferent, if not hostile, market. Again, this view survives on a grain of truth and a generous helping of self-interest.

The grain of truth is that the poor do face an uphill struggle as they grapple with markets that are at best indifferent and at worst deliberately rigged against them. Lacking assets, connections, access, and sometimes business expertise, poor people often have great difficulty riding market forces out of poverty, as chapter 5 explains.

The self-interest is that if the poor cannot save themselves, then someone else must save them, and by grabbing power in the name of the many, the few have often done very well. U.S. academic James Scott (1998) points out that in order to make human beings manageable by the state, the complex realities of their lives have to be reduced to a simple picture that the state can "see." This simplification makes problems amenable to solutions of what he calls "bureaucratic high modernism"—programs that classify, quantify, and follow rules. The vision of a top-down effort to eliminate poverty—by reducing it to technical problems of program and policy design, finding *the solution* that can be implemented by a modern Weberian bureaucracy, and funding that solution adequately—has great seductive power. In limited spheres, such top-down programs have often had laudable results, leading, for example, to the massive expansions of education and public health. But the attempt to eradicate poverty by eradicating messiness and complexity, and in the process limiting choice and the use of markets, has often led to disappointing, if not tragic, results.

Nearly everyone who works on development issues recognizes the inadequacy of these two metanarratives of poverty. While some think they are straw men, and we hope that they are, nevertheless some straw men are, like the Hindu demon Ravana, worth burning each year.[1]

If our findings do not support these metanarratives, can we suggest a more useful way of thinking about poverty? An alternative framing of poverty, however simplified, does emerge from the narratives of the poor and the formerly poor that we gathered.

In our study of communities around the world, poverty is not a problem of "the poor" but is much broader. It is a problem of the many, not the few. Poverty is fluid: it is a situation or a condition people find themselves in, not a permanent characteristic. Most people living in poverty do not suffer from fatalism or low aspirations; rather, they take initiative to change their conditions, and most are confident that with hard work they will prevail. Poor people value freedom and their social relationships, and they want to use them to improve their well-being in a variety of ways. But their initiatives, whether individual or collective, often come up against blocked opportunities, whether in the context of rigged markets or local democracies captured by the elite. The key to poverty reduction lies in the intersection of initiative and opportunity.

Practical Implications

We offer in conclusion some ideas about how the results of this study could inform development practice. We do so with some trepidation, as the study was not designed to isolate and examine the impact of popularly debated programs, like microcredit, or controversial policies, like free trade. Nor could we, with our data, evaluate the relative returns to specific projects—whether a road would be better here or there, or whether input subsidies are more or less useful than technical training for increasing productivity.

What we can do is relate the findings to four current approaches to poverty and then to three principles that we believe should inform poverty reduction efforts. We outline these principles in the full knowledge that no study sees the whole picture and that there are no simple answers.

In the continuously roiling debates among actors concerned in one way or another with poverty reduction—development practitioners, human rights activists, NGO workers, entrepreneurs, philanthropists, economists, and finance ministers, almost all of them nonpoor, the authors of this book included—one can distinguish four major approaches.

National growth is all, and policy is the key to growth. One view is that the primary determinant of how many people move out of poverty is how rapidly economic output in the country they live in is growing. Although there might be churning of individuals and there might be local variations, in the end most people are pulled up by rising wages and expanding employment. These are the result not of individual actions but of market forces. Poverty reduction thus depends on policies that allow and encourage free-market forces to do their work.

Although there is some substance to this viewpoint, as we showed in chapter 5, it does not capture the whole picture. As Joseph Stiglitz (2005) puts it, "Growth may be everything, but it's not the only thing." Our study brings two caveats to the fore.

First, a growing economy does create opportunities, but access to those opportunities is far from equitable. Poor people do not enjoy equal access to free markets, where an invisible hand works in everyone's interest. Rather, a visible hand often works to hold poor people back. Sometimes this visible hand is that of government, imposing restrictions that have the effect (if not the intent) of thwarting poor people's initiatives. Sometimes the visible hand is of powerful private actors who collude to rig markets in their own favor.

Second, the national economy is important, but there are wide differences among localities. Seventy-three percent of the variation in net prosperity between our communities is within study regions. Where one lives can make a great difference in how much one benefits from national economic growth. Bringing the lagging localities up to speed can both help sustain growth and create local opportunity where it matters most.

Poverty policy is about safety nets and programs. Another view, one focusing on the instruments directly under the control of governments, considers poverty reduction a matter of creating the right set of redistributive transfers, income generation programs, and expenditures on social services (such as health and education) used by the poor. Again, this approach has some merit, as we show in chapters 6 and 7. Certainly programs that support poor people and address their vulnerabilities are important dimensions of public policy. But our study suggests three considerations.

First, our community mobility matrixes reinforce what has been emerging from various data sets that have tracked households over time: poverty transitions are very fluid, and "the poor" are not in fact a stable, identifiable group of people. There is much rising and falling. No static formula for targeting programs—by region, age, education, even current poverty status—is going to predict accurately who will be poor, even in the near future. And transfers (grants, loans) have to be fairly large to stabilize families, reduce vulnerability, and end the cycling in and out of poverty.

Second, even accounting for people's natural tendency to overstate their own role in their achievements, it was striking how few people credited external programs of any type as instrumental in their move out of poverty. Although it is exciting to find programmatic initiatives that seem to be making a difference in particular contexts, it is nonetheless sobering to note that NGOs were mentioned as a cause of moving out of poverty *by only 0.3 percent* of our respondents—barely more than those who mentioned "illegal activities." People most often cite new jobs, new agricultural initiatives, and new businesses as routes out of poverty. Externally assisted programs need to play a part, however small, in enabling people to scale up their livelihood activities into self-sustaining and market-worthy initiatives. Unless they can do so, they offer only mitigation, not sustained reduction, of poverty.

Third, social services are important, but their impact on poverty reduction varies. In the case of education, while it obviously plays a large role, most people have received by early adulthood all the formal education they are ever going to have. Poverty reduction has to reduce poverty for those people, not simply ask them to wait until their more educated children can escape poverty.

Health plays a large role, but generally in a negative sense. Good health by itself is almost never sufficient to move people up and out of poverty. Bad health, on the other hand, bleeds resources and can wipe a family out financially. Bad health keeps poor people from moving out of poverty, and among those who are not poor, a serious health shock can trigger a fall into poverty. This finding is of key importance, because reducing falling can dramatically increase the numbers moving out of poverty.

Abject poverty is a challenge for philanthropy. A third approach, less common in development agencies but looming large in the public mind in rich and poor countries, is the view that "the poor" are beyond any help but direct charity. This view defines poverty downward to include only the poorest of the poor, the chronically destitute. In this case, it is easy to characterize poor people as needing and deserving the charity of the well-to-do.

Our study really did not speak to this view of poverty. We allowed our respondents to define poverty, and this view is not how they see poverty or how most of the poor people in the study see themselves. Across study sites, the chronically destitute are at most a very small fraction of those who are in poverty, so our participants had little to say on this score.

There is certainly nothing wrong with wanting to help those who cannot help themselves. The danger of this view is that it redirects attention from poverty as a global and mass-based phenomenon, affecting more than half the world's population, and redefines it as a narrow problem that can be solved with individual acts of charity or corporate largesse. Instead of demanding that markets and governments create fair and equitable access to opportunity, it lets them off the hook for a public relations pittance.

Poverty reduction will be driven by external actors. As noted above, some view poverty as the result of a system that is biased against the poor, a system so powerful that it strips poor people both collectively and individually of any agency in bringing about change. This view lends itself to solutions featuring either large-scale redistribution of income or replacement of the market as an economic system.

When the poor are viewed as a powerless mass, this denies the power of their individual initiative and downplays the importance of freedom. An unspecified "we" must help "them," as they are incapable of overcoming the powerful systemic forces holding them down. Again, there is something to be said for this view. Those in poverty do often face an uphill battle against powerful economic and political forces and formal systems seemingly biased against them.

But overwhelmingly, poor people in their narratives do not see themselves as trapped. Again and again our respondents told stories of overcoming obstacles by using their freedom to seize opportunities. They see maintaining their own freedom and power as essential to finding their way out of poverty. We come away from this study with the conviction that any initiative that does not start at the root, by looking at the initiative and opportunities of those in poverty, is bound to be misguided.

Given the flaws in these four approaches, what are the principles that should inform poverty reduction?

The first principle is that all actions should seek to *expand the scope for people in poverty to use their agency.* The view of the poor as people with "needs" to be filled pervades development thinking. While there is no question that people have needs, reducing people to their needs undermines their ability to help themselves. People have needs but they also have dreams, ambitions, plans, skills, ideas, and preferences—and people experiencing poverty are no exception. Despite the obstacles they face, the overwhelming majority of people in poverty believe that the future will be better for themselves and for their children, and they see hard work and initiative as the means to achieve that future.

This expansion of agency applies equally to the public and private spheres. Just as human beings cannot be reduced to their animal needs, neither are human beings reducible to the private sphere of *homo economicus* and all else is intrusion. Rather, this expansion of agency takes into account that people are embedded—in a family, in a location, in overlapping communities and identities, and as citizens in local and national governments. Expanding agency is not code for *laissez faire;* it applies to expanding agency in social and political spheres of life as well.

Poor women, men, and youths exercise their agency as individuals as well as collectively through groups and organizations that sometimes achieve scale. External actors often find it difficult to invest in organizations of the poor without trying to control these organizations. Moreover, investment in organizing, whether for political or economic reasons, rarely yields immediate returns; hence the tremendous underinvestment. However, such investment is critical. When poor people are aggregated into linked groups and organizations, their sheer numbers increase their bargaining power in markets and local democracies and bring them fairer returns.

The second principle is that actions should seek to *transform markets into ones that poor people can access and participate in fairly*. A very large number of poor people see market-based initiative as a means to advancement. But poor people do not enjoy equal opportunities in free markets. The solution is not to eliminate markets but to expand access to them in equitable ways. Among many NGOs, there is deep skepticism about markets, although some business interests lack respect for NGOs and for poor people as able business partners. More equitable markets, particularly in rural areas, are more likely to emerge when these unlikely partners work together to innovate and create new business models and move poor people's production activities higher up the value chain.

The very small scale of most poor people's enterprises creates great disadvantages in the marketplace. To the extent that their tiny livelihood activities can be linked and scaled up through organizations of poor people, the playing field will become more level. Moreover, many poor people struggle with a lack of connectedness—roads to reach markets, electrical connections, channels to bring water for irrigating farms. Improving connectedness, especially for communities in rural areas, can greatly increase people's ability to take advantage of economic opportunities. Another piece of the puzzle is credit and financial services. The microloans typically available to the poor are often too small and too immediate in repayment terms to be used for productive purposes that help amass wealth. Finally, connections to market information and market know-how are vital.

The third principle is that *well-functioning local democracies can help people move out of poverty*. People in poverty seek freedom and power over their lives. But governance at the local level all too often turns into a zero-sum contest for spoils. Corruption is pervasive, creating opportunities for some and barriers for others. The combination of fair elections, improved access to information, and collective action can enable poor people to demand accountability from local leaders. Fair, accountable local democracies and local leaders can do much to liberalize economies from below.

Poor people are already working to change their world. They hope, they work, they risk, they challenge, they take initiative, they fail, and they try over and over again to make the world better—for themselves, their children, their families, their communities, and their countries. Despite their experiences, poor people still believe in markets and governments that are equitable and just. What can we do to make this a reality?

Notes

1. In Hinduism, Ravana is seen as the principal antagonist to Lord Rama in the Hindu epic *Ramayana*. Head of the Rakshasas or demons, he was defeated in a battle of good over evil by Rama. The occasion is celebrated in India by burning him in effigy during a yearly festival.

Appendix 1: Researchers and Institutions Involved in Country Studies

Country	Lead researchers	Other researchers	Research institutes
Afghanistan	Philibert de Mercey, Alejandra Val Cubero, Najibullah Ziar	ACNielsen India, Masooma Essa, Aliya Wahdat, Mohammad Zarif Sediqqi, Shingul Kaliwal, Abdul Wahdood, Besmellah Alokozay, Sayed Awlia	Altai Consulting
Bangladesh	Shahana Rahman, Fatima Jahan Seema, Nishat Sharmin, Gautam Shuvra Biswas	Habiba Lavoni Suvra, Mostafizur Rahman, Hummayan Kabir, Mahamudur Rahman, Sabera Tabassum, Toufiqul Islam, Shamima Sultana, Mahamud Kollol, Mujib Ul Hasan, Shakhawat Hossain, Khadiza Begum, Anis Uj Zaman, Nahida Hasan, Sabera Tabsumm, Shamima Nasrin, Sanker Kumer Roy, Md. Abdullah-Al-Mamun, A. M. Anisuzzaman, Sabera Tabassum, Mohammad Delwar Hossain, Debashis Fani, Wahid Sarker, Habiba Lavoni Suvra, Nazma Yeasmin, Saleh Akram, Pritylata Biswas	PROSHIKA
Cambodia	So Sovannarith, Ingrid FitzGerald	Chan Sophal, Kem Sithen, Tuot Sokphally, Pon Dorina, Kem Sithen, Ann Sophapim, Chea Sovann, Chen Soportea, Chey Nath, Chheang Vuntha, Choun Chanthoura, Chim Charya, Hang Vannara, Heng Daravuthy, Hov Idh, Keo Ouly, Kim Sithy, Khun Chandavy, Long Kolab, Men Sam On, Ouk Leakhana, Pean Pancy, Ros Channak, Sek Vuthy, Sok Saroeun, Tang Kruy, Thun Sean Heng, Yous Samrith, K. A. S. Murshid, Pon Dorina, Chhay Pidor, Brett Ballard, Neak Samsen	Cambodia Development Resource Institute (CDRI)
Colombia	Ana María Ibáñez, María Teresa Matijasevic, Sergio Iván Prada, Carlos Ariel García	Liliana Velásquez, Mónica Ramírez, Carolina Villada, Miguel Ángel Rivera, Adriana Quiceno, Lina Isabel Trujillo, Alejandra Velásquez	Centro de Estudios Regionales, Cafeteros y Empresariales (CRECE)
India	Deepa Narayan, Binayak Sen	ACNielsen India, Sandeep Ghosh, Bharat M. Shah, Devendra Tyagi, Mukund Chandran, Sarfaraz Nasir, Ruchika Kapoor, Vishnu Shankar Tiwari, Saveena Khan, Arjit Mukhopadhyay, Kamath Gopalkrishnan	World Bank; ACNielsen India

Country	Lead researchers	Other researchers	Research institutes
India: Andhra Pradesh	Deepa Narayan, Soumya Kapoor, Giovanna Prennushi	Devendra Tyagi, Gopalakrishnan Kamath, Mukund Kumar Chandan, Ghouse, Rajender, Santhosh, Niranjan	World Bank; ACNielsen India
India: Assam	Deepa Narayan, Binayak Sen, Ashutosh Varshney	Arijit Mukhopadhyay, Debnath Bhadra, Arijit Mukherjee, Pankaj Deka, Tilak Kalita, Chandan Das, Rupjyoti Borah, Prasanna Hazarika, Rahul Barman, Shankar Thakuria, Deuti Hazarika, Hiren Bhattacharjee, Chandan Sarma, Kamal Lodh, Bidya Sinha, Sanjay Das, Utpal Saibia, Rama Kanta Barman, Rapjuyoti Ratna, Maqbul Ali	World Bank; ACNielsen India
India: Uttar Pradesh	Soumya Kapoor, Deepa Narayan, Saumik Paul, Nina Badgaiyan	Saveena Khan, Vishnu Shankar Tiwari, Devendra Pratap Singh, Arvind Kumar Singh, Rajesh Singh, Bhawana Nainwal, Sher Bahadur Prajapati, Narendra Pandey, Ram Singh Mourya, Jaiprakash Bajpai, Pankaj Srivastav, Anand Kumar Mourya, Minoti Mitra, Ruby Nainwal, Pankaj Kumar Verma, Raj Kumar Yadav	World Bank; ACNielsen India
India: West Bengal	Binayak Sen, Deepa Narayan, Klaus Deininger	Saptarshi Guha, Mukund Kr Chandan, Debashish Basu, Arijit Mukhopadhyay, Atanu Dey, Jaya Mandal, Sujay Majumder, Bismita Das, Bratin Banerjee, Ujjala Biswas, Paramita Sasmal, Amit Chowdhury, Pranab Das, Arnab Bose	World Bank; ACNielsen India
Indonesia	Sri Kusumastuti Rahayu, Vita Febriany	Ruly Marianti, Wawan Munawar, Didit Wicaksana, Mutmainah, Khoirul Rosyadi, Suroso, Akhmadi, Mutmainah, Ari Ratna, Ivanovich Agusta, Heri Rubianto, Widy Taurus Sandi, Erfan Agus Munif, Sulton Mawardi, Syahidussyahar, Ervan Abdul Kadir, Nurdewa Safar, Muhlis A. Adam, Musriyadi Nabiu, Salha Marasaoly, Abdulgani Fabanjo, Edy Nasriyanto Hatari, Muhammad Noor, Nurdewa Safar, Abdul Kadir Kamaluddin	SMERU Research Institute

Country	Lead researchers	Other researchers	Research institutes
Malawi	Maxton Grant Tsoka, John Kadzandira, Manohar Sharma	James Mwera, Nozgechi Phiri, Veronica Mbulaje, Augustine Harawa, Macdonald Chitekwe, Andrew Zulu, James Mwera, Mapopa Nyirongo, Massy Chiocha	University of Malawi Centre for Social Research; International Food Policy Research Institute (IFPRI)
Mexico	Trine Lunde, Vicente García Moreno, Alejandro Ramírez	Abraham Jahir Ortiz Nahón, Vicente García, Marianne Isazkun Bernat Aznar, Larissa Bosh Paullada, Israel Morales de la Peña, Abraham Ortiz, Etoile Garcia, David Gallardo, José Guillermo Hernández, Miguel Venegas, Rodolfo García, Rafael Pech	
Morocco	Abdesselam Fazouane, Aziz Chaker, Miria Pigato, Jose Lopez-Calix, Nora Dudwick, Deepa Narayan	Mohamed Ahlibou, Naima Hajji Rachid Harimi, Az-Eddine El Abbassi, Achour Boulal	Social and Economic Development Group, Middle East and North Africa Region, World Bank
Philippines: Bukidnon	Agnes R. Quisumbing, Chona R. Echavez, Erlinda Montillo-Burton, Scott McNiven	Research Institute for Mindanao Culture, Xavier University; CGIAR Systemwide Program on Collective Action and Property Rights (CAPRi), University of Wisconsin–Madison	IFPRI
Philippines: conflict (Mindanao)	Erlinda Montillo-Burton, Chona R. Echavez, Imelda G. Pagtulon-an	Jennefer Lyn Bagaporo, Vergil Boac, Donna Sanchez, Conralin Yap, Adonis Gonazales, Carla Vergara, Marie Clarisse Gomos, Michael Lou Montejo, Lourdes Wong, Prospercora Vega, Vicky Regidor, Betty Aposakas, Lucia Sabanal, Carol Pagtulon-an, Roxendo Ucat, Marlo Reyes, Esther Briones, Rowena Abilja	Research Institute for Mindanao Culture, Xavier University
Senegal	Mamadou Daffé, Souleymane Guèye, Soukèye Thiongane, Aïssatou Ba	Chimère Diaw, Aminata Diop, Moustapha Ly, Sidy Bouya Bâ, Aïssatou Sakho Diop, Jean Pierre Yvon Fall, Daba Ndiaye, Alioune Sarr, Awa Ndao, Henriette Baldé, Moustapha Ka, Demba Ndong, Abdoul Gnimana Diallo, Waly Clément	Senagrosol Consult

Country	Lead researchers	Other researchers	Research institutes
Sri Lanka: conflict	Prashan Thalayasingam	Gayathri, Sujatha, Gayan, Chathura, Siriwardane, Dayal, Indira, Munas, Vigitha, Sivadeepan, Sivaharan, Rathan, Leo, Azam, Shehan, Suchith, Baanu, Shahim, Rahuman, Kosalai, Sudarshan, Braveena, Niroshan, Kannan	Centre for Poverty Analysis (CEPA), AC Nielsen Lanka Pvt. Ltd.
Sri Lanka: tea estates	Neranjana Gunetilleke, Sanjana Kuruppu, Susrutha Goonesekera	Sanjana, Dulani, Suranjith, Nishantha, Sandika, Sujatha, Shahim, Munas, Sandika, Sanjitha, Susrutha, Gayathri, Nishantha, Mansi	Centre for Poverty Analysis (CEPA)
Tanzania: Kagera	Joachim De Weerdt	Adalbertus Kamanzi, Respichius Mitti, Khamaldin Mutabazi, Hanneke Honer, Adela Katunzi, Josien de Klerk, Leonard Kyaruzi, James Mitchener, George Musikula, Thaddeus Rweyemamu	Economic Development Initiatives (EDI)
Tanzania: Ruvuma	Flora Kessy, Oswald Mashindano, Dennis Rweyemamu, Prosper Charle	Kim Kayunze, Justin Urassa, Dennis Rweyemanu, Monica Kimaro, Rosemary Kamugisha, Esther Michael, Timothy Lucas, Swide Mashina, Salvastory Mkama	Economic and Social Research Foundation (ESRF)
Thailand	Priyanut Piboolsravut, Somsakdi Arjprachan, Prasopsee Sookmark, Rajana Netsaengtip	Niwes Laechart, Kesinee Banjong, Morakot Supalak	National Economic and Social Development Board; Local Development Foundation (LDF); Local Knowledge Management Institute (LMI); National Statistical Office of Thailand
Uganda	Richard Ssewakiryanga	Akim Okuni, Frank Muhereza, Nsubuga Charles, Simon Rutabajuuka, Frank Muhereza, Joseph Enyimu, Rossetti Nabbumba, Diego Angemi, David Lawson, Kristen Himelein, Paul Mpuga, James Muwonge, Byron Twesigye, Anthony Matovu, Hassan Wasswa, Joseph Robert Bugembe	Ministry of Finance, Planning and Economic Development; Uganda Participatory Poverty Assessment Project (UPPAP); Centre for Basic Research

Appendix 2: Technical Note on Household Regressions

This note addresses technical issues pertaining to the use of data from the household survey carried out as part of the Moving Out of Poverty study. In particular, it discusses the use of the household responses in a multivariate regression to examine the correlates at the individual and village levels of moving out of poverty. It looks at the sampling frame, the construction of the dependent and independent variables, and the multivariate regression functional form and weights. The full regressions are reported in appendix 6, and the results are discussed in the text of the book in the appropriate sections.

Description of the Study

The Moving Out of Poverty (MOP) study is a large, complex research program carried out in 21 diverse study regions in 15 countries around the world. The study combines both qualitative and quantitative work in an attempt to unpack from below the processes, interactions, and sequencings associated with household transitions out of poverty. The focus is on learning from men and women who have managed to move out of poverty over the past decade about the factors and processes that came together for their asset accumulation and the role of broader community institutions, if any, in supporting or obstructing their mobility.

Choosing the study regions

In selecting countries and regions within countries to participate in the study, an effort was made to ensure that a variety of contexts would be covered. As shown in table A.1, the 15 countries differ in terms of their income levels, national growth rates, and governance environments. Not surprisingly, while there is considerable variation along the dimensions, some cells of the table are empty: for example, there are no low-income/high-governance countries in the study.

Selection of regions also took into account the availability of local research institutes with the interest and capacity to carry out the multidisciplinary study, as well as interest on the part of national governments and World Bank country teams.

Sampling for communities (villages, neighborhoods)

In addition to a broad set of hypotheses, the study addressed specific policy questions that are of current concern in each study region. The focus was on one or two variables that are central to understanding growth and poverty reduction in the local context. These variables were identified through an iter-

TABLE A.1

Countries in the MOP study stratified by income, growth, and governance

Economy	High governance	Low governance	Very low governance
Low income (US$825 or less)			
High growth		India, Malawi, Senegal	Bangladesh, Cambodia, Tanzania, Uganda
Low growth			Afghanistan
Lower middle income (US$826–US$3,255)			
High growth	Philippines, Thailand	Indonesia, Morocco, Sri Lanka	
Low growth		Colombia	
Upper middle income (US$3,256–US$10,065)			
High growth		Mexico	
Low growth			

Note: Income figures are per capita gross national income. Growth and governance classifications reflect the growth rate in 2004 and the average governance rating for 1996–2004. A growth rate <= 3 indicates a low-growth country. High governance rating refers to a governance average > 0 and < 2.5; low governance rating, a governance average < 0 and > –0.5; very low governance rating, a governance average < –0.5 and > –2.5. Governance average is the simple average of six components (voice and accountability, political stability, rule of law, government effectiveness, regulatory quality, and control of corruption) of the governance dataset in "Governance Matters IV: Governance Indicators for 1996–2004."

ative process that was based on data availability and discussion with different actors familiar with the growth and poverty debate in the region, including national and state-level policy actors and poverty and growth experts within government, research institutes, civil society, and donor agencies. The Malawi study, for instance, explores the impact on mobility of access to social and economic infrastructure. In the state of Uttar Pradesh, India, the study examines the role of caste in facilitating or hindering people's movements out of poverty. The Indonesia study focuses on local-level conflicts to understand how conflict in different growth contexts affects people's ability to move out of poverty. The focus in Thailand is on growth and inequality.

Three different sampling strategies were employed for districts/blocks/villages to identify study sites within the 21 regions, which were grouped in three categories (table A.2):

- *Study regions with a preexisting panel data set.* In regions where panel data were available, the communities that had been in the previous panel

TABLE A.2
Choosing locations within study regions

Study region	Provinces/districts	Selection criteria		No. of communities	No. of household surveys
		Blocks	Communities		
India: Andhra Pradesh	Panel study			60	839
Cambodia	Panel study			9	—
Philippines: Bukidnon	Panel study			10	259
Uganda	Panel study			18	724
Tanzania: Kagera	Panel study			8	—
India: Uttar Pradesh	Growth	Irrigation and caste	Random	110	1,635
India: West Bengal	Purposive using government survey	% of land reform beneficiaries	Random	80	1,200
Bangladesh	Poverty headcount	Average landholding and literacy rates	Women's empowerment, food security, and growth in agricultural wages	16	862
Sri Lanka: tea and rubber estates	Crop type, geographic spread, poverty headcount	Ownership of estate (private/state), population size, remoteness, labor supply (resident/nonresident)		20	—
Thailand	Growth and income inequality	Growth and income inequality		40	600

Study region	Selection criteria			No. of communities	No. of household surveys
	Provinces/districts	Blocks	Communities		
Mexico	Yucatán and Oaxaca		Communities with high % of indigenous population, varying in growth	12	346
Morocco	Growth and migration		3 communities (2 rural, 1 urban) selected in each of 3 provinces	9	—
Tanzania: Ruvuma	Growth		Distance to district headquarters, population size	8	332
Malawi	Access to infrastructure and markets			15	139
Senegal	Access to infrastructure			15	301
India: Assam	Growth and conflict	Conflict		50	746
Sri Lanka: conflict	Growth and conflict	Conflict	Conflict	9	—
Afghanistan: conflict	Conflict, proximity to city or borders, cultivation and trade of poppy, degree of exposure to international aid			6	91
Indonesia: conflict	Type of conflict (ethnic, religious, local)	Growth	Conflict and ethnic/religious composition	10	372
Colombia: conflict	Growth, conflict, and whether communities were either receiving displaced populations or were themselves displaced	Growth		8	252
Philippines: conflict	Study conducted only in the Mindanao region	Growth	Conflict	10	300
Total				523	8,998

Note: In all conflict regions, districts with a very high level of active conflict at the time of the survey were not chosen for reasons of safety of the field team.

were revisited. This was the method used in five regions: Cambodia; the Bukidnon region of the Philippines; the Kagera region of Tanzania; Uganda; and the state of Andhra Pradesh, India.

- *Study regions with a particular focus.* Where the focus was on a specific theme, this theme informed sampling. The desire was to select provinces/districts, blocks, and communities that differed substantially in the thematically relevant dimensions. This was the method used in 10 regions.
- *Study regions with conflict.* The MOP study included a separate substudy with an emphasis on conflict. It was carried out in six regions: Afghanistan, Colombia (with an emphasis on the displaced population), Indonesia, Sri Lanka, the Philippines, and the state of Assam in India. In these regions, the spatial sampling was devoted to finding communities within the broader region with higher and lower levels of conflict.

All local-level communities in the study (villages, barrios, etc.) are identified by pseudonyms in this book. Higher-level entities (blocks, provinces, districts, regions, states, and countries) are identified by their real names.

Sampling for household questionnaires: The community mobility matrix

The MOP study consists of several different instruments, one of which is the household quantitative questionnaire (see appendix 3 for a list of data collection methods). For studies that used panel data, the questionnaires were conducted by revisiting panel households and interviewing the same person who was interviewed for the panel before. Where panel data were unavailable, the selection of informants for the household questionnaire was based on a household sorting exercise undertaken during a focus group discussion called the "ladder of life." The discussion, conducted in each study community, proceeded in four steps:

1. The focus group first discussed events and factors that had affected their community's prosperity over the past 10 years.
2. The group then constructed a figurative ladder of life for their community. Each step of the ladder corresponded to a category of household well-being that the group defined in terms of specific household characteristics (land ownership, assets, occupation, living conditions, and social prestige, among others). The process did not force a set number of ladder steps, and the focus groups varied in the number of steps they defined for their communities.

3. As part of this discussion, each group developed its own definition of a poverty line, called the community poverty line (CPL). The CPL marked the step on the ladder above which people were considered no longer poor in their community.

4. Once it had created the ladder in the abstract, the focus group did a household sorting activity. Every household on a list of up to 150 households residing in the community (developed prior to the discussion) was mapped onto the ladder to denote its status both 10 years ago (1995) and today (at the time of the survey, 2005). Based on these rankings, a community mobility matrix was developed (see chapter 3 for examples). The matrix showed which households had moved up or down the ladder or stayed at the same step over the 10-year study period. The MOP study's community mobility matrixes are similar in many ways to standard transition matrixes that are based on measured income or consumption, except that they are based on community-defined categories (not constructed categories like quintiles of income) and on community recall.

Because the matrix was based on the sorting of 100–150 individual households in a community, it provided a useful source for selecting respondents for the household survey. Four mobility groups were considered:

- *Movers*: households that were poor in 1995 but had moved out of poverty by 2005
- *Chronic poor*: households that were poor in 1995 and remained poor in 2005
- *Never poor*: households that were not poor in 1995 and remained not poor in 2005
- *Fallers*: households that were not poor in 1995 but fell into poverty by 2005

In each case, "poor" means below the locally defined community poverty line and "not poor" means above it.

Once households in the matrix were stratified into these groups, a minimum of 15 households in each community were selected for the survey. We deliberately oversampled movers and the never poor because of the study's interest in learning from those who had moved out of poverty and those who had been able to maintain their wealth. Table A.3 shows the approximate desired distribution for sampling the household questionnaires in each community.

Adherence to this distribution depended on availability of sufficient numbers of households in each of the four mobility groups. Sometimes it

TABLE A.3
Desired distribution of households across mobility groups

	Now	
10 years ago	*Poor or worse off*	*Nonpoor or better off*
Poor or worse off	Chronic poor: 20%	Movers: 40%
Nonpoor or better off	Fallers: 10%	Never poor: 30%

was not possible to match the target percentages: in very poor communities, for instance, the number of movers was limited; therefore, fewer movers were interviewed. Panel studies were an exception to the distribution rule. The questionnaires were conducted by revisiting panel households and interviewing the same person that was interviewed for the panel before.

The questionnaires were conducted mainly with adults between 30 and 60 years of age. The aim was to identify and understand the range of factors that helped or hindered the mobility of individuals within the larger context of their households and communities. The multimodule questionnaires were innovative in that they collected information on the individual respondent's social capital, personal aspirations, and perceptions of local governance, freedom, crime, insecurity, and violence, in addition to the usual demographic and economic information on assets, expenditure, health, and education. While many of the questions on expenditure and assets related to the household, the subjective questions were about the individual. The far-right column in table A.2 summarizes the number of household surveys collected in the different study regions. These households varied from only 91 in Afghanistan to over 1,600 in Uttar Pradesh, for a total of 8,998 household surveys in the entire study.

Two points are worth noting. First, the study made no attempt to create a nationally representative sample. In the discussion, country names are used merely as a shorthand way of identifying data from the study regions within those countries. Thus, by "Indonesia," it should be clear that we mean "the communities/households sampled for our study within the selected regions of Indonesia." As noted on page xxiv, we try to provide in our abbreviations and acronyms both a country and a study focus in order to remind the reader that the unit is the study region, not the country.

Second, the household surveys were not used to estimate numbers of poor or nonpoor or movers. Those numbers are estimated in the community mobility matrix. The household surveys had two main uses. One was to reveal difference in reported characteristics, attitudes, behaviors, and outcomes between the movers out of poverty and other groups. The second was to run multivariate regressions using the household's mobility status, as ascribed by the focus group, to establish associations between household mobility and characteristics of the household and locality. We made no attempt to establish causality or make causal claims based on these regressions, though that is one possible way to interpret the associations.

Background to the Regressions: Dependent and Independent Variables

To construct the regressions, we first specify (a) a measure for the dependent variable (i.e., "movement out of poverty" or "mobility of the poor"), (b) measures for each of the conceptual variables, (c) the way we propose to distinguish between private and community impacts of some of the conceptual variables (particularly the local democracy and agency measures), and (d) the control variables included in the regressions.

Examining measures for movement out of poverty and mobility of the poor (MPI)

Because the study is about the mobility of poor people, only those households that were poor 10 years ago, at the beginning of the study period, were included for purposes of regression analysis. Within this "initial poor set," the objective was to differentiate between those who moved up from poverty over the 10 years and those who did not. Two dependent variables were used for the regression analysis:

- MOP: households that were initially poor and moved up and out of poverty over 10 years, crossing the community poverty line
- MPI: households that were initially poor and moved up any distance over 10 years, irrespective of whether they crossed the community poverty line

The data offered two measures that could be used to calculate the dependent variables. The first was status of and change in the household's rank on the ladder of life, now compared to 10 years ago, as identified by the ladder of life focus group discussion. The second was status of and change in the household's self-assessed rank on the ladder of life, now compared to 10 years ago, as identified by the respondent himself or herself in the household questionnaire.

Both dependent variables were constructed using the first measure— community perceptions of the household's mobility on the ladder of life. It is important to note that the mobility ratings were *not self-assessed*. This was to avoid endogeneity biases or "halo effects" that might arise in regressing a household's own perception of movement against its perception of variables measuring the conceptual categories. For instance, it may well be that people who subjectively *feel* they have more control over decision making also subjectively *feel* they are moving up—even if others perceive them as economically stagnant. By using the *community's* perception of mobility as the dependent variable and the *individual's* responses about the household as measures of the right-hand-side variables, this particular problem is attenuated, if not eliminated.

Construction of MOP score. The ladder of life discussion group developed mobility rankings of each household that received the survey. Focus group members recalled the household's placement on the well-being ladder 10 years ago and then determined its current step on the ladder. Based on these mobility ranks and the community poverty line, the MOP score was constructed as a binary variable (yes/no) using the following formula:

$$MOP^{h,j} = \begin{cases} 1 & if \quad step_{t-n}^{h,j} < CPL^j, step_t^{h,j} \geq CPL^j \\ 0 & otherwise \end{cases}$$

where *step* is the step on the ladder of life constructed by the focus group and CPL is the community poverty line set by the group and *n* is the (roughly 10-year) recall period.

Construction of MPI score. Any score constructed for movement out of poverty is subject to the placement of a threshold line that can vary across communities and contexts. Given problems that relative lines like the CPL pose, a broader score of upward MPI was also used as the dependent variable using the following formula:

$$MPI^{h,j} = \begin{cases} 1 & if \quad step_t^{h,j} > step_{t-n}^{h,j} \\ 0 & otherwise \end{cases}$$

Using measures for conceptual categories of independent variables

The MOP and MPI dependent variables were regressed against various independent variables to produce the partial associations (no attribution of causality is expressed or implied). These variables included both household variables and community variables. A list of all of the variables, their sources, and coding is presented in appendix 4.

Household-level standard control variables. In estimating the regressions, we control for variables that may influence household mobility but that are not a major focus of the study. These are mainly well-known correlates of mobility and are included mainly to distinguish the influence of various other variables that may be correlated. For instance, more educated households may feel more empowered or may have more influence over their local governments. In each multivariate regression, the household demographic and economic characteristics included a proxy for the household's initial wealth. Ownership at the beginning of the study period was included for (a) house, (b) collection of household assets, (c) livestock, and (d) farmland. The education level of the respondent and reported health shocks experienced by the household over 10 years were also included as variables in each regression.

Household variables unique to the study. In addition to the usual covariates, there are several variables from the household questionnaire that are of special interest to this study (see appendix 4):

- *Aspirations.* Respondents were asked two questions, one about aspirations for the respondent and one about aspirations for future generations. These answers were combined into a single index using PCA.
- *Personal agency.* Respondents were asked two questions about their level of agency, one about control over everyday decisions and one about their position on a ladder of power and rights. Again, the two questions were combined into a single index with principal components analysis.
- *Responsiveness of the local government.* Respondents were asked four questions about (a) their trust in local government officials, (b) their satisfaction with local democracy, (c) the extent to which local government takes into account people's concerns, and (d) their ability to influence the actions of the local government. These answers were combined into an index using principal components analysis (see below for more detail on PCA).
- *Fairness of the economy.* Respondents were asked four questions about (a) farmers getting fair prices, (b) fairness in treatment by the law, (c) whether the respondent had been denied credit, and (d) whether he or she expected to be denied credit. Again, these answers were combined

into a single index of fairness for each respondent based on weights from PCA.

- *Violence against women.* Respondents were asked about their perception of the prevalence of violence against women in their community.

We also included a policy focus variable for each of the study regions. In Uttar Pradesh, for example, proxies are included for the caste of each household.

For the household-level variables, we used the respondent's recollection of conditions 10 years ago rather than current levels. This is an attempt to mitigate the endogeneity bias of using current perceptions, as current conditions are certainly affected by changes over the past 10 years. One can easily imagine that households that moved out of poverty would be likely to report, for example, higher empowerment scores because of that move. Of course, given that our only option was to use recall data, there is no guarantee that currently reported perceptions of the past are not also affected by events.

In addition to the household variables, there are community-level variables of two types. One set comes from the community instruments, such as the focus group. The other comes from using the household responses and computing leave-out means.

Community variables from community instruments. Seven community-level variables were used in the regressions that were drawn either from the community-level information provided by key informants or from the focus group discussions. These were (mostly) created by combining questions into indices using PCA.

- *Corruption.* The key informant questionnaire included two questions about corruption, one about officials at the national level and one about officials at the local or community level. In addition, the focus group discussion produced an estimate of corruption among government officials in the community.
- *Initial strength of the economy.* Key informants were asked about the strength of the local economy, the presence of private employers, and the difficulty of finding a job 10 years ago.
- *Change in economic prosperity over 10 years.* The focus group discussions were asked about trends in community prosperity, trends in available economic opportunities, trends in access to such opportunities, and whether it was easier or harder to make a living.

- *Collective action.* Key informants were asked two questions, one about the likelihood of the community coming together to solve water problems and one about community members coming together to assist each other.
- *Social stratification.* Key informants were asked one question about the divisions among people based on locally relevant social categories (e.g., ethnicity, caste).
- *School inequality.* Key informants were asked about trends over 10 years in the extent of discrimination in schools based on (a) ethnic or religious factors and (b) gender.
- *Access to networks or associations.* Focus groups were asked to estimate whether access to networks and associations within the village had increased or decreased (or had remained the same) over 10 years.

Community variables constructed from household survey instrument. The household questionnaire contains several questions about household perceptions, including perceptions of the responsiveness of the local democratic structure and perceptions of the household's own empowerment and aspirations. An average of household responses for these questions cannot be treated as an indicator of a responsive local democracy or of an empowered community. At best, the responses are indicators of the "perception of democracy" or "perception of empowerment" based on the sample surveyed within a community.

Furthermore, it could well be that some households answered that their local democracy is responsive because they have had an opportunity to participate in it or derive benefits from it. However, one household's participation can have a strong "chilling" or "crowding out" effect on other households in the same community. The association of the average or net perception therefore may not necessarily be the sum of individual perceptions (Alatas, Pritchett, and Wetterberg 2007).

To distinguish between private effects (association of the own household's perceptions with outcomes) and social effects (impact of one household on other households), we use the fact that our sampling is by communities. We can, therefore, calculate for each community both the perception of each household (private effect) and perceptions of all *other* households in the community (social effect). Consider as an example the response to the following question: "Compared to 10 years ago, does the local government now pay more, less, or about the same attention to what people like you think when it decides what to do?" The leave-out mean for a given individual is simply the perception of local government responsiveness of all other individuals in their community, leaving out that one person.

The use of leave-out means is an attempt to disentangle social effects from private effects or pure household perceptions by aggregating all individual responses in community j, except for household i. Suppose there were a linear, causal relationship between the mobility of poor household i in village j and whether it reports higher local government responsiveness and the perceptions of government responsiveness of all other households in the community.

$$\text{MPI}^{i,j} = \alpha + \beta_{HH}(\text{LG}^{i,j}) + \beta_{LOM}(\text{LG}^{-i,j})$$

The *private* impact of the ith household's perceptions of the local government on the likelihood that it moves up is the coefficient β_{HH}.

The impact of the ith household's perceptions of the local government on all other households in the community is to raise the "community less household" average by $1/N^j$ for each household. The *social* impact of the ith household's perceptions of the local government is then β_{LOM}/N^j on each other household in the community. This could be zero if there is no interaction at all. However, if the ith household's positive perceptions of responsiveness are influenced by the benefits it derives from a zero-sum public good, say a local public works program from which the ith household benefits by excluding others, the social impact on others could be negative (in fact, it would have to be negative). In this case, the net impact on mobility of the poor associated with the ith household's perceptions of local government responsiveness is just the sum of the private and social impacts—but it cannot be assumed to be the sum of the individual coefficients alone.

Using principal components to combine conceptually related variables

For many of the phenomena that the analyst might wish to elicit and examine, it is impossible to know with any precision which question will produce the most reliable responses. Hence, questionnaires often include questions on closely related concepts. When data are to be used in multivariate regressions, this leaves the analyst with four options. We chose to combine conceptually similar questions into a single index using principal components.

A word about the three options rejected. One is "profligacy," simply including in the regressions all of the possible variables. This has the advantage of "letting the data decide," but it has the disadvantages of creating regressions with 50 or more individual variables and of producing massive multicollinearity if the variables are in fact closely related conceptually. A second option is to choose the "best" indicator for each conceptual category. This can be done a priori, which runs the risk of choosing the empirically least successful (e.g., most subject to measurement error), or it can be done based on "horse races" of available candidates, which is the very definition of data mining. The third option is to use some index based on a weighted average of the questions. This has the advantage of reducing the numbers of variables and avoids data mining, but the weights are arbitrary. A common practice of using "equal" weights has nothing in particular to recommend it.

The technique of principal components is a commonly used data reduction technique that reduces a set of variables to a single variable. Principal components analyzes the correlations between a set of variables and produces a set of weighted averages of the underlying variables such that (a) each captures the maximum common variation among the set of variables, and (b) each additional factor after the first is orthogonal to the previous factor. So the first factor is a linear weighted average of the set of N variables with weights chosen so as to maximize the overall common variance of all the variables.

While in many ways the index produced is arbitrary, this does have three advantages. First, it is not data mining, as it does not use any information about the dependent variable in choosing the specification. Second, it chooses weights that, if the set of N variables are truly conceptually related, statistically best capture the common variation. Third, because it is a linear index, it is relatively easy to map back from the underlying variable through the regression coefficient to the association with the dependent variable.

We did the principal components analysis study region by study region, rather than imposing common weights across all study regions. The results for each study region for each PCA-constructed variable are presented in appendix 5. First, whenever there are only two variables, PCA just produced equal weights. Second, the results are mostly in accord with expectations. All variables are recoded so that movements in the same direction numerically represent movement in the same conceptual direction (this is not necessarily true in the raw questions). We see that most of the PCA, therefore, produces, as expected, indexes with all positive weights, often nearly equal. But third, there is considerable variation across countries in the weights, including some negative values. Rather than attempt to choose the "best" fit for each study region, we just implemented the data reduction technique for each and used the weights produced.

The only way in which this process differed from the perfectly garden-variety PCA was that we wanted an index of conditions 10 years ago. But rather than using the PCA weights from 10 years ago, we did PCA on the current variables and then used those weights to construct an index for 10 years ago, while using the values of the underlying variables from that time.

Once we had the PCA scores, we could infer the estimate associated with each individual component variable in that index with the dependent variable (MOP or MPI). To do so, we proceeded in two steps. First, we used the PCA weights to calculate how much a change in an individual component of the index would change the index (which involved the variance of the component because PCA norms the raw variables) would produce in the PCA score. Next, we multiplied this value with the ordinary least squares regression coefficient for the PCA score to estimate the concomitant associated change in MOP or MPI.

Here is an example of going from raw component to estimated association when PCA has been used. Take the case of the study region in Afghanistan, where aspirations had a significant positive association with an initially poor household's ability to move out of poverty over 10 years. Considering the individual components of the aspirations index, we find that a 2-unit increase in beliefs about one's own future (1 = worse off, 3 = better off) is associated with a change of nearly 2 units in the aspirations index using the following formula:

Change in PCA index = (loading on individual component × range of individual component)/standard error of individual component

(for aspirations in Afghanistan) = (0.7071 × 2)/0.708

The subsequent change of 2 units in the PCA index for aspirations when multiplied with the OLS regression coefficient for household aspirations in Afghanistan (0.11) is associated with an increase of nearly 21 percent in the likelihood of escaping poverty. A 2-unit increase in aspirations for one's children nearly doubles the probability of exit from poverty to 42 percent (range = 2, standard error = 0.36).

Functional Form and Weights

Functional form

An OLS model was used for running regressions. Because the dependent variable is a binary outcome (0/1), this is sometimes referred to as the linear probability model (LPM). It is well known that with a limited dependent variable, there are estimation techniques (such as probit and logit) that are more statistically efficient. This is because by imposing in estimation the constraint (which must be true) that the predictions of outcomes by the regression techniques have to be strictly between zero and one, these techniques produce lower standard errors than OLS.

We did not do this, however, for three reasons. First, the loss from not using a logit or probit estimator is only efficiency (a second-order property of estimators), not consistency, and we suspect that, in this case, the gains to precision are not particularly meaningful. Second, the LPM has ease of interpretation, particularly when moving from the underlying PCA-constructed indexes to the reporting of outcome associations. Third, with nonlinear functional forms like logit and probit, the use of the leave-out means is much more complicated.

All of the standard errors used the standard adjustment to be consistent with cluster-based sampling using the cluster techniques available in Stata data analysis software.

While a complete specification was run for the study regions in India, a relatively parsimonious model was used for the non-India study regions, where sample sizes were much smaller. The sparse specification excluded the PCA index on fairness, the PCA index for social inequality in schools, and ownership of land. Leave-out means were only included for the responsiveness of local democracy and personal agency PCAs.

Weighted versus unweighted regressions

The structure of the sampling of those who were interviewed for the household instrument produces four issues about weights, even though in this appendix, we are focused on the regressions.

Let us use a simple example to illustrate these issues. Suppose in a given country 25 percent of the population consists of red people and 75 percent of blue people. Red people are taller on average than blue people. Suppose an instrument contains observations on height and weight. Finally, assume the sample was chosen to have equal numbers of red and blue people (so red people were oversampled).

First, since sampling was not random, the overall averages from the household surveys of any characteristic are not consistent estimates of the sampled population. The unweighted average height would be wrong about the average height of the population, as red people are taller and are over-sampled. In the MOP study, this example shows that because the movers were oversampled, if they are different, the overall averages of characteristics from household surveys are not estimates of the overall average of the population characteristics.

Second, as long as the individuals *within* the groups are chosen randomly, then summary statistics of the *differences* across the groups on an unweighted basis are consistent. In the example, comparing red people's average height to blue people's average height is a consistent estimate of the subpopulation heights.

Third, all of the regression results reported are unweighted. For the regressions themselves, because we assume a linear functional form, the issue of weighted versus unweighted regressions is an issue of estimator efficiency (in that the weighted estimates might produce lower standard errors), but not one of consistency.

Returning to the example, suppose that there is a linear relationship between height and weight and that this linear relationship is the same for red and blue people. In this case, an unweighted regression would produce a consistent estimate of the relationship between height and weight, even though red people are oversampled.

It is possible that using sampling weights would produce a more efficient (lower standard errors) estimator, but our view is that these gains are likely to be small. We don't want to give ourselves over to *t*-statistic fetishism in any case. That is, if the difference between "statistical significance" (usually taken as rejecting the null hypothesis at some standard significance level such as 5 percent or 1 percent) is whether estimates are weighted or unweighted, it would be questionable to make much of the relationship in any case. This is a general point about reported empirical work, not about our report, because in most instances, there are large deviations of the actually applied statistical procedures and the conditions under which the classic theory of hypothesis testing are valid.

Moreover, if the weighted and unweighted partial association estimates were to differ—which they do not, for the most part, in the cases where this has been explored—this would not be an indication that the weighted results are to be preferred. In fact, heuristically, the differences between unweighted and weighted results can be thought of as a Hausman-like (1978) test for model specification. Because under the maintained null used in estimating an OLS regression the unweighted and weighted are both consistent for the "true" coefficient, this implies that they should also converge (in large samples) to be "near" one another. Hence, a large difference (where "large" would be normed for statistical tests by the appropriate variance-covariance matrix of the difference between the two estimators) between weighted and unweighted results suggests model misspecification. But as this type of test is an omnibus specification test (that is, it has power against many forms of misspecification), a difference between weighted and unweighted to first order is difficult to interpret and cannot be taken to mean the weighted result is "better."

Fourth, there is a tricky final issue, not about the weighting of the regressions in general but about leave-out means. These are used, in some sense, as "community characteristics," and thus although they are not reported, they might seem to fall under the first category of not using the unweighted results to estimate summary statistics of characteristics. But there are two points. One, this does maintain the assumption of the linearity of the effect, so we assume that in the leave-out mean the impact on a mover of having a higher value of the variable of a faller or never poor person is the same, so in that case, the same issue of linearity discussed above applies. Second, as long as the sampling was done consistently across villages, the bias as community variables of the sample should be (roughly, on average) constant across villages.

Results

The regression results for each of the study regions are reported in appendix 6, with MOP and then MPI as the dependent variable. As expected, the results vary considerably across study regions in terms of both the magnitude of the coefficients and their associated standard errors.

In the body of the text, these results are usually presented using a graph that displays the OLS-LPM coefficient and one and two standard error bounds around the point estimate. This allows the reader to assess both the magnitude and the associated precision across countries.

Appendix 3: Data Collection Methods

Activity	Data collection method	Purpose	Sources of information
1	Selective literature review	• Provide background to the key growth and poverty puzzles in the country. • Help design the study.	Secondary sources
2	Key informant interview or workshop: national timeline	• Identify policy questions to be addressed by the study. • Develop a national timeline of key events and policies that have helped or hindered people's movements out of poverty.	Policy experts from government, civil society, and private sector
3	Community profile	• Identify community-level factors that have helped or hindered movement out of poverty and the overall prosperity of the community over the past 10 years. • Quantify and code data emerging from focus discussions on the basis of their ratings of issues ranging from community prosperity to freedom and inequality.	Key informants Focus group discussion
4	Key informant interview: community timeline	• Understand community-level events or factors that have helped or hindered movement out of poverty and the overall prosperity of the community. • Gain an understanding of the local context.	2–4 key informants in a group or individually

Activity	Data collection method	Purpose	Sources of information
5	Focus group discussion: ladder of life	• Identify the range of factors that help or hinder movement out of poverty or prosperity over time at the community level. • Identify the range of factors that help or hinder movement out of poverty or prosperity over time at the household level, and the reasons for movement at the different levels. • Identify the sequencing and interaction among factors at the household level that enable movement between different steps of the ladder of life. • Identify the mobility status of specific households in the community.	1 focus group of adult men 1 focus group of adult women
6	Focus group discussion: livelihoods, freedom, power, democracy, and local governance	• Understand trends in economic opportunities for the community. • Understand the impact of government rules and regulations and other factors on access to economic opportunities. • Explore people's understanding of the concepts of freedom, power, and inequality, and how these concepts relate to economic mobility and well-being. • Explore people's understanding of democracy and how democracy is working at the local level.	1 focus group of adult men 1 focus group of adult women Depending on the local context, this activity can be conducted as one discussion, or there can be 2 sections discussing (a) sources of economic opportunities and the role of governance, and (b) freedom, power, inequality, and democracy. If there are 2 sections, a total of 4 focus group discussions per community will be needed for this activity.

Activity	Data collection method	Purpose	Sources of information
7	Focus group discussion: aspirations of youth	• Explore youths' aspirations for earning a living and steps they are taking to prepare for their future. • Explore youths' understanding of the concepts of freedom, power, inequality, and democracy, and how these concepts relate to economic mobility and well-being.	1 focus group of male youths 1 focus group of female youths
8	Two mini-case studies: community-wide events and factors affecting mobility	• Provide in-depth analysis from a range of perspectives on two important events or factors affecting the overall economic prosperity of the community over the past 10 years.	Key informants and focus group discussions
9	Household questionnaire	• Identify the range of factors that help or hinder mobility of households.	For countries with panel data: Depending on panel sample size and sampling strategy chosen, the team should revisit panel households and interview an adult member of the household (30–60 years of age). If it is not possible to identify a large enough sample from the panel, individuals may be randomly selected from households identified by the ladder of life focus group discussion as belonging to a particular mobility category. For countries without panel data: Select informants based on the household sorting exercise undertaken during the ladder of life focus group discussion.

Activity	Data collection method	Purpose	Sources of information
10	Open-ended interviews: individual life stories	• Understand how and why some individuals escaped poverty, and the factors and processes that led to their escape.	Adults (men or women) 30–60 years of age. It is important that a household questionnaire be completed with each informant who provides an individual life story. Identification of informants follows a process similar to selection of informants for the questionnaire.
		• Understand how and why some individuals managed to stay out of poverty, and the factors and processes that helped them maintain their wealth.	
		• Understand how and why some individuals remained trapped in chronic poverty, and the factors and processes that kept them in poverty.	
		• Understand how and why some individuals fell into poverty, and the factors and processes that led to their decline.	
		• Understand the factors and processes that come together for accumulation or depletion of assets and savings.	

Appendix 4: List of Variables for Household Regressions

Explanatory variable	Source	Coding/directionality
Economic opportunity		
Initial strength of economy (PCA index[a])		
Strength of local economy 10 years ago (rc205b)	KI	very weak=1, very strong=5
Presence of private employers 10 years ago (rc208b)	KI	yes=1, no=0
Difficulty of finding a job 10 years ago (rc209b)	KI	very difficult=1, very easy=6
Changes in economic prosperity (PCA index)		
Whether easier or harder to make a living (rc904)	FGD	harder=1, easier=2
Trend in community prosperity (rc903)	FGD	less prosperous=1, more prosperous=3
Trend in available economic opportunities (rc912)	FGD	fewer=1, more=3
Trend in access to economic opportunities (rc917)	FGD	fewer have access=1, more have access=3
Local democracy		
Responsiveness of local democracy (PCA index)		
Trust in local government officials (rh415bi)	HH	not at all=1, to a very great extent=5
Satisfaction with democracy in local government (rh511)	HH	very dissatisfied=1, very satisfied=4
Extent to which local government takes into account concerns (rh502b)	HH	less=1, more=3
Ability to influence actions of local government (rh504)	HH	decreased=1, increased=3
Corruption (PCA index)		
Corruption in government officials at the country level (c505b)	KI	almost none=1, almost all=4
Corruption in government officials in village (c506b)	KI	almost none=1, almost all=4
Corruption in government officials in community (c924)	FGD	almost none=1, almost all=4

Explanatory variable	Source	Coding/directionality
Fairness		
Fairness (PCA index)		
Farmers getting fair prices (rh240b)	HH	deteriorated=1, improved=3
Fairness in treatment by law in community (rh606b)	HH	yes=1, no=0
Denied credit (h234)	HH	yes=1, no=2
Expectation of denial of credit (h236)	HH	yes=1, no=2
Violence against women		
Violence against women in households 10 years ago (h609b)	HH	none at all=1, very much=4
Individual agency		
Personal agency (PCA index)		
Initial position on 10-step ladder of power and rights (h708)	HH	scale from 1 to 10
Control over everyday decisions (trend) (rh501b)	HH	less=1, more=3
Household aspirations (PCA index)		
Aspirations for self (rh716)	HH	worse off=1, better off=3
Aspirations for future generation (rh717)	HH	worse off=1, better off=3
Collective agency		
Index of collective action (PCA index[a])		
Coming together to solve water problems 10 years ago (rc412b)	KI	very unlikely=1, very likely=4
Coming together to assist each other 10 years ago (rc413b)	KI	very unlikely=1, very likely=4
Access to networks and associations		
Change in access to networks and associations within the community (rc919)	FGD	less access=1, more access=3
Social stratification		
Extent of social divisions in the village 10 years ago		
Differences between people based on ethnicity, caste, etc., 10 years ago (c414b)	KI	no division=1, to a very great extent=5
School inequality measure (trend)		
Ethnic/religious discrimination in schools (c305b)	KI	improved=1, deteriorated=3
Gender discrimination in schools (c304b)	KI	improved=1, deteriorated=3

Explanatory variable	Source	Coding/directionality
Control variables		
Present education status of household head[b] (h106)	HH	no schooling=1, university=8
Health shocks over 10 years (rh305)	HH	yes=1, no=0
Initial landholding (h204 i+ii+iii+iv)b[c]	HH	number of hectares owned
Ownership of house 10 years ago (rh206b)	HH	whether owned (yes=1, no=0)
Initial assets index (PCA index[a] of assets owned 10 years ago) (rh201 i–xiii)b	HH	whether owned (yes=1, no=0)
Initial livestock index (PCA index[a] of assets owned 10 years ago) (rh203 i–x)b	HH	whether owned (yes=1, no=0)

Note: Reference questions in the community questionnaire are indicated by *c* and in the household questionnaire by *h*. Prefix *r* means variable was recoded. Suffix *a* means current (at time of the study); *b* means initial (approximately 10 years ago). KI = key informant; FGD = focus group discussion; HH = household.

a. A PCA was first done on current conditions, and weights were applied to initial conditions 10 years ago. A weighted average of initial conditions (with current weights) was then used as an explanatory variable.

b. In the survey, the education level of the household head is measured in 2005, but it is unlikely to have changed significantly over the previous 10 years for an adult head of household.

c. The symbols i, ii, iii, and iv signify irrigated land, unirrigated temporary crop land, unirrigated permanent crop land, and grazing land/wasteland, respectively.

Appendix 5: Weights for the PCA-Constructed Indexes, by Study Region

	UP Caste	WB Landdist	AP SHG	BAN Empow	UGA Panel	MAL Infra	SEN Infra	TAN Ruv	PHI Panel	THAI Ineq	MEX Ethn	COL Conf	AFG Conf	INDO Conf	PHI Conf	ASSAM Conf
Initial strength of local economy																
Strength of local economy, 10 years ago (rc205b)	0.47	0.72	0.57	0.52	0.55	0.49	0.71	0.59	0.68	0.24	0.54	0.44	used directly	0.70	0.41	−0.05
Presence of private employers, 10 years ago (rc208b)	0.60	0.17	0.54	−0.42	0.46	0.56	0.71	0.60	0.31	0.68	0.61	0.69	—	0.42	0.72	0.71
Difficulty in finding a job, 10 years ago (rc209b)	0.65	0.68	0.62	0.75	0.69	0.67	—	−0.54	0.66	0.70	0.57	−0.58	—	0.58	−0.56	0.70
	1.72	1.56	1.73	0.84	1.71	1.72	1.41	0.66	1.65	1.61	1.73	0.55	0.00	1.70	0.57	1.36
Changes in economic prosperity																
Trend in community prosperity (rc903)	0.58	0.55	0.15	0.53	0.45	0.57	0.55	−0.07	0.16	0.64	0.50	0.44	0.35	−0.03	0.37	0.50
Whether easier or harder to make a living (rc904)	0.42	0.66	0.69	0.38	0.14	0.50	0.63	0.54	−0.51	0.55	0.50	0.46	0.45	0.51	0.39	0.44

	UP Caste	WB Landdist	AP SHG	BAN Empow	UGA Panel	MAL Infra	SEN Infra	TAN Ruv	PHI Panel	THAI Ineq	MEX Ethn	COL Conf	AFG Conf	INDO Conf	PHI Conf	ASSAM Conf
Trend in available economic opportunities (rc912)	0.54	0.41	0.70	0.52	0.64	0.40	0.46	0.62	0.59	0.36	0.49	0.46	0.67	0.62	0.55	0.49
Trend in access to economic opportunities (rc917)	0.45	0.30	0.10	0.55	0.61	0.52	-0.31	0.56	0.61	0.39	0.50	0.62	0.47	0.59	0.64	0.56
	1.98	1.92	1.65	1.98	1.84	1.99	1.33	1.66	0.85	1.95	2.00	1.98	1.94	1.69	1.95	1.99

Responsiveness of local democracy

	UP Caste	WB Landdist	AP SHG	BAN Empow	UGA Panel	MAL Infra	SEN Infra	TAN Ruv	PHI Panel	THAI Ineq	MEX Ethn	COL Conf	AFG Conf	INDO Conf	PHI Conf	ASSAM Conf
Trust in local government officials (rh415bi)	0.39	0.51	0.47	0.24	—	0.04	—	-0.29	0.49	0.19	0.44	0.10	-0.22	0.60	0.37	0.36
Satisfaction with democracy in local government (rh511)	0.53	0.57	0.47	0.50	0.51	0.53	0.56	0.45	0.64	0.54	0.51	0.41	0.61	0.63	0.58	0.57

	UP Caste	WB Landdist	AP SHG	BAN Empow	UGA Panel	MAL Infra	SEN Infra	TAN Ruv	PHI Panel	THAI Ineq	MEX Ethn	COL Conf	AFG Conf	INDO Conf	PHI Conf	ASSAM Conf
Extent to which local government takes into account concerns (rh502b)	0.58	0.22	0.56	0.59	0.55	0.60	0.59	0.61	0.59	0.57	0.49	0.56	0.59	0.39	0.55	0.51
Ability to influence actions of local government (rh504)	0.49	0.61	0.49	0.59	0.66	0.60	0.58	0.58	0.06	0.59	0.55	0.71	0.48	0.29	0.48	0.54
	1.98	1.90	1.99	1.91	1.72	1.77	1.73	1.35	1.78	1.89	1.99	1.78	1.47	1.92	1.97	1.98
Corruption																
Corruption in government officials at the country level (c505b)	0.67	0.70	0.65	0.71	0.71	—	0.71	0.65	-0.71	—	-0.71	0.58	0.61	0.70	0.71	0.68
Corruption in government officials in village (c506b)	0.69	0.71	0.68	0.71	0.71	—	0.71	0.63	0.71	used directly	used directly	0.64	0.57	0.71	0.70	0.73

	UP Caste	WB Landdist	AP SHG	BAN Empow	UGA Panel	MAL Infra	SEN Infra	TAN Ruv	PHI Panel	THAI Ineq	MEX Ethn	COL Conf	AFG Conf	INDO Conf	PHI Conf	ASSAM Conf
Corruption in government officials in community (c924)	0.28	0.09	0.35	—	—	used directly	—	-0.43		—	0.71	0.51		0.08	-0.09	0.06
LOM: HH:	1.64	1.50	1.67	1.41	1.41	0.00	1.41	0.84	0.00	0.00	0.00	1.73	0.55	1.49	1.31	1.47

	UP Caste	WB Landdist	AP SHG	BAN Empow	UGA Panel	MAL Infra	SEN Infra	TAN Ruv	PHI Panel	THAI Ineq	MEX Ethn	COL Conf	AFG Conf	INDO Conf	PHI Conf	ASSAM Conf
Fairness																
Farmers getting fair prices (rh240b)	0.13	0.32	−0.18	0.52	—	—	0.71	−0.16		0.71	0.25	−0.15	0.02	0.42	0.13	0.23
Fairness in treatment by law within community (rh606b)	0.23	0.50	0.43	0.66	−0.03	0.29	0.71	−0.08	0.41	0.71	0.21	−0.19	0.24	0.01	−0.29	0.08
Denied credit (h234)	0.67	0.69	0.65	—	0.71	0.67	—	0.70	0.64	—	0.66	0.68	0.70	0.64	0.67	0.70
Expectation of denial of credit (h236)	0.70	0.41	0.60	0.54	0.71	0.68	—	0.69	0.65	—	0.68	0.69	0.68	0.64	0.67	0.68
	1.72	1.92	1.50	1.72	1.38	1.65	1.41	1.16	1.70	1.41	1.79	1.02	1.63	1.72	1.18	1.68
Personal agency																
Step on ladder of power and rights, 10 years ago (h708)	0.71	0.71	0.71	0.71	0.71	0.71	0.71	0.71	0.71	0.71	0.71	0.71	0.71	0.71	0.71	0.71
Control over everyday decisions (rh501b)	0.71	0.71	0.71	0.71	0.71	0.71	0.71	0.71	0.71	0.71	0.71	0.71	0.71	0.71	0.71	0.71
	1.41	1.41	1.41	1.41	1.41	1.41	1.41	1.41	1.41	1.41	1.41	1.41	1.41	1.41	1.41	1.41

	UP Caste	WB Landdist	AP SHG	BAN Empow	UGA Panel	MAL Infra	SEN Infra	TAN Ruv	PHI Panel	THAI Ineq	MEX Ethn	COL Conf	AFG Conf	INDO Conf	PHI Conf	ASSAM Conf
Household aspirations																
Aspirations for self (rh716)	0.71	0.71	0.71	0.71	0.71	0.71	0.71	0.71	0.71	—	0.71	0.71	0.71	0.71	0.71	0.71
Aspirations for future generation (rh717)	0.71	0.71	0.71	0.71	0.71	0.71	0.71	0.71	0.71	—	0.71	0.71	0.71	0.71	0.71	0.71
	1.41	1.41	1.41	1.41	1.41	1.41	1.41	1.41	1.41	0.00	1.41	1.41	1.41	1.41	1.41	1.41
Collective action																
Coming together to solve water problems, 10 years ago (rc412b)	0.71	0.71	0.71	0.71	0.71	0.71	used directly	0.71	0.71	0.71	0.71	−0.71	0.71	0.71	0.71	0.71
Coming together to assist each other 10 years ago (rc413b)	0.71	0.71	0.71	0.71	0.71	0.71	—	0.71	0.71	0.71	0.71	0.71	0.71	0.71	0.71	0.71
	1.41	1.41	1.41	1.41	1.41	1.41	0.00	1.41	1.41	1.41	1.41	0.00	1.41	1.41	1.41	1.41

	UP Caste	WB Landdist	AP SHG	BAN Empow	UGA Panel	MAL Infra	SEN Infra	TAN Ruv	PHI Panel	THAI Ineq	MEX Ethn	COL Conf	AFG Conf	INDO Conf	PHI Conf	ASSAM Conf
School inequality																
Ethnic/ religious discrimination in schools (c305b)	0.71	0.71	0.71	0.71	0.71	0.71	0.71	0.69	−0.71	0.66	0.71	0.71	−0.71	0.71	—	0.71
Gender discrimination in schools (c304b)	0.71	0.71	0.71	0.71	0.71	0.71	0.71	0.69	0.71	0.66	0.71	0.71	—	0.71	—	0.71
LOM: Change in equality in schools (h303b, 3=improved, 1=deteriorated)								0.20		0.35			0.71			
	1.41	1.41	1.41	1.41	1.41	1.41	1.41	1.59	0.00	1.67	1.41	1.41	0.00	1.41	0.00	1.41

Appendix 6: Regression Results Tables for MOP and MPI

Full OLS Regression Results with MOP as Dependent Variable

Independent variables associated with MOP	UP Caste	WB Landdist	AP SHG	BAN Empow	UGA Panel	MAL Infra	SEN Infra	TAN Ruv	PHI Panel	THAI Ineq	MEX Ethn	COL Conf	AFG Conf	INDO Conf	PHI Conf	ASSAM Conf
Initial strength of economy (PCA rc205b, rc208b, rc209b)	-0.02 (0.02)	0.01 (0.01)	-0.02 (0.05)	0.03* (0.01)	0.11 (0.11)	-0.12** (0.04)	0.04 (0.03)	-0.19*** (0.03)	-0.18*** (0.05)	0.08 (0.06)	0.05* (0.03)	0.02* (0.01)	-0.10*** (0.02)	-0.04*** (0.01)	0.18** (0.06)	0.04 (0.03)
Change in economic prosperity (PCA rc904m, rc903m, rc912m, rc917m)	-0.01 (0.01)	-0.01 (0.01)	0.00 (0.04)	0.07*** (0.02)	0.13** (0.05)	0.01 (0.03)	-0.00 (0.01)	0.32*** (0.05)	0.03 (0.12)	0.04 (0.05)	0.04 (0.03)	0.02 (0.02)	0.08*** (0.03)	0.07*** (0.01)	0.06 (0.05)	0.01 (0.02)
Responsiveness of local democracy (PCA rh504, rrh415bi, rh511, rh502b)	0.04** (0.01)	0.03* (0.01)	-0.02 (0.02)	0.06** (0.02)	0.01 (0.02)	-0.05 (0.07)	-0.02 (0.04)	0.01 (0.03)	0.08* (0.04)	-0.04 (0.03)	-0.01 (0.03)	-0.00 (0.01)	-0.04 (0.04)	-0.01 (0.03)	0.04 (0.03)	0.04* (0.02)
LOM of responsiveness of local democracy (locdemocracylom)	-0.03 (0.02)	-0.04 (0.02)	0.13* (0.05)	-0.17*** (0.06)	0.37* (0.18)	-0.10* (0.06)	-0.17*** (0.03)	0.77*** (0.17)	0.85*** (0.27)	0.04 (0.12)	0.06 (0.08)			0.27*** (0.05)	0.16* (0.08)	-0.11* (0.04)
Corruption (PCA c505b, c506b, c924m)	-0.03 (0.01)	0.01 (0.01)	-0.04 (0.04)	-0.07*** (0.01)	-0.09* (0.05)	0.21* (0.10)	-0.08*** (0.01)	0.09*** (0.01)	-0.02 (0.08)	-0.01 (0.10)	-0.03*** (0.01)			0.09*** (0.03)		0.03 (0.03)
Fairness index (PCA rh240b, rh606b, h234, h236)	0.03* (0.01)	0.04* (0.02)	0.05 (0.05)													0.04 (0.02)

388

Independent variables associated with MOP	UP Caste	WB Landdist	AP SHG	BAN Empow	UGA Panel	MAL Infra	SEN Infra	TAN Ruv	PHI Panel	THAI Ineq	MEX Ethn	COL Conf	AFG Conf	INDO Conf	PHI Conf	ASSAM Conf
LOM of fairness index (fairindexlom)	-0.02 (0.03)	-0.03 (0.03)														0.00 (0.05)
Personal agency index (PCA rh501b, h708)	0.04* (0.02)	-0.01 (0.03)	0.01 (0.03)	0.07** (0.03)	0.04* (0.02)	-0.07 (0.06)	-0.01 (0.03)		0.06 (0.07)	0.03 (0.03)	-0.03 (0.05)	0.05 (0.04)	0.03 (0.04)	0.05* (0.03)	-0.06 (0.05)	0.08** (0.03)
LOM of personal agency index	-0.08 (0.06)	0.03 (0.04)	-0.23* (0.09)	0.00 (0.08)	0.14 (0.36)	0.01 (0.15)	-0.10* (0.05)		0.48 (1.00)	0.13 (0.18)	0.14 (0.16)			0.97*** (0.21)		0.06 (0.09)
Household aspirations (PCA rh716, rh717)	0.14** (0.01)	0.25** (0.02)	-0.04* (0.02)	0.01 (0.02)	0.03* (0.02)	-0.02 (0.05)	0.00 (0.03)	0.03 (0.03)	-0.01 (0.04)	n.a.	0.01 (0.03)	-0.02 (0.02)	0.11* (0.06)	0.01 (0.03)	0.03 (0.03)	0.09** (0.02)
LOM of household aspirations (hhsasplom)	-0.18** (0.03)	-0.19** (0.03)	0.05 (0.05)													-0.10 (0.06)
Index of collective action, 10 years ago (PCA rc412b, rc413b)	-0.03* (0.01)	-0.01 (0.02)	-0.11* (0.05)	-0.04*** (0.01)	0.05 (0.07)	n.a.	0.15** (0.05)	-0.25*** (0.05)	-0.21* (0.09)	n.a.	-0.07* (0.03)	0.00 (0.02)	0.06** (0.02)	0.11*** (0.03)	n.a.	0.01 (0.02)
Change in access to networks and associations (rc919m, 1=less, 3=more)	-0.01 (0.01)	0.00 (0.01)	n.a.	-0.28*** (0.06)	n.a.	0.10 (0.07)	n.a.	-0.56*** (0.10)	0.06 (0.48)	n.a.	-0.05 (0.10)	-0.15*** (0.02)	n.a.	-0.34*** (0.06)	-0.08 (0.06)	-0.04 (0.05)

Independent variables associated with MOP	UP Caste	WB Landdist	AP SHG	BAN Empow	UGA Panel	MAL Infra	SEN Infra	TAN Ruv	PHI Panel	THAI Ineq	MEX Ethn	COL Conf	AFC Conf	INDO Conf	PHI Conf	ASSAM Conf
Extent of social divisions in the village, 10 years ago (c414b, 1=no division, 5=to a great extent)	-0.01 (0.01)	0.00 (0.01)	0.03 (0.04)	0.06** (0.02)	0.01 (0.07)	-0.10 (0.09)	-0.09 (0.06)	n.a.	0.02 (0.29)	-0.07 (0.08)	0.31** (0.13)	0.10*** (0.01)		-0.38*** (0.05)	0.17* (0.09)	0.02 (0.02)
Violence against women in households, 10 years ago (h609b, 1=none, 4=much)	0.04 (0.02)	-0.08* (0.04)	-0.08** (0.03)	n.a.	n.a.	-0.02 (0.11)	n.a.	0.03 (0.03)	-0.08 (0.08)	0.01 (0.08)	0.02 (0.04)	0.03 (0.02)	-0.02 (0.04)	0.06 (0.04)	0.02 (0.07)	0.09** (0.03)
LOM of violence against women in households, 10 years ago (h609blom)	-0.07 (0.05)	0.08 (0.05)														-0.15** (0.05)
School inequality measure, trend (PCA c304b, c305b)	0.00 (0.01)	0.00 (0.01)	0.05 (0.04)													0.00 (0.02)
Present education status of household head (educ2005)	0.04** (0.01)		-0.01 (0.01)	0.03** (0.01)	n.a.	n.a.	n.a.	n.a.	n.a.	n.a.	0.07** (0.03)	0.01 (0.03)	n.a.	0.06* (0.03)	n.a.	0.04** (0.01)
Health shocks, over 10 years (healthshock, 1=yes, 0=no)	-0.02 (0.04)	-0.04 (0.04)	0.00 (0.04)	-0.09** (0.03)	-0.04 (0.08)	0.06 (0.20)	n.a.	(-0.00) (0.07)	0.03 (0.06)	-0.07 (0.08)	0.06 (0.06)	0.05 (0.06)	-0.12 (0.17)	-0.05 (0.07)	-0.05 (0.07)	-0.09* (0.05)

Independent variables associated with MOP	UP Caste	WB Landdist	AP SHG	BAN Empow	UGA Panel	MAL Infra	SEN Infra	TAN Ruv	PHI Panel	THAI Ineq	MEX Ethn	COL Conf	AFG Conf	INDO Conf	PHI Conf	ASSAM Conf
Initial landholding (land1995)	0.02** (0.01)		0.00 (0.00)													-0.01 (0.01)
Ownership of house, 10 years ago (ownhouse1995, 1=yes, 0=no)	0.16 (0.12)	0.07 (0.04)		0.12** (0.05)	n.a.	-0.16 (0.23)	0.15*** (0.03)	-0.13 (0.09)	-0.03 (0.06)	0.04 (0.08)	-0.05 (0.07)	-0.01 (0.04)	0.15 (0.12)	0.04 (0.12)	(−0.21)* (0.10)	0.16 (0.15)
Initial assets index (PCA rh201ib–rh201xiiib)	-0.01 (0.04)	0.05** (0.02)	0.00 (0.02)	0.12** (0.05)	0.07 (0.06)	0.13* (0.06)	n.a.	0.08* (0.04)	0.08 (0.09)	-0.09* (0.04)	0.05* (0.03)	-0.01 (0.02)	0.01 (0.08)	0.23*** (0.04)	0.10** (0.04)	0.03 (0.04)
Initial livestock index (PCA rh203ib–rh203xib)	0.00 (0.01)	0.03 (0.01)	0.01 (0.01)	0.01*** (0.00)	n.a.	0.03 (0.07)	n.a.	(−0.03) (0.04)	-0.04 (0.04)	n.a.	-0.02 (0.03)	0.03 (0.02)	0.09 (0.11)	0.00** (0.00)	0.01 (0.06)	0.00 (0.02)
Policy variable	-0.09* (0.04)	-0.03 (0.03)	0.02 (0.02)			-0.06 (0.05)	-0.05* (0.02)	(−0.07)** (0.02)				0.20*** (0.01)	-0.05 (0.03)	-0.08* (0.04)	-0.15*** (0.02)	
Constant	0.44** (0.15)	0.54** (0.06)	0.72** (0.25)	1.11*** (0.17)	0.44*** (0.18)	0.34* (0.19)	0.07 (0.27)	1.90*** (0.13)	0.28 (0.20)	0.62* (0.31)	0.24 (0.24)	-0.10 (0.15)	0.70* (0.27)	1.40*** (0.25)	0.89*** (0.18)	0.35 (0.32)
Observations	969	620	531	501	217	75	200	233	100	217	261	211	67	238	167	452
R^2	0.32	0.41	0.17	0.18	0.17	0.09	0.20	0.16	0.44	0.09	0.12	0.51	0.20	0.19	0.36	0.30

Note: Cluster-robust standard errors in parentheses. n.a. = not available.

*p < .10   **p < .05   ***p < .01   (White heteroscedasticity-consistent standard errors)

391

Full OLS Regression Results with MPI as Dependent Variable

Independent variables associated with MPI	UP Caste	WB Landdist	AP SHG	BAN Empow	UGA Panel	SEN Infra	TAN Ruv	AFG Conf	INDO Conf	PHI Conf	COL Conf	MEX Ethn	PHI Panel	THAI Ineq	ASSAM Conf
Initial strength of economy (PCA rc205b, rc208b, rc209b)	-0.01 (0.01)	0.01 (0.01)	0.01 (0.05)	0.01 (0.02)	0.08 (0.06)	-0.05** (0.02)	-0.15*** (0.01)	-0.03* (0.02)	-0.09*** (0.01)	0.15*** (0.03)	-0.07*** (0.01)	-0.00 (0.06)	-0.00 (0.04)	0.04 (0.07)	0.07** (0.02)
Change in economic prosperity (PCA rc904m, rc903m, rc912m, rc917m)	0.00 (0.01)	-0.01 (0.01)	-0.01 (0.05)	0.06*** (0.02)	0.07 (0.04)	-0.05** (0.02)	-0.33*** (0.06)	0.02 (0.02)	0.03*** (0.01)	0.01 (0.03)	0.03** (0.01)	0.02 (0.02)	-0.12 (0.10)	0.05 (0.05)	0.01 (0.02)
Responsiveness of local democracy (PCA rh504, rh415bi, rh511, rh502b)	0.04** (0.01)	0.03* (0.01)	-0.03 (0.02)	0.05** (0.02)	0.00 (0.02)	0.01 (0.03)	0.00 (0.02)	0.02 (0.02)	0.03 (0.03)	0.08*** (0.02)	-0.00 (0.03)	-0.02 (0.03)	0.04 (0.07)	-0.04 (0.03)	0.04* (0.02)
LOM of responsiveness of local democracy (locdemocracylom)	-0.03 (0.02)	-0.02 (0.02)	0.20** (0.05)	-0.27*** (0.07)	0.11 (0.13)	-0.16** (0.05)	-0.55*** (0.14)		0.29*** (0.04)	0.16*** (0.04)		0.09 (0.08)	0.90** (0.30)	-0.06 (0.10)	-0.09** (0.03)
Corruption (PCA c505b, c506b, c924m)	-0.01 (0.01)	0.01 (0.01)	-0.01 (0.04)	-0.06** (0.02)	-0.03 (0.04)	-0.02 (0.03)	0.21*** (0.01)		-0.03 (0.02)			-0.04** (0.02)	0.07 (0.05)	0.02 (0.15)	0.01 (0.02)

Independent variables associated with MPI	UP Caste	WB Landdist	AP SHG	BAN Empow	UGA Panel	SEN Infra	TAN Ruv	AFG Conf	INDO Conf	PHI Conf	COL Conf	MEX Ethn	PHI Panel	THAI Ineq	ASSAM Conf
Fairness index (PCA rh240b, rh606b, h234, h236)	0.02 (0.02)	0.04* (0.02)	-0.01 (0.05)												0.05** (0.02)
LOM of fairness index (fairindexlom)	0.02 (0.03)	-0.02 (0.03)													-0.08 (0.06)
Personal agency index (PCA rh501b, h708)	0.04* (0.02)	-0.01 (0.03)	0.02 (0.04)	0.05* (0.02)	0.02 (0.02)	-0.01 (0.03)		0.01 (0.05)	0.02 0.04	-0.09 (0.05)	0.03** (0.01)	-0.04 (0.04)	0.12* (0.06)	0.03 (0.03)	0.07* (0.03)
LOM of personal agency index	-0.08 (0.05)	0.04 (0.05)	-0.12 (0.11)	0.14* (0.08)	-0.44* (0.24)	0.04 (0.05)			0.36* 0.21			0.16 (0.14)	1.46 (0.98)	-0.13 (0.17)	-0.03 (0.08)
Household aspirations (PCA rh716, rh717)	0.13** (0.01)	0.24** (0.02)	-0.04 (0.02)	-0.01 (0.01)	0.02 (0.03)	0.01 (0.02)	0.01 (0.04)	0.10** (0.04)	0.00 0.05	0.03 (0.03)	0.02 (0.02)	0.00 (0.03)	-0.02 (0.04)	n.a.	0.11** (0.02)
LOM of household aspirations (hhsasplom)	-0.17** (0.03)	-0.17** (0.04)	0.04 (0.07)												-0.09 (0.06)
Index of collective action, 10 years ago (PCA rc412b, rc413b)	-0.01 (0.01)	-0.02 (0.02)	-0.11 (0.06)	-0.00 (0.01)	0.06 (0.05)	0.17*** (0.05)	(-0.02) (0.04)	0.06*** (0.02)	0.19*** 0.01		0.04 (0.03)	-0.01 (0.05)	-0.18* (0.09)	n.a.	-0.03 (0.02)

Independent variables associated with MPI	UP Caste	WB Landdist	AP SHC	BAN Empow	UGA Panel	SEN Infra	TAN Ruv	AFG Conf	INDO Conf	PHI Conf	COL Conf	MEX Ethn	PHI Panel	THAI Ineq	ASSAM Conf
Change in access to networks and associations (rc919m, 1=less, 3=more)	0.01 (0.01)	-0.01 (0.01)	n.a.	-0.11 (0.08)	n.a.	n.a.	(-0.02) (0.11)	n.a.	-0.27*** 0.06	0.00 (0.03)	-0.04 (0.03)	-0.05 (0.08)	0.40 (0.37)	n.a.	-0.05 (0.04)
Extent of social divisions in the village, 10 years ago (c414b, 1=no division, 5=to a great extent)	-0.01 (0.01)	0.02 (0.01)	-0.01 (0.03)	0.10** (0.04)	0.07 (0.04)	0.07 (0.08)	n.a.		-0.18*** 0.05	0.10** (0.03)	-0.10*** (0.02)	-0.07 (0.16)	-0.16 (0.22)	-0.09 (0.07)	-0.001 (0.02)
Violence against women in households, 10 years ago (h609b, 1=none, 4=much)	0.04 (0.02)	-0.07 (0.04)	-0.05 (0.04)	n.a.	n.a.	n.a.	0.00 (0.04)	0.02 (0.05)	-0.02 0.05	0.01 (0.07)	0.03* (0.01)	-0.02 (0.03)	-0.10 (0.09)	-0.01 (0.05)	0.07** (0.03)
LOM of violence against women in households, 10 years ago (h609blom)	-0.05 (0.04)	0.02 (0.05)													-0.15** (0.05)
School inequality measure, trend (PCA c304b, c305b)	0.01 (0.01)	0.00 (0.01)	0.06* (0.03)												0.01 (0.02)

Independent variables associated with MPI	UP Caste	WB Landdist	AP SHG	BAN Empow	UGA Panel	SEN Infra	TAN Ruv	AFG Conf	INDO Conf	PHI Conf	COL Conf	MEX Ethn	PHI Panel	THAI Ineq	ASSAM Conf
Present education status of household head (educ2005)	0.03**		−0.01	0.03***	n.a.	n.a.	n.a.	n.a.	0.06***		−0.03*	0.05	n.a.	n.a.	0.03*
	(0.01)		(0.01)	(0.01)					0.01		(0.02)	(0.03)			(0.02)
Health shocks, over 10 years (healthshock, 1=yes, 0=no)	−0.04	−0.02	−0.04	−0.06*	0.04	n.a.	(0.01)	−0.27	−0.07	(−0.13)*	0.03	−0.03	0.11	−0.07	−0.08
	(0.04)	(0.04)	(0.04)	(0.03)	(0.08)		(0.07)	(0.20)	0.07	(0.06)	(0.02)	(0.05)	(0.08)	(0.08)	(0.04)
Initial landholding (land1995)	0.01*		0.00*												−0.01
	(0.01)		(0.00)												(0.01)
Ownership of house, 10 years ago (ownhouse1995, 1=yes, 0=no)	0.09	0.04		0.14**	n.a.	0.10***	−0.02	0.10	0.03	−0.19	0.08	−0.01	−0.01	0.04	0.19
	(0.11)	(0.05)		(0.06)		(0.03)	(0.09)	(0.11)	0.12	(0.13)	(0.07)	(0.06)	(0.17)	(0.06)	(0.17)
Initial assets index (PCA rh201ib–rh201xiiib, with current weights)	−0.01	0.04*	0.02	0.02	0.04	n.a.	0.10**	0.02	0.15***	0.07	0.04	0.02	0.01	−0.08	0.03
	(0.04)	(0.02)	(0.02)	(0.04)	(0.05)		(0.04)	(0.07)	0.05	(0.05)	(0.04)	(0.03)	(0.07)	(0.05)	(0.04)
Initial livestock index (PCA rh203ib–rh203xib)	0.00	0.03*	0.04	0.01	n.a.	n.a.	(−0.03)	0.18***	0.00	0.06	−0.01	−0.03	0.02	n.a.	−0.02
	(0.01)	(0.01)	(0.02)	(0.00)			(0.02)	(0.03)	0.00	(0.05)	(0.01)	(0.03)	(0.05)		(0.02)

395

Independent variables associated with MPI	UP Caste	WB Landdist	AP SHG	BAN. Empow	UGA Panel	SEN Infra	TAN Ruv	AFG Conf	INDO Conf	PHI Conf	COL Conf	MEX Ethn	PHI Panel	THAI Ineq	ASSAM Conf
Policy variable	-0.08*	-0.03	0.02			-0.03	1.01***	-0.07***	-0.15***	-0.08***	0.07**				0.03
	(0.03)	(0.03)	(0.01)			(0.04)	(0.02)	(0.01)	(0.02)	(0.01)	(0.02)				(0.02)
Constant	0.33*	0.63**	0.80*	0.68***	0.50***	-0.01	-3.06***	0.99***	0.82***	0.84***	1.06***	0.96***	0.41**	0.83**	0.54
	(0.13)	(0.08)	(0.32)	(0.22)	(0.11)	(0.28)	(0.19)	(0.26)	(0.24)	(0.18)	(0.13)	(0.23)	(0.16)	(0.32)	(0.30)
Observations	969	620	531	501	217	200	233	67	238	167	211	261	100	217	452
R^2	0.28	0.38	0.15	0.14	0.11	0.13	0.15	0.22	0.14	0.22	0.41	0.14	0.27	0.091	0.32

Note: Cluster-robust standard errors in parentheses. n.a. = not available.

*p < .10   **p < .05   ***p < .01   (White heteroscedasticity–consistent standard errors)

Notes

1. The basic specification includes variables on economic opportunity, local democracy, collective action, agency, aspirations, violence against women, and extent of social divisions in the village.
2. Also included are household characteristics (assets, livestock, house ownership, education level, health shocks).
3. The standard errors reported for all regressions are corrected for cluster-based sampling. Seed set at 123 for imputations.
4. Non-India regressions: Because of small sample sizes, the basic model has been reduced to include a limited set of variables under each block or concept. Fairness, school inequality, and ownership of land have been dropped.
5. Regressions combine the variables on power and rights and control over decision making into a personal agency index.
6. Leave-out means (LOM) are included only for the democracy and personal agency indexes. LOMs for violence against women, fairness, and aspirations have been dropped except for India.
7. Conflict countries include a variable for conflict.
8. In some conflict countries, corruption, social divisiveness, and the LOM variables had to be dropped because of high multicollinearity with the conflict variable.
9. In Malawi, the absolute ranks for each household on the mobility matrix were not consistently entered. It was not possible, therefore, to calculate upward mobility (MPI) for each household. However, the status of each household as ranked by the mobility matrix (i.e., whether mover, faller, chronic poor, or never poor) was available and was used for the MOP household regressions.

Country notes

UP (Caste): Policy variable is whether household belongs to scheduled caste (1=yes, 0=no).

WB (Landdist): Policy variable is whether village had a land reform program in the past 10 years (1=yes, 0=no).

AP (SHG): Policy variable is number of groups household belonged to 10 years ago.

BAN (Empow): Violence against women: n.a. Corruption index includes only c505b and c506b. Initial assets index (PCA h201ib, iib, ivb, vib, viiib, with current weights). Initial livestock index (h203iib, h203vb, h203viiib, with current weights). No policy variable is included.

UGA (Panel): Change in access to networks, violence against women, education status of household head, ownership of house, initial livestock index: n.a. Responsiveness of local democracy does not include rh415bi. Corruption index includes only c505b and c506b. Initial assets index = mean of assets 10 years ago. No policy variable is included.

MAL (Infra): Index of collective action, education status of household head: n.a. Change in economic prosperity includes only rc912 and rc917. For corruption, c924 used directly. Policy variable is access to growth facilities.

SEN (Infra): Change in access to networks, violence against women, initial livestock index, initial asset index, education status of household head, health shocks: n.a. Initial strength of economy includes only rc205b and rc208b. Responsiveness of local democracy does not include rh415bi. Corruption index does not include c924. For ownership of house, housing conditions used as proxy (PCA rh207). For collective action, rc412 used directly. Policy variable is access to social infrastructure (1=less, 3=more).

TAN (Ruv): Education status of household head, extent of social divisions in the village: n.a. Personal agency index and its LOM dropped as a result of low variance. Initial strength of economy includes only rc205b and rc208b. Corruption index does not include c924. Imputed variables: household aspirations, responsiveness of local democracy, violence against women, ownership of house, health shocks. Policy variable is log (distance to main centers).

PHI (Panel): Education status of household head: n.a. Corruption index does not include c924. No policy variable is included.

THAI (Ineq): Household aspirations, index of collective action, change in access to networks, education status of household head, initial livestock index: n.a. Imputed variables: responsiveness of local democracy, personal agency index, violence against women, initial assets, ownership of house, health shocks. No policy variable is included.

MEX (Ethn): All variables except for the initial asset index, initial livestock index, and education status of household head were imputed. Corruption index does not include c506b. No policy variable is included.

COL (Conf): Policy variable is impact of conflict (0=no conflict, 4=large harmful effect). Corruption, LOM of responsiveness of local democracy, and LOM of personal agency index dropped because of high multicollinearity with the conflict variable. Imputed variables: initial strength of economy, responsiveness of local democracy, household aspirations, violence against women, ownership of house.

AFG (Conf): Policy variable is impact of conflict on functioning of markets (1=no effect, 4=large harmful effect). Education status of household head: n.a. Change in access to networks is not included because of lack of variation. Corruption, social divisions, and both LOMs are dropped because of high multicollinearity with the conflict variable. Initial strength of economy: rc205b used directly. Imputed variables: responsiveness of local democracy, personal agency index, household aspirations, ownership of house.

INDO (Conf): Policy variable is impact of conflict on functioning of markets (1=no effect, 4=large harmful effect). Imputed variables: household aspirations.

PHI (Conf): Index of collective action and education status of household head: n.a. Policy variable is impact of conflict on functioning of local markets (1=no effect, 4=large harmful effect). LOM of personal agency index and corruption dropped due to high multicollinearity with the conflict variable.

ASSAM (Conf): Policy variable is conflict trajectory (1=peace to peace; 2=conflict to peace; 3=peace to conflict; 4=conflict to conflict).

References

Acemoglu, D., and J. A. Robinson. 2008. "Persistence of Power, Elites, and Institutions." *American Economic Review* 98 (1): 267–93.

Agarwal, B., J. Humphries, and I. Robeyns, eds. 2006. *Capabilities, Freedom, and Equality: Amartya Sen's Work from a Gender Perspective.* New Delhi: Oxford University Press.

Aiyar, S., D. Narayan, and K. Raju. 2007. "Empowerment through Self-Help Groups: Andhra Pradesh Shows the Way in India." In *Ending Poverty in South Asia: Ideas That Work*, ed. D. Narayan and E. Glinskaya, 104–35. Washington, DC: World Bank.

Alatas, V., L. Pritchett, and A. Wetterberg. 2007. "Voice Lessons: Evidence on Social Organizations, Government Mandated Organizations, and Governance from Indonesia's Local Level Institutions Study." In *Membership-Based Organizations of the Poor*, ed. M. Chen, R. Jhabvala, R. Kanbur, and C. Richards, 313–51. New York: Routledge.

Alderman, H., P. Chiappori, L. Haddad, J. Hoddinott, and R. Kanbur. 1995. "Unitary Versus Collective Models of the Household: Is It Time to Shift the Burden of Proof?" *World Bank Research Observer* 10 (1): 1–19.

Alesina, A., and G. Angeletos. 2005. "Fairness and Redistribution." *American Economic Review* 95 (4): 960–80.

Alesina, A., and E. Glaeser. 2004. *Fighting Poverty in the U.S. and Europe: A World of Difference.* New York: Oxford University Press.

Alesina, A., E. Glaeser, and B. Sacerdote. 2001. "Why Doesn't the United States Have a European-Style Welfare State?" *Brookings Papers on Economic Activity* 32 (2001–02): 187–278.

Alkire, S. 2002. *Valuing Freedoms: Sen's Capability Approach and Poverty Reduction.* New York: Oxford University Press.

———. 2008. "Concepts and Measures of Agency." Working Paper 9, Oxford Poverty and Human Development Initiative, University of Oxford, Oxford, UK.

Alsop, R., and N. Heinsohn. 2005. "Measuring Empowerment in Practice: Structuring Analysis and Framing Indicators." Policy Research Working Paper 3510, World Bank, Washington, DC.

Appadurai, A. 2004. "The Capacity to Aspire: Culture and the Terms of Recognition." In *Culture and Public Action*, ed. V. Rao and M. Walton, 59–84. Stanford, CA: Stanford University Press.

Arrow, K. J. 1971. *Essays in the Theory of Risk-Bearing.* Amsterdam: North-Holland.

Ashforth, A. 2005. *Witchcraft, Violence, and Democracy in South Africa.* Chicago: University of Chicago Press.

Axelrod, R. 1984. *The Evolution of Cooperation.* New York: Basic Books.

Baiochhi, G. 2005. "Inequality and Innovation: Decentralization as an Opportunity Structure in Brazil." In *Decentralization and Local Governments in Developing Countries: A Comparative Perspective,* ed. P. Bardhan and D. Mookherjee. Cambridge, MA: MIT Press.

Bandura, A. 1995. "Comments on the Crusade against the Causal Efficacy of Human Thought." *Journal of Behavior Therapy and Experimental Psychiatry* 26 (3): 179–90.

———. 1998. "Personal and Collective Efficacy in Human Adaptation and Change." In *Advances in Psychological Science,* vol. 1, *Social, Personal, and Cultural Aspects,* ed. J. G. Adair, D. Belanger, and K. L. Dion, 51–71. Hove, UK: Psychology Press.

Banerjee, A., and E. Duflo. 2006. "The Economic Lives of the Poor." Discussion Paper 5968, Centre for Economic Policy Research, London.

Banfield, E. 1958. *The Moral Basis of a Backward Society.* New York: Free Press.

Bardhan, P. 1999. "Democracy and Development: A Complex Relationship." In *Democracy's Value,* ed. I. Shapiro and C. Hacker-Cordón, 93–111. New York: Cambridge University Press.

———. 2002. "Decentralization of Governance and Development." *Journal of Economic Perspectives* 16 (4): 85–205.

Bardhan, P., and D. Mookherjee. 2004. "Poverty Alleviation Efforts of West Bengal Panchayats." *Economic and Political Weekly,* February 28, 965–74.

———. 2006. "Pro-poor Targeting and Accountability of Local Governments in West Bengal." *Journal of Development Economics* 79 (2): 303–27.

Barro, R. 1994. "Democracy and Growth." Working Paper 4909, National Bureau of Economic Research, Cambridge, MA.

Barron, P., R. Diprose, and M. Woolcock. 2007. "Local Conflict and Development Projects in Indonesia: Part of the Problem or Part of a Solution?" Policy Research Working Paper 4212, World Bank, Washington, DC.

Baulch, B., and N. McCulloch. 2002. "Being Poor and Becoming Poor: Poverty Status and Poverty Transitions in Rural Pakistan." *Journal of Asian and African Studies* 37 (2): 168–85.

Bebbington, A., L. Dharmawan, E. Fahmi, and S. Guggenheim. 2006. "Local Capacity, Village Governance, and the Political Economy of Rural Development in Indonesia." *World Development* 34 (11): 1958–76.

Beegle, K., J. De Weerdt, and S. Dercon. 2006. "Orphanhood and the Long-Term Impact on Children." *American Journal of Agricultural Economics* 88 (5): 1266–77.

Bénabou, R., and J. Tirole. 2006. "Belief in a Just World and Redistributive Politics." *Quarterly Journal of Economics* 121 (2): 699–746.

Bertrand, M., and S. Mullainathan. 2001. "Do People Mean What They Say? Implications for Subjective Survey Data." *American Economic Review* 91 (2): 67–72.

Besley, T., and R. Burgess. 2002. "The Political Economy of Government Responsiveness: Theory and Evidence from India." *Quarterly Journal of Economics* 117 (4): 1415–51.

Besley, T., R. Pande, and V. Rao. 2007. "Just Rewards? Local Politics and Public Resource Allocation in South India." Development Economics Paper 49, Suntory and Toyota International Centres for Economics and Related Disciplines, London School of Economics and Political Science.

Bester, H. 1985. "Screening vs. Rationing in Credit Markets with Imperfect Information." *American Economic Review* 75 (4): 850–55.

———. 1994. "The Role of Collateral in a Model of Debt Renegotiation." *Journal of Money, Credit and Banking* 26 (1): 72–86.

Bhide, S., and A. K. Mehta. 2004. "Chronic Poverty in Rural India: Issues and Findings from Panel Data." *Journal of Human Development* 5 (2): 195–209.

Booth, C. 1889. *Life and Labour of the People in London.* London: Macmillan.

Boudon, R. 1973. *L'inégalité des chances: La mobilité sociale dans les sociétés industrielles.* Paris: Colin.

Bourdieu, P., and J. C. Passeron. 1970. *La Reproduction.* Paris: Editions de Minuit.

Bovens, M. 2006. "Analysing and Assessing Public Accountability: A Conceptual Framework." European Governance Papers (EUROGOV), no. C-06-01. http://www.connex-network.org/eurogov/.

Carter, M. R., and M. Ikegami. 2007. "Looking Forward: Theory-Based Measures of Chronic Poverty and Vulnerability." Working Paper 485, Chronic Poverty Research Centre, Manchester, UK.

Carter, M. R., and J. May. "One Kind of Freedom: Poverty Dynamics in Post-apartheid South Africa." *World Development* 29 (12): 1987–2006.

CGAP (Consultative Group to Assist the Poor) 2007. "CGAP Reflections on the Compartamos Initial Public Offering: A Case Study on Microfinance Interest Rates and Profits." Focus Note 42, CGAP, Washington, DC.

Chambers, R. 2002. "Power, Knowledge, and Policy Influence: Reflections on an Experience." In *Knowing Poverty: Critical Reflections on Participatory Research and Policy*, ed. K. Brock and R. McGee, 135–65. London: Earthscan.

———. 2003. "Deliberative Democratic Theory." *Annual Review of Political Science* 6: 307–26.

Chen, S., and M. Ravallion. 2000. "How Did the World's Poorest Fare in the 1990s?" Policy Research Working Paper 2409, World Bank, Washington, DC.

———. 2007. "Absolute Poverty Measures for the Developing World, 1981–2004." *Proceedings of the National Academy of Sciences of the United States of America* 104 (43): 16757–62.

Chronic Poverty Research Centre. 2008. *Chronic Poverty Report, 2008–09: Escaping Poverty Traps.* Manchester, UK: CPRC.

CIFOR (Center for International Forest Research). 2005. *Contributing to African Development through Forests: CIFOR's Strategy for Engagement in Sub-Saharan Africa.* Bogor, Indonesia: CIFOR.

Cohen, J., and C. Sabel. 1997. "Directly Deliberative Polyarchy." *European Law Journal* 3 (4): 313–42.

Cord, L. 2005. *Pro-Poor Growth in the 1990s: Lessons and Insights from 14 Countries.* World Bank: Washington, DC.

Crook, R., and J. Manor. 1998. *Democracy and Decentralization in South Asia and West Africa: Participation, Accountability, and Performance.* New York: Cambridge University Press.

Dahl, R. 1989. *Democracy and Its Critics.* New Haven, CT: Yale University Press.

Daily, C. M., and M. J. Dollinger. 1992. "An Empirical Examination of Ownership Structure in Family and Professionally Managed Firms." *Family Business Review* 5 (2): 117–36.

Deaton, A. 2004. "Measuring Poverty." Working Paper 170, Woodrow Wilson School of Public and International Affairs, Research Program in Development Studies, Princeton University, Princeton, NJ.

Deininger, K., and J. Okidi. 2003. "Growth and Poverty Reduction in Uganda, 1992–2000: Panel Data Evidence." *Development Policy Review* 21 (4): 481–509.

Deininger, K., and L. Squire. 1996. "A New Data Set Measuring Income Inequality." *World Bank Economic Review* 10 (3): 565–91.

Dercon, S. 2004. "Growth and Shocks: Evidence from Rural Ethiopia." *Journal of Development Economics* 74: 309–29.

Dercon, S., with J. De Weerdt, T. Bold, and A. Pankhurst. 2006. "Group-Based Funeral Insurance in Ethiopia and Tanzania." *World Development* 34 (4): 685–703.

Dercon, S., and P. Krishnan. 2000. "Vulnerability, Seasonality, and Poverty in Ethiopia." In *Economic Mobility and Poverty Dynamics in Developing Countries*, ed. B. Baulch and J. Hoddinott. London: Frank Cass.

de Soto, H. 2000. *The Mystery of Capital: Why Capitalism Triumphs in the West and Fails Everywhere Else.* New York: Basic Books.

Diamond, L. 2002. "Elections Without Democracy: Thinking about Hybrid Regimes." *Journal of Democracy* 13 (2): 21–35.

———. 2005. "Empowering the Poor: What Does Democracy Have to Do with It?" In *Measuring Empowerment: Cross-Disciplinary Perspectives*, ed. D. Narayan, 403–25. Washington, DC: World Bank.

Diener, E., and R. Biswas-Diener. 2005. "Psychological Empowerment and Subjective Well-Being." In *Measuring Empowerment: Cross-Disciplinary Perspectives*, ed. D. Narayan, 125–40. Washington, DC: World Bank.

Di Tella, R., and R. MacCulloch. 2007. "Why Doesn't Capitalism Flow to Poor Countries?" Working Paper 13164, National Bureau of Economic Research, Cambridge, MA.

Dyrberg, T. B. 1997. *The Circular Structure of Power: Politics, Identity, Community.* New York: Verso.

Ferguson, J. 1999. *Expectations of Modernity: Myths and Meanings of Urban Life on the Zambian Copperbelt.* Berkeley: University of California Press.

Fields, G. S. 2001. *Distribution and Development: A New Look at the Developing World.* Cambridge, MA: MIT Press; New York: Russell Sage Foundation.

Foster, A., and M. Rosenzweig. 2001. "Democratization, Decentralization and the Distribution of Local Public Goods in a Poor Rural Economy." Department of Economics, Brown University, Providence, RI.

Freire, P. 1974. *Education for Critical Consciousness.* Trans. M. Marshall, M. B. Ramos, and L. Bigwood. London: Sheed and Ward.

Friedman, B. 2005. *The Moral Consequences of Economic Growth.* New York: Knopf.

Fukuyama, F. 1995. *Trust: The Social Virtues and the Creation of Prosperity.* New York: Free Press.

Fung, A., and E. O. Wright. 2003. "Thinking about Empowered Participatory Governance." In *Deepening Democracy: Institutional Innovations in Empowered Participatory Governance*, ed. A. Fung and E. O. Wright, 3–42. New York: Verso.

Galasso, E., and M. Ravallion. 2005. "Decentralized Targeting of an Anti-Poverty Program." *Journal of Public Economics* 85 (April): 705–27.

Galbraith, J. K. 1983. *The Anatomy of Power*. Boston: Houghton Mifflin.

Gersick, K. E., J. A. Davis, M. M. Hampton, and I. Lansberg. 1997. *Generation to Generation: Life Cycles of the Family Business*. Cambridge, MA: Harvard Business School Press.

Gibbs, M., R. Lindner, and A. Fischer. 1986. "Reliability of Two Survey Techniques: A Study of Innovation Discovery by Farmers." *Statistician* 35 (4): 429–39.

Gladwell, M. 2000. *The Tipping Point: How Little Things Can Make a Big Difference*. New York: Backbay Books.

Glewwe, P., and G. Hall. 1998. "Are Some Groups More Vulnerable to Macroeconomic Shocks than Others? Hypothesis Tests Based on Panel Data from Peru." *Journal of Development Economics* 56: 181–206.

Grootaert, C., and R. Kanbur. 1995. "The Lucky Few Amidst Economic Decline: Distributional Change in Côte d'Ivoire as Seen through Panel Data Sets, 1985–1988." *Journal of Development Studies*, 31 (4): 603–19.

Gugerty, M. K. 2007. "You Can't Save Alone: Commitment in Rotating Savings and Credit Associations in Kenya." *Economic Development and Cultural Change* 55 (2): 251–82.

Gupta, D., and K. L. Sharma, eds. 1991. *Country-Town Nexus: Studies in Social Transformation in Contemporary India*. Jaipur: Rawat.

Hammer, J., and L. Pritchett. 2006. "Scenes from a Marriage: World Bank Economists and Social Capital." In *The Search for Empowerment: Social Capital as Idea and Practice at the World Bank*, ed. A. Bebbington, M. Woolcock, S. Guggenheim, and E. Olson, 63–90. Bloomfield, CT: Kumarian Press.

Harrison, L. E., and S. P. Huntington, eds. 2000. *Culture Matters: How Values Shape Human Progress*. New York: Basic Books.

Hausman, J. A. 1978. "Specification Tests in Econometrics." *Econometrica* 46 (6): 1251–71.

Heyer, J., F. Stewart, and R. Thorp, eds. 2002. *Group Behavior and Development: Is the Market Destroying Cooperation?* New York: Oxford University Press.

Himmelfarb, G. 1992. *Poverty and Compassion: The Moral Imagination of the Late Victorians*. New York: Vintage.

Hirschman, A. O., and M. Rothschild. 1973. "The Changing Tolerance for Income Inequality in the Course of Economic Development." *Quarterly Journal of Economics* 87 (4): 544–66.

Hoff, K., and P. Pandey. 2004. "Belief Systems and Durable Inequalities: An Experimental Investigation of Indian Caste." Policy Research Working Paper 3351, World Bank, Washington, DC.

———. 2006. "Discrimination, Social Identity, and Durable Inequalities." *American Economic Review* 96 (2): 206–11.

Hunt, J. 2007. "Bribery in Health Care in Peru and Uganda." Working Paper 13034, National Bureau of Economic Research, Cambridge, MA.

Huntington, S., and J. Nelson. 1976. *No Easy Choice: Political Participation in Developing Countries*. Cambridge, MA: Harvard University Press.

Ibrahim, S., and S. Alkire. 2007. "Agency and Empowerment: A Proposal for Internationally Comparable Indicators." *Oxford Development Studies* 35 (4): 379–403.

Isham, J., D. Narayan, and L. Pritchett. 1994. "Does Participation Improve Performance? Establishing Causality with Subjective Data." *World Bank Economic Review* 9 (2): 175–200.

Jalan, J., and M. Ravallion. 2000. "Is Transient Poverty Different? Evidence for Rural China." *Journal of Development Studies* 36 (6): 82–99.

———. 2002. "Geographic Poverty Traps? A Micro Model of Consumption Growth in Rural China." *Journal of Applied Econometrics* 17: 329–46.

Johnston, D., and J. Morduch. 2007. "Microcredit vs. Microsaving: Evidence from Indonesia." Paper presented at World Bank conference on Access to Finance, Washington, DC, March 15–16.

Kabeer, N. 1999. "Resources, Agency, Achievement: Reflections on the Measurement of Women's Empowerment." *Development as Change* 30 (3): 435–64.

———. 2001. "Reflections on the Measurement of Women's Empowerment: Theory and Practice." In *Discussing Women's Empowerment: Theory and Practice*. Sida Studies 3. Stockholm: Swedish International Development Cooperation Agency.

Kahneman, D., and A. Krueger. 2006. "Developments in the Measurement of Subjective Well-Being." *Journal of Economic Perspectives* 20 (1): 3–24.

Kanbur, R. 2008. "Globalization, Growth and Distribution: Framing the Questions." Working Paper 2008-3, Department of Applied Economics and Management, Cornell University, Ithaca, NY.

Karelis, C. H. 2007. *The Persistence of Poverty: Why the Economics of the Well-Off Can't Help the Poor*. New Haven, CT: Yale University Press.

Kaufman, A. 1968. "Participatory Democracy: Ten Years Later." *La Table Ronde*, no. 251–252: 216–28. Reprinted in *The Bias of Pluralism*, ed. W. E. Connolly. New York: Atherton Press, 1971.

Kaufmann, D., A. Kraay, and M. Mastruzzi. 2005. "Governance Matters IV: Governance Indicators for 1996–2004." Policy Research Working Paper 3630, World Bank, Washington, DC.

Keefer, P. 2002. "Clientelism, Credibility, and Democracy." Development Research Group, World Bank, Washington, DC.

Keefer, P., and R. Vlaicu. 2008. "Democracy, Credibility, and Clientelism." *Journal of Law, Economics, and Organization* 24 (2): 371–406.

Khandker, S. R. 1998. *Fighting with Microcredit: Experience in Bangladesh*. New York: Oxford University Press.

———. 2005. "Microfinance and Poverty: Evidence Using Panel Data from Bangladesh." *World Bank Economic Review* 19 (2): 263–86.

Khemani, S. 2001. "Decentralization and Accountability: Are Voters More Vigilant in Local than in National Elections?" Policy Research Working Paper 2557, World Bank, Washington, DC.

Knack, S. 2000. "Social Capital and the Quality of Government: Evidence from the U.S. States." Policy Research Working Paper 2504, World Bank, Washington, DC.

———. 2005. "Empowerment as a Positive-Sum Game." In *Measuring Empowerment: Cross-Disciplinary Perspectives,* ed. D. Narayan, 365–81. Washington, DC: World Bank.

Knack, S., and P. Keefer. 1997. "Does Social Capital Have an Economic Payoff? A Cross-Country Investigation." *Quarterly Journal of Economics* 112 (4): 1251–88.

Kraay, A. 2006. "When Is Growth Pro-poor? Evidence from a Panel of Countries." *Journal of Development Economics* 80: 198–227.

Krishna A. 2002. *Active Social Capital: Tracing the Roots of Development and Democracy.* New York: Columbia University Press.

———. 2004. "Escaping Poverty and Becoming Poor: Who Gains, Who Loses, and Why?" *World Development* 32 (1): 121–36.

———. 2006. "Pathways Out of and Into Poverty in 36 Villages of Andhra Pradesh, India." *World Development* 34 (2): 271–88.

Krishna, A., M. Kapila, M. Porwal, and V. Singh. 2005. "Why Growth Is Not Enough: Household Poverty Dynamics in Northeast Gujarat, India." *Journal of Development Studies* 41 (7): 1163–92.

Krueger, A., and D. Schkade. 2007. "The Reliability of Subjective Well-Being Measures." Working Paper 13027, National Bureau of Economic Research, Cambridge, MA.

Kynch, J., and A. Sen. 1983. "Indian Women: Well-Being and Survival." *Cambridge Journal of Economics* 7 (3/4): 363–80.

Lane, R. 1959. "The Fear of Equality." *American Political Science Review* 53 (1): 35–51.

Lanjouw, P., O. Jean, C. Elbers, and G. Demombynes. 2007. "How Good a Map? Putting Small Area Estimation to the Test." Policy Research Working Paper 4155, World Bank, Washington, DC.

Lankina, T., A. Hudalla, and H. Wollmann. 2007. *Local Governance in Central and Eastern Europe: Comparing Performance in the Czech Republic, Hungary, Poland, and Russia.* New York: Palgrave Macmillan.

Lerner, M. 1982. *The Belief in a Just World: A Fundamental Delusion.* New York: Plenum Press.

Lewis, O. 1959. *Five Families: Mexican Case Studies in the Culture of Poverty.* New York: Basic Books.

———. 1966. *La Vida: A Puerto Rican Family in the Culture of Poverty—San Juan and New York.* New York: Random House.

Lieten, G. 1996. "Panchayats in Western Uttar Pradesh." *Economic and Political Weekly,* September 28, 2700–5.

Loury, G. 1977. "A Dynamic Theory of Racial and Income Differences." In *Women, Minorities, and Employment Discrimination,* ed. P. Wallace and A. LaMond, 153–88. Lexington, MA: Heath.

Lukes, S. 1974. *Power: A Radical View.* New York: Palgrave Macmillan.

Marshall, A. 1890. *Principles of Economics.* London: Macmillan.

Mathew, G., and R. Nayak. 1996. "Panchayats at Work: What It Means for the Oppressed?" *Economic and Political Weekly,* July 6, 1765–71.

Mayhew, H. 1851. *London Labor and the London Poor.* London: G. Woodfall.

Mayoux, L. 2003. "Women's Empowerment, Participation, and Micro Finance: Issues, Evidence, and Ways Forward." In *Sustainable Learning for Women's Empowerment: Ways Forward in Micro-Finance,* ed. L. Mayoux. New Delhi: Samskriti.

Mehta, P. B. 2003. *The Burden of Democracy*. New Delhi: Penguin India.

Molnar, A., A. White, and A. Khare. 2008. "Forest Rights and Asset-Based Livelihoods: Catalyzing Rural Economies and Forest Conservation through Policy Reform and Collective Action." In *Assets, Livelihoods, and Social Policy*, ed. A. Dani and C. Moser, 257–78. Washington, DC: World Bank.

Moser, C., and A. Norton. 2001. "To Claim Our Rights: Livelihood Security, Human Rights, and Sustainable Development." Overseas Development Institute, London.

Mosse, D. 1997. "The Symbolic Making of a Common Property Resource: History, Ecology, and Locality in a Tank-Irrigated Landscape in South India." *Development and Change* 28: 467–504.

Munshi, K., and M. R. Rosenzweig. 2005. "Why Is Mobility in India So Low? Social Insurance, Inequality, and Growth." CID Working Paper 121, Center for International Development, Harvard University, Cambridge, MA.

Murray, C. 1984. *Losing Ground: American Social Policy, 1950–1980*. New York: Basic Books.

Narayan, D. 1999. "Social Capital and the State: Complementarity and Substitution." Policy Research Working Paper 2167, World Bank, Washington, DC.

———. 2002a. "Bonds and Bridges: Social Capital and Poverty." In *Social Capital and Economic Development: Well-being in Developing Countries*, ed. J. Isham, T. Kelly, and S. Ramaswamy. Cheltenham, UK: Edward Elgar.

———, ed. 2002b. *Empowerment and Poverty Reduction: A Sourcebook*. Washington, DC: World Bank.

———, ed. 2005. *Measuring Empowerment: Cross-Disciplinary Perspectives*. Washington, DC: World Bank.

Narayan, D., R. Chambers, M. Shah, and P. Petesch. 2001. *Voices of the Poor: Crying Out for Change*. New York: Oxford University Press and the World Bank.

Narayan, D., D. Nikitin, and B. Richard. 2009. "Assets Gained and Lost: Understanding Mobility through Life Stories." In *Moving Out of Poverty: The Promise of Empowerment and Democracy in India*, ed. D. Narayan. New York: Palgrave Macmillan; Washington, DC: World Bank.

Narayan, D., and D. Nyamwaya. 1996. "Learning from the Poor: A Participatory Poverty Assessment in Kenya." Environment Department Paper 34, Social Policy and Resettlement Division, World Bank, Washington, DC.

Narayan, D., R. Patel, K. Schafft, A. Rademacher, and S. Koch-Schulte. 2000. *Voices of the Poor: Can Anyone Hear Us?* New York: Oxford University Press and the World Bank.

Narayan, D., and P. Petesch. 2002. *Voices of the Poor: From Many Lands*. New York: Oxford University Press and the World Bank.

Narayan, D., and P. Petesch, eds. 2007. *Moving Out of Poverty: Cross-Disciplinary Perspectives on Mobility*. New York: Palgrave Macmillan; Washington, DC: World Bank.

Narayan, D., P. Petesch, and S. Paul. 2009. "Communities Where Poor People Prosper." In *Moving Out of Poverty: The Promise of Empowerment and Democracy in India*, ed. D. Narayan. New York: Palgrave Macmillan; Washington, DC: World Bank.

Narayan, D., and L. Pritchett. 1997. "Cents and Sociability: Household Income and Social Capital in Rural Tanzania." Policy Research Working Paper 1796, World Bank, Washington, DC.

North, D. C. 1990. *Institutions, Institutional Change, and Economic Performance*. New York: Cambridge University Press.

Nussbaum, M. 2000. *Women and Human Development: The Capabilities Approach*. New York: Cambridge University Press.

O'Brien, D. J., J. L. Phillips, and V. V. Patsiorkovsky. 2005. "Linking Indigenous Bonding and Bridging Social Capital." *Regional Studies: Journal of the Regional Studies Association* 39 (8): 1041–51.

Olken, B. 2004. "Monitoring Corruption: Evidence from a Field Experiment in Indonesia." Working Paper 11753, National Bureau of Economic Research, Cambridge, MA.

Olson, M. 1965. *The Logic of Collective Action: Public Goods and the Theory of Groups*. Cambridge, MA: Harvard University Press.

Ostrom, E. 1990. *Governing the Commons: The Evolution of Institutions for Collective Action*. New York: Cambridge University Press.

Ottaway, M., and M. Riley. 2006. "Morocco: From Top-down Reform to Democratic Transition?" Carnegie Paper 71, Carnegie Endowment for International Peace, Washington, DC.

Paul, S. 2007. "Citizen Report Cards in Bangalore, India: A Case Study in Accountability." In *Ending Poverty in South Asia: Ideas that Work*, ed. D. Narayan and E. Glinskaya, 347–77. Washington, DC: World Bank.

Petesch, P., C. Smulovitz, and M. Walton. 2005. "Evaluating Empowerment: A Framework with Cases from Latin America." In *Measuring Empowerment: Cross-Disciplinary Perspectives*, ed. D. Narayan, 39–67. Washington, DC: World Bank.

Pew Global Attitudes Project. 2007. *Global Opinion Trends, 2002–2007: A Rising Tide Lifts Mood in the Developing World*. Washington, DC: Pew Research Center.

Portes, A. 1998. "Social Capital: Its Origins and Applications in Modern Sociology." *Annual Review of Sociology* 24: 1–24.

Pottier, J. 1988. *Migrants No More: Settlement and Survival in Mambwe Villages, Zambia*. Bloomington: Indiana University Press; London: International African Institute.

Powis, B. 2007. "Systems of Capture: Reassessing the Threat of Local Elites." Social Development Paper 109, South Asia Series, World Bank, Washington, DC.

Pretes, M. 2002. "Microequity and Microfinance." *World Development* 30 (8): 1341–53.

Pritchett, L., A. Suryahadi, and S. Sumarto. 2000. "Quantifying Vulnerability to Poverty—A Proposed Measure, with Application to Indonesia." Development Economics Working Paper 83, East Asian Bureau of Economic Research, World Bank, Washington, DC.

Prud'homme, R. 1992. "Informal Local Taxation in Developing Countries." *Government and Policy* 10: 1–17.

———. 1995. "The Dangers of Decentralization." *World Bank Research Observer* 10 (2): 201–20.

Przeworski, A., M. Alvarez, J. Cheibub, and F. Limongi. 2000. *Democracy and Development: Political Institutions and Well-Being in the World, 1950–90.* New York: Cambridge University Press.

Putnam, R. 1993. *Making Democracy Work: Civic Traditions in Modern Italy.* With Robert Leonardi and Raffaella Nannetti. Princeton, NJ: Princeton University Press

———. 2007. "E Pluribus Unum: Diversity and Community in the Twenty-first Century." *Scandinavian Political Studies* 30 (2): 137–74.

Putterman, L. 1995. "The Role of Ownership and Property Rights in China's Economic Transition." *China Quarterly* 144: 1047–64.

Qian, Y. 2003. "How Reform Worked in China." In *In Search of Prosperity: Analytical Narratives on Economic Growth*, ed. D. Rodrik, 297–333. Princeton, NJ: Princeton University Press.

Rao, V. 2008. "Symbolic Public Goods and the Coordination of Collective Action: A Comparison of Local Development in India and Indonesia." In *The Contested Commons: Conversations between Economists and Anthropologists*, ed. P. Bardhan and I. Ray. Malden, MA: Blackwell.

Rao, V., and M. Walton, eds. 2004a. *Culture and Public Action.* Stanford, CA: Stanford University Press.

———. 2004b. "Culture and Public Action: Relationality, Equality of Agency, and Development." In Rao and Walton 2004a, 3–36.

Ravallion, M. 1995. "Growth and Poverty: Evidence for Developing Countries in the 1980s." *Economic Letters* 48 (July): 411–17.

———. 2001. "Growth, Inequality, and Poverty: Looking Beyond Averages." *World Development* 29 (11): 1803–15.

———. 2004. "Competing Concepts of Inequality in the Globalization Debate." Policy Research Working Paper 3243, World Bank, Washington, DC.

Ravallion, M., and S. Chen. 1997. "What Can New Survey Data Tell Us about Recent Changes in Distribution and Poverty?" *World Bank Economic Review* 11 (2): 135–52.

———. 2004. "How Have the World's Poorest Fared Since the Early 1980s?" *World Bank Research Observer* 19 (2): 141–70.

Ravallion, M., S. Chen, and P. Sangraula. 2008. "Dollar a Day Revisited." Policy Research Working Paper 4620, World Bank, Washington, DC.

Ravallion, M., G. Datt, and D. van de Walle. 1991. "Quantifying Absolute Poverty in the Developing World." *Review of Income and Wealth* 37 (December): 345–61.

Rawls, J. 1993. *Political Liberalism.* John Dewey Essays in Philosophy, no. 4. New York: Columbia University Press.

Ray, D. 2006. "Aspirations, Poverty, and Economic Change." In *Understanding Poverty*, ed. A. Banerjee, R. Bénabou, and D. Mookherjee, 409–22. New York: Oxford University Press.

Reinikka, R., and J. Svensson. 2005. "Fighting Corruption to Improve Schooling: Evidence from a Newspaper Campaign in Uganda." *Journal of the European Economic Association* 3 (2/3): 259–67.

Robeyns, I. 2007. "When Will Society Be Gender Just?" In *The Future of Gender*, ed. Jude Browne. New York: Cambridge University Press.

Roodman, D., and U. Qureshi. 2006. "Microfinance as Business." Working Paper 101, Center for Global Development, Washington, DC.

Rowntree, B. S. 1901. *Poverty: A Study of Town Life*. London.

Rubio, M. 1997. "Perverse Social Capital: Some Evidence from Colombia." *Journal of Economic Issues* 31 (3): 805–16.

Santos, B. D. 1998. "Participative Budgeting in Porto Alegre: Towards a Redistributive Democracy." *Politics and Society* 26 (4): 461–510.

Schattscheiner, E. 1963. *Politics, Pressures, and the Tariff*. Hamden, CT: Archon Books.

Schulman, B. 1994. *From Cotton Belt to Sunbelt: Federal Policy, Economic Development, and the Transformation of the South, 1938–1980*. Durham, NC: Duke University Press.

Schulze, W., M. Lubatkin, and R. Dino. 2003. "Toward a Theory of Agency and Altruism in Family Firms." *Journal of Business Venturing* 18: 473–90.

Scott, J. 1985. *Weapons of the Weak: Everyday Forms of Peasant Resistance*. New Haven, CT: Yale University Press.

———. 1998. *Seeing Like a State: How Certain Schemes to Improve the Human Condition Have Failed*. New Haven, CT: Yale University Press.

Seabright, P. 1996. "Accountability and Decentralization in Government: An Incomplete Contracts Model." *European Economic Review* 40: 61–89.

Sen, A. 1985. "Well-Being, Agency, and Freedom: The Dewey Lectures." *Journal of Philosophy* 82 (4): 169–221.

———. 1990. "Gender and Cooperative Conflict." In *Persistent Inequalities: Women and World Development*, ed. Irene Tinker, 123–49. New York: Oxford University Press.

———. 1992. *Inequality Re-examined*. Oxford, UK: Clarendon Press

———. 1993. "Capability and Well Being." In *The Quality of Life*, ed. M. Nussbaum and A. Sen, 30–53. Oxford, UK: Clarendon Press.

———. 1999. *Development as Freedom*. New York: Knopf

Sen, B. 2003. "Drivers of Escape and Descent: Changing Household Fortunes in Bangladesh." *World Development* 31 (3): 513–34.

Shah, A., and T. Thompson. 2004. "Fiscal Decentralization in Developing and Transition Economies: Progress, Problems, and the Promise." Policy Research Working Paper 3282, World Bank, Washington, DC.

Sisk, T., ed. 2001. *Democracy at the Local Level: The International IDEA Handbook on Participation, Representation, Conflict Management, and Governance*. Stockholm: International IDEA.

Smith, A. 1776. *An Inquiry into the Nature and Causes of the Wealth of Nations*. London: Methuen.

Stewart, F. 2001. "Horizontal Inequalities: A Neglected Dimension of Development." CRISE Working Paper 1, Center for Research on Inequality, Human Security, and Ethnicity, University of Oxford, Oxford, UK.

Stiglitz, J. E. 2005. "The Ethical Economist." *Foreign Affairs*, November/December, 129.

Stiglitz, J. E., and A. Weiss. 1981. "Credit Rationing in Markets with Imperfect Information." *American Economic Review* 71 (3): 393–410.

Tilly, C. 1999. *Durable Inequality*. Berkeley: University of California Press.

———. 2006. *Why?* Princeton, NJ: Princeton University Press.

Tommasi, M., and F. Weinschelbaum. 1999. "A Principal-Agent Building Block for the Study of Decentralization and Integration." Working Paper, Universidad de San Andres, Buenos Aires.

Turner, V. 1982. Introduction to *Celebration: Studies in Festivity and Ritual*, ed. V. Turner. Washington, DC: Smithsonian Institution Press.

Van den Berghe, L. A. A., and S. Carchon. 2003. "Agency Relations within the Family Business System: An Exploratory Approach." *Corporate Governance: An International Review* 11 (3): 171–79.

Varshney, A. 2005. "Democracy and Poverty." In *Measuring Empowerment: Cross-Disciplinary Perspectives*, ed. D. Narayan, 383–401. Washington, DC: World Bank.

———. 2007. "India's Democratic Challenge." *Foreign Affairs*, March/April.

Vollmann, W. T. 2007. *Poor People.* New York: Ecco.

Ward, J. L. 1987. *Keeping the Family Business Healthy: How to Plan for Continuous Growth, Profitability, and Family Leadership.* San Francisco: Jossey Bass.

Weber, M. 1947. *The Theory of Social and Economic Organization.* Trans. A. M. Henderson and T. Parsons. Glencoe, IL: Free Press.

———. 1968. *Economy and Society: An Outline of Interpretive Sociology.* New York: Bedminster Press.

Winters, A., and S. Yusuf. 2007. *Dancing with Giants: China, India, and the Global Economy.* Washington, DC: World Bank.

Withey, S. B. 1954. "Reliability of Recall Income." *Public Opinion Quarterly* 18 (2): 197–204.

Woolcock, M. 1998. "Social Capital and Economic Development: Toward a Theoretical Synthesis and Policy Framework." *Theory and Society* 27 (2): 151–208.

World Bank. 1990. *World Development Report 1990: Poverty.* New York: Oxford University Press.

———. 2003. *World Development Report 2004: Making Services Work for Poor People.* New York: Oxford University Press.

———. 2006. *World Development Report 2006: Equity and Development.* New York: Oxford University Press.

———. 2007. *Doing Business 2008.* Washington, DC: World Bank.

———. 2008. *India: Self-Help Groups, Savings Mobilization, and Access to Finance.* New Delhi: World Bank.

Wright, G. 1974. "The Political Economy of New Deal Spending: An Econometric Analysis." *Review of Economics and Statistics* 56 (1): 30–38.

Yilmaz, S., Y. Beris, and R. Berthet. 2008. "Local Government Discretion and Accountability: A Diagnostic Framework for Local Governance." Social Development Paper 113, Local Governance and Accountability Series, World Bank, Washington, DC.

Zhuravskaya, E. 2000. "Incentives to Provide Local Public Goods: Fiscal Federalism, Russian Style." *Journal of Public Economics* 76 (3): 337–68.

Index

Boxes, figures, notes, and tables are denoted by b, f, n, and t, following the page numbers.

CDD (community-driven development), 315–17, 328
cell phones and economic opportunities, 207–8
Chambers, Robert, 43
change over time, 8. *See also* mobility
Chen, S., 183
children's future, aspirations for, 22, 54–56, 55*f*, 56*f*, 154–55
China
　cultural values of, 54
　family businesses in, 296
　leaders' role in economic transformation in, 272
　poverty line in, 103*b*
　poverty reduction in, 183–84, 219–20
choice, freedom of, 77–78, 78*b*
chronic poor
　aspirations of, 54, 55, 56, 56*f*, 153, 154*f*
　asset ownership and, 160
　children's aspirations, 157
　collective action and, 305
　defined, 12
　democracy and, 257
　estimates of, 98
　factors creating trap of chronic poverty, 98
　families and, 283, 329*n*2
　happiness rating of, 63, 63*f*
　hard work as way out of poverty for, 59–60, 59*f*
　health shocks and, 164, 165*f*, 169*f*
　initiative taking by, 20, 65, 66*t*
　quantifying personal agency of, 145, 146*f*, 148*f*
　self-confidence and, 27–28, 27*f*
Chronic Poverty Research Centre, 98
Circular Structure of Power (Dyberg), 145
citizenship level and chronic poverty, 98
civil conflicts, 192, 284*b*, 324, 326
　displacement due to. *See* displaced households in Colombia
　responsive local democracies and, 238, 240
civil liberties. *See* freedom
civil society organizations. *See* nongovernmental organizations (NGOs)

Clinton Global Initiative, 49*n*5
coffee market and growers, 38–39, 195–96, 308–9
Cohen, J., 230–31
collective action, 33, 281–331
　collective agency, 115–16
　community activities and assistance, 43–45, 44*f*, 301–7
　community-driven development (CDD), 315–17, 328
　limitations of poor people's groups, 301–6
　purposes of community groups, 301–2, 302*f*
　rich organizing against poor, 306–7, 329*n*8
　spontaneous groups, 301
　cooperation around local public goods, 318–27, 331*nn*21–22
　accountability, 324
　interaction with states, 325–27, 325*f*
　physical environment improvements, 323
　security improvements, 320–23
　corporations of poor people, 317–18, 319*b*
　democracy and, 231–32
　effectiveness of, 38–41, 44*f*
　for moving out of poverty, 46–47, 46*f*, 304–6, 305*f*, 306*f*, 328
　engagement in community, 82–85, 326
　external groups, links to, 307–11, 337
　family unit. *See* families
　friendships and, 298–99, 300*b*
　literature on, 281–82
　low profile of NGOs in, 311–13, 338
　microcredit groups, 313–15
　scaling up, 311–18, 338
Colombia
　aspirations in, 54, 153
　"bad power" in, 139
　business licensing in, 199
　community engagement in, 84, 329*n*8
　corruption in, 164
　credit availability in, 212, 302
　guerrilla factions in, 140, 326
　hard work as way out of poverty in, 60
　health shocks in, 170

insecurity and chronic poverty, 98
"invisible hand" theory and market
access, 192–201
Isham, J., 331*n*22
Italy, family interests in, 296
ITC, 220

J
Jalan, J., 101
Janmabhoomi program (India), 119,
125*n*15, 326
jealousy of other's gains, 130, 142–44,
240
Johnston, D., 330*n*15, 331*n*17
justice, 230, 232

K
Kaiser Family Foundation survey on
causes of poverty, 73
Kanbur, R., 101
Karelis, Charles, 19
Kashmir, migration to, 289*b*
Kaufman, A., 277*n*10
Kecamatan Development Program
(Indonesia), 209, 313, 316,
331*n*18
Keefer, P., 278*n*21, 325
Kennedy School of Government
survey on causes of poverty,
73
Kenya, savings and credit associations
in, 330*n*11
Khandker, S. R., 331*n*16
Kipling, Rudyard, 76–77
Knack, S., 279*n*28, 325, 331*n*22
Kraay, A., 183
Krishna, P., 100
Kynch, J., 329*n*4

L
ladder of life
community mobility matrix. *See*
community mobility matrix
(CMM)
data collection methods, 10, 12–13,
48*n*3, 88, 124*n*3
household dynamics on, 92–95, 93*t*,
94*f*, 96*f*, 124*n*4
samples from Andhra Pradesh and
Uganda, 14–15*t*

land
government program giving land to
the poor, 236
importance of in moving out of
poverty, 160
reform and titling of, 214–18, 215*f*
Latin America. *See also individual
countries*
aspirations in, 54
NGOs in, 330*n*14
social solidarity and mobility in,
330*n*10
study sites in, 9
law and order, 236, 237*f*
community policing, 321*b*
leadership
in democracy, 258–59
moral leadership, 138, 254–55
lessons from poor people, 41–42, 333
Lewis, Oscar, 19, 53, 333
liberalization, need for, 33, 37, 219
licensing. *See* business licensing
Lijjat Papad (Indian company),
317–18
local context
agency and, 115–16
democracy and, 33–38, 35*f*, 42, 115.
See also democracy
differences among communities, 25,
116, 118–21
economic opportunities and, 115,
186–89
importance of, 8, 42, 47, 88, 105–15,
333
pseudonyms used to protect
identities, 48*n*1
public works projects and local
prosperity, 216, 216*f*
location as factor in economic
opportunities, 186–89, 219,
221*n*4
Lok Capital, 331*n*20
Loury, G., 329*n*9
Lubatkin, M., 329*n*7
luck's role in moving up, 67*f*, 68–72
Lukes, S., 130, 131–32

M
Macaulay, Lord, 76
MacCulloch, R., 249